Sanborn's Travelog Series:

MEXICO'S
SOUTH PACIFIC COAST

A Driver's Guide

Wanderlust Publications
2009 S. 10th McAllen TX 78503
Ph: (956) 682-7433
Fax: (956) 686-0732

Wanderlust Publications, McAllen, Texas

Inquiries should be addressed to: Wanderlust Publications, 2009 South 10th Street, McAllen, TX 78503-5405 Ph: (956) 682-7433 Fax: (956) 686-0732.

Our web page address: http://www.sanbornsinsurance.com

E-mail: info@sanbornsinsurance.com

First Edition: July, 1998

First Reprint: May, 2000

Second Reprint: March, 2001

Third Reprint: March, 2002

Second Edition: July, 2003

Printed in the United States of America

Mexico's South Pacific Coast: A Driver's Guide

Sanborn's Travelog Series

ISBN: 1-878166-29-8

If you've got a minute ...

We truly hope you had a wonderful trip and that our *Travelog* helped. You can help other folks by passing on information you may have learned. It's from your feedback that we can improve, so send us your suggestions and observations. If possible, please refer to name of book, page #, and the mile #. The whole *Travelog* covers all of Mexico and is contained in nine books, so we need some way to track it. **YOUR PHONE #, POR FAVOR!** We may have a question, or want to thank you personally!

Praise or complaints for Mexican individuals or companies should be sent to : **Secretaria de Turismo, Dirección General de Servicios al Turismo, Presidente Masaryk – 3er Piso, C.P. 11587, Mexico D.F.** Each year, the government honors a citizen who helped tourists. Your complaint or praise will be recorded and sent to the right agency. You'd be surprised at what good it can do.

Hasta luego from all the staff at Sanborn's.

Today's date:_____ Date entered Mexico: _____ Exit date: _____

Which Sanborn's office served you? _____

Were they friendly?_____ Helpful?_____ Knowledgeable?_____ How could they improve service? _____

_____

_____

Did you have a good time – overall? YES! _____NO _____Was any facility or individual especially helpful? _____

Was your *Travelog* in order? YES_____NO_____ Did it make sense? YES_____ NO_____

Excellent? _____ Good? _____ Fair?_____

Was the **HIGHWAY INFORMATION** essentially accurate? YES_____NO_____

Do you have new info for us?_____

_____

_____

_____

Was the **EAT & STRAY** section essentially accurate? YES_____ NO_____

Do you have new places for us or some that should be edited?_____

_____

_____

_____

_____

What would YOU like to see that WASN'T there?_____

Will you return to Mexico some day?_____

Name:_____

Address, City, State, Zip :_____

Country_____**TELEPHONE** # (_____)_____

How many travelling?_____ First trip? YES_____NO_____

Where did you hear about Sanborn's?_____

_____

FROM:

BUSINESS REPLY MAIL
FIRST CLASS PERMIT NO. 57 McALLEN, TEXAS

POSTAGE WILL BE PAID BY ADDRESSEE

SANBORN'S
MEXICO INSURANCE SERVICE
DEPT. COMMENTS
P.O. BOX 310
McALLEN, TX 78505-0310

Table of Contents

General Information viii

Maps

Map of Puerto Vallarta 1
Map of Manzanillo 5
Map of Guadalajara 6
Map of Colima 9
Map of Ixtapa 13
Map of Zihuatanejo 14
Map of Acapulco 17
Map of Mexico City Downtown 19
Map of Mexico City 20
Map of Cuernavaca 22
Map of Puerto Escondido 27
Map of Salina Cruz 30
Map of Toluca 34
Map of Ixtapan de la Sal 36
Map of Taxco 39
Map of Puebla 43
Map of Oaxaca 46
Map of Downtown Oaxaca 47
Map of Uruapan 58
Map of Tehuacán 73
Map of Cuautla 85

Logs

LOG 1 --------- START: Puerto Vallarta, Jal -------------- END: Melaque Jct, Jal 2
LOG 2 --------- START: Melaque Jct, Jal ------------------ END: Tecomán Jct, Col 3
LOG 3 --------- START: Guadalajara, Jal ------------------ END: Tecomán Jct, Col 7
LOG 4 --------- START: Tecomán Jct, Col --------------- END: La Mira Jct, Mich 10
LOG 5 --------- START: La Mira Jct, Mich -------------- END: Ixtapa, Gro 12
LOG 6 --------- START: Ixtapa, Gro ---------------------- END: Acapulco, Gro 15
LOG 7 --------- START: Mexico City, DF ---------------- END: Cuernavaca, Mor 18
LOG 8 --------- START: Cuernavaca, Mor --------------- END: Iguala, Gro 23
LOG 9 --------- START: Iguala, Gro ---------------------- END: Acapulco, Gro (Toll) 24
LOG 10 -------- START: Acapulco, Gro ------------------ END: Pto. Escondido, Oax 25
LOG 11 -------- START: Pto. Escondido, Oax ----------- END: Tehuantepec, Oax 28
LOG 12 -------- START: Tehuantepec, Oax -------------- END: La Ventosa, Oax 31
LOG 13 -------- START: Palmillas Jct, Qro -------------- END: Toluca, Mex 32
LOG 14 -------- START: Toluca, Mex -------------------- END: Ixtapan de la Sal, Mex 35
LOG 15 -------- START: Ixtapan de la Sal, Mex --------- END: Iguala, Gro 37
LOG 16 -------- START: Iguala, Gro --------------------- END: Acapulco, Gro (Free) 40
LOG 17 -------- START: Mexico City, DF ---------------- END: Puebla, Pue 41
LOG 18 -------- START: Puebla, Pue --------------------- END: Oaxaca, Oax 44
LOG 19 -------- START: Oaxaca, Oax -------------------- END: Tehuantepec, Oax 48

Specials

LOG 20 -------- START: Guadalajara, Jal ----------------- END: Melaque Jct, Jal 50
LOG 21 -------- START: Melaque, Jal --------------------- END: Guadalajara, Jal 52

LOG 22 ------- START: Tecomán Jct, Col ---------------- END: Jiquilpan, Mich 54

LOG 23 ------- START: Jiquilpan, Mich ---------------- END: Tecomán Jct, Col 55

LOG 24 ------- START: La Mira Jct, Mich ------------- END: Uruapan, Mich 57

LOG 25 ------- START: Uruapan, Mich ----------------- END: La Mira Jct, Mich 59

LOG 26 ------- START: Ixtapa, Gro --------------------- END: Cd. Altamirano, Mich 61

LOG 27 ------- START: Cd. Altamirano, Mich ---------- END: Toluca, Mex 62

LOG 28 ------- START: Toluca, Mex -------------------- END: Mexico City, DF 63

LOG 29 ------- START: Mexico City, DF ---------------- END: Toluca, Mex 64

LOG 30 ------- START: Toluca, Mex -------------------- END: Cd. Altamirano, Mich 66

LOG 31 ------- START: Cd. Altamirano, Mich ---------- END: Ixtapa, Gro 67

LOG 32 ------- START: Pochutla, Oax ------------------ END: Oaxaca, Oax 68

LOG 33 ------- START: Oaxaca, Oax -------------------- END: Pochutla, Oax 69

LOG 34 ------- START: Oaxaca, Oax -------------------- END: Tehuacán, Pue 71

LOG 35 ------- START: Tehuacán, Pue ------------------ END: Oaxaca, Oax 74

LOG 36 ------- START: Cuernavaca, Mor --------------- END: Izucar de Matamoros, Pue 76

LOG 37 ------- START: Izucar de Matamoros, Pue ------ END: Huajuapan de León, Oax 78

LOG 38 ------- START: Huajuapan de León, Oax ------- END: Oaxaca, Oax 79

LOG 39 ------- START: Oaxaca, Oax -------------------- END: Huajuapan de León, Oax 81

LOG 40 ------- START: Huajuapan de León, Oax ------- END: Izucar de Matamoros, Pue 83

LOG 41 ------- START: Izucar de Matamoros, Pue ------ END: Cuernavaca, Mor 84

LOG 42 ------- START: Izucar de Matamoros, Pue ------ END: Puebla, Pue 87

LOG 43 ------- START: Puebla, Pue -------------------- END: Izucar de Matamoros, Pue 88

LOG 44 ------- START: Esperanza, Pue ----------------- END: Tehuacán, Pue 89

LOG 45 ------- START: Tehuacán, Pue ------------------ END: Huajuapan de León, Oax 90

LOG 46 ------- START: Huajuapan de León, Oax ------- END: Tehuacán, Pue 92

LOG 47 ------- START: Tehuacán, Pue ------------------ END: Esperanza, Pue 93

LOG 48 ------- START: Toluca, Mex -------------------- END: Tres Marías, Mor 94

LOG 49 ------- START: Tres Marías, Mor --------------- END: Toluca, Mex 95

LOG 50 ------- START: Cuernavaca, Mor --------------- END: Ixtapan de la Sal, Mex 96

LOG 51 ------- START: Taxco, Gro --------------------- END: Jct Hwy 95D, Mor 98

Eat & Strays

Barra de Navidad 99

Manzanillo 101

Colima 103

Ixtapa 104

Zihuatanejo 107

Acapulco 110

Puerto Escondido 119

Puerto Angel 121

Huatulco 122

Salina Cruz 124

Toluca 125

Ixtapan de la Sal 126

Taxco 127

Cuernavaca 128

Cuautla 132

Tehuacán 133

Oaxaca 134

Return Logs

LOG 52 -------- START: La Ventosa, Oax ---------------- END: Tehuantepec, Oax 138

LOG 53 -------- START: Tehuantepec ---------------------- END: Pto. Escondido, Oax 138

LOG 54 -------- START: Pto. Escondido, Oax ------------ END: Acapulco, Gro 140

LOG 55 -------- START: Acapulco, Gro-------------------- END: Ixtapa, Gro 142

LOG 56 -------- START: Ixtapa, Gro ---------------------- END: La Mira, Mich 144

LOG 57 -------- START: La Mira Jct, Mich ------------- END: Tecomán Jct, Col 145

LOG 58 -------- START: Tecomán Jct, Col ---------------- END: Melaque Jct, Jal 147

LOG 59 -------- START: Melaque, Jal END: ------------- Puerto Vallarta, Jal 148

LOG 60 -------- START: Tecomán Jct, Col --------------- END: Guadalajara, Jal 150

LOG 61 -------- START: Acapulco, Gro------------------- END: Iguala, Gro 152

LOG 62 -------- START: Iguala, Gro --------------------- END: Ixtapan de la Sal, Mex 153

LOG 63 -------- START: Ixtapan de la Sal, Mex --------- END: Toluca, Mex 154

LOG 64 -------- START: Toluca, Mex -------------------- END: Palmillas Jct, Qro.................................. 156

LOG 65 -------- START: Iguala, Gro --------------------- END: Cuernavaca, Mor 157

LOG 66 -------- START: Cuernavaca, Mor --------------- END: Mexico City, DF 158

LOG 67 -------- START: Tehuantepec, Oax -------------- END: Oaxaca, Oax... 159

LOG 68 -------- START: Oaxaca, Oax -------------------- END: Puebla, Pue (toll) 161

LOG 69 -------- START: Puebla, Pue --------------------- END: Mexico City, DF 164

Index 166

WELCOME TO MEXICO!

HOW TO READ THIS BOOK

First of all, take some time to get familiar with our format. The information is presented in varying detail, depending on where you are in your journey. In cities, we tend to give you several landmarks in case one has disappeared since our last visit.

Remember, always read ahead in the log! You should look at it the night before to plan your trip and mark appropriate highlights. On the road, the navigator should read ahead about four or five entries, but don't give them all to the driver. Work this out with your pilot.

With this *Travelog*, we have attempted to include every route that you could take while exploring this region of Mexico. Since there is sometimes more than one way you could go, we've included alternate routes. Every time you come to a major intersection or a major new highway, there should be a new log. Pay special attention to the **"IF TO:"** paragraphs which will indicate a page number if the next log you need is on a different page.

The mileage numbers represent miles and kilometers, respectively. We've listed both so our Canadian friends can use this book. The numbers start at 0.0 at a major intersection. The "KM XXX" stands for the kilometer markings you'll see on Mexico's highways. They aren't always visible, but when they are, they give you a great reference point.

Not every gas station is listed. There are just too many of them these days. The ones we list all have unleaded gasoline. Diesel is found at all the larger ones. Neither is every little town listed, a departure from our original way of doing things.

The scenic ratings of roads are subjective. A "5" is very close to heaven. A "0" is either hell or a tollroad. These have nothing to do with driving ease. Some toll roads are actually pretty, but most are not. Take the scenic route if you want to take your time and enjoy. Take the direct route if you just want to get from point A to point B in a hurry.

EAT AND STRAY LEGEND

We gave up listing exact prices years ago. That's the one thing that people are most likely to complain about in any guidebook. Prices change but often stay within the same range. A moderately priced restaurant or hotel will stay in the same category relative to others in the same city.

AE = American Express, MC = MasterCard, VI = Visa, SATV = Satellite TV.

PRICES – Please don't take these as gospel. Prices increase at least once a year, but we give you a fighting chance to hold on to your bucks. Always look at the room first and ask for the best price. If a hotel has a disco and you want to sleep, ask for a room far away in another galaxy, perhaps. If the room's too noisy, think nothing of asking to change. Be sure to ask for the *sub-gerente* since the *gerente* will be home asleep. Prices are in U.S. Dollars.

ECON – under $25 MOD – $25-$60 UPPER $60 and above

Restaurants are rated for quality and service. Prices are approximate for two people to eat dinner there. Drinks, tips and appetizers are not included. If breakfast is the specialty, cut prices in half.

ECON – under $10 MOD – $10-$25 UPPER – $25 and above

For RV parks, we list approximate rates when known.

ECON – under $8 MOD – $8-10 UPPER – $10 and above

CAR PERMITS AND IMMIGRATION DOCUMENTS

If you are driving your car or a rented car from the border, you'll need a vehicle permit to drive to the interior of Mexico with the exception of Baja California (If you fly to the interior and rent a car, you won't need a permit).

To get your Tourist Card (FMT) you must present a passport or a certified copy of your birth certificate and pay a fee of $22.00 pesos. Everyone must have proof of citizenship: A picture ID with a birth certificate, voter's registration card or a notarized proof of citizenship. Even little children must have birth certificates. If a child is traveling with only one parent, it is necessary to have notarized permission of the absent parent (even if divorced). Pets need current vaccination records and health certificates.

To get your vehicle permit, you'll need the vehicle title or registration, which must be in the same name as your credit card (Visa©, MasterCard©, American Express© or Diner's Club©). If your chariot is financed, you'll need a notarized letter of permission from the lien holder to take it into Mexico. You can't loan your car to a friend. If you have a boat and a trailer, they must also be in the same name as the vehicle. You need the credit card to pay a $22 fee to Banjército for your permit. If you don't have a credit card, you can still get a permit by posting a bond, which amounts to 2 to 3 percent of the value of your vehicle plus a $150 dollar deposit. You get a refund of the deposit but not the bond. Get a credit card if you possibly can. The permit is good for multiple entries during 180 days.

You must turn in your permit and tourist card before you leave the country for the last time. Forgetting to do so could result in your being refused entry again or subject you to a high fine. You must turn in your permit at the Banjército office, either at the 21 kilometer checkpoint or at the border station. The Banjército offices are generally close to the bridge. Sometimes you have to park a block or two away and scout it out first. Don't expect to just get in line at the bridge going to the U.S. and expect the toll taker to help you out. That's not his job or department. You do not need to return to the U.S. at the same border crossing where you started.

WHAT CAN I TAKE INTO MEXICO?

When crossing into Mexico, if you have no merchandise to declare, you must go through the stop and go light check point. A green light means proceed ahead without inspection. A red light means stop for inspection.

When you travel to Mexico by airplane or by ship, you are allowed to import duty free one or various items worth up to $300 dollars per person (including children). For example, a family of five members consisting of the parents and three minor children, can import up to $1,500 Dollars worth of merchandise, duty free. However, if you are traveling by land, you are allowed only $50.00 Dollars (per person) worth of merchandise duty free.

When you bring items whose value exceeds the above mentioned limits, but not more than $1,000.00 Dollars, you can pay your personal taxes. If your merchandise is worth more than $1,000.00 Dollars, you must use the services of a customs broker.

If the flight by which you arrive come from the border zone you are allowed only $50.00 Dollars of new items per person.

If you are a resident in Mexico you are allowed to bring in free of duty the following items for your personal use: One camera or video camera if it can be carried by the passenger; up to 12 rolls of virgin film, video cassettes, or photographic materials; one article of sports equipment or a used set of equipment that can be hand carried; books and magazines; 20 packages of cigarettes or 50 cigars or 250 grams of tobacco; 3 liters of wine, beer or liquor (adults only); medicines for personal use or with a doctor's prescription if it is a controlled substance, and the suitcases to carry baggage.

If you are a resident of a foreign country (USA, Canada, or other), in addition to the above you are allowed to take a set of binoculars, a photographic camera, a television, a radio or radio-cassette tape or disc player, up to 20 recording tapes or discs, a typewriter, a portable computer, a musical instrument that can be hand carried, a camping tent and camping equipment, a set of fishing equipment, a pair of skis, 5 used toys for minors, two tennis rackets, a motorless boat less than 5 1/2 meters long or surf board with or without a sail.

If you are inspected and are discovered with items of greater value than is permitted and you have not paid duty on them, you risk having to pay a high fine (of up to four times the value of each item). If weapons or ammunition are found, the penalty includes imprisonment.

The following are products you can take into Mexico without previous authorization: Dehydrated or canned foods, bamboo (dry), roasted coffee (packaged), fresh or dry meats (beef, sheep or goat from US or Canada), candy (not lactic), dried spices, dry herbal medicines, dry or preserved insects, canned jellies or fruit preserves, nuts, straw articles or artifacts, dried fish, cheese (processed in US or Canada), canned or processed sauces, soups without meat, canned or processed vegetables, dogs or cats (with a recent health certificate and vaccination record).

CAN I BRING IT BACK?

You are not allowed to bring back more than $10,000 in cash. If you bring back more than $500.00 in merchandise you must declare it, fill out importation documents and have it inspected at the customs house where the large trucks cross.

Declare all agricultural items. Failure to do so may result in delays and fines of $25.00 or more. Fruits, vegetables, meats and birds taken from the U. S., to Mexico may not be allowed to re-enter. Check in advance with U.S.D.A. inspectors. Also declare all medicines or prescription drugs bought in Mexico.

Prohibited Fruits and vegetables: Potatoes: cooked OK. Plants and seeds: Special permits are required and some are prohibited. Check in advance. (Except dried plant parts, such as for medicinal purposes, permitted) Meats and Game: Raw or cooked pork, including sausages, cold cuts, skins and pork tacos (except shelf-stable, canned pork and hard-cooked pork skin cracklings). Poultry: Raw meat from domesticated and game fowl (except well-cooked poultry). Game: Check in advance. Other meat: imports limited to 50 pounds per person. Eggs are prohibited (except boiled and cooked eggs). Live birds: Wild and domesticated birds, including poultry. To import personally owned pet birds, check in advance. Straw is generally prohibited including wheat straw, seeds and all other articles made from them including animal feed.

Permitted fruits and vegetables: Avocados without seeds, except in California, bananas, blackberries, cactus fruits, dates, dewberries, grapes, lycheés, melons, papayas, pineapples, and strawberries. Most vegetables permitted except those listed above. Okra, however, is subject to certain restrictions. Nuts: acorns, almonds, cocoa beans, chestnuts, coconuts (no husks or milk), peanuts, pecans, piñones (pinenuts), tamarind beans, walnuts and waternuts.

GAS AND GAS STATIONS

UNLEADED GAS and DIESEL are abundant everywhere in Mexico. Unleaded gas is called Magna Sin (87 octane). Also a higher octane (93) Premium unleaded gas is sold in most stations. Nova (leaded gas) has been phased out. There is only one brand, PEMEX, which stands for PEtroleos MEXicanos. Prices are the same throughout the interior. Diesel is also found at most stations. The diesel pumps are in a different part of the station and are red. The best diesel is *centrifugado*, or centrifuged. Diesel Sin has lower sulfur content.

It's still a good idea to make sure that the pump has reset to zero before the attendant starts pumping. Stay at the pump until the operation is finished. Don't just rush off to the bathroom. Although most stations still do not take credit cards, more and more are accepting MC and VI cards (but don't count on it).

The bathrooms used to be filthy, but lately they have embarked on a cleanup effort. Often there will be an attendant. Tipping them is a nice thing to do. A personal supply of toilet paper is smart, though not always necessary.

Speaking of restrooms, in Mexico *his* will be called *Caballeros* and *hers* will be *Damas* (sometimes W.C. for water closet). In the bathrooms of many Mexican hotels, you'll notice the initials C on one faucet and F on the other. Bear in mind that C means *caliente* (hot) and F means *fría* (cold).

AUTO PARTS AND REPAIRS

You'll find lots of spare parts in Mexico, though not always the right ones. Fords, Chevys, Dodges and Nissans are all made there. Many of the parts are interchangeable. The best thing to do is to have a good, honest mechanic check out your car before you go and to pay particular attention to the brakes, tires, front end, U-joints, belts (carry spares) and any "computer" parts. Please do not even think about messing with your catalytic converter. Get a tune-up, including new spark plug wires etc. Your car is going to be your servant for the next few thousand miles. Don't let it be the other way around.

Goodyear is in every town and can do a good job with brakes, front ends, etc. You'll find shade tree mechanics, identified by a "*taller mecánico*" sign beside the road. Taller has nothing to do with his height. It means shop. If they don't have the brake pads you need, they will make them.

Carry: belts (all), fuel filters (4), air filters (2), a good set of tools, windshield washer fluid (lots), auto transmission fluid (1 qt.), fuel injector cleaner (5 bottles). Diesels should have (5) filters and any additive that might combat water and the buildup of sulfuric acid in your crankcase.

A spare gas can should only be necessary if you are going four wheeling. Carrying gas is too dangerous and smelly. Ninety-nine per cent of folks won't need it. Also make sure your tires (including spare) are in good shape. Mexican tires are excellent, but the sizes are slightly different.

RENTING A CAR

Over 3,000,000 people fly to Mexico, and then rent cars for all or part of their trip while 1,500,000 drive from the U.S. or Canada. These "more than average" tourists have realized that driving is the most practical way to get around, offering unlimited freedom. Renting a car in Mexico is similar to renting one anywhere in the world with a few caveats. You must have a major credit card. All the major rental car agencies are located at major airports. Their rates vary, so shop around. There are also some independent rental car agencies at many airports. Sometimes they offer a better deal and sometimes not. Again, shop around.

 Please check the vehicle carefully! Any little ding not noted will be charged to you as if you damaged their car on purpose. Make sure all lights, signals and especially the horn work. Unlimited mileage is the exception rather than the rule, so be sure to ask if it is available. In Mexico City, all vehicles are prohibited from circulating one day a week, based on the last number of their license tag. This applies to rental cars, too. A good rental car company will swap cars so you don't lose a day's driving. We have heard that some rental companies will try to switch license tags and tell you it's okay. It's not. Make sure they agree to give you another legal car for that day. There should be a decal in the back window with the license tag number on it. Be sure they match or refuse the car. Renting in one city and then dropping off in another is expensive. The car rental company will charge you a per kilometer fee that may double you bill.

MONEY MATTERS

Pay with your credit card whenever possible to take advantage of the best exchange rate. Credit cards like Visa© and MasterCard© are accepted almost everywhere. Discover© is not accepted anywhere. American Express©, Diner's Club© and Carte Blanche© are accepted only at the finer establishments. You can get cash advances on the Visa© and MasterCard© at some ATMs. Pesos bills come in denominations of $10, $20, $50, $100, $200, $500 and probably bigger. Coins are 5¢, 10¢, 20¢, 50¢ (*centavos*) and $1,$2, $5, $10, and $20 pesos.

TRAVEL TIPS

If you wish to catch up on the news in the States, there is one daily English language newspapers published in Mexico City called *The News*. It carries all the latest U.S. and world news as well as sports columns, editorials and your favorite comics.

Many of the hotels in Mexico have self-operated elevators.Remember that the main floor or lobby is PB (*Planta Baja*), not the first (1) floor.

Topes or speed bumps, sometimes called *vibradores,* are the common speed control devices used in Mexico. All you really need to know about them is that you do not want to hit them going over five miles an hour. Both pilot and navigator should keep an eye out for them as you approach any small town. They will be at the entrance and somewhere in the middle. Don't be lulled into a false sense of security by the fact that some of them have signs marking their location. If traffic is slowing down for no apparent reason, you'll find out why when you get closer.

Most railroad crossings in Mexico have STOP signs. All trucks and busses must stop. It doesn't follow that you have to stop, but slow down and watch for tailgating traffic.

Commonly nicknamed "Moctezuma's Revenge," diarrhea is sometimes developed by tourists while visiting Mexico. One must realize that traveler's diarrhea can be caused by several factors and can occur anywhere in the world. Overeating, overdrinking and overexertion at high altitudes are typical causes. However, drinking impure water is the main cause for contracting the *turista*. Avoid tap water (even for brushing your teeth). Use purified water or agua *purificada* available in gas stations and small stores, just like in the States. In supermarkets, it can be purchased in one-gallon plastic containers. Mineral water, while perfectly safe, has the effect of a mild laxative on some individuals due to its mineral content. So be sure and ask for purified water at hotels, motels and restaurants. Avoid eating from street carts and sidewalk vendors.

NEED TO CALL HOME?

Calling home from Mexico has gotten easier. We recommend that you purchase international long distance phone cards available at most pharmacies and grocery stores. Pay phones that use phone cards are quite common. Simply insert the card and dial 001 + Area Code + Phone Number. You may also use your personal telephone calling card to call home from your hotel or a pay phone.

POLICE

You've probably heard nothing but bad stories about Mexican police. Most of them are helpful, polite and honest. While it's true that many years ago, *mordida* (a little bite, meaning a bribe) was a way of life, things have changed. The best advice is to approach each policeman with the attitude that he is honest and just doing his job. If, however, you encounter one from the old school who is looking for a bribe, ask for his badge number. Always carry a note pad and a pen.

MISSING LICENSE PLATES? — There is one sure way to know that your car is over parked or illegally parked – your license plate will be missing. There's a practical reason for this. Paper parking citations can be ignored and fines forgotten. However, when the police possess a license plate, drivers are compelled to go to the station and pay their fine to reclaim their plates (*placas*). Our Rita Meter maid carries a book of tickets. In Mexico, she carries a screw driver. Although fines are not usually costly and officials are courteous, it's better to avoid the problem.

Most policemen are honest. Some travelers have told us about policemen who went out of their way to help them or guide them out of town when they were lost. Should you encounter one who's not so liberated, don't panic. Get his badge number and insist you want to see his *jefe*. The phrase is "*Vamos a la comandancia.*" Another is, "*Hablemos con su jefe.*" Usually that will start a negotiating process. Stick to your guns, so to speak, as long as you are sure you didn't do anything wrong. If you insist on going to the police station, bogus infractions will vanish. However, if you have broken a law, he has every right to take your license plates. You must go to the station to pay your fine. If it's a weekend, you may have to wait until Monday. Although we do not recommend it, some old-timers prefer to pay the fine "on the spot" to save the aggravation. If a policemanc asks you for a bribe, report him. The government is very concerned about officers "on the take" and treat all reports seriously. You should report the officer's badge number and when and where the incident occurred. Send any complaints about policemen, other officials, hotels, restaurants, etc. (or praise for those who went out of their way to help you) to: Departamento de Quejas, Dirección General de Turismo, Presidente Masaryk #172, Mexico, DF. In Mexico City, call: (55) 5604-1240. The Policia Federal de Caminos are quite professional and honest. They can be your best friend in an emergency.

U.S. CONSULATES

CD. JUÁREZ, CHIH — López Mateos #924-N CP. 32000 Tel: (656) 613-4048 or 613-5050 Fax: (656) 616-9056 Duty Officer: (915) 526-6066 (in El Paso, TX) Office Hours: 08:00 to 15:45 Mailing Address: American Consulate Apdo. Postal #1681 32000 Cd. Juárez, Chih.

GUADALAJARA, JAL — Progreso 175, Col. Americana Guadalajara, Jalisco ZP C. 44100. Tel: (01-33) 3825-2700; Fax: (01-33) 3826-6549 Duty Officer and after hours calls: (33) 3626-5553.

HERMOSILLO, SON — Monterrey #141 entre las calles Rosales y Galeana, Col. Esqueda, Hermosillo, Sonora, México 83260 Ph: (662) 217-2575 Fax: (662) 217-2578.

MATAMOROS, TAM — Calle Primera #2002 y Azaleas, Matamoros, Tamaulipas 87330. Tel.: (868) 912-4402/03/08 Fax: (868) 912-2171 Office Hours: 08:00 to 12:00 and 13:00 to 17:00 Mailing Address: American Consulate Apdo. Postal #451, 87350 Matamoros, Tamps.

MÉRIDA, YUC — Paseo Montejo #453 por Avenida Colon, Merida, Yucatan, Mexico 97000. Ph: (999) 925-5011 Fax: (999) 925-6219.

MONTERREY, NL — Avenida Constitución #411 Pte. Monterrey, N.L. Mexico 64000. Tel.: (81) 8345-2120 Fax: (81) 8345-7748 Mailing Address: P.O. Box #3098 Laredo, TX 78044-3098.

NVO. LAREDO, COAH — Calle Allende #3330, Colonia Jardín, Nuevo Laredo, Tamps. Mexico 88260. Tel.: (867) 714-0696 or 714-0512 Fax: (867) 714-0696 Office Hours: 8:00 a.m. - 12:30 p.m. / 1:30 p.m. - 5:00 p.m. Principal Officer: Thomas Armbruster

TIJUANA, BCN — Tapachula 96, Colonia Hipodromo, Tijuana, Baja California, Mexico 22420. Tel.: (dialing from the U.S.) 011-52-(664) 622-7400 Fax: (dialing from the U.S.) 011-52-(664) 681-8016. U.S. Mailing Address: P.O. Box 439039, San Diego, CA 92143-9039.

U.S. CONSULAR AGENTS

ACAPULCO, GRO — Alexander Richards, Hotel Acapulco Continental, Costera M. Alemán 121 Local 14, Acapulco, Gro. 39670 Tel: (744) 469-0556, Tel./Fax: (744) 484-0300. Email: consular@prodigy.net.mx

CABO SAN LUCAS, BCS — Michael J. Houston, Blvd. Marian Local C-4, Plaza Nautica, Centro, Cabo Sal Lucas, B.C.S. 23410. Tel.: (624) 143-3566 Fax: (624) 143-6750. Email: usconsulcabo@hotmail.com

CANCÚN, Q ROO — Lynnette Belt, Segundo Nivel #320-3232, Plaza Caracol Dos, Blvd. Kukulcán, Zona Hotelera, Cancún, Q. R. 77500. Mailing Address: Apdo. Postal 862., Concun, Q.R. Tel.: (998) 883-0272, Fax: (998) 883-1373 Email: uscons@prodigy.net.mx, Lynnette@usconscancun.com

Cd. ACUNA/DEL RIO, COAHUILA — Elvira Morales, Ocampo No. 305 (corner with Morelos), Centro, Ciudad Acuña, Coahuila 26200. Tel.: (877) 772-8661, Fax: (877) 772-8179 Email: elviramz@msn.com

COZUMEL, QR — Anne R. Harris, Offices 8 & 9, "Villa Mar" Mall - Between Melgar and 5th. Ave., Cozumel, QR. 77600. Tel.:(987) 872-4574/872-4485 Fax: (987) 872-2339. Email: usgov@cozumel.net, usca@cozumel.net Mailing Address: Av. 35 Norte No. 650 (between 12 bis and 14 Norte), Cozumel, QR. 77622

IXTAPA / ZIHUATANEJO — Elizabeth Williams, Local 9, Plaza Ambiente, Ixtapa, Zihuatanejo. Tel.: (755) 553-2100 Fax: (755) 554-6276 Email: liz@lizwilliams.org, Lizpersonal@bigfoot.com Mailing Address: Apdo. Postal 169, Zihuatanejo, Gro. 40880

MAZATLÁN, SIN — Patti Fletcher, Hotel Playa Mazatlán, Playa Gaviotas No. 202, Zona Dorada, Mazatlán, Sinaloa 82110 Ph & Fax: (669) 916-5889 , Email: mazagent@mzt.megared.net.mx

OAXACA, OAX — Mark Arnold Leyes, Macedonia Alcala # 407, Office 20, Oaxaca, Oax. 68000. Tel.: (951)514-3054 or 516-2853. Fax: (951) 516-2701 Email: conagent@prodigy.net.mx.

PIEDRAS NEGRAS, COAHUILA — Dina L. O'Brien, Prol. General Cepeda No. 1900, Fraccionamiento Privada Blanca. Piedras Negras, Coahuila 26700. Tel.: (878) 795-1986, 795-1987, 795-1988. Off. U.S. (830) 773-9231. Email: obriendina@hotmail.com

PTO. VALLARTA, JAL — Kelly Anne Trainor, Plaza Zaragoza #160, Piso 2 Oficina18, Puerto Vallarta, Jal.48300 Tel.: (322) 223-0074. Fax: (322) 223-0074. Email: amconpv@prodigy.net.mx

REYNOSA, TAMPS. — Roberto Rodríguez, Calle Monterrey No. 390 (corner with Sinaloa), Col. Rodríguez, Reynosa, Tamps., 88630. Tel.: (899) 923-9331, 923-8878, 923-9245. Email: usconsularagent@hotmail.com

SAN LUIS POTOSÍ, SLP — Carolyn H. Lazaro,Edificio "Las Terrazas" Ave. Venustiano Carranza 2076-41, Col. Polanco, San Luis Potosi, S.L. P., 78220. Tel.: (444) 811-7802 Fax: (444) 811-7803 Email: usconsulslp@yahoo.com

GENERAL SOCIAL RULES

If someone invites you to dine with them or come to their house, they are sincere. To refuse without giving good reason is bad manners. In general, whenever a specific place and time are mentioned, the invitation is sincere. Their sense of time (except in business situations) is different than ours, so allow thirty minutes to an hour for acceptable tardiness.

Never make fun of someone's station in life or what they have or don't have. People are proud of themselves and their possessions, no matter how meager they may appear to your eyes.

Please, don't ask, "How much is it in real money?" Often people will quote you in dollars to be polite. Also, don't worry too much about being short changed. People are a lot more honest than you might suspect.

WAITING IN LINE — Chances are that someone will cut in. You politely say, *Desculpe, la fila sigue atrás,* to tell them that the end of the line is somewhere behind you. Unfortunately, Mexicans are no different than people anywhere in the world. Some rude people will just ignore you, but most people are polite and will go farther back in the line and try again.

PARKING ATTENDANTS — In small towns there are still some guys who are wearing khaki clothing and official looking hats that are as old as they are and will direct you to a parking space. They are not police officers but will watch your car. Pay them the peso equivalent of fifty cents or so.

PARKING LOTS — Many hotels have underground lots that are narrow and have low ceilings. You will not be able to use them if you have a tall camper. If you have an extended cab pickup with a long bed, it will take some maneuvering to get in and out, but it can be done if you have the patience. Find another open-air lot if possible. At some parking lots you will get a time ticket. Make sure you know the price before leaving and don't lose the ticket.

TIPPING — It's customary to tip the gas pump attendant the peso equivalent of a quarter. Remember that your U.S. coins are useless to anyone in Mexico, so don't use them for tips. The kids who wash your windshield get a quarter and porters get fifty cents a bag. Maids should get a dollar a day. Waiters get 10-15% average and exceptional service, of course, gets up to 20%. Please use common sense and don't overtip like an ugly American or undertip like a cheapskate.

WOMEN TRAVELING ALONE

While many people enjoy their trips more with a companion, traveling alone in Mexico should be no more daunting than doing so anywhere in the U.S. Use common sense, dress conservatively, don't sleep in your car and you will find the Mexican people to be very hospitable. As in any country, how you are treated often depends on the signals you give out. Don't dress provocatively. Places to be careful are ruins and other tourist attractions close to closing time, bars, lonely beaches (Please don't camp on one) or anywhere you would not go back home. Use common sense and you'll have a good time.

DON'T DRIVE AT NIGHT!

Please don't drive at night — You are quite safe in terms of personal safety on Mexico's highways. A number of factors make night driving hazardous; On older, two lane roads, you could hit a chuckhole with no warning that could seriously damage your suspension. Shoulders are narrow or sometimes nonexistent. Drivers of broken down vehicles often place rocks on the road to "warn" you that they are taking up a lane ahead. Even if you see the rocks in time, it may be too late. Long after they are gone, the rocks often remain, despite signs telling you not to leave them. These rocks can tear up your car or send you careening off a mountain.

Mexico has a lot of open range. Cows, burros, goats and horses think they have the right of way. You can't see a black cow at night. Cows, burros etc. don't wear taillights. Outside of cities, some drivers may drive without headlights, thinking they can see better or that they will conserve their lights by not using them. Others may have only one (or no) taillights. There is often a high drop from the pavement to the shoulder that could cause you to roll over. The famous Green Angels don't drive at night.

Many people in Mexico have never or seldom been in a vehicle. They walk everywhere they go, usually in the brush very close to the edge of highway pavement. frequently, they suddenly step out of the brush onto the highway placing themselves in the immediate path of an automobile. Because they have no conception fo the speed and weight of a vehicle, they are unaware of the danger. Most of them have never owned a flashlight and trust thier instincts to walk and find their way in the dark. In the daytime, small children often sit on the very edge of highway pavement with their backs to passing traffic only inches away from trucks buses and cars passing at high speeds.

GREEN ANGELS

Green Angels are trained mechanics who roam all the major highways to assist disabled travelers. This is a free service provided by Mexico's Department of Tourism. You'll see their bright green panel trucks driving slowly down every major highway. They cover each route twice a day. If you break down, they will find you, or you can call them on your CB, channel 9. There are over 800 "Angels" covering 230 routes. If one of them helps you, his service is free, but he will have to charge you for any parts you need or gasoline. He can also provide emergency medical aid, so a tip is recommended and always well received. **If you need help and a phone is nearby, call the Green Angel central radio room 01-55-5250-8221.**

MORE DRIVING ADVICE

TOLL ROADS — Take the toll roads whenever possible as they can save a lot of time, although some are quite expensive especially if you're on a budget. We no longer post them in this Travelog because they go up so often. You can find the latest tariff rates on the internet at the following web site: http://www.capufe.gob.mx/tarifas.html

CUTTING IN — This is very common. If you are in a line of traffic and it doesn't seem to be moving and cars are passing you on the dirt on the right, chances are they are cutting in front of the line. In city traffic when someone wants to turn right or left (from any lane), one of the passengers (or driver) will stick an arm out and indicate with hand signals the direction of an intended turn. It's customary to let them. When you are in a traffic jam and someone acts like they are going to cut in but point their finger straight in front of them, they're indicating that they are crossing the line of traffic, not trying to cut in. They are usually telling the truth. Let them in.

BUSES — Passing a long distance bus (not the little local *colectivos* and *lecheros* or second class stop-and-go varieties) is usually an invitation to a duel. Do so at your own risk, or better yet, don't. They will always go faster than you. Bus drivers really seem to be bothered if you use high beams of even fog lights or drive during the day with your headlights on. They will flash you if they are feeling pleasant, but if not, they will blind you with their forty-seven running lights and two million candlepower sets of quad-headlights. It's an awesome sight on a lonely road. When passing buses discharging passengers, slow down and be prepared for them to dash in front of you. Non-drivers don't comprehend velocity.

FLAGMEN — You're bound to encounter a few sets of these. Sometimes the flagman may be only an inattentive young man with a faded red rag who is supposed to warn you about upcoming dangers. Whenever you see a guy on the side of the road with a red rag, assume you'd better slow down as there could be a myriad of dangers ahead.

TRAFFIC SIGNALS — When a light changes from green to yellow to red, sometimes the green will start flashing, turn yellow, then red. Mexicans tend to inch forward before the red changes to green. When there are four lights on a signal (and a left turn lane), one is probably a protected left turn signal. Be careful if there is no left turn lane because the fourth signal may indicate a right turn or just be an extra green.

RIGHT TURN ON RED — This is not universally allowed, unless there is a sign, usually a right arrow with the words *Continua con precaución.*

LEFT TURNS — There are at least 4 kinds.

The first is easy — When you are in a city, there will be a left turn lane (usually, not always) and a traffic signal with four lights. The far left one is a protected turn signal. You must wait for the left turn arrow. You cannot turn left when the coast is clear on only a green light. You must wait for the protected arrow.

Left turn type two — There is a sign with an arrow indicating you should exit, then it turns left in front of traffic. What on earth does that mean? You should exit right onto a lateral or access road on a divided street. Stay in the left lane. Go to a stoplight. Turn left across the street you were just on. It's easier to do than it sounds.

Left turn type three — You are on a two-lane open road. If there is traffic coming, do not put on your left turn blinker and stop in the middle of an intersection to turn left. Just before you get there, you'll see a paved shoulder to the right. You should exit right, pull around until you are heading in the direction you want to turn. When traffic is clear, scoot across the highway.

Left turn type four — This is easy and familiar. You are on a divided highway. There is a break in the median and a sign that says *retorno.* You guessed it — a turnaround.

Well, now you have had a good introduction to what it's really like to drive in Mexico. The bottom line is go and have a good time. The Mexican people are friendly and don't get all uptight if you make a few mistakes. Remember: "If you want to <u>have</u> friends you must <u>be</u> friendly."

SANBORN'S COMPANY BIOGRAPHY

Sanborn's Mexico Insurance traces its roots to 1948 when Dan Sanborn, a newspaperman from Kankakee, Illinois, began writing a unique highway guide to Mexico for his friends.

In the early 1950's, he opened a roadside stand to sell citrus juice, curios, Mexico insurance and "horned toads" (lizards that shoot blood from their eyes). With the insurance, each customer got a *Travelog*, Dan's mile-by-smile highway guide of Mexico, custom-made for the customer's itinerary.

Today, Sanborn's has more than 40 agencies located at major US-Mexico border crossings, and in Mexico. Customers can purchase insurance by using our Faxinsure or Phoneinsure service, in addition to our walk-in and mail order service. We also sell Central American insurance. It's a "family-style" business with old-fashioned values and courtesy. Each customer is "one of the family."

Tourists need Mexican insurance because neither U.S. nor Canadian insurance is recognized in Mexico. We sell Seguros del Centro insurance, underwritten by GE and sold on a daily or inexpensive six-month or annual basis. Claims are settled in the U.S., and we have adjusters throughout Mexico (Our U.S. claims service will pay to fix vehicles in the U.S.A.).

Today, the *Travelog* is a series of 9 guidebooks to all Mexico with incredibly detailed directions, history, customs and humor, which get people where they're going safely and helps them enjoy the historic routes they drive. Detailed maps of most tourist towns are included, as well as lists of hotels, restaurants and RV parks. All price ranges are covered.

TEMPERATURE CONVERSION TABLE

Fairenheit	100	95	85	80	75	70	65	60	55	50	45	40	35	32
Celcius	37.3	35	29.4	46.6	23.8	21.1	18.3	15.5	12.7	10	7.2	4.2	1.6	0

CONVERTING KILOGRAMS TO POUNDS: Simply double the kilogram figure, then add 10%. For example, if a man's weight is 80 kilos, double this (160) and add 10% (16). His weight would be 176 pounds.

CONVERSION OF METRIC WEIGHTS AND MEASURES

1 gram = 0.035 ounces
1 kilogram = 2.205 pounds
1 metric ton = 1.102 tons
1 milliliter = 0.033 fluid ounces
1 deciliter = 3.381 fluid ounces
1 liter = 1.056 quarts

1 millimeter = 0.039 inch
1 centimeter = 0.393 inch
1 decimeter = 3.937 inches
1 meter = 3.289 feet
1 kilometer = 0.621 miles

TIRE PRESSURE:

Kilos	2.1	2	1.9	1.8	1.7	1.6
Pounds	32	30	28	26	24	22

CONVERTING KILOMETERS TO MILES

Kilometers	1	5	10	20	30	40	50	60	70	80	90	100	120
Miles	0.62	3.1	6.2	12.4	19	25	31	37.5	44	50	56	62.5	75

CONVERTING LITERS TO GALLONS

Liters	1	4	10	15	20	30	40	50	60	70	80	90
Gallons	0.26	1.06	2.64	3.97	5.28	7.92	10.6	13.2	15.8	18.5	21.1	23.8

Wanderlust Publications

P.O. Box 310, McAllen, Texas 78505-0310 Ph: (210) 682-7433 Fax: (210) 686-0732

Mexico's Colonial Heart

_____ This travelog covers all overland routes linking Central Mexico's Colonial region from Guadalajara to Veracruz. Highlights include Chapala, Morlia, Patzcuaro, Guanajuato, San Miguel de Allende, Querétaro and Mexico City. ISBN: 1-878166-49-2 — 216 pages — soft cover $24.95 plus $3.50 S & H.

Mexico's Pacific Coast & Copper Canyon

_____ All overland routes from Nogales, Arizona to Mazatlán, Pto. Vallarta, Guadalajara and back. It includes details on the Copper Canyon, Pto. Peñasco, Kino Bay, San Carlos, Alamos and El Fuerte. ISBN: 1-878166-41-7 — 204 pages — soft cover $24.95 plus $3.50 S & H.

Mexico's Gulf Coast & Costa Esmeralda

_____ All overland routes from the US border at McAllen / Brownsville to Acayucan, Veracruz and back. It includes the beautiful Costa Esmeralda, El Tajín archeological ruins and Jalapa, the capital of Veracruz. ISBN: 1-878166-43-3 — 116 pages — soft cover $24.95 plus $3.50 S & H.

Mexico's Ruta Maya

_____ All overland routes from Veracurz through the Yucatan Peninsula and Chiapas, including Merida Cancun, Villahermosa, Palenque, Chetumal, Belize, the Guatemala Border and offbeat beaches. ISBN: 1-878166-45-X — 166 pages — soft cover $24.95 plus $3.50 S & H.

Northeastern Mexico

_____ Enjoy a short trip from the Texas border at McAllen, Roma, Laredo, Eagle Pass, or Del Rio to Monterrey —Mexico's third largest city, Saltillo, Montemorelos, Linares Cd. Victoria, or Matehuala. ISBN: 1-878166-48-4 — 152 pages — soft cover $24.95 plus $3.50 S & H.

Mexico's Huasteca Potosina & Central Highlands

_____ All overland routes from Saltillo and Cd. Victoria thru San Luis Potosí to Guadalajara , Mexico City and Puebla including side trips and special routes between Zacateca and Tampico. ISBN 1878166-50-6 — 228 pages —soft cover $24.95 plus $3.50 S & H.

Mexico's South Pacific Coast

_____ All overland tourist routes from Puerto Vallarta and Guadalajara thru Manzanillo, Acapulco and Pto. Escondido to Tehuantepec as well as from Toluca and Mexico City thru Oaxaca to Tehuantepec. ISBN: 1-878166-29-8 —192 pages — soft cover $24.95 plus $3.50 S & H.

Mexico's Baja, North & South

_____ All overland routes from the border to Cabo San Lucas and back; includes Tijuana, Ensenada, San Felipe, La Paz, and Cabos. ISBN: 1-878166-33-6 — 136 pages — soft cover $24.95 plus $3.50 S & H.

Mexico's Central Route and Copper Canyon

_____ All overland routes from El Paso, Douglas and Prisidio thru Chihuahua, Torreón, Hidalgo del Parral and Durango to Mazatlán and Zacatecas. ISBN: 1-878166-30-1 — 152 pages — soft cover $24.95 plus $3.50 S & H.

Sanborn's Recreational Guide to Mexico

_____ The most complete directory of RV & camping facilities and fishing and hunting resorts in Mexico. ISBN: 1-878166-36-0 — 135 pages — soft cover $24.95 plus $3.50 S & H.

Name:_____Phone:_____

Street:_____City:_____State:_____Zip:_____

Quantity	Description	Price	Extended Price
_____	_____	_____	_____
_____	_____	_____	_____
_____	_____	_____	_____
_____	_____	_____	_____
_____	_____	_____	_____
_____	_____	_____	_____
	Texas Residents add tax	@ 8.25%	_____
(1-2 books = $3.50, 3-4 books = $6.00, 5 or more = $8.00)		___ S & H	_____
		Total	_____

METHOD OF PAYMENT

_____ Please find enclosed a check/money order or _____ Bill my VISA_____ MasterCard_____

Name of Cardholder:_____

Card No.: _____ Exp. Date: _____/_____/_____

Signature: _____

FROM:

BUSINESS REPLY MAIL
FIRST CLASS PERMIT NO. 57 McALLEN, TEXAS

POSTAGE WILL BE PAID BY ADDRESSEE

SANBORN'S
MEXICO INSURANCE SERVICE
DEPT. BOOKS
P.O. BOX 310
McALLEN, TX 78505-0310

TO AIRPORT, NUEVO VALLARTA & TEPIC

MEX 200

TO LA MOJONERA

SANBORN'S ®
TOURIST MAP OF
PUERTO VALLARTA
COPYRIGHT © TRAVCO SERVICES, INC.
UD-039
(not to scale)

N
Sí
SANBORN'S ®

SIERRA PLAZA PTO. VALLARTA
PLAZA IGUANA
MELIA

TACHO'S RV PARK

PLAYA DE ORO

KRYSTAL VALLARTA

TENNIS CLUB VALLARTA

CASA GRANDE VALLARTA

RAMADA PLAZA (HOLIDAY INN)

FIESTA AMERICANA
LOS TULES

PTO. VALLARTA RV PARK

PELICANOS
LAS PALMAS

PLAZA LAS GLORIAS
CONTINENTAL PLAZA
JOHN NEWCOMB

COSTA DEL SOL

EL CONQUISTADOR

BUGAVILIAS SHERATON

BAHIA BANDERAS

Av. México

Brasilia
Guatemala
San Salvador
Nicaragua
Honduras
Panamá
Uruguay
Venezuela
Argentina
31 de Octubre
Allende
Italia

BUENAVENTURA

SUITES EL PESCADOR

ROSITA

LOS CUATRO VIENTOS

Morelos
Libertad
Lázaro Cárdenas

Bypass

Olas Altas

EL SET

Río Cuale

MEX 200

TO BARRA DE NAVIDAD & MANZANILLO

Francisco Villa
Viena

MOBY DICK
ROSITA
EL JARDIN SHOPPING CENTER
CEBOLLA ROJA
CARLOS O'BRIAN'S

MOCAMBO

ZAPATA
CASA DEL ALMENDRO
BRAZZ
POST OFFICE
CITY HALL

CHEF ROGER'S

MUSEUM

MOLINA DE AGUA

POSADA RIO CUALE

DAIQUIRI DICK'S

PLAYA LOS ARCOS

FONTANA DEL MAR

COSTA ALEGRE

TROPICANA

Díaz Ordáz
Morelos
Abasolo
Galeana
Mina
Iturbide
Juárez
Hidalgo
A. Rodríguez

31 de Octubre
Allende
Pipila
Leona Vicario
Domínguez
Aldama
Corona
Matamoros
Miramar
LA SIESTA
LOS CUATRO VIENTOS
Zaragoza
Carranza
Emiliano
Libertad
Guerrero

Isla Cuale
3 de Febrero
A. Serdán
Fco. Madero
Lázaro Cárdenas
Olas Altas
Olas Altas
Río Cuale

LE BISTRO
THEATER
LA LAGUNA
Carranza

PIZZA JOE'S

Río Suárez
Vallarta
Constitución
Insurgentes
Aguacate
M. Diéguez

LAS CAZUELAS

ROBERTO'S

POSADA ROGER
Fco. Rodríguez
Rodolfo Gómez
Pulpito
Amapas
Pilitas

SEÑOR CHICO'S

LOG 1 *START:* **Puerto Vallarta, Jal** *END:* **Melaque Jct, Jal**

UD-087

130.5 MI or 208.8 KM
DRIVE TIME 3 – 4 HOURS
SCENIC RATING – 3

This very important coastal highway is a great shortcut and has contributed much to the growth of the Tenacatita-Melaque-Santiago-Manzanillo resort areas. Formerly it was necessary to go all the way from Tepic to Guadalajara and then down to Barra de Navidad. The highway is quite winding in spots with deep cuts and big fills (watch for rocks on pavement), but there are also some nice long straight stretches mixed in. All in all, it's a nice road.

MI	KM	
0.0	0.0	After Hotel Camino Real, up a bit past lovely home ahead on right.
1.0	1.6	Now wind alongside Pacific on pretty tropical drive.
2.5	4.0	Luxury Hotel Garza Blanca (White Heron) at right and across street at left are hotel's hillside chalet-type suites, each with pool.
3.3	5.3	Presidente Inter-Continental Hotel at right.
4.3	6.9	Note Los Arcos (The Arches) in rocks at right. **KM 201**. Then La Jolla de Mismaloya Resort and Spa at right.
5.3	8.6	Mismaloya Playa (beach) at right. Also at right is Restaurant-Bar La Noche de la Iguana, named after the movie "Night of the Iguana" that put "PV" on the map. At left a half-mile upstream is El Rinconcito, a thatched-roof restaurant serving outstanding seafood including crab, crayfish, octopus, lobster, scampi, etc. Then Lomas de Mismaloya Subdivision development.
8.5	13.6	Village of Boca de Tomatlán down at right. Road goes inland and over couple of bridges.
10.5	16.8	Note cascade thru rocks 'way down at right.
11.5	18.4	More cascades at right.
12.0	19.2	Over bridge and thru settlement of Lomas de Paraíso (Paradise Hills) and famous Chico's Paraíso, an interesting restaurant set on tropical hillside overlooking waterfall.
21.3	34.1	Now nice skyline drive thru pines. Watch for livestock ahead.
26.0	41.6	Skirt edge of El Tuito, mostly at right. Topes. Then, of all things, a mile of straight. Hotel Real Del Valle at left.
32.0	51.2	Over bridge over Río Las Juntas.
42.3	67.7	Pass dirt side road (left) to San Rafael and past handful of little stores at left.
45.5	72.8	Thru settlement of El Tesquesquite.
51.5	82.4	Nice headquarters for workers on Río Tamatlán irrigation and land clearing project.
53.5	85.6	Thru settlement of José María Pino Suárez. Topes. **KM 125**.
59.0	94.4	Cross wide Río Tomatlán on long bridge and then pass side road (left) to Tomatlán, 12 kilometers, and thru La Cumbre (The Top or Summit). **GAS**, at right. Incidentally, the first tomato is said to have been cultivated in the area around Tomatlán by the Aztecs, so the legend goes. Mango and papaya orchards at left.
67.0	107.2	Over two bridges.
68.0	108.8	Over two more bridges and thru Campo Acosta, another booming farm village. **KM 100**.
75.5	120.8	Thru José María Morelos, still another farming village. Topes.
77.5	124.0	Over long bridge over Río San Nicolás. Golf ball washer on bridge.
78.4	125.4	Pass side road (right) to Las Alamandas.
80.0	128.0	Note Pacific in front and then off to right.
83.0	132.8	Pass dirt side road (right) to beaches of Perula and La Fortuna. Playa Dorada, 18 bungalows and 18 rooms and pool. Perula town and La Punta Perla.
85.3	136.5	Pass side road (right) to Villa Polinesia RV Campground (8 spaces with all hookups; camping; showers; toilets; BBQ grills; palapas; laundromat; Ph: 33-3622-3940 in Guadalajara). Thru farming community of Juan Pérez. Suites Chamela: 5 stories with pool and jacuzzi.
86.5	138.4	Catch glimpse of beach and Pacific at right and pass drug store (*farmacia*) and restaurant and **GAS** at left. Bungalows Naryar Chamela: 18 bungalows, 2 bedroom, Ph: 33-3363-7318 or 33-3644-0044 in Guadalajara.
90.5	144.8	Pass side road (right) to Chamela and over bridge. Curve right and another bridge.
91.5	146.4	Nice truck-stop Restaurant Don Lupe's at left.
94.3	150.9	Pass side road (left) to University of Mexico's (UNAN) biology station.
98.0	156.8	Cobblestone side road (right) to top-notch Hotel Plaza de Careyes (see below) and to Club Mediterranean/Playa Blanca (the latter for members only) a little farther inland.

HOTEL PLAZA DE CAREYES, styled after a Mediterranean village, is an excellent facility whose grounds cover 3,700 acres and include 8 miles of protected coastline. There are 104 air-con rooms, suites, and kitchens; nice pool; restaurant; bar; disco; movie; "Noche Mexicana" with mariachis and cockfights on Saturday nights; horses; fishing; sailing; shops; AE, MC, VI.

MI	KM	
101.0	161.6	Now curve right and over one of those curved bridges. Then over still another.
103.5	165.6	Pass side dirt road (right) to Cuitzmala, 2 kilometers, and over big bridge over Río Cuitzmala. Topes.
106.0	169.6	Thru little village of Emiliano Zapata, mostly at left, and over twin bridges. More Topes. **KM 40**.
110.3	176.5	Pass paved side road (right) to Hotel El Tecuane, 6 miles thru beautiful mango trees; 32 rooms; restaurant; bar; pool; 2 landing strips; 4 miles of beach frontage; several RV spaces with no hookups; AE, MC, VI. Ph: (315) 337-0132. In Guadalajara Ph: 33-3615-8872 or 33-3616-0085.
112.0	179.2	Curve right with settlement of Agua Caliente at right. **KM 30**.
113.0	180.8	Over long bridge over Río Purificación and pass side road (right) to Tenacatita.
118.0	188.8	Entrance right to Fiesta Americana de los Angeles Locos (The Crazy Angels), a nice, secluded hotel (221 air-con rooms; restaurants; bars; satellite TV; pool; nice beach; AE, MC, VI; Ph: 315-317-0221). **KM 20**.
120.3	192.5	Curve left past side road (right) to Hotel Bahia de Tenacatita down on nice beach among stately palms, not functioning, and to Boca de Iguanas RV Park: 50 spaces among palms on beach/lagoon; some water and electrical hookups; showers; toilets; camping; fishing. Then pass grove of tall, tall palms.
122.0	195.2	Curve left past side road (right) to La Manzanilla, 2 kilometers away.
125.0	200.0	Top! Now down – not too fast! **KM 7**.
125.2	200.3	Road down to right goes to El Tamarindo, a private club.
126.5	202.4	Over two little bridges and community of Aguacatillo, a handful of houses at right.
127.5	204.0	Nice view off to left of valley and ocean.
130.0	208.0	Thru village of Emiliano Zapata.
130.5	208.8	Come now to junction Hwy #80. **GAS**, at left. This is Melaque Junction.

IF TO: Manzanillo, etc., TURN RIGHT and start Melaque Jct. Tecomán Log.

IF TO: Guadalajara, etc., TURN LEFT and start Melaque Jct - Guadalajara Log (page 52).

End of Log 1

LOG 2 *START:* Melaque Jct, Jal *END:* Tecomán Jct, Col

UD-087

72.3 MI or 115.7 KM
DRIVE TIME 1 1/2 - 2 1/2 HOURS

0.0	0.0	From junction, proceed south toward ocean for three-fourths mile.
0.8	1.3	Turn left here.

IF TO: Hotels Melaque, Vista Hermosa, etc. continue straight ahead. See Barra de Navidad Eat & Stray (page 99) for a listing of accommodations in the area.

1.0	1.6	Seaside village of San Patricio at right.
1.8	2.9	Cross pair of bridges over little Río Jaluco.
2.3	3.7	Pass side road right to seashore village of Barra de Navidad (population 10,000). If you'd like to drive down for a look at this rather interesting place, hop to it – it's 2 miles and offers nice Hotel Cabo Blanco plus some other hotels, and you can usually buy nice big clusters of coral in the little shop on main corner. On highway, ahead and thru little village of Jaluco. **GAS** at right.
4.8	7.7	Thru village of El Aguacate (The Avocado). Topes. Note banana plantations and coconut palms.
5.3	8.5	Over couple of bridges over Arroyo Seco.
6.5	10.4	Pass side road (right) to La Culebra (The Snake). At right, also, is huge coconut palm forest – what a terrific view! **KM 5**.
10.0	16.0	LP gas at right. Then cemetery at right and into town of Cihuatlán (population 25,000). Technological School at left and then plaza ahead at left with pretty white church behind. Then up and over wide Río Marabasco on big Cihuatlán Bridge. Goodyear right. Crossing Río Marabasco, you also cross state line – leave Jalisco and enter Colima.
12.3	19.7	Pass community of Río Marabasco at left.
14.8	23.7	Thru village of Chavarín.
15.5	24.8	Straight here past side road (right) to Manzanillo's airport.

MI	KM	
17.8	28.5	Ejido Emiliano Zapata at right. Then thru La Cienega. Goat crossing. **KM 34**.
20.0	32.0	Cobblestone road right to Playa de Oro, 7 kilometers.
24.3	38.9	Bear right thru Ejido La Central.
26.0	41.6	Village of Naranjo at left, and enter Manzanillo (population 100,000).
27.8	44.5	Up over Río Miramar and pass Vida del Mar Condominium resort and club Bahia de Santiago resort development and golf club at right. Then settlement of Miramar at left.
28.3	45.3	Sharp curve left past ruins of our U.S. World War II infirmary and convalescent camp on left. Our Allied warships and freighters used to transfer their sick, mostly those suffering from tropical disease, to Manzanillo. **KM 18**. Then overpass.
28.8	46.1	Club Maeva at left, a Mediterranean-style village consisting of 440 white-and-blue villas.
29.3	46.9	Pass side street right goes to Hotel Casablanca Alamar. Then Restaurant El Dorado at right.
30.3	48.5	Thru village of Santiago (population 7,000).
31.3	50.1	After Santiago bridge, come to side road right that leads down to Hotel Playa de Santiago. See Manzanillo Eat & Stray (page 101) accommodation in the area.
31.5	50.4	**GAS**, left and come to side road (right) to fabulous Moorish-style Hotel Las Hadas, complete with golf course. Incidentally, it's very expensive. Side road also leads to Don Felipe RV Park. See area map (page 5) for location of these places.
31.8	50.9	Pass village of Salahua mostly at left.
32.5	52.0	Arco Iris Motel at right. (Arco Iris is Spanish for rainbow.)
32.8	52.5	Motel Marbella over at right on beach.
33.0	52.8	Posada del Sol at right, a condominium.
33.3	53.3	Pass Condominium Mar y Mar at right. Sports center and school at left.
34.5	55.2	Military garrison at left. **GAS**, at right. Then take left here at glorieta of sail boat for bypass around Manzanillo proper.

IF TO: Rancho Luna, Roca del Mar Condominium, and popular La Posada Inn, continue straight ahead.

35.3	56.5	Come to junction with large auditorium over on left.
36.3	58.1	Come to another monument junction. **GAS** at right. A right goes to downtown. Straight to Colima.
36.5	58.4	Veer right if to downtown Manzanillo and TURN LEFT with arrow to Colima and Tecomán.
37.0	59.2	Over bumpy railroad crossing. Then pass exit right to puerto interior. **KM 5**.
37.6	60.2	Veer right for toll road. Left is for free road.
45.0	72.0	Cross bridge over Arroyo Las Adjuntas.
50.0	80.0	Laguna de Cuyutlán shows up again at right.
55.8	89.3	Come to tollhouse and pay toll (car $40, 2-axle $80, 3-axle $120).
56.1	89.8	Pass exit (right) to Cuyutlán on coast, 7 kilometers. This is the place where late in April and in early May the famous "green wave" is supposed to roll in, a magnificent natural phenomenon.
56.4	90.2	Now thru lime-growing area. Then cross bridge over railroad.
59.0	94.4	Cross a couple of bridges over Río Palo Verde. **KM 56**.
64.5	103.2	Pass side road (right) to El Paraíso and free road.
65.9	105.4	Cross bridge over Río Armeria.
66.9	107.0	Pass exit right to Armeria (population 28,000).
68.6	109.8	**GAS** on left.
72.3	115.7	Come now to Tecomán Junction with Hwy 110.

IF TO: Colima, Guadalajara, etc., take left fork and start Tecomán - Guadalajara Toll road Log (page 150), which is the short route (via corta) to Guadalajara.

IF TO: Playa Azul, Ixtapa-Zihuatanejo, Acapulco, etc., exit right into town of Tecomán and start Tecomán Jct - La Mira Jct Log (page 10). **GAS** ahead.

End of Log 2

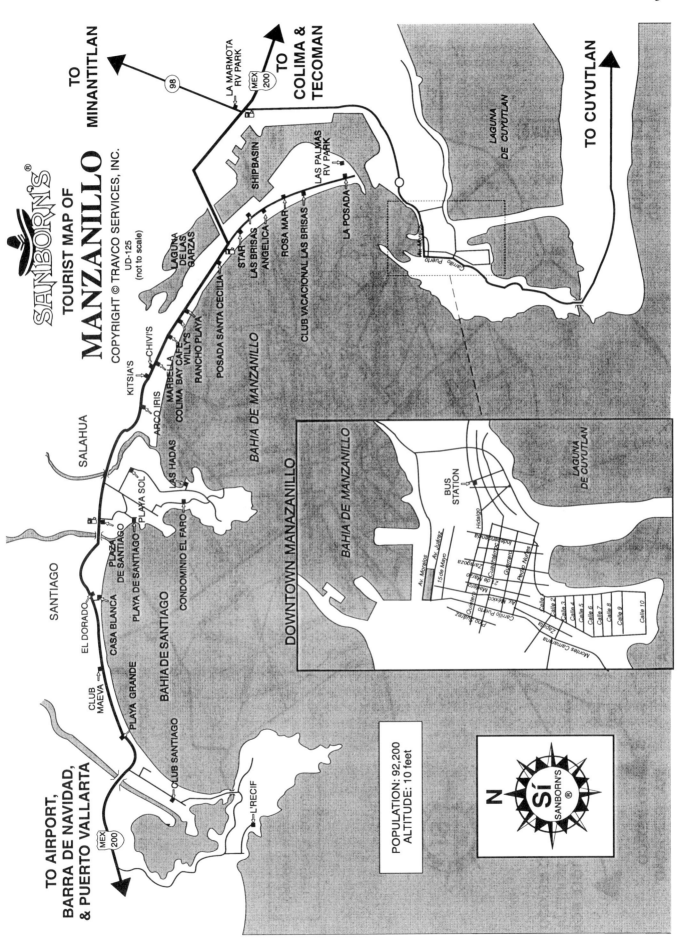

SANBORN'S®
TOURIST MAP OF
MANZANILLO
COPYRIGHT © TRAVCO SERVICES, INC.
UD-125
(not to scale)

TO
MINANTITLAN

98

LA MARMOTA RV PARK

MEX 200

TO
COLIMA &
TECOMAN

TO CUYUTLAN

LAGUNA DE CUYUTLAN

SHIPBASIN

LAS PALMAS RV PARK

LAGUNA DE LAS GARZAS

STAR
LAS BRISAS
ANGELICA
ROSA MAR

POSADA SANTA CECILIA

CLUB VACACIONAL LAS BRISAS

LA POSADA

MARBELLA
COLIMA BAY CAFE
WILLY'S
RANCHO PLAYA

CHIVI'S
KITSIA'S

ARCO IRIS

SALAHUA

LAS HADAS

PLAYA SOL

BAHIA DE MANZANILLO

CONDOMINIO EL FARO

PLAZA DE SANTIAGO
PLAYA DE SANTIAGO

SANTIAGO

EL DORADO

CASA BLANCA

CLUB MAEVA

PLAYA GRANDE

BAHIA DE SANTIAGO

CLUB SANTIAGO

L'RECIF

TO AIRPORT,
BARRA DE NAVIDAD,
& PUERTO VALLARTA

MEX 200

DOWNTOWN MANAZANILLO

BAHIA DE MANZANILLO

BUS STATION

LAGUNA DE CUYUTLAN

Av Morelos
Av Juárez
15 de Mayo
Hidalgo
Independencia
2 de Mayo
Zaragoza
Guerrero
Cuauhtémoc
Pedro Núñez
Mexico
Carrillo Puerto
Av Mexico
Zapata
Quintero
Benito Juárez
Montes Camarena

Calle 2
Calle 3
Calle 5
Calle 6
Calle 7
Calle 8
Calle 9
Calle 10

POPULATION: 92,200
ALTITUDE: 10 feet

N

Sí
SANBORN'S®

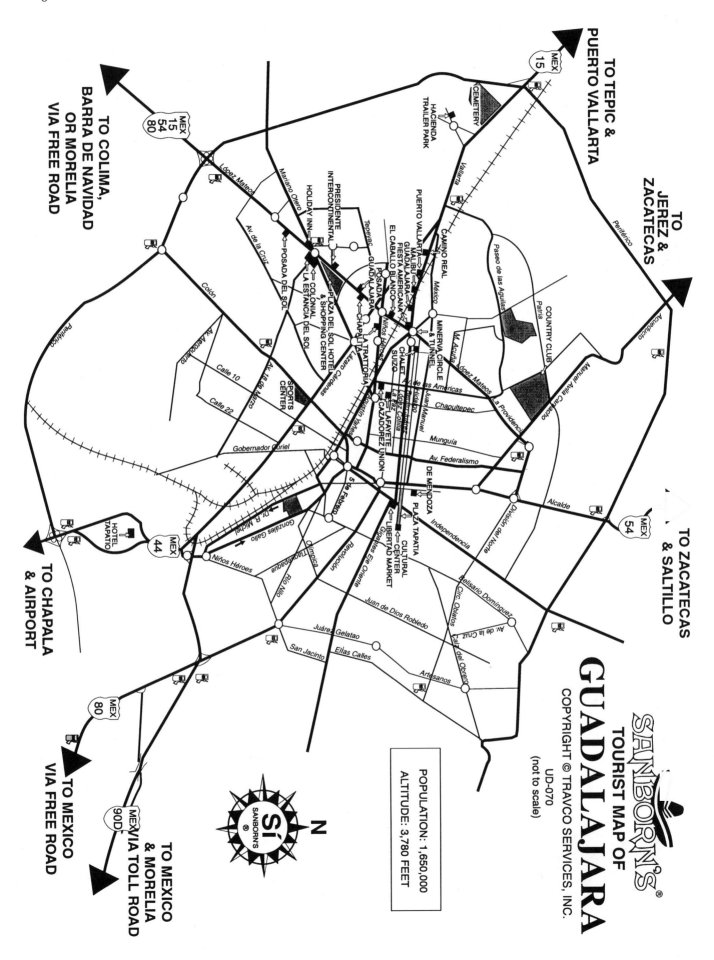

SANBORN'S®
TOURIST MAP OF
GUADALAJARA
COPYRIGHT © TRAVCO SERVICES, INC.
UD-070
(not to scale)

POPULATION: 1,650,000
ALTITUDE: 3,780 FEET

TO TEPIC &
PUERTO VALLARTA

TO
JEREZ &
ZACATECAS

TO ZACATECAS
& SALTILLO

TO COLIMA,
BARRA DE NAVIDAD
OR MORELIA
VIA FREE ROAD

TO CHAPALA
& AIRPORT

TO MEXICO
VIA FREE ROAD

TO MEXICO
& MORELIA
VIA TOLL ROAD

LOG 3 *START:* Guadalajara, Jal *END:* Tecomán Jct, Col

UD-087

146.3 MI or 234.1 KM
DRIVE TIME 2 1/2 TO 3 HOURS
SCENIC RATING — 2

From Minerva Glorieta (Mile 0) to Mile 21 of this log, this highway is labeled #15-80 where it branches off (southeast) into Hwy # 15 and (west) into Hwy #80-54. Then, about a mile further west (Mile 23 1/4) you'll come to Hwy #54 (and the bypass around Acatlán) which branches off south while Hwy #80 continues westward. (So don't become confused when you don't see any "Hwy #54" signs for the first 22 miles of this log.)

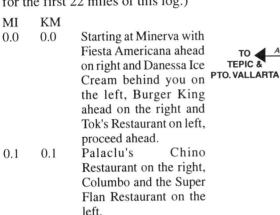

MI	KM	
0.0	0.0	Starting at Minerva with Fiesta Americana ahead on right and Danessa Ice Cream behind you on the left, Burger King ahead on the right and Tok's Restaurant on left, proceed ahead.
0.1	0.1	Palaclu's Chino Restaurant on the right, Columbo and the Super Flan Restaurant on the left.
0.2	0.3	Veer left and down on the divided freeway, under railroad thru Restaurant Row. El Caballo Restaurant will be on right along with Price Club. Firestone is on the left just before the traffic light.
0.5	0.8	You'll see a VW agency on left and after several stoplights there will be a **GAS** station on the left.
0.7	1.2	Here you'll go under Lázaro Cárdenas Street.
1.0	1.6	Motel Campo is on left, Motel Chapalita beyond, and Posada Guadalajara on the right.
1.2	1.9	Gigante department store on the right.
1.3	2.0	There is a pretty fountain on the right.
2.0	3.2	Exit here for Holiday Inn Crown Plaza and pass statue of Mariano Otero at left. Plaza del Sol shopping center and Hotel Plaza del Sol are on the left.
2.3	3.7	You pass Holiday Inn at right and Motel Plaza del Sol at left.
2.5	4.0	Chrysler dealer is on the left and Ford on the right.
2.7	4.3	Guadalajara Grill at left.
2.9	4.6	Exit here for Hyatt Hotel.
3.3	5.3	Bolerama La Calma on right.
3.4	5.4	Holiday Suites del Real on right.
3.5	5.6	You pass thru impressive eagle road markers (which used to be the city limits of Guadalajara).
3.6	5.7	Administration Bldg. for Zapopan.
3.7	5.9	Gigante on right.
4.2	6.7	Restaurante Real Cazadores on right. Also **GAS** at right, but there's a better station 10 miles ahead.
4.4	7.0	Comercial Mexicana, left.
4.6	7.3	Coca Cola on right.
5.0	8.0	Careful now! Coming to junction with Periférico (There is usually a traffic cop here.) which goes to the Chapala road (Hwy #44) to the left (exit right after overpass) and to Tepic road (Hwy #15) to right. On left is a Mercedes Benz dealer; under Pedestrian crossing is Restaurant and Bar La Camarada.
6.0	9.6	Pass side road (right) to Ciudad Bugambilias and shopping center.
7.0	11.2	Pass side road (right) to El Palomar. Gigante is on right.
7.7	12.3	Pass side lane (right) to San José del Tajo Trailer Resort.

MI	KM	
8.6	13.8	Good **GAS** on right.
9.4	15.0	Pass side road (right) to fabulous Santa Ana Golf Course and subdivision.
10.6	17.0	Pass Garden Hotel at right.
11.3	18.1	Fancy new Dunas Motel on right.
15.1	24.2	Town of Santa Cruz. **GAS** on both sides. Balneario Escondido and Vegetarian school at right.
16.6	26.6	Restaurant Mi Ranchito at right. Industrial park off to left.
18.0	28.8	Enter village of Buena Vista Take curve and wind on up.
19.1	30.6	Birriera Los Chavos at right.
22.0	33.6	Exit right to Morelia and Jocotepec. Right for Barra de Navidad also. Stay in left lane for Colima.
22.7	36.3	Topes! Pay Toll (car $44, 2-axle $54, 3-axle $75). Toll road begins here. Altitude: 1,370 m or 4,506 feet.
23.2	37.1	Bypass little town of Acatlán de Juárez. Note town down to right.
26.0	41.6	Thru the marshlands you may see egrets with no regrets or a brawny Brahma.
44.2	70.7	Pass sign that says Laguna Sayula begins.
45.2	72.3	Pass exit (right) to village of Techaluta.
53.5	85.6	Pass exit (right) to towns of Tapalpa and Atoyac over at left. Signs say this is a sand storm region.
62.4	99.8	**GAS** at right and at left.
63.5	101.6	Curve right and pass exit (right) to Sayula and Usmajac. **KM 65**.
66.0	105.6	Bypass town of Usmajac (or Uxmajac, the Indian spelling).
68.5	109.6	Thru cut and start winding for a spell. Watch for rocks on pavement.
70.5	112.8	Now for a nice straight stretch. Famous Mt. NEVADA DE COLIMA ahead to right (14,000 ft.).
75.0	120.0	Rest area and snack stand at right. **KM 85**.
77.4	123.8	Pass exit (right and up onto overpass) to Cd. Guzmán. Fertilizer plant at left. **KM 87**.
80.2	128.3	Note electrical generator plant at right.
90.4	141.4	Pass exit (right) to Atenquique and free road, but it's closed. **KM 107**.
92.0	147.2	Cross two magnificent bridges over deep canyons, Antenquique I and II.
92.3	147.7	Puente Las Agates. **KM 113**.
93.1	149.0	Cross El Nuevo bridge. Pass paper mill town of Antenquique.
94.1	150.6	Puente Los Hornos. Doesn't the rock formation on left look like an Indian guarding the bridge?
97.2	155.5	Puente Pialla, altitude 3,200 ft. Pass Mountain top town of Pialla. **KM 117**.
98.5	157.6	Viaducto Beltrán, Pass village of Volcán. **KM 120**.
100.3	160.5	Come to tollbooth and pay toll (car $46, 2-axle $58, 3-axle $79).
104.8	167.7	Cross bridge over Barranca del Muerto. This is the state line. Leave state of Jalisco and enter state of Colima.
106.2	169.9	Puente Los Lobos (The Wolves). **KM 131**.
111.6	178.6	Over puente Cuauhtémoc.
112.2	179.5	Pass exit (right) to airport and Cuauhtémoc. **KM 140**.
114.2	182.7	**GAS** on left. **KM 143**.
115.8	185.3	Pass exit (right) to free road to Guadalajara.
116.0	185.6	Pass exit (right) to Chiapa.
116.7	186.7	Pass side road (left) to town of El Trapiche. Note crosses in center of road. Divided highway begins.
119.8	181.7	Traffic going to Manzanillo keep in left lane and turn left onto bypass around Colima. For accommodations see Colima Eat & Stray (page 103).

IF TO: Manzanillo left, straight for downtown Colima.

120.8	193.3	Pass another entrance into Colima at right.
121.0	193.6	Colima over on right, a peaceful city Don't hesitate to stop if it is growing late in the evening.
121.2	193.9	Come to junction (right) to downtown Colima and (left) to Jiquilpan and North Hwy #110.

IF TO: Manzanillo, continue ahead.

IF TO: Jiquilpan, exit right, go under overpass and onto Hwy #110 and join Tecomán - Jiquilpan Log (page 54) at mile 25.

121.6	194.6	Pass exit (right) back into Colima.
122.2	195.5	Start down some dangerous curves.
122.5	196.0	Pass exit (right) to town of Coquimatlán. Restaurant Rancho Grande at right.
122.8	196.5	**GAS** on left, accessible at retorno. Then pass Colima golf course at right.
124.4	199.0	Pass retorno and side road (left) to Loma de Fátima.
128.1	205.0	**GAS** at right.
128.4	205.4	Sign says Manzanillo 85 km, Armeria 38 km. **KM 12**.
129.0	206.4	Pass side road (left) and left turn lane to Los Asmoles. **KM 13**.
130.8	209.3	Pass another road (left) into Los Asmoles.

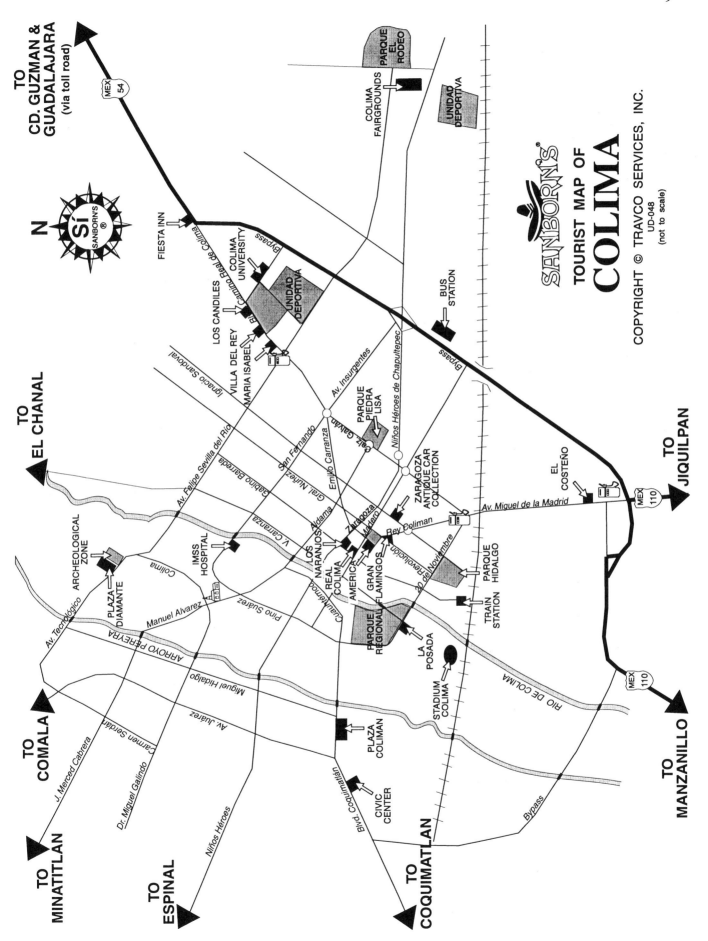

TOURIST MAP OF
COLIMA

COPYRIGHT © TRAVCO SERVICES, INC.
UD-048
(not to scale)

MI	KM	
133.2	213.1	Top and begin steep downgrade.
137.3	219.7	Pass side road (left) to Ixtlahuacan. **KM 26.**
139.2	222.7	Pass town of Tecolapa over to right.
142.9	228.6	Pass road (right) to Caleras and Madrid. Then thru coconut palms.
145.1	232.2	Note large Coca Cola bottling plant on right.
146.3	234.1	Pass exit (right) to railroad station and to town of Tecomán. This is the junction with Hwy #200 that goes south to Acapulco. Then pass a retorno left also to Tecomán.

IF TO: Playa Azul, Acapulco, exit right, crossing over highway on overpass and into Tecomán. Start Tecomán - La Mira Jct Log.

IF TO: Manzanillo, continue ahead on toll road and join Tecomán - Melaque Jct Log (page 147) at mile.

End of Log 3

LOG 4 START: Tecomán Jct, Col END: La Mira Jct, Mich

UD-087

172.1 MI or 275.4 KM
DRIVE TIME 5 HOURS
SCENIC RATING – 3

0.0	0.0	Having exited Hwy #110 at junction, proceed ahead on 4-lane into Tecomán.

Incidently during the pre-Cortés era, Tecomán was known as "Caxitlán," and it was the capital of this region. In 1523, Captain Gonzalo de Sandoval conquered it under Cortés' orders and called it "San Sebastián."

1.5	2.4	**GAS** on left.
2.0	3.2	At right is Motel Real (A/C, Restaurant, pool, parking, Ph: (313) 134-0100 Fax: (313) 134-1581. Then pass hotel Plaza on left.
2.5	4.0	Come to fork Left fork goes into downtown Tecomán TAKE RIGHT FORK to Hwy #200 Then pass Restaurant La Hacienda grill on left.
3.1	5.0	Turn left and follow signs that say Playa Azul.
4.0	6.4	Turn right onto Hwy #200, left goes back into Tecomán. **GAS** at right.
5.3	8.5	Pass road (right) to Tecuanillo, 10 Km. (6.2 mi.) on Pacific Coast.
7.3	11.7	Thru Cofradía de Morelos, mostly at left.
8.7	13.9	Pass road (right) to Cerro de Aguilar, 3 Km. **KM 260.**
10.6	17.0	Microwave relay station La Primavera ("Spring") on left. **KM 256.**
11.0	17.6	Pass side road (right) to Valle Nuevo and pass Rancho 19 on left.
14.2	22.7	Curve left and over Arroyo Zanja Prieta.
18.8	30.0	TAKE RIGHT FORK here. Slow for topes as there is a school at right. Straight is to Cerro de Ortega (population 4,000). Sign says it's 246 Km (153 mi) to Playa Azul.
20.7	33.1	Pass side road (right) to Boca de Apiza, 4 km, a settlement on the Pacific. Ahead through lush banana and coconut plantations.
22.1	35.4	Cross Río Coahuayana which is also the state line. Leave state of Colima (Mexico's third smallest state) and enter state of Michoacán.
22.9	36.6	Come to crossroads: Right is to settlement of Apiza and San Vicente and left is to village of Coahuayana.
25.8	41.3	**GAS** at right and side road (left) to village of El Ranchito and then over puente Ticuiz.
28.5	45.6	Curve right and nice view of Pacific at right and begin gradual climb.
30.5	48.8	Now down. Look at the blue ocean and the white crest of waves just ahead.
33.5	53.6	Village of San Juan de Alma with huge white sand beach. Over little bridge and more curves ahead.
36.5	58.4	"El Mirador" (where you can pull off and soak up the panorama).
38.4	61.4	Pass side trail (left) to villages of Aquila and Maquili. Stop for Army inspection checkpoint.
41.8	66.9	Cross bridge over Río Aquila and enter little town of La Placita (population 8,500). Hotel Rosales on right.
42.1	67.4	Hotel de la Costa on right. Slow for topes. Then **GAS** on left. Over another bridge. Sign says that Playa Azul is now 208 Km (129 Mi) away.
43.5	69.6	Cross triple set of bridges and start winding section ("tramo sinuoso")
44.0	70.4	Curve up and right. Again a glimpse of the beautiful Pacific. Now down.
49.4	79.0	Pass side road (left) to Ostula, curve left, and cross bridge over Río Ostulo.
53.4	85.4	Thru village of Ixtapilla and cross bridge over Río Ixtapilla. Curve right and over another bridge.
55.7	89.1	Pass side road (right) to settlement of El Zapote. ("Zapote" is Spanish for sapodilla, a tropical evergreen bearing an edible fruit and yielding chicle.) Curve left and over bridge.

MI	KM	
58.3	93.3	Pass side trail (right) to El Faro ("The Lighthouse") and curve right and over bridge.
62.2	99.5	Now thru little village of Motín de Oro down at right. Then cross twin bridges over Río Motín.
64.6	103.4	Down steep grade thru Chinapa on beach and curve right and up.
66.2	105.9	Curve right again and over another pair of bridges. Now enter zone where marine turtles are protected – this area has become a refuge because in recent years fishermen have mercilessly slaughtered them, creating a worldwide reaction.
68.0	108.8	Thru village of Colola, mostly at right, and over San Isidro Bridge.
73.2	117.1	Over Río Maraota and past settlement of Maraota at right with paved airstrip near beach.
77.2	123.5	Paso de Noria, a handful of houses at right, and over Paso de Noria Bridge.
84.0	134.4	Thru Cachán and cross big bridge over Río Cachán and curve right and up.
88.5	141.6	Thru cut. Careful for rocks on pavement.
95.2	152.3	Over Río Chocola and curve right.
101.3	162.1	Thru little village of Tizupa (population 269). Then over Tizupa Bridge and curve right and out.
107.4	171.8	Over Cuilala Bridge. From this point, you'll encounter many bridges. (You can now readily understand why it took so long to complete this section of Hwy #200!).
110.7	177.1	Over El Aguijote Bridge
111.6	178.6	Note palapa and mirador overlooking the ocean at right.
114.5	183.2	Cross long Huahua Bridge and thru village of Huahua (population 454).
115.8	185.3	Over Tinaja Bridge and a half mile farther cross El Mezquite Bridge.
117.0	187.2	Over Manzanilla II Bridge. **KM 81.**
118.7	189.9	La Colorada Bridge.
120.5	192.8	Cross El Tanque ("The Tank") Bridge.
122.2	195.5	Over curving Tupitina Bridge.
126.3	202.1	Thru settlement of El Chico Michoacán, mostly at left, and thru papaya groves. Then cross El Chico Bridge.
127.5	204.0	Mexiquillo Bridge. Then curve left and wind up and over Majahuta Bridge.
130.1	208.2	Over El Bejuco II Bridge, then Bejuco I, and another ahead, El Salado. Thru a handful of houses forming settlement of El Salado.
134.6	215.4	Cross long bridge over Río Nexpa. Then over Hornos Bridge and note beautiful beach at right with coconut palms.
137.4	219.8	Cross Boca de Campos Bridge and curve right and thru cut and up. Then pass little village of Caleta de Campos at right on beach. **KM 50.**
139.7	223.5	Over Teolán Bridge, curving to right.
143.3	229.3	Cross Majahua, La Manzanilla I and Playas Cuates Bridges. **KM 42.**
145.4	232.6	Over Mexcalhuacan Bridge and past little settlement of Mexcalhuacan at right. Then over La Soledad Bridge with magnificent view of La Soledad Beach at right.
149.8	239.7	Settlement of Chuquiapan at right and over bridge of same name.
153.9	246.2	Chuta Bridge over Río Carrizal and thru settlement of Chuta. Then two mor bridges ahead, El Fallado and Popoyuta.
157.8	252.5	Wide spot of El Bejuco at right and over bridge of same name.
158.4	253.4	Rangel Bridge and thru little fishing village of Las Peñas at right with several primitive restaurants and a secluded cove just right for camping.
162.1	259.4	Curve left and thru little community of El Cayaco surrounded by palms and papayas.
166.0	265.6	Hamlet of El Habillal at right and curve left.
169.6	271.4	Cross Acalpican Bridge, Wide spot of Acalpican, and El Bordón Bridge.
170.5	266.5	Careful now as you approach junction (right) to Playa Azul.

IF TO: If to Playa Azul (and Playa Azul Hotel and R V Park Ph: (753) 536-0024 and 536-0001 and nice Hotel María Teresa Jericó, Independencia #626. Restaurant. Pool. MC, VI. Ph: (753) 536-0005 Fax: 536-0055), turn right; there's **GAS** at Playa Azul down road at left past topes.

IF TO: Uruapan, Ixtapa-Zihuatanejo, or Acapulco, turn left and ahead.

172.1	275.4	Come now to La Mira (population 12,700).

IF TO: Uruapan, straight ahead and start La Mira - Uruapan Log (page 57).

IF TO: Ixtapa- Zihuatanejo, Acapulco, Puerto Escondido, turn right and follow Lázaro Cárdenas and Zihuatanejo signs. Start La Mira - Ixtapa Log.

End of Log 4

LOG 5 *START:* La Mira Jct, Mich *END:* Ixtapa, Gro

UD-087

68.0 MI or 108.8 KM
DRIVING TIME 1 1/2 HOURS
SCENIC RATING — 3

Although overall this is a fair stretch of highway, there are sections of rough, chuck-holed pavement so exercise caution in these areas.

MI	KM	
0.0	0.0	Here at La Mira (population 12,700) and junction with Hwy #37; proceed southeast on Hwy #200 to Zihuatanejo, Ixtapa, Acapulco, etc.
1.7	2.7	**GAS** at left. Careful for topes.
3.1	5.0	Careful for more topes.
7.3	11.7	Pass side road (right) to Sicartsa.
7.8	12.5	Come now to junction. Straight goes into port city of Lázaro Cárdenas. After passing under overpass, exit right and up over overpass for Zihuatanejo, etc. Then pass subdivision of La Orilla and airport at right. Begin 4-lane divided highway for a stretch

LAZARO CARDENAS is the location of one of Latin America's largest steel mills, called "Las Truches" or "Sicartsa," owned by the government. During its construction the town's population swelled to over 100,000! Today, however, only a mere 20,000 reside here. The nicest hotel in the area is CASTEL HACIENDA JACARANDAS (120 a/c rooms; restaurant-bar; pool; AE, MC, VI; Phone 2-3555).

9.4	15.0	Come to fork. Left fork goes into growing village of Guacamayas. TAKE RIGHT FORK for bypass and over railroad crossing.
10.1	16.2	Cross over Guayacamas twin bridges and topes.
11.0	17.6	Pass another road (left) into Guacamayas. 4-lane divided highway ends.
12.0	19.2	Begin gradual climb and curve right and left.
13.0	20.8	Note powerhouse at right and gates of José María Morelos Dam (Presa Villita).
13.5	21.6	Come to state line. Leave state of Michoacán and enter state of Guerrero.
15.2	24.3	Thru settlement of Tamacuas.
16.3	26.1	Pass side road (right) to Zacatula.
18.6	29.8	Thru little community of El Naranjito and more coconut palms.
21.7	34.7	Pass side road (left) to Elías Calles Then cross canal de Llamada. Sign says Zihuatanejo 190 km.
22.2	35.5	Thru village of Petacalco. School at right. Then over puente Petacalco.
26.0	41.6	Now cross big bridge over Río Zorcua. Then thru little village of same name.
30.6	49.0	Pass community of Coyucuila on left and over puente Coyucuila.
34.0	54.4	Pass rural road (left) to Feliciano. Over Río Feliciano.
37.9	60.6	Thru village of Joluta. Pass side trail (right) to El Atracadero. Then over Joluto bridge.
40.5	64.8	Over puente El Chico. Then thru settlement of El Chico.
44.0	70.4	Cross bridge over Río La Unión.
45.4	72.6	Pass side road (left) to La Unión.
48.7	77.9	Pass side road (left) to Chutla, 4 kilometers. Then over Río Chutla.
53.7	85.9	Thru settlement of Los Llanos and over Río Los Llanos.
57.2	91.5	Thru village of Lagunillas and over river of same name. (Lots of villages named for rivers thru here.)
59.5	95.2	Pass side road (right) to Troncones. At this little town is an RV park and a restaurant on the beach called Burro Borracho (drunken donkey). They have beach bungalows. Ph: (755) 553-0809 Fax: 553-2417.
62.5	100.0	Thru community of Buena Vista. Restaurant Compadres on left.
65.7	105.1	Cross bridge over Río Pantla. Then thru village of Pantla.
67.7	108.3	Pass side trail (right) to Barrio Nuevo.
68.0	108.8	Thru community of La Salitrera and come to junction (left) Hwy #134 to Cd. Altamirano and Toluca. Ixtapa is just 5 miles ahead on Hwy #200.

IF TO: Ixtapa, Zihuatanejo, Acapulco, etc., continue straight and start Ixtapa - Acapulco Log.

IF TO: Cd. Altamirano, Toluca, etc., turn left and start Ixtapa - Cd. Altamirano Log (page 61).

End of Log 5

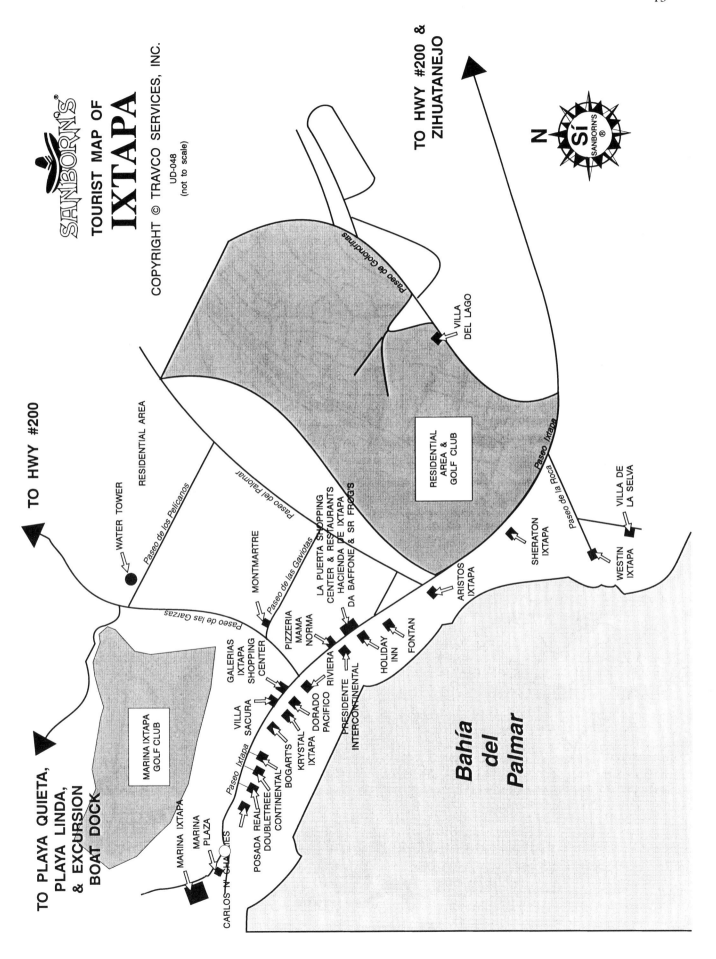

SANBORN'S
TOURIST MAP OF
IXTAPA
UD-048
(not to scale)
COPYRIGHT © TRAVCO SERVICES, INC.

N

TO HWY #200

TO HWY #200 &
ZIHUATANEJO

TO PLAYA QUIETA,
PLAYA LINDA,
& EXCURSION
BOAT DOCK

RESIDENTIAL AREA

WATER TOWER

Paseo de los Pelicanos

Paseo del Palomar

Paseo de las Garzas

MARINA IXTAPA
GOLF CLUB

MARINA IXTAPA
MARINA PLAZA

CARLOS 'N CHARLIES

Paseo Ixtapa

POSADA REAL
DOUBLETREE
CONTINENTAL

BOGART'S

KRYSTAL
IXTAPA

DORADO
PACIFICO

VILLA
SACURA

GALERIAS
IXTAPA
SHOPPING
CENTER

PIZZERIA
MAMA
NORMA

MONTMARTRE

Paseo de las Gaviotas

RIVIERA

PRESIDENTE
INTERCONTINENTAL

HOLIDAY
INN

FONTAN

LA PUERTA SHOPPING
CENTER & RESTAURANTS
HACIENDA DE IXTAPA
DA BAFFONE & SR FROG'S

ARISTOS
IXTAPA

RESIDENTIAL
AREA &
GOLF CLUB

Paseo de Golondrinas

Paseo Ixtapa

VILLA
DEL LAGO

SHERATON
IXTAPA

Paseo de la Roca

WESTIN
IXTAPA

VILLA DE
LA SELVA

Bahía
del
Palmar

14

TO
IXTAPA &
PLAYA AZUL

MEX
200

TO
ACAPULCO

MEX
200

SANBORN'S®

TOURIST MAP OF
ZIHUATANEJO

COPYRIGHT © TRAVCO SERVICES, INC.

UD-048
(not to scale)

AVILA

BAHIA
ZIHUATANEJO

Morelos

Altamirano

Vicente Guerrero

Benito Juárez

Nava

Catalina

Ejido

LA TORTUGA

Bravo

CASA
MARINA

AEROMEXICO

Juan Alvarez

VILLAS
MIRAMAR
IRMA

BUNGALOS
ALLEC & LEY

FISHERMAN'S
CO-OP

BRISAS
DEL MAR

CANAIMA

PLAYA LA MADERA

PLAYA PRINCIPAL

RAUL
TRES MARIAS

N

Sí
SANBORN'S
®

CASA QUE
CANTA

SOTAVENTO
& CATALINA

PLAYA
CONTRAMAR

ZIHUATANEJO
BAY

PLAYA DE LA ROPA

FIESTA
MEXICAN

VILLA
DEL SOL

PLAYA LAS GATAS

LA GAVIOTA

PACIFIC OCEAN

PLAYA LAS GATAS
CLUB

LIGHTHOUSE

LOG 6 *START:* Ixtapa, Gro *END:* Acapulco, Gro

UD-087

162.0 MI or 259.2 KM
DRIVE TIME 3 1/2 - 4 HOURS
SCENIC RATING — 3

MI	KM	
0.0	0.0	Here at La Salitrera and junction Hwy #134, proceed ahead toward Ixtapa-Zihuatanejo on Hwy #200.
0.6	1.0	Over Río Salitrera. Then thru village of Salitrera.
5.0	8.0	Pass side road (right) to Ixtapa, but a better, more scenic road is 2 miles ahead.
6.5	10.4	Pass side trail (left) to El Pozquelite, 2 kilometers.
7.4	11.8	Nice view of Ixtapa, and its sparkling bay at right.
7.7	12.3	Pass "mirador," also at right, where you can pull off and stop and enjoy the view. Then come to junction with road to Ixtapa. Zihuatanejo is just over 2 miles ahead.

IF TO: Ixtapa, turn right onto this "scenic" road which will take you into town. For accommodations, see Ixtapa Eat & Stray (page 104).

9.0	14.4	Then apartment complex village of Agua de Correa at left. Then come to fork.

IF TO: Zihuatanejo, take right fork into town. For accommodations, see Zihuatanejo Eat & Stray (page 107).

IF TO: Acapulco take left fork and ahead.

9.6	15.4	Pass another entrance into town at right.
10.0	16.0	Come to large monument *glorieta* Straight is to Acapulco.
10.7	17.1	Note monument made of blue blocks at left. Then **GAS** at right.
12.0	19.2	The highway is being widened for a stretch.
14.3	22.9	Pass motel Reyes on right.
16.8	26.9	Pass exit (right) to Ixtapa-Zihuatanejo international airport. Then **GAS** at right.
20.0	32.0	Down thru Los Achotes and over puente Los Achotes. Then pass side road (left) to El Zorco, 2 kilometers.
25.2	40.3	Pass little cemetery up at left. Then thru village of San Jerónimo.
26.7	42.7	Onto bridge over Río Cueros and thru Palos Blancos.
30.2	48.3	Pass a Guerrero state college at right. Then **GAS** at left
31.0	49.6	Enter town of Petatlán (population 18,000).
31.5	50.4	Over big and then small bridge over Río Petatlán.
32.4	51.8	**GAS** at left.
36.8	58.9	Over puente El Tuzal.
38.5	61.6	Cross bridge over Río Juluchuca and then thru village of same name. **KM 195**.
41.2	65.9	Sea water evaporation plant for salt at right, and thru stretched-out village of Las Salinas, set among coconut palms.
42.6	68.2	Thru settlement of Loma Bonita. Then Pacific Ocean at right.
46.4	74.2	Thru tropical coconut groves past El Cayacal.
47.0	75.2	Nice drive alongside Pacific and past whistle-stop restaurant at right.
48.0	76.8	Pass "mirador" at right - pull off for a breather if you like.
51.0	81.6	Thru Arroyo Seco.
55.4	88.6	Thru village of Coyuquilla Norte and over river of same name.
57.7	92.3	Thru Los Laureles and village of Coyuquilla Sur at right.
59.3	94.9	Thru little town of Papanoa (population 3,500) with **GAS** at left.
60.4	96.6	Sawmill and lumber yard at left. Then road seesaws alongside Pacific.
61.5	98.4	Thru village of Cayaquitos with Hotel Club Papanoa and Balneario Cayaquitos at right.
63.4	101.4	Pass side road (right) to Puerto Vicente Guerrero.
70.6	113.0	Thru stretched-out village of El Llano, more properly referred to as "El Llano Rancho Alegre."
71.7	114.7	Pass Motel/Balneario La Cabaña at right.
72.5	116.0	Over puente El Trapiche
74.5	119.2	Thru San Luis La Loma and cross bridge over Río Grande.
75.7	121.1	Thru village of San Luis San Pedro. **GAS** at right.
79.1	126.6	Pass side road (left) to Guayabillo, 6 kilometers.
83.8	134.1	Take left fork here to bypass Nuxco. Then cross bridge over Río Nuxco.
86.0	137.6	Thru village of Rodecia.

MI	KM	
89.0	142.4	Pass settlement of Tenexpa at right.
91.0	145.6	Careful for "topes" and thru villages of El Cuchil and Colonia Ramos.
93.0	148.8	Enter town of Tecpan de Galeana (population 75,000). Pass fancy church at right and slow for "vados." Cemetery at right and then **GAS**, also at right. Then school at right and take leave of town.
98.0	156.8	Pass side road (right) to Tetitlán and beach. Pass truck-stop restaurant at left.
107.0	171.2	Thru village of San Jerónimo at right. Then village of El Ticul at left and over Río Atoyac.
108.0	172.8	Pass side road (right) to Hacienda de Cabañas, 8 kilometers, and then **GAS** at left.
110.0	176.0	Skirt edge of Atoyac de Alvarez to left, straight ahead and over bridge. Then community of El Ciruelar.
111.5	178.4	Thru little community of Buenos Aires and over another bridge. Then thru village of Alcholoa.
113.0	180.8	Pass side road (left) to Ixtla, 3 kilometers.
116.3	186.1	Thru village of Cacalutla and over bridge.
118.0	188.8	Thru Colonia Cuauhtémoc.
119.0	190.4	Over bridge and thru village of Zacualpan.
122.0	195.2	Thru Vicente Guerrero. (Vicente Guerrero, 1783-1831, was an independence fighter born in Tixtla, Guerrero, and the state is named in his honor. Like many Mexican heroes, he died by execution.)
124.3	198.9	Thru village of El Cayaco and over bridge.
125.5	200.8	Thru tropical village of El Papayo.
129.3	206.9	Over bridge and thru big village of El Zapote.
131.3	210.1	Thru Las Tranquitas and on thru El Zapotillo.
135.5	216.8	El Carrizal and Bungalows at right.
137.3	219.7	Now cross big bridge over Río Coyuca and enter town of Coyuca (population 50,000). **GAS** at right.
139.3	222.9	Government coconut oil extracting plant at right. Then series of curves.
140.5	224.8	Aserradero Las Salinas (Salinas Sawmill) at left.
145.3	232.5	Thru community of El Embarcadero and over bridge.
145.8	233.3	Come to junction with bypass of Acapulco.

IF TO: Junction Hwy #95 toll road and bypass Acapulco or enter Acapulco from the north side thru toll tunnel, turn left and start stub log below. This way into Acapulco is about 8 miles longer, but it will save time by avoiding downtown city traffic.

BYPASS OF ACAPULCO

0.0	0.0	Having turned left, continue ahead on nice wide 2-lane road. Begin climbing.
11.0	17.6	Restaurant Económica on right.
12.1	19.4	Large LP gas plant on right.
12.9	20.6	Cross long bridge over a river.
13.6	21.8	Come to junction with free road between Iguala and Acapulco. Iguala and Mexico City is to the left and Acapulco to the right. Continue straight to toll road.
15.2	24.3	Continue down hill. AA center on right. Then over river Alfredo Mendizabel.
16.6	26.5	**GAS** on left. Then thru Los Organos.
17.4	27.8	Thru village of El Quemado.
18.3	29.3	Come to Autopista del Sol toll road. Merge left.
18.8	30.1	Pass monument on right.

IF TO: Iguala, Mexico City, stay in left lane and exit at retorno just ahead.

19.5	31.2	At left is the retorno (left) to go to Mexico City. Then under Acapulco welcome sign "Bienvenidos a Acapulco, Paraíso del Pacífico."
19.9	31.8	Lala milk plant on right.
20.4	32.6	Pass exit left to suburb of Renacimiento. **GAS** at left. Decide here if you want to enter Acapulco via La Cima (right lane) or the toll tunnel. Keep to left for tunnel.
21.1	33.8	Go up over overpass. The road to La Cima goes down to right. Follow signs that say to Pto. Marquez.
21.4	34.2	Pass exit (right) to Pto. Marquez and come to tollbooth and pay toll (cars $20, buses $37, trucks $61, residents pay half price).
21.6	34.6	Enter the big maxi-tunnel of Acapulco. Turn your headlights on. Speed limit 80 Kmph or 50 Mph.
23.5	37.6	Come out of tunnel. EXIT RIGHT for Costera Miguel Alemán and Diana circle. Straight is Av. Cuauhtémoc Centro.
24.0	38.4	Cross overpass and down to right.
24.3	38.9	Pass Sam's Club on right. Then Comercial Mexicana on right.
24.5	39.2	Come to Diana monument glorieta with Tony Roma and Continental Plaza on left.

End Stub Log

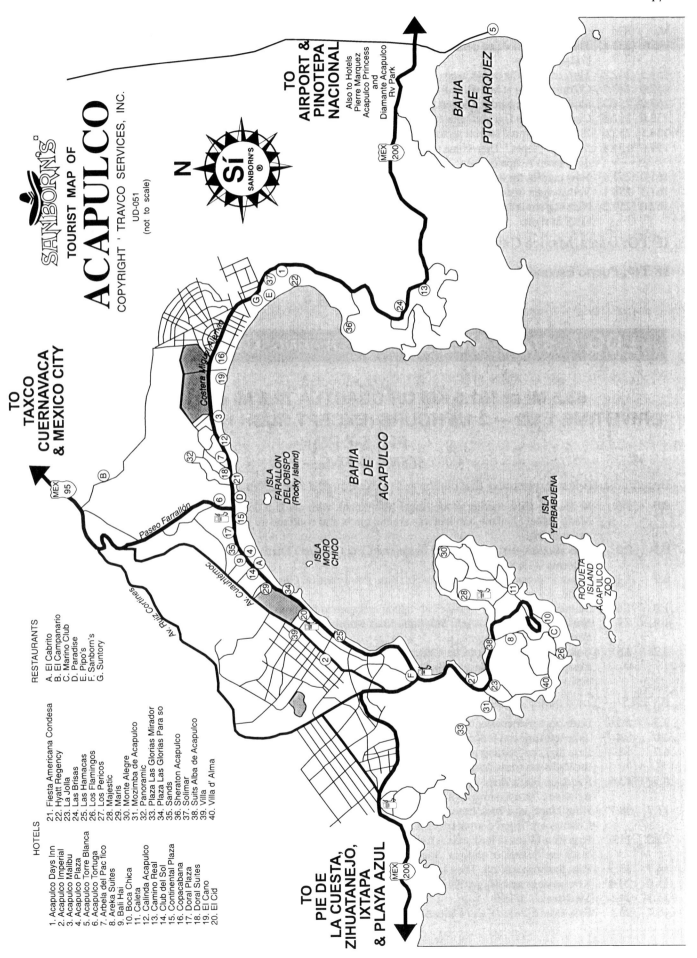

SANBORN'S
TOURIST MAP OF
ACAPULCO
COPYRIGHT ' TRAVCO SERVICES, INC.
UD-051
(not to scale)

N
Sí
SANBORN'S ®

TO
AIRPORT &
PINOTEPA
NACIONAL

Also to Hotels
Pierre Marquez
Acapulco Princess
and
Diamante Acapulco
Rv Park

MEX 200

BAHIA
DE
PTO. MARQUEZ

5

TO
TAXCO
CUERNAVACA
& MEXICO CITY

MEX 95

Costera Miguel Alemán

Paseo Farrallón

Av. Ruiz Cortines

Av. Cuauhtémoc

ISLA
FARALLON
DEL OBISPO
(Rocky Island)

ISLA
MORO
CHICO

BAHIA
DE
ACAPULCO

ISLA
YERBABUENA

ROQUETA
ISLAND
ACAPULCO
ZOO

TO
PIE DE
LA CUESTA,
ZIHUATANEJO, IXTAPA
& PLAYA AZUL

MEX 200

HOTELS

1. Acapulco Days Inn
2. Acapulco Imperial
3. Acapulco Malibu
4. Acapulco Plaza
5. Acapulco Torre Blanca
6. Acapulco Tortuga
7. Arbela del Pacífico
8. Areka Suites
9. Bali Hai
10. Boca Chica
11. Caleta
12. Calinda Acapulco
13. Camino Real
14. Club del Sol
15. Continental Plaza
16. Copacabana
17. Doral Plaza
18. Doral Suites
19. El Cano
20. El Cid

21. Fiesta Americana Condesa
22. Hyatt Regency
23. La Jolla
24. Las Brisas
25. Las Hamacas
26. Los Flamingos
27. Los Pericos
28. Majestic
29. Maris
30. Monte Alegre
31. Mozimba de Acapulco
32. Panoramic
33. Plaza Las Glorias Mirador
34. Plaza Las Glorias Para so
35. Sands
36. Sheraton Acapulco
37. Solimar
38. Suits Alba de Acapulco
39. Villa
40. Villa d' Alma

RESTAURANTS

A. El Cabrito
B. El Campanario
C. Marino Club
D. Paradise
E. Pipo's
F. Sanborn's
G. Suntory

MI	KM	
146.0	233.6	Thru village of Bajos del Ejido and come to a PGR inspection station. Your car may be checked. Then over bridge over río.
151.5	242.2	Thru edge of Pie de la Cuesta and then Barra de Coyuca, both suburbs of Acapulco.
152.0	243.2	Colonia Jardín at left. Note Pacific Ocean at right.
157.0	251.2	Slow, and turn hard to the left (follow MEXICO signs) and ahead.
158.0	252.8	Curve right and up and note Acapulco Bay over to right.
158.5	253.6	ISSSTE Hospital (social security) at right.
159.0	254.4	Slow for "topes." Then come to intersection with Hwy 95, turn 180 degrees to right, and wind down toward downtown Acapulco.
161.0	257.6	Now careful for oncoming traffic and turn left onto Costera Miguel Alemán, Acapulco's main drag.
161.3	258.1	Volkswagen agency at right.
162.0	259.2	Nice supermarket at right and Hotel Continental, also at right. Then come to Diana Circle and end of log. **GAS** at right.

IF TO: Iguala, Mexico City, etc., start Acapulco - Iguala Log (page 152).

IF TO: Puerto Escondido or Huatulco, etc., start Acapulco - Puerto Escondido Log (page 25).

End of Log 6

LOG 7 *START:* Mexico City, DF *END:* Cuernavaca, Mor

UD-087

63.5 MI or 101.6 KM OR CUAUTLA 72.3 MI or 115.7 KM
DRIVE TIME 1 1/2 — 2 1/4 HOURS (EXCEPT RUSH HOUR: 7-9:30 AM, 2-4 PM, 5-7 PM)
SCENIC RATING — 3

Beautiful multi-lane expressway that climbs and goes through a forest. Well engineered. Some steep grades.

0.0	0.0	In Mexico City, starting at the Angel Monument, with the U.S. Embassy over to right across from Hotel María Isabel Sheraton. Go halfway around circle and continue up Reforma. Stick to the middle lane — it's easier going.
0.3	0.5	Pass another pretty landscaped circle and Cine (Theater) Diana at right. Then Banca Confía, left. Signs: Reforma — Lomas straight.
0.7	1.1	Signs: Polanco — Periférico straight. Now thru beautiful Chapultepec Park, one of the prettiest parks in the world.
1.0	1.6	Statue of the rain god "Tlaloc" at right at entrance to fabulous Anthropological Museum.
1.7	2.7	National auditorium at left. Stoplight. Start working your way to the left for a left turn just ahead. Follow Perisur or Viaducto signs.
2.2	3.5	Come to Nuevo Bosque de Chapultepec exit. Veer left and curve down and around to right and under overpass. Caution! Merge with Periférico expressway traffic. Work you way to the middle lane and wind easily thru Chapultepec Park.

RV'ERS — You'd better stick to the far right lane that's for heavy traffic.

3.3	5.3	Note big roller coaster at right. Start working to left lane. The next exit right is for Toluca.
4.0	6.4	Take left fork and following Cuernavaca/San Angel signs ignoring all others.
6.7	10.7	Pass highrise housing project at right with tall trees alongside railroad industrial spur. The following exit is for Radisson Plaza hotel.
8.5	13.6	Radisson Plaza Hotel at right. Under Camino al Desierto overpass. Then under Altavista overpass. Stay in right lane for upcoming exit to Cuernavaca in 3 miles.
11.7	18.7	Note black lava rock hereabouts. This are is called "Pedregal." Now exit right at "Colegio Militar — Cuernavaca" signs onto access road, If you miss it, the next exit will do.
13.5	21.6	Pass Hotel Paraíso Radisson at right. Take exit right to Colegio Militar and Cuernavaca. Then veer right. Big black movie theater on tight. Sometimes traffic congested here. You are now on Insurgentes sur.
14.7	23.5	Pass Sanborn's at left. Then La Mansión Restaurant at left. Restaurant Arroyo at right.
15.0	24.0	KFC at right and Burger King, left
15.3	24.5	McDonald's at left.
15.7	25.1	Pass exit (right) to Calz. Tlalpan. Get ready for next exit. Be in right lane.

19

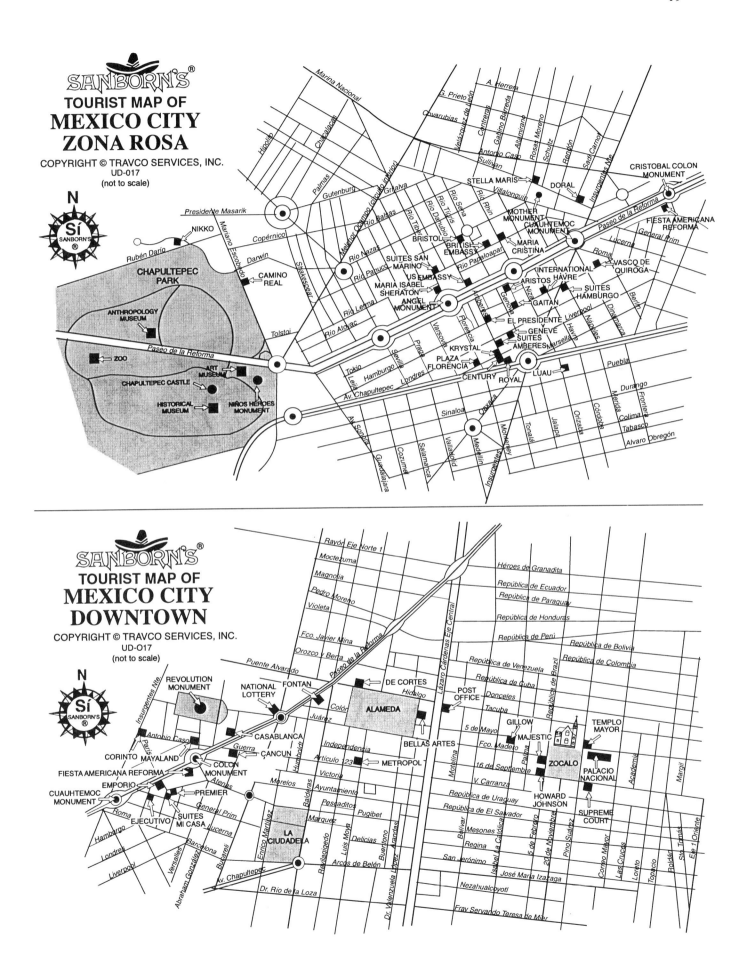

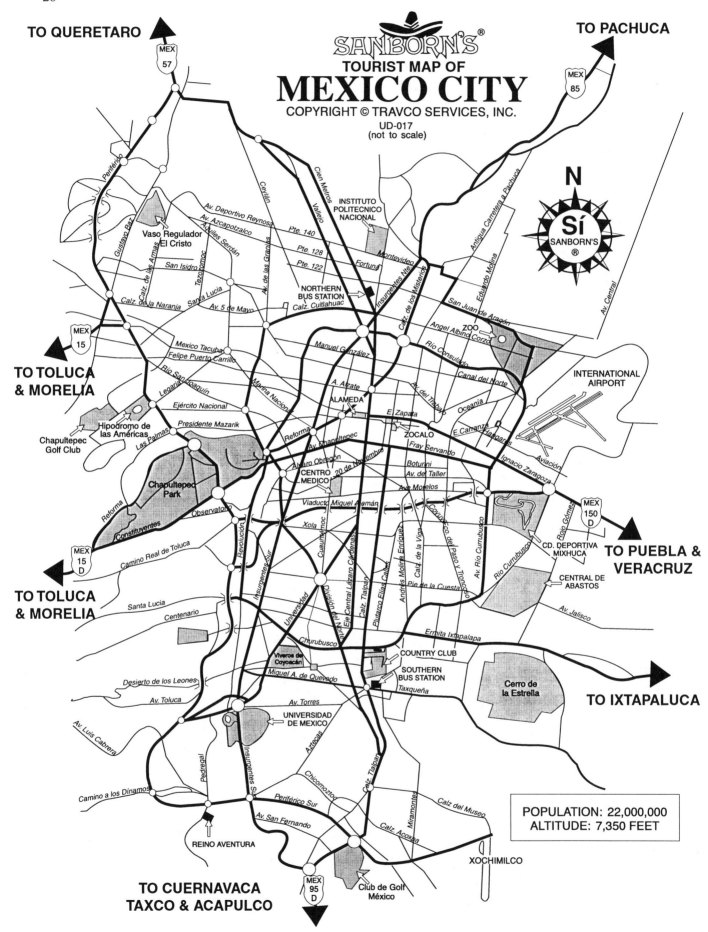

20

TO QUERETARO

MEX 57

TO PACHUCA

MEX 85

SANBORN'S®
TOURIST MAP OF
MEXICO CITY
COPYRIGHT © TRAVCO SERVICES, INC.
UD-017
(not to scale)

N
Sí
SANBORN'S
®

Periférico

Av. Deportivo Reynosa
Av. Azcapotzalco
A. Villes Serdán

Cien Metros
Vallejo
Cevián

Pte. 140
Pte. 128
Pte. 122

INSTITUTO
POLITECNICO
NACIONAL

Antigua Carretera a Pachuca
Eduardo Molina
Av. Central

Vaso Regulador
El Cristo

San Isidro
Calz. de las Armas
Santa Lucia
Tezozomoc

Calz. de la Naranja
Av. 5 de Mayo

Gustavo Baz

NORTHERN
BUS STATION
Calz. Cuitlahuac

Fortuna
Montevideo

Insurgentes Nte.

San Juan de Aragón

ZOO

MEX 15

TO TOLUCA & MORELIA

Mexico Tacuba
Felipe Puerto Carrillo
Rio San Joaquín

Manuel González

Calz. de los Misterios

Angel Albino Corzo

Rio Consulado

Canal del Norte

INTERNATIONAL
AIRPORT

Legaria
Ejército Nacional

Marina Nacional

A. Alzate
ALAMEDA

Av. del Trabajo

Oceania

Presidente Mazarik

E. Zapata
ZOCALO
Fray Servando

E. Carranza
Hangares

Aviación

Hipódromo de
las Américas
Chapultepec
Golf Club

Las Palmas

Reforma
Av. Chapultepec

Alvaro Obregón
CENTRO
MEDICO
20 de Noviembre

Boturini
Av. del Taller

Ave Morelos

Ignacio Zaragoza

MEX 150 D

TO PUEBLA & VERACRUZ

Chapulteped
Park

Reforma

Observatorio

Viaducto Miguel Alemán

CD. DEPORTIVA
MIXHUCA

CENTRAL DE
ABASTOS

Constituyentes

Revolución

Xola

Cuauhtémoc

Calz. de la Viga

Río Currubusco

Río Currubusco

Av. Jalisco

MEX 15 D

TO TOLUCA & MORELIA

Camino Real de Toluca

Santa Lucia
Centenario

Insurgentes Sur

Universidad

División del Norte

Eje Central Lázaro Cárdenas

Calz. Tlalpan

Plutarco Elías Calles

Andrés Molina Enríquez

Covuxco del paso y Troncoso

Pie de la Cuesta

Ermita Ixtapalapa

Cerro de
la Estrella

TO IXTAPALUCA

Churubusco
Viveros de
Coyoacán
Miguel A. de Quevedo

COUNTRY CLUB

SOUTHERN
BUS STATION
Taxqueña

Desierto de los Leones
Av. Toluca

Av. Torres
UNIVERSIDAD
DE MEXICO

Aztecas

Calz. Tlalpan

Av. Luis Cabrera

Pedregal

Insurgentes Sur

Chicomoztod

Miramontes

Calz. del Museo

Calz. Acoxpa

POPULATION: 22,000,000
ALTITUDE: 7,350 FEET

Camino a los Dínamos

Periférico Sur

Av. San Fernando

REINO AVENTURA

XOCHIMILCO

**TO CUERNAVACA
TAXCO & ACAPULCO**

MEX 95 D

Club de Golf
México

MI	KM	
16.2	25.9	EXIT RIGHT. Immediately work to right lane and take first right. Then merge left on to highway to Cuernavaca.
18.3	29.3	Pass exit (right) to military academy (Mexico's West Point).
21.0	33.6	After a couple of topes, come to tollhouse and pay toll (car —$40, 2 axle — $80, 3 axle — $120, extra axle — $20) and start winding up past village of San Pedro Mártir over on right. Along this road are emergency phones every 2 miles. Ahead you'll pass "retornos" or wide spots where you can park and enjoy the view — or where you can turn around and go back if you forgot your wife in Mexico City.
22.0	35.2	Note stadium way over to left and down.
25.7	41.1	Thru little town of Topilejo. Hospital at left. Nice skyline drive for a spell.
33.0	52.8	Village of Parres over to right on railroad.
34.0	54.4	This left curve is the highest point on the highway (9,900 feet). Brrrr! Where's sunny Mexico? It gets windy and cold up here.
37.0	59.2	Come now to state line. Leave Distrito Federal and enter state of Morelos. Then pass big park and monument to General Morelos up at right, one of Mexico's Top heroes of the revolution against the Spaniards, and of whom Napoleon said, "Give me five generals like Morelos and I'll conquer the world!" Continue on down under overpass.
40.3	64.5	Cross bridge over railroad and then curve left thru little town of Tres Cumbres (Three Peaks) also known as Tres Marías (Three Marys), which by the way is an ice cream dish. Now along nice skyline drive.
43.0	68.8	Dead ahead in distance on a clear day you can see famed Popocatepetl and Ixtaccihuatl volcanoes.
47.8	76.5	Stop at right and take in view. Then wind down and slow for famous right horseshoe curve called "La Pera" (The Pear). Then a left curve and straight away thru lava beds.
51.5	82.4	Come to turnoff to Cuautla.

IF TO: Cuernavaca, Acapulco, continue ahead and follow stub log below.

IF TO: Cuautla, Oaxaca, TAKE RIGHT EXIT AND SKIP DOWN TO CONTINUATION OF MAIN LOG.

STUB LOG TO CUERNAVACA and on to ACAPULCO

56.5	90.4	**GAS**, at right and left.
57.3	91.7	Chrysler dealer, left.
58.2	93.1	Exit (right) to Ahuatepec and Tepoztlán.

IF TO: Oaxtepec Vacation center, RV park and Hotel Hacienda Cocoyoc, exit here and follow log in Cuernavaca Eat & Stray (page 128).

59.0	94.4	Cross bridge over railroad. Then exit right for Cuernavaca RV Park.
62.5	100.0	Firestone dealer at left.
63.0	100.8	Colonia Lomas del Paraíso at left.
63.5	101.6	Come to Cuernavaca East interchange and old road to Cuautla.

IF TO: Acapulco, Taxco, continue ahead and start Cuernavaca - Iguala Log (page 23).

IF TO: Ixtapan de la Sal, Taxco, start Cuernavaca - Ixtapan de la Sal Log (page 96).

IF TO: Cuautla, Izucar de Matamoros turn off here, go left under overpass onto old road to Cuautla and start Cuernavaca - Izucar de Matamoros Log (page 76).

IF TO: Downtown, turn off right here and follow CIVAC signs.

IF TO: Hotel Camino Real Sumiya, turn off here, go left under overpass on old road to Cuautla. Go one block, and turn right.

END OF STUB LOG

Continuation of main log:

50.5	80.8	Careful! Sharp turnoff. Follow 115-D Cuautla or Cuautla-Oaxtepec signs.
51.3	82.1	Slow and bend right. End of divided highway, from here on it'll be 4-lane but not divided.
51.5	82.4	Over railroad and note how it goes right up a hill at left. Then wind down.
55.3	88.5	Curve right and slow for topes and come to tollbooth and pay toll. Proceed ahead and curve past Tepoztlán turnoff (right), which, by the way, has a very interesting historical convent and worthwhile museum.

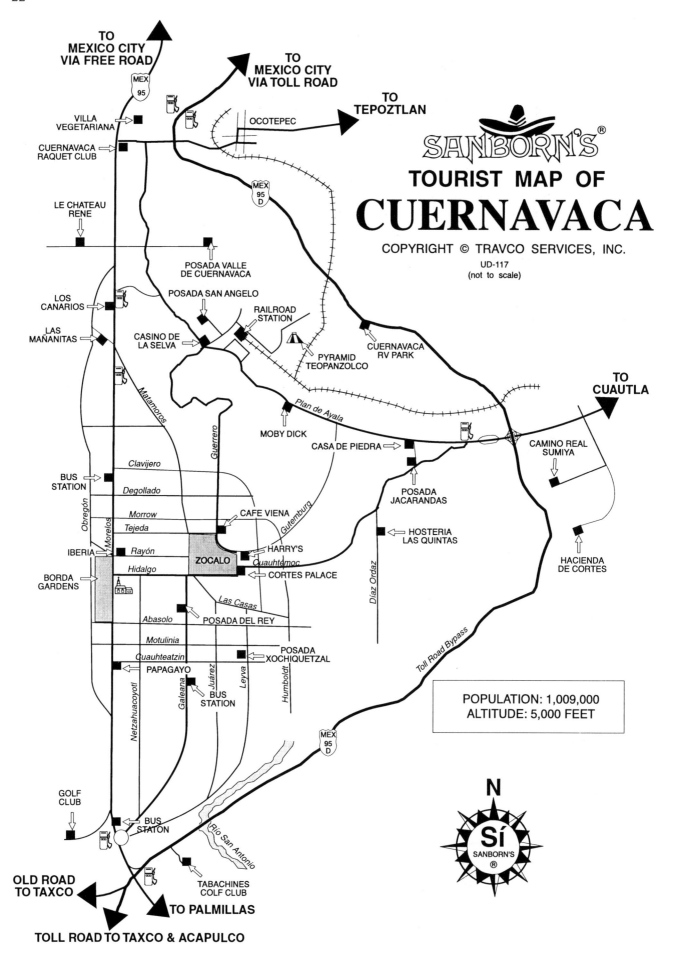

TO
MEXICO CITY
VIA FREE ROAD

MEX
95

TO
MEXICO CITY
VIA TOLL ROAD

TO
TEPOZTLAN

OCOTEPEC

SANBORN'S®
TOURIST MAP OF
CUERNAVACA
COPYRIGHT © TRAVCO SERVICES, INC.
UD-117
(not to scale)

VILLA
VEGETARIANA

CUERNAVACA
RAQUET CLUB

LE CHATEAU
RENE

MEX
95
D

POSADA VALLE
DE CUERNAVACA

POSADA SAN ANGELO

RAILROAD
STATION

LOS
CANARIOS

LAS
MAÑANITAS

CASINO DE
LA SELVA

CUERNAVACA
RV PARK

PYRAMID
TEOPANZOLCO

TO
CUAUTLA

Matamoros

Plan de Ayala

MOBY DICK

CASA DE PIEDRA

CAMINO REAL
SUMIYA

Clavijero

Guerrero

BUS
STATION

Degollado

POSADA
JACARANDAS

Obregón

Morrow

Gutemburg

CAFE VIENA

Tejeda

Morelos

Rayón

IBERIA

ZOCALO

Harry's

HOSTERIA
LAS QUINTAS

Cuauhtemoc

Hidalgo

Díaz Ordaz

HACIENDA
DE CORTES

BORDA
GARDENS

CORTES PALACE

Las Casas

Abasolo

POSADA DEL REY

Motulinia

Toll Road Bypass

Cuauhteatzin

POSADA
XOCHIQUETZAL

Netzahuacoyotl

PAPAGAYO

Galeana

Juárez

Leyva

Humboldt

BUS
STATION

MEX
95
D

POPULATION: 1,009,000
ALTITUDE: 5,000 FEET

GOLF
CLUB

N

BUS
STATON

Sí
SANBORN'S
®

Rio San Antonio

OLD ROAD
TO TAXCO

TABACHINES
COLF CLUB

TO PALMILLAS

TOLL ROAD TO TAXCO & ACAPULCO

MI	KM	
58.0	92.8	Wind down past little río at left. Note interesting rocky mountains thru here.
61.3	98.1	That's fertile Yautepec Valley down to right.
64.8	103.7	Slow over topes and come to another tollhouse. Pay toll and continue ahead under a couple of overpasses.
65.0	104.0	Under another overpass and then note ancient aqueduct over at left.
66.1	105.8	See ruins of fabulous old sugarcane hacienda at left! What possibilities!
67.4	107.8	**GAS**, at left.

IF TO: Hacienda Cocoyoc Hotel or Oaxtepec Vacation Center, turn off right here (See descriptions in Cuautla Eat & Stray, page 132).

IF TO: Cuautla, bend left and then straight ahead over overpass

71.5	114.4	Take right fork here and ahead. Then curve right as you merge with Hwy #160 at left, coming from Mexico City. Then proceed into suburb of Cuautlixco.
72.0	115.2	OK **GAS**, station at right.
72.3	115.7	Come now to junction with old road to Cuernavaca at right (Hwy #115).

IF TO: Hacienda Cocoyoc, turn right and go four miles.

IF TO: Cuautla, Oaxaca, continue ahead and join Cuernavaca - Izucar de Matamoros Log (page 76) at mile 26.0.

End of Log 7

LOG 8 *START:* Cuernavaca, Mor *END:* Iguala, Gro

UD-087

60.3 MI or 96.5 KM
DRIVE TIME 1 1/4 HOURS
SCENIC RATING – 1

The main log takes you to Iguala via the old toll road. The stub log takes you down the toll road.

0.0	0.0	Starting here in Cuernavaca at east interchange at junction to old road to Cuautla and turn off to Sumiya Hotel, proceed southbound on Hwy #95 bypass. Hotel Cuernavaca at left. Sign says "Acapulco Via Corta – 268 km, free road – 340 km." **KM 92**.
1.7	2.7	Pass exit (right) to Tabachines. **KM 93**.
2.5	4.0	Come to south interchange. Acapulco toll road is to left. Iguala free road is straight ahead. Downtown Cuernavaca on Av. Morelos is to right.
2.8	4.5	Acapulco via toll road, VEER LEFT, go under overpass and curve right. Iguala free exits to right.
3.8	6.1	Take leave of Cuernavaca.
4.5	7.2	Burgos subdivision at left.
6.0	9.6	Las Brisas subdivision off to left.
9.3	14.9	Suburban community of Xochitepec over at right. For El Paraíso RV Park, take next exit. Turn right, Go about 2 miles (east) towards Chiconcoac, then turn right (south) towards Zacatepec. After 1 1/2 miles, turn right (SW) towards Atlacholoaya. Entrance to trailer park will be on you right after about 1/2 mile.
11.3	18.1	Retorno at left to pull over for a stop. Over Río Zacatepec. Then curve left.
14.7	23.5	**GAS**, right and left.
15.3	24.5	Come to Alpuyeca tollhouse. Slow for topes and pay toll (cars –$38, extra axle – $19, 2 axle – $76, 3 axle – $114). For a visit to Vista Hermosa (5 miles), Jojutla or to Lake Tequesquitengo (9 miles), turn off right.
16.7	26.7	Acapulco (Autopista del Sol) toll road, veer left and follow stub log below. Old Iguala toll road CONTINUE STRAIGHT AHEAD and skip down to mile 17.4. Road narrows to 2 lanes. Also at right is an exit for Tianguistenco.

STUB LOG AUTOPISTA DEL SOL

0.0	0.0	Having veered left, continue ahead on divided 4-lane.
6.3	10.1	Pass exit (right) to Taxco and Iguala (free).
11.9	19.0	Pass exit (right) to Lake Tequesquitengo and Tehuixtla.
26.3	42.1	Cross state line – leave state of Morelos and enter state of Guerrero.
39.4	63.0	Come to tollbooth and pay toll (car – $61, extra axle – $40, 2 axles – $122, 3 axles – $183). Now come to the Iguala junction.

IF TO: Acapulco, continue ahead on Autopista and start Autopista del Sol toll stub log in Iguala - Acapulco Log (page 24).

End of Autopista del Sol at Iguala

MI	KM	
17.4	27.8	Village of Zacatepec over to right.
19.3	30.9	Free road parallels this toll road on left. Pass a retorno where you can pull off for a breather.
20.0	32.0	Thru little settlement with **GAS**, and tow service at right. **KM 37**.
23.8	38.1	Pass town of Puente de Ixtla at left Then over Río Ixtla.
24.5	39.2	Cross another bridge over Río Ixtla.
26.4	42.3	Sign says, "Taxco and Zoofari exit 2 km."
27.1	43.3	Go down long hill.
27.7	44.3	Under pedestrian crossing. Restaurant Michoacán at right. Come to Amacuzac interchange. EXIT RIGHT (follow ACAPULCO CUOTA and TAXCO CUOTA signs). It's a sharp right curve and then a very sharp left curve and under overpass. Straight for Taxco – Iguala Free. **KM 44**.
28.5	45.6	Pass little town of Amacuzac over to left and cross bridge over Río Amacuzac.
30.7	49.1	Thru Casahuatlán.
32.5	52.0	Cross state line – leave state of Morelos and enter state of Guerrero. **KM 52**.
35.8	57.3	Dangerous curve right.
37.0	59.2	Pass exit right to Taxco toll road. Then follow along railroad for a spell.
47.0	75.2	Stone quarry up at left.
48.0	76.8	Cross bridge over railroad.
51.3	82.1	Summit – 4,300 feet. Then start winding down.
57.3	91.7	There's Lake Tuxpan off and over to left.
59.8	95.7	Slow for tope and stop at tollbooth to pay toll (car – $7, 2-axle – $13, 3-axle - $19, extra axle – $6). Clean restrooms at tollbooth. Then TAKE LEFT FORK for Acapulco. Right fork goes to Iguala and back to Taxco.

IGUALA is the "Philadelphia of Mexican Independence" –where Iturbide drafted his Plan of Three Guarantees and where independence was proclaimed on February 24, 1821. It was here that the Mexican flag was first hoisted over a government building. There are a couple of emergency hotels here (downtown) – the Royalty and the Velasco, but the best in the area is La Cabaña Motel/Restaurant near the junction.

| 60.3 | 96.5 | Come now to big **GAS** station, at right. |

IF TO: Acapulco, take left fork and start Iguala - Acapulco Log.

IF TO: Ixtapan de la Sal, Taxco, take right fork and start Iguala - Ixtapan de la Sal Log (page 152).

End of Log 8

LOG 9 *START:* Iguala, Gro *END:* Acapulco, Gro (Toll)

UD-087

144.0 MI or 230.4 KM
DRIVE TIME 4 – 4 1/2 HOURS
SCENIC RATING - 1

NOTE: Having taken the left fork here at Iguala junction, proceed ahead past **GAS**, at right. If you have decided to take the Autopista del Sol to Acapulco, follow ACAPULCO CUOTA signs and start this log below. For free road turn to Iguala - Acapulco Log Free (page 40). The free road is for the adventurous, is curvy and is often in poor shape. Toll road is for the rich.

0.0	0.0	Starting here at Iguala junction at entrance to toll road with **GAS**, on right and left, proceed ahead on 4-lane divided.
17.0	27.2	Retorno to left. This highway goes thru many rock cuts and hills but is flat with no sharp curves.
26.4	42.2	Cross bridge over Río Mezcala. **KM 221**.
34.5	55.2	Scenic pullover at right and left.
37.0	59.2	Pass exit (left) to free road to Chilpancingo. Careful for high winds thru here. **KM 237**.
54.5	87.2	Pass exit (right) for free road to return to Iguala. **KM 267**.
55.1	88.2	Pass exit (right) to Chichualca.

MI	KM	
59.5	95.2	Pass exit (right) to Chilpancingo. **KM 276**.
60.7	97.1	**GAS**, at right. No ice cream. Hotel/restaurant with clean restrooms. Also pass exit to Tierra Colorada. We're now in Chilpancingo.
61.4	98.2	Pass exit (right) to Petaquillas.
67.6	108.2	Come to tollbooth and pay toll (cars – $55, extra axle – $27, 2 axle – $110, 3 axle – $165). **KM 289**.
122.0	195.2	Come to last tollbooth and pay toll (cars – $25, extra axle – $12, 2 axle – $50, 3 axle – $75).
122.5	196.0	At left is the retorno (left) to go back to Mexico City. Then under Acapulco welcome sign "Bienvenidos a Acapulco, Paraíso del Pacífico."
122.9	196.6	Lala milk plant on right.
123.4	197.4	Pass exit left to suburb of Renacimiento. **GAS** at left. Decide here if you want to enter Acapulco via La Cima (right lane) or the toll tunnel. Keep to left for tunnel.
124.1	198.6	Go up over overpass. The road to La Cima goes down to right. Follow signs that say to Pto. Marquez.
124.4	199.0	Pass exit (right) to Pto. Marquez and come to tollbooth and pay toll (cars $20, buses $37, trucks $61, residents pay half price).
124.6	199.4	Enter the big maxi-tunnel of Acapulco. Turn your headlights on. Speed limit 80 Kmph or 50 Mph.
126.5	202.4	Come out of tunnel. Exit right for Costera Miguel Alemán and Diana circle. Straight is Av. Cuauhtémoc Centro.
127.0	203.2	Cross overpass and down to right.
127.3	203.6	Pass Sam's Club on right. Then Comercial Mexicana on right.
127.5	204.0	Come to Diana monument glorieta with Tony Roma and Continental Plaza on left. For info on accommodations see Acapulco Eat & Stray (page 110)

Welcome to Acapulco!
End of Log 9

LOG 10 *START:* Acapulco, Gro *END:* Pto. Escondido, Oax

UD-077

261.4 MI or 418.2 KM
DRIVE TIME 6 – 6 1/2 HOURS
SCENIC RATING – 3

Careful for livestock in right-of-way. This section of the Pacific Coast south of Acapulco is known as "Costa Chica" (Little Coast), a country of low hills and open grasslands reminiscent of the African veld. And speaking of Africa, along this highway in Cuajinicuilapa and surrounding area resides Mexico's only Black population. Also along this route you'll encounter military checkpoints, part of Mexico's campaign against arms and drug smuggling.

MI	KM	
0.0	0.0	Here in Acapulco at Diana Circle heading eastward along Costera M. Alemán, pass **GAS**, at left. Then begin long concrete jungle of hotels – Fiesta Tortuga, Condesa del Mar, El Presidente, Holiday Inn, etc.
1.0	1.6	Acapulco sports center at left.
1.3	2.1	Convention center at left housing restaurants, cafes, bars, theaters, discos, and more.
2.0	3.2	Pass Romano's Le Club Hotel at right.
2.3	3.7	Come now to "glorieta" (circle). Go three-quarters way around and out and divided ends. Follow PTO. MARQUEZ, PINOTEPA NACIONAL, and AEROPUERTO signs.
4.0	6.4	Past entrance (left) to unique Hotel Las Brisas.
5.5	8.8	Nice view of Puerto Marquez down at right. This sparkling bay is where many pirates who sailed the Pacific anchored in the olden days for provisions as well as for protection from enemies and storms.
7.5	12.0	Slow as you approach exit (right) to Pinotepa Nacional or Pto. Marqués. Left lane takes you to airport and Acapulco Princess. For Pinotepa Nacional, stay in right lane and at signal light TURN LEFT. A right turn here takes you to Pto Marqués.
10.0	16.0	Pass Motel Paraíso on right.
11.8	18.9	TAKE RIGHT FORK and follow "Pinotepa Nacional" (245 km) sign. Left is to Acapulco and Mexico City.
12.2	19.5	Thru settlement of El Cayaco. Restaurant Entre Amigos ("Among Friends") on right.
13.0	20.8	Coca cola bottling plant on left. Then thru Tunzingo.
15.0	24.0	Thru another settlement, this one called Tres Palos.
16.4	26.2	Cross bridge over a 4-lane divided highway. No signs.
17.0	27.2	Thru Nicolás Bravo.
18.1	29.0	Thru San Pedro de las Playas.
18.4	29.4	El Nuevo Paraíso Restaurant, up on hill at left.

MI	KM	
19.5	31.2	Over puente El Bejuco and thru settlement of El Bejuco ("The Rattan").
24.2	38.7	Thru village of San Antonio.
28.9	46.2	Over bridge over Río Papagayo ("Parrot River").
32.8	52.5	Thru little hamlets of San Juan Grande first and San Juan Chico following.
36.9	59.0	Over El Cortés Bridge and thru settlement of El Cortés.
41.0	65.6	Thru La Estancia ("The Stay") and over La Estancia Bridge.
46.5	74.4	Enter village of San Marcos (population 10,000). Emergency Hotel and Restaurant Lecarma at right and cemetery at left. Careful for topes.
53.1	85.0	Acamiel honey processing plant on right.
60.2	96.3	Thru town of Las Vigas, ("The Beams"). Population: 4,500. Then over Las Vigas Bridge.
62.8	100.5	Thru Las Lomitas and over Nexpa Bridge. Thru little hamlet of El Porvenir ("The Future").
70.8	113.3	Thru village of Cruz Grande. Then the 48th infantry battalion garrison at right.
71.4	114.2	**GAS** at left. Next 13 miles are low, rolling hills.
74.8	119.7	Over Jalapa Bridge. (Incidentally, bridge in Spanish is "puente").
83.2	133.1	Curve left, then right and over Río Copala.
84.3	134.9	Pass town of Copala at left and highway begins to climb alongside base of Sierra Madres.
95.9	153.4	Over one bridge and then another over Río Marquelia and thru little sea-level town of Marquelia (population 10,000) – Pacific is a few miles to right.
109.6	175.4	Thru village of Juchitán.
120.3	192.5	Over bridge over Río Quetzalán. Then pass side road (left) to Ometepec, once a gold-mining center and still quite charming. (Medical missionaries of the Southern Presbyterian Church operate small "Hospital de la Amistad" ("friendship") here – visitors welcome.
127.1	203.4	Village of Milpillas at right and over bridge over Río Santa Catarina.
132.8	212.5	Over Barajillas Bridge and thru village of same name.
136.8	218.9	Enter little town of Coajinicuilapa. **GAS** at left. (If you're ready for a breather, Restaurant Lucy at left is OK; clean restrooms; friendly; interesting paintings).

Here in Coajinicuilapa dwells Mexico's only Black population, some of whom are descendants of African Bantu tribesmen while others trace their origin back to Zanzibar, where Ambrosio González, a Spanish noble (and once owner of these lands) brought them to replace the Indians who worked the mines and sugar plantations. The town was founded in 1562 by 40 families of African slaves who were freed in these parts; today this capitol of Afro-Mexico has grown to a population of 4,500. Many old customs still survive and are evidenced by the round huts, the long tunics worn by the older women, the young women carrying their infants on one hip, and their peculiar Spanish accent (similar to the Castilian spoken by Cuban Blacks).

MI	KM	
138.3	221.3	Take leave of the town of Coajinicuilapa. Then pass side road (right) to Punta Maldonado.
142.4	227.8	Come now to state line. Leave state of Guerrero and enter state of Oaxaca.
151.5	242.4	Thru La Estancia with its cemetery at left. **KM 222**.
152.8	244.5	Pass side road (right) to El Ciruelo.
154.8	247.7	Thru settlement of Lagunillas.
165.0	264.0	Thru little village of Mancuernas.
166.1	265.8	LP gas on right.
166.6	266.6	Pass road (left) to Cacahuatepec and Tlaxiaco (Hwy #125).
168.8	270.1	Military garrison at right housing the 47th Infantry Battalion. Then **GAS** at left.
169.9	271.8	Motel Las Gaviotas on left. Then Pepe's hotel and restaurant also on left.
170.6	273.0	Motel Carmona on right and into Pinotepa Nacional, a tropical town of 40,000 and a busy farm center for the Amusgo Indians with their colorful Sunday market (note stalls on both sides of highway). Pass nice Restaurant and Club Campestre (enter thru white arches at right; good sandwiches and meals; pool; nice setting).
171.8	274.9	Take leave of Pinotepa Nacional.
174.0	278.4	Curve left and over bridge. Note waterfall at left.
179.0	286.4	Thru village of Rancho Viejo.
182.3	291.7	Thru village of Huaxpaltepec.
190.3	304.5	Now thru village of Jamiltepec. **KM 30**.
190.6	305.0	**GAS** at right.
189.5	303.2	Cross twin bridges over Río Verde. **KM 50**.
209.3	334.9	Thru village of San José del Progreso. A mile farther on pass Industrial Citrícola ("citrus industry") de Oaxaca. Laguna de Chicahua Bird Refuge toward Pacific at right.
214.8	343.7	Thru village of Santa Rosa de Lima. Then **GAS** at right.
229.5	367.2	Over bridge and enter Río Grande (population 12,000). Then over bridge, curve to right, and out.
230.6	269.0	Pass Hotel Paraíso Río Grande at right and take leave of Río Grande.
235.2	376.3	Cross Hidalgo bridge over big river.

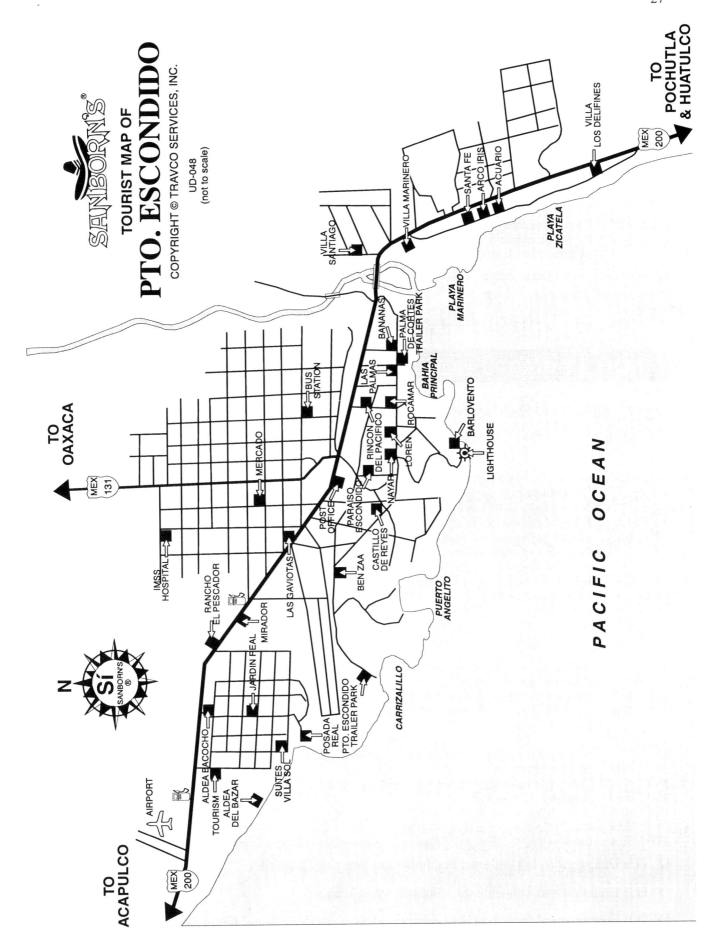

SANBORN'S®

TOURIST MAP OF

PTO. ESCONDIDO

COPYRIGHT © TRAVCO SERVICES, INC.

UD-048
(not to scale)

TO
POCHUTLA
& HUATULCO

MEX
200

VILLA
LOS DELIFINES

SANTA FE
ARCO IRIS
ACUARIO

VILLA MARINERO

PLAYA
ZICATELA

VILLA
SANTIAGO

BANANAS

PALMA
DE CORTES
TRAILER PARK

PLAYA
MARINERO

LAS
PALMAS

BAHIA
PRINCIPAL

ROCAMAR

BARLOVENTO

RINCON
DEL PACIFICO

LOREN

BUS
STATION

LIGHTHOUSE

MERCADO

POST
OFFICE

PARAISO
ESCONDIDO

NAYAR

CASTILLO
DE REYES

TO
OAXACA

MEX
131

BEN ZAA

PUERTO
ANGELITO

PACIFIC OCEAN

IMSS
HOSPITAL

RANCHO
EL PESCADOR

LAS GAVIOTAS

MIRADOR

CARRIZALILLO

N

Sí
SANBORN'S
®

JARDIN REAL

POSADA
REAL

PTO. ESCONDIDO
TRAILER PARK

AIRPORT

TOURISM

ALDEA BACOCHO

ALDEA
DEL BAZAR

SUITES
VILLA SOL

TO
ACAPULCO

MEX
200

28

MI	KM	
251.2	401.9	Pass La Isla del Gallo (Rooster Island).
251.4	402.2	Pass Instituto Bíblico Genesaret at right. Then Aguaje el Zapote.
255.8	409.3	One more big bridge, this one over Río Chila.
259.6	415.4	Puerto Escondido's airport at left. Then **GAS**, left.
260.1	416.2	Tourist information house about 1/2 block down on right.
260.5	416.8	Hotel Aldea Bacocho on right and pass side road (right) to Fraccionamiento ("subdivision") Bacocho at right and to Castel Puerto Escondido and also Hotel Jardín Real. Then Hotel El Camino del Sol, left.
260.9	417.4	Hotel Rancho El Pescador at left. Then enter city limits of Puerto Escondido (population 38,200).
261.1	417.8	Puerto Angelito – Carrizalillo beach and tourist office at right. Then Restaurant Tolteca, left. Agencia Municipal, right. Big Coca Cola sign on building at left. For Puerto Escondido Trailer Park on beach, turn right here, go one block, then right again and down partially paved road. Nice view of Puerto Escondido Bay at right.
261.4	418.2	Come to junction (left) with Hwy #131 to Oaxaca which has recently been resurfaced. To right is road into delightful seaside town of Puerto Escondido ("Hidden Port"). For info on accommodations see Puerto Escondido Eat & Stray (page 119).

IF TO: Pochutla, Puerto Angel, Oaxaca, Salina Cruz, Tehuantepec, etc., continue ahead and start Pto. Escondido - Tehuantepec Log.

End of Log 10

LOG 11 *START:* Pto. Escondido *END:* Tehuantepec, Oax

UD-087

170.0 MI or 272.0 KM
DRIVE TIME 3-4 HOURS
SCENIC RATING – 2

MI	KM	
0.0	0.0	Here at junction with Hwy #131 to Oaxaca (left) and also side road (right) into idyllic tropical town of Puerto Escondido, proceed ahead on Hwy 200. Careful for topes and curve right with white sandy beach down at right. Hotel San Juan, right. Very nice. Then pass Hotel Villa Escondida at right.
0.3	4.8	Bilingual cultural institute at left. Then Hotel-Restaurant Doña Vito also on left.
0.5	0.8	Military garrison at left where the 54th Infantry Battalion is stationed. Over puente Regadillo.
0.7	1.1	Pass side road (right) to Zicatelo, Marinero beach, Búngalos Villa Marinero, Santa Fe Hotel, and vegetarian restaurant downhill to right on Calle de la Morro. Cabañas Eda at right. Sign says "Pochutla, 70 Km."
1.4	2.2	Hotel Il Villandante at left. Zicatelo beach to right.
1.6	2.6	Villa del Mar, right.
1.9	3.0	Pass exit right to Hotel Villa Bay.
2.7	4.3	Pass another exit (right) to Zicatelo beach.
3.0	4.8	Las Tortugas Ecological area at left.
3.3	5.3	**GAS** at right.
3.8	6.1	Village of Barra de Colotepec and curve left and over big bridge over river of same name. Road is straight with some ups and downs.
15.8	25.3	Over Río Valdeflores. Settlement of Valdeflores.
18.8	30.1	Big topes in and out of settlement of Santa Elena at right. Pass side road (left) to village of San Bernardino and Cozoaltepec.
20.3	32.5	Curve left, then straight, with view of Pacific at right.
23.5	37.6	Over Río Cozoaltepec and another view of beach at right.
29.2	46.7	Over Puente La Gartero.
33.8	54.1	Curve right thru village of San Isidro and over big bridge. Pass wide spot of El Venado (The Deer) at right.
36.9	59.0	Restaurant El Paso, right.
38.5	61.6	Thru village of San Antonio. **KM 198**.
39.0	62.4	Pass El Coco school at right. **KM 200**.
44.0	70.4	Come to junction Hwy #175. Sign says: "Salina Cruz 185 km, Huatulco 40 km." **KM 210**.

IF TO: Oaxaca, turn left and start Pochutla - Oaxaca Log (page 68).

IF TO: Huatulco and Tehuantepec, continue straight ahead.

IF TO: Puerto Angel, turn right. For accommodations see Pto. Angel Eat & Stray (page 121).

PUERTO ANGEL, at the end of a winding stretch of 8 miles, is a quaint little village reflecting itself in the blue waters of a small bay where fishing boats and naval ships doze. Besides the naval base, a few seafood restaurants, and its colorful fishing market (at mid morning on the dock upon the fishing boats' arrival), Puerto Angel offers two swimming beaches – "Zipolite," long and easily accessible where everybody wears a swim suit and "Playa del Amor" (Love Beach), small and encircled by hills and reached only by a brisk walk, where only birthday suits are used, this being the first public nudist beach in Mexico!

MI	KM	
48.5	77.6	Over bridge over Río El Aguacate (The Avocado) which curves around to left and pass side road right to village of Zapotengo, 2 miles away, and curve left. Look at those rocks on hillside at left. Careful for rocks on road – this is a landslide area "zona de derrumbes." There are lots of burned-out cases in Mexico a la Graham Greene. More good folks have "found" themselves here than you'd suspect.
53.7	85.9	Thru village of El Pinal. **KM 227.**
54.0	86.4	Come to crossroads: (right) to village of Coyula, and (left) to settlement of El Limón.
58.6	93.8	Over bridge over Río Coyula curving to left. Goat crossing. **KM 233.**
61.0	97.6	Another crossroads. This is not your exit for Huatulco, the resort. Pass side road (left) to big village of Sta. María Huatulco (but there is an RV park and economic hotels) while right is to village of El Arenal (sandy ground) and on to San Augustín. The latter is perched on a nice bay, but unless you drive a four-wheel vehicle, those 5 miles separating the highway from the bay are treacherous.
61.7	98.7	Thru wide spot of Agua el Zapote. Over Río Cuajiniquil (the pronunciation could kill you).
62.0	99.2	Huatulco's airport, left. **GAS**, right.
64.8	103.7	Over one more river, this one named Río del Xuchitl.
70.0	112.0	Pass side road (right) to Bahía Santa Cruz de Huatulco, 3 1/2 miles. This is the resort. It's maybe one of the prettiest places around. See Huatulco Eat & Stray (page 122) for accommodations. There's **GAS,** in town. Sign say "Salina Cruz, 145 Km."
71.2	113.9	Over puente Chaguey.
71.5	114.4	Pass side road (right) that takes you to Club Med and Tangolunda, Sheraton and other Huatulco hotels. Go under overpass to get there.
72.6	116.2	Over another river, this one named Río Tangolunda. Sometimes (depending on the time of year) any or all of these bridges will have bad surfaces. Keep alert. Pass side road (right) to Tangolunda.
78.4	125.4	One more bridge over Río Copalita and thru village of Copalita at right.
78.9	126.2	Restaurant Norma at right. Very windy road thru here.
85.7	137.1	Over bridge that curves around to right over Río Zimatán.
88.9	142.2	Then over Río Chacalapa. **KM 280.**
91.3	146.1	Pass side road (left) to village of Chacalapa. Then pass huge rock on right called Piedra del Rosario.
98.5	157.6	Over big bridge and then small bridge over Río Ayuta.
100.0	160.0	Straight stretch for a spell.
104.7	167.5	Over Río Coyul. 3 big TOPES. Thru settlement of El Coyul. Nice little humble Restaurant Romita for snacks and soft drinks on right. **KM 299.**
105.8	169.3	Curve left and over big bridge and two smaller ones.
109.3	174.9	Thru little village of Tapanala and out over bridge over Río Tapanala. Careful for pigs, really.
112.1	179.4	Settlement of Santa María Huamelula (population 7,600) and out over big bridge curving to right over Río Huamelula. **KM 317.**
114.5	183.2	Village of Santiago Astata (population 2,200) at right.
115.1	184.2	Pass side road (left) to San Pedro Huamelula and over bridge over Río Huamelula.
122.0	195.2	Salt drying beds, right. **KM 332.** The isthmus ahead, by the way, was once a contender for the "big ditch" that ended up going thru Panama. Strong winds begin to blow thru here. RV'rs beware!
133.3	213.3	Note beautiful beach down to right – what a terrific spot for a resort. (Venerable Dan wrote that, back in the 1960's. I reckon he knew a good thing when he saw it!)
135.3	216.5	Over three bridges and then little village of Rincón Bamba down at left. Pass side road (right) to Concepción on Bamba beach (2 km away).
139.6	223.4	Settlement of Santa ("Sta.") Gertrudis Miramar at right.
141.6	226.6	Pass side road (left) to Aguascalientes (There's no hot water.) and Santa Clara.
143.5	229.6	Thru little village of El Morro Mazatán. Restaurant Mari at left has a good breakfast. Now you'll enter the red-rock country. **KM 365.**
151.3	242.1	Over puente Corralito.
152.4	243.8	Pass road (right) to Guillaguiche.
158.5	253.6	Hotel-Restaurant Playa del Marquez, right.
159.5	255.2	Up and thru a couple of cuts and then nice view of Salina Cruz Bay, its naval base, and Pemex storage dock. Then wind on down. See Salina Cruz Eat & Stray (page 123) for accommodations in the area.
161.3	258.1	TOPES. Careful and cross Trans-Isthmus Railroad and merge with Hwy #185. Come to "T" and turn left when coast is clear. Right goes into Salina Cruz (population 61,760). Restaurant Hawaii 03 at left – very good seafood. Red cross at right. **KM 393.**

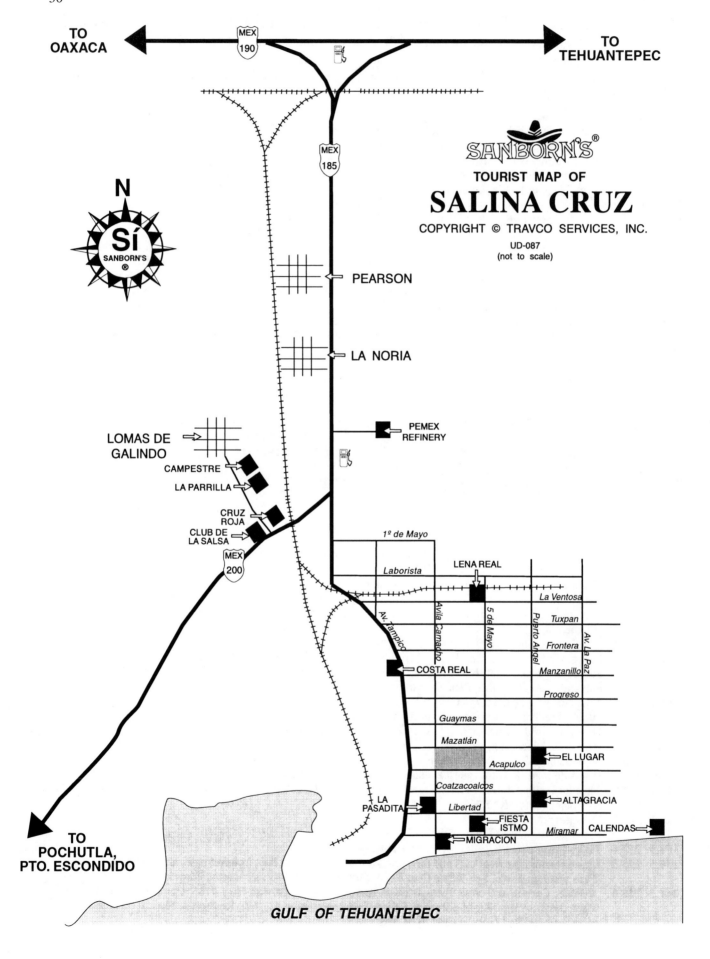

TO OAXACA

TO TEHUANTEPEC

MEX 190

MEX 185

N
Sí
SANBORN'S ®

SANBORN'S ®
TOURIST MAP OF
SALINA CRUZ
COPYRIGHT © TRAVCO SERVICES, INC.
UD-087
(not to scale)

PEARSON

LA NORIA

PEMEX REFINERY

LOMAS DE GALINDO

CAMPESTRE

LA PARRILLA

CRUZ ROJA

CLUB DE LA SALSA

MEX 200

1º de Mayo

Laborista

LENA REAL

La Ventosa

Av. Tampico

Avila Camacho

5 de Mayo

Puerto Angel

Av. La Paz

Tuxpan

Frontera

Manzanillo

COSTA REAL

Progreso

Guaymas

Mazatlán

Acapulco

EL LUGAR

Coatzacoalcos

LA PASADITA

Libertad

ALTAGRACIA

FIESTA ISTMO

MIGRACION

Miramar

CALENDAS

TO POCHUTLA, PTO. ESCONDIDO

GULF OF TEHUANTEPEC

MI	KM	
161.8	258.9	Budget Rent-A-Car at left and a school on right.
162.1	259.4	**GAS** at right. Slow for TOPES. Then restaurant El Campestre on right that serves BBQ.
162.8	260.5	Pass Hotel and Restaurant El Parador on right.
163.2	261.1	Entrance right to Pemex refinery, one of Mexico's largest. Ford dealer, right. **KM 295**.
164.1	262.6	**GAS** at right. Restaurant Dos Oceanos.
164.9	263.8	Pass Chrysler/Dodge dealer on right. Then pass Hotel El Pescador on left.
165.7	265.1	Big Hotel Cid del Mar on right. Watch for topes.
166.1	265.8	Motel El Encanto with air condition on right.
168.3	269.3	Restaurant Tocolava at right.
168.5	269.6	Hospital at right.
170.0	272.0	Come now to Tehuantepec and junction Hwy #200 and #190). **GAS**, ahead at left.

IF TO: Oaxaca, turn left and start Tehuantepec - Oaxaca Log (page 159).

IF TO: Downtown Tehuantepec, La Ventosa Junction, take right fork and start Tehuantepec - La Ventosa Log.

End of Log 11

LOG 12 *START:* Tehuantepec, Oax *END:* La Ventosa, Oax

UD-087

26.6 MI or 42.6 KM
DRIVE TIME 1/2 – 1 HOUR
SCENIC RATING –2

Between Tehuantepec and La Ventosa, the road is flat and wide, straight and fast. However, November thru March there are very stiff north winds in the La Ventosa area that can blow even the largest trailers and motorhomes off the road as they can reach almost hurricane force: So, if you're an RV'er, exercise caution!

0.0	0.0	Here on edge of Tehuantepec at junction with Hwys #190 and #200, with **GAS** on left, take right fork, bend slightly, and ahead. TOPES.
0.5	0.8	Cross steel frame bridge over Río Tehuantepec with railroad bridge alongside at right. Then pass street (right) to downtown Tehuantepec (population 142,000) - take a look if you wish.

Here, as in Juchitán, just 16 miles ahead, you'll see the dark and statuesque local women wearing handsomely embroidered dresses with starched ruffles and white-lace blouses called "huipils," mainly in the colorful market areas. Incidentally, Zapotec is still widely spoken here.

1.0	1.6	Pass another entrance (right) to downtown.
2.0	3.2	Come now to Hotel Calli at left (3 story, 8O room layout; restaurant; pool; pets OK; MC, VI; best around). Then pass side road (left) to Mixtequilla. You'll enjoy this nice, wide highway for next 20 miles.
13.0	20.8	Pass road (left) to air base.
14.0	22.4	Pass road (left) to Santa Almería Xadani.
17.0	27.2	Hotel Del Río on left. Over steel frame bridge as you enter Juchitán (population 66,530). Vibrators. Pass Coca Cola Bottling plant at right. Then **GAS** station at right. Pass side road (left) to Ixtepec.
17.6	28.2	Cement factory on left. Over railroad bridge.
18.5	29.6	LP gas at right.
24.3	38.9	Pass "cal" (lime) plant at left and power plant at right.
25.7	41.1	Agricultural experiment station at right.
26.6	42.6	Come now to community of La Ventosa Junction and end of log.

IF TO: Tuxtla Gutiérrez or Tapachula, take RIGHT FORK and start La Ventosa Jct - Tapanatepec Log. See Mexico's Ruta Maya book (page 59). **GAS**, just ahead at right.

IF TO: Acayucan across Isthmus of Tehuantepec, take LEFT FORK, curve left, and start La Ventosa - Acayucan Log. See Mexico's Ruta Maya book (page 70). **GAS**, here at junction.

End of Log 12

LOG 13 START: Palmillas Jct, Qro END: Toluca, Mex

UD-057

82.5 MI or 132.0 KM
DRIVE TIME 2 1/2 – 3 1/2 HOURS
SCENIC RATING – 2

Besides being a good shortcut highway to Morelia, Taxco and Acapulco (even though it is a little winding in spots and often congested with slow moving trucks), this is also a most historical road because it was along this route that Padre Miguel Hidalgo marched his rag-tag revolutionary army from Dolores Hidalgo-San Miguel de Allende-Querétaro to Toluca and then across toward Mexico City.

MI	KM	
0.0	0.0	Having turned off Hwy #57, proceed ahead thru high meadow farming country.
1.8	2.9	CAREFUL! Slow for a sharp left curve. Then right and up and up. Cross state line at a little bridge – leave state of Querétaro and enter state of México.
3.8	6.1	CAREFUL! SHARP RIGHT!
4.8	7.7	Past Río Blanco "barranca" (canyon) over to right.
5.3	8.5	**GAS** left.
16.1	25.8	Little community of Nado. Pass side road (left) to Aculco. Altitude about 8,000 ft.
16.5	26.4	Old stone aqueduct on left.
16.8	26.9	Thru a beautiful stand of trees!
19.3	30.9	Thru rocky community of El Bosque (The Forest). For the next few miles, you'll climb and climb and wind and wind.
20.5	32.8	Old stone hacienda off to left. Sometimes pretty bumpy for next 30 miles.
23.0	36.8	El Acosten to right. GO STRAIGHT.
26.0	41.6	Picturesque church, right. Wide vista of farming valley below.
28.8	46.1	Wind down. Emergency hotel. Straight thru edge of town of Acambay.
31.4	50.2	**GAS**, right.
34.0	54.4	CAREFUL! SHARP LEFT! Then RIGHT. BUMPY! BE READY FOR CURVY ROAD. IT'S REALLY CURVY and DANGEROUS FOR A FEW MILES.
35.2	56.3	CAREFUL! SHARP LEFT! Up and curve left.
39.3	62.9	Top. 8,500 feet. Now down on winding road.
41.3	66.1	Come to exit (right) to Morelia toll road. READ AHEAD for directions to Toluca.

IF TO: Morelia and on to Guadalajara, via toll road – exit here. Exit right following "Maravativo, Morelia" signs. It's a dandy road. If you want to save time (and are willing to pay for it), then hop to it.

41.5	66.4	Pass fringes of Atlacomulco. Get in left lane for Toluca.
43.0	68.8	CAREFUL FOR CONFUSING INTERSECTION AND COPS. Stoplight, which may not be working. Turn LEFT for Toluca.
43.5	69.6	Toluca via toll road (recommended), straight for one block. At next light (careful), TURN LEFT for Toluca and spa.
43.9	70.2	**GAS**, and highway patrol, left. Uniroyal, right. Ahead, shopping center with Super Kompras, left. **KM 63**. Watch your speed. Cops abound.
44.0	70.4	At right is Hotel-Spa Fiesta Mexicana. It has some spa services with Swedish showers, jacuzzi, steam, massage, facials, weight reduction etc. They also have a nice hotel with 44 rooms and 6 suites with jacuzzi, restaurant, tennis courts, pool, and gym. It's not worth a special trip, but if you are in the neighborhood, it's a nice enough place. Ph: (712) 122-2236, 122-2238 Fax: 122-2337. **KM 61**.
44.2	70.7	Pass Corona agency. Extinct volcano at left.
45.5	72.8	**GAS**, left.
45.8	73.3	Slow for topes. Pay toll at tollhouse. Four lane divided.
46.0	73.6	Pass exit to S.A. Enchise. Lots of cops on this road. Watch your speed.
49.8	79.7	Little village of Mavoro over to left.
52.3	83.7	**GAS**, at right, then overpass.
54.0	86.4	Pass big factory at right. They make electrical things like switch boxes, meters and insulation material, etc.
55.0	88.0	In distance ahead, on a clear day, you can see pretty snow-capped Mt. Nevado de Toluca – it's Mexico's fourth highest peak (1.) Orizaba, 2.) Popo, 3.) Ixta or Sleeping Lady).
59.0	94.4	Veer left to bypass village of Ixtlahuaca. Note red-winged blackbirds thru here. **KM 38**.
61.9	99.0	Hacienda La Purísima to right.
66.8	106.9	Cross stone bridge over Río Lerma. **KM 24**.
71.4	114.2	Pass tollbooth (toll booths still not open when we came thru).

MI   KM
73.0   116.8   Slow now. LOOK-&-LISTEN as you cross the bumpy railroad.
77.0   123.2   **GAS**, at right. Pass side road (right) to village of Calixtlahuaca. Real Hacienda La Puerta at right. **KM 3**.

A short way beyond this village, there are archeological discoveries called CALIXTLAHUACA. They're interesting, but not worth a special trip.

77.2   123.5   Fedomex plant at right and left. Enter outskirts of Toluca, capital of the state of Mexico and one of the largest cities in Mexico – close to 1,000,000 folks call this home, though the population sign says 480,630. Traffic is intense and cops are ambitious here, so keep alert and be careful. Altitude about 8,800 feet. See Toluca Eat & Stray (page 124) for accommodations.
77.6   124.2   John Deere at right. Holanda (ice cream distributor), right.

IF TO: Anywhere except Morelia, be ready to turn LEFT onto Paseo Tollocan bypass in 1 mile. GET IN MIDDLE LANE FOR NOW. FOLLOW MEXICO, IXTAPAN SIGNS.

IF TO: Morelia, stay out of left lane. Just keep going straight.

78.0   124.8   College of Engineers at right. WATCH YOUR SPEED.
78.4   125.4   Retorno and KM 1 – you're 1 KM from bypass. Toluca straight.
78.7   125.9   You should be in LEFT LANE to get on bypass. Cemento Cruz Azul at right.

IF TO: Ixtapan de la Sal, Cuernavaca, Taxco, or Mexico City, Turn LEFT. Careful as you cross over highway. FOLLOW SIGNS FOR MEXICO, IXTAPAN DE LA SAL.

IF TO: Downtown Toluca straight.

IF TO: Morelia – Veer right and begin Toluca – Morelia Free Log. See Mexico's Colonial Heart book (page 190).

BEGIN TOLUCA BYPASS

HEAVY TRAFFIC FROM 7-9 AM and 4-7 PM.

78.9   126.2   Having taken left turn, cross over very bumpy railroad crossing. At left is building with Quaker State sign. Basketball court and red housing project at right. Follow Mexico, Ixtapan de la Sal signs.
79.3   126.9   You are now proceeding SE on Paseo Tollocan or Alfredo Velez (it changes names). Airport exit, left.
79.9   127.8   Pass intersection of Via José López Portillo. Toluca Centro to right. **GAS**, left. Stoplight. FOR MEXICO CITY EXIT, GET IN RIGHT LANE. EVERYONE: AVOID LEFT LANE!
80.3   128.5   Pass residential Colonia Las Torres at right. Stoplight.
81.2   129.9   GM plant and **GAS**, at left. Then Mercedes dealer, left and Ford dealer, right.

IF TO: MEXICO CITY, EXIT RIGHT. Start Toluca - Mexico City Log (page 63).

81.3   130.1   Under overpass. Stay in middle lane.
81.5   130.4   Pass exit (right) to downtown. Then under overpass and curve right and come to exit (right) to Mexico City by modernistic sculpture.

IF TO: Mexico, EXIT right and start Toluca – Mexico City Log (page 63).

81.7   130.7   Bus station, left. Over overpass. STAY IN MIDDLE OR LEFT LANES. RIGHT LANE ENDS SOON.
81.8   130.9   Pass McDonald's on left – too hard to get to. Snow-covered Nevado de Toluca, left. START WORKING OVER TO LEFT LANE FOR IXTAPAN.
82.0   131.2   Pass Comercial Mexicana, right. RIGHT LANE ENDS. Curve left. Watch merging traffic from right.
82.2   131.5   **GAS**, and Super-Compras at right. Then straight at overpass and past Hotel Central, at left. GET IN LEFT LANE FOR IXTAPAN.
82.5   132.0   Wal-Mart, left. GET IN LEFT LANE. NEXT EXIT LEFT IS FOR IXTAPAN.
82.6   132.2   ISSTE Hospital, left. Exit here for Ixtapan de la Sal.

IF TO: Cd. Altamirano, Ixtapa, continue straight and start Toluca - Cd. Altamirano Log (page 66).

IF TO: Ixtapan de la Sal, Taxco, Iguala, Acapulco, CAREFUL FOR DIFFICULT EXIT. DO NOT TURN LEFT AT FIRST LIGHT! TURN LEFT AT SECOND LIGHT. Toks's Restaurant, right. Turn onto Pino Suárez. After turn, there will be a big hardware store on your right. **GAS**, left. Start Toluca - Ixtapan de la Sal Log.

End of Log 13

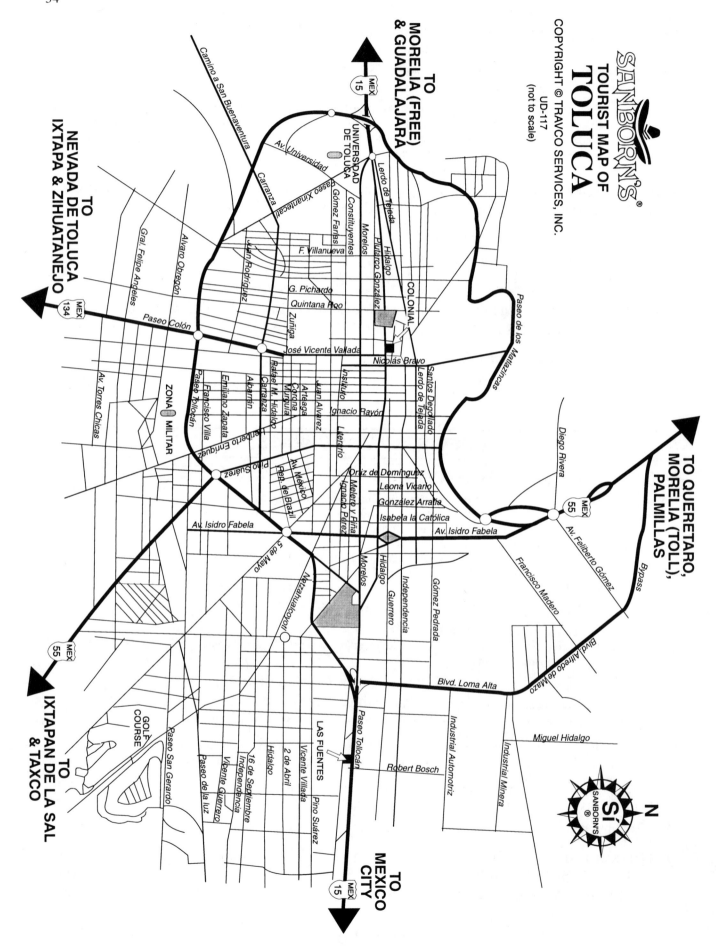

SANBORN'S®
TOURIST MAP OF
TOLUCA

COPYRIGHT © TRAVCO SERVICES, INC.

UD-117
(not to scale)

LOG 14 *START:* Toluca, Mex *END:* Ixtapan de la Sal, Mex

UD-O77

55.8 MI or 89.3 KM
DRIVE TIME 1 1/2 – 2 1/2 HOURS
SCENIC RATING – 3

Wind thru farmland, then forested mountains. You also go thru many flower farms which raise carnations and daisies. There are many downhill grades where you must brake with motor.

MI	KM	
0.0	0.0	Here at Paseo Tollocan bypass around town and junction Hwy #15, proceed ahead. Hardware store, right. Big **GAS** station, left.
0.5	0.8	Come to stoplight. Stay in right lane. Follow Metepec signs.
0.8	1.3	Refraccionaria California to right. Las Carnitas restaurant, bar and grill at left.
1.0	1.6	You're now in Metepec. Get in middle lane. Slow for school zone. Topes. Metepec is best known for its famous pottery depicting colorful tree-of-life works. Their Monday morning market is good.
1.3	2.1	VW dealer at left.
1.7	2.7	Topes. Plaza Las Americas shopping center on left. Burger King, VIPS, Toks, Gigante and Sam's Club. Then pass glass tower office building at right. More topes. **KM 2**.
2.4	3.8	Over vibrators. Straight to Ixtapan de la Sal. Zoológico Metepec, right. **KM 5**.
3.1	5.0	Topes just before overhead sign. Then 1/4 mile later, Hotel Metepec Plaza. Inexpensive but nice.
3.8	6.1	Nice view of Nevado de Toluca at right. Mexico's fourth highest mountain of 14,900 feet and an extinct volcano – you can drive right up to the crater's rim! The Indian name for this ex-volcano is "Xianatecatl," meaning Naked Man. Incidentally, Mexico's tallest mountain is Orizaba at 18,851 feet; second is "Popo" at 17,761 feet, and third is "Ixta" (Sleeping Lady) at 17,343 feet.
4.6	7.4	**GAS**, left and right. Pass side road (left) to town of Metepec.
5.1	8.2	Come to where the Tres Marías-Toluca special exits us. It's a shortcut to Cuernavaca.

IF TO: Cuernavaca via shortcut, veer left here and start the Toluca-Tres Marías Special (page 94).

IF TO: Ixtapan de la Sal via toll road, veer right and ahead. Follow stub log below. For free road, continue straight and skip down to continuation of main log. We like this scenic route, but haven't logged it in years. There probably are very few changes, except for some bypasses around towns and more **GAS** stations.

TOLUCA – IXTAPAN DE LA SAL TOLL ROAD

Drive time: 45 minutes to an hour. This is a pretty congested toll road and there are a lot of slow-moving trucks on it.

7.6	12.2	Road narrows to two lanes. Pass restaurant Las Codornices (The Quail).
10.6	16.7	TOPES, big ones both sides. **KM 13**.
11.6	18.6	**GAS** left. **KM 18**.
12.6	20.2	Pass exit (right) to Ixtapan via free road.

IF TO: IXTAPAN, exit right. Toll road continues straight.

13.1	21.0	Come to tollhouse and pay toll (car – $10; 2 axle – $13.5; extra axle – $7).
25.8	41.3	Pass exit (right) to Villa Guerrero. There's a restaurant here.
32.6	52.2	Veer right onto divided.
33.1	53.0	Back to two lanes.
33.5	53.6	**GAS**, at left.
40.6	65.0	Enter Ixtapan de la Sal on nice divided parkway. Then pass entrance to Balneario Ixtapan de la Sal. Join main log at mile 50.3. For info on accommodations see Ixtapan de la Sal Eat & Stray (page 125).

IF TO: Taxco, straight and start Ixtapan de la Sal – Iguala Log (page 37).

END IXTAPAN DE LA SAL TOLL ROAD

CONTINUATION OF (FREE ROAD) LOG.

6.5	10.4	Thru edge of Mexicalcingo.

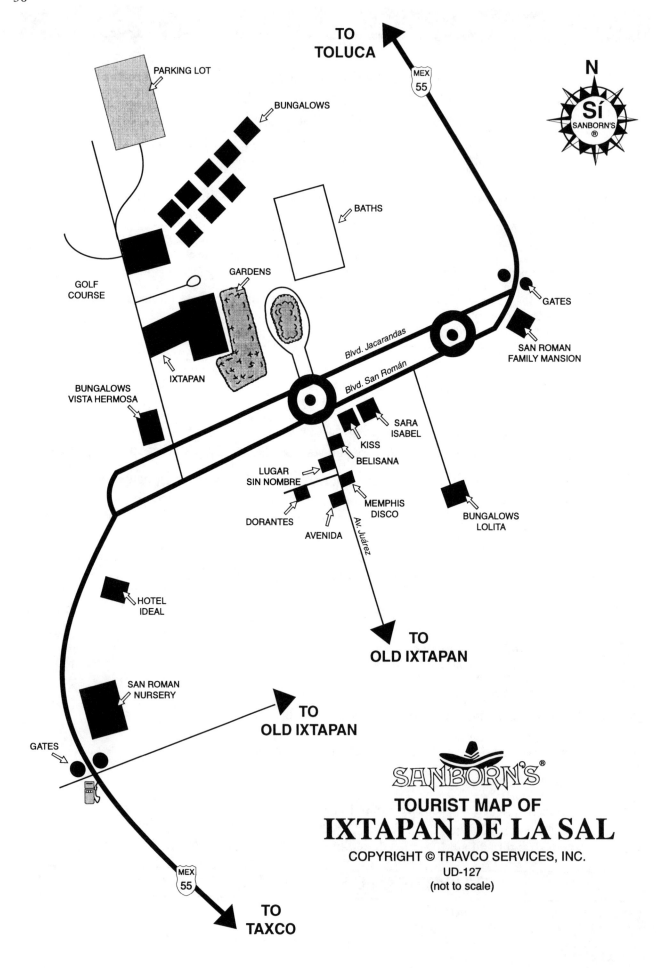

TO TOLUCA

MEX 55

PARKING LOT

BUNGALOWS

BATHS

N
Sí
SANBORN'S
®

GOLF COURSE

GARDENS

GATES

IXTAPAN

Blvd. Jacarandas

SAN ROMAN FAMILY MANSION

Blvd. San Román

BUNGALOWS VISTA HERMOSA

SARA ISABEL

KISS

BELISANA

LUGAR SIN NOMBRE

MEMPHIS DISCO

Av. Juárez

DORANTES

AVENIDA

BUNGALOWS LOLITA

TO OLD IXTAPAN

HOTEL IDEAL

SAN ROMAN NURSERY

TO OLD IXTAPAN

GATES

MEX 55

TO TAXCO

SANBORN'S ®
TOURIST MAP OF
IXTAPAN DE LA SAL
COPYRIGHT © TRAVCO SERVICES, INC.
UD-127
(not to scale)

MI	KM	
10.0	16.0	Fruit-processing plant at right. Curve right past village of San Antonio la Isla at left.
14.8	23.7	End 4-lane divided. Then at right is archeological site of TEOTENANGO. Into outskirts of Tenango de Valle over to right. **GAS**, at right.
15.5	24.8	Curve right.
17.8	28.5	Little town of Atlatlahuca over to right.
21.0	33.6	Thru edge of San Pedro Zictepec, mostly up and over to left.
23.3	37.3	Pass side road left to MALINALCO archeological zone, equipped with a public campground (no hookups). Now wind up. Top.
24.3	38.9	Slow for a couple of sharp right curves.
29.8	47.7	Slow now as you approach Tenancingo de Degollado, usually called "Tenancingo," known for its fruit wines, "rebozos" (made of cotton, rayon, and silk), and tropical hardwood. It is also the home of Ken Baldin, a pre-Columbian artist and naturalist. His studio (or gallery) is up at right – worthwhile, but parking is a problem. Church. VW agency at right. Then in and down and curve left. Past Morelos monument circle. Restaurant Vel-Mar at left. It used to be a balneario. Stop and eat at tables outside by the swimming pool.
30.5	48.8	Pretty shady park at left. Soccer field at left, then continue ahead. Turn right onto divided parkway and up past Allende Monument. **GAS**, at right. Power station at right.
31.5	50.4	Pass plaza at left. Then halfway around Hidalgo Monument and thru town on one-way Hidalgo. Furniture factory at left and right. Leave town proper.
32.8	52.5	Wind up. Curve left-right at far end. Down thru little town of Santa Ana. Buy your sweetie a bunch of flowers from here.
34.3	54.9	Slow for left curving bridge. **KM 54**.
36.0	57.6	Careful! Traffic exiting for bypass around little town of Villa Guerrero.
37.3	59.7	Careful for traffic merging from town.
38.8	62.1	Thru stretched out community of San Francisco.
43.3	69.3	Now straight for a change.
44.8	71.7	Wind down. Curve left and slow over one-way Calderón Bridge and left.
45.5	72.8	Down alongside Nenetzingo Canyon at left. Then thru community of Llano de la Unión. Pass side road (right) to Porfírio Díaz.
45.8	73.3	Over Arroyo Llano de la Unión and sharp left.
47.5	76.0	Wind down and horseshoe curve left. Village of San Diego down at left.
49.0	78.4	Up and nice view off to left.
50.3	80.5	Wind and curve right. Thru gates and enter Ixtapan de la Sal. Note San Roman family mansion at left just before exit gates. (The San Román family owns hotel Ixtapan.) For info on accommodations see Ixtapan de la Sal Eat & Stray (page 125).
50.8	81.3	Come to Bungalows Lolita to left. Pass hotel Sara Isabel at left with hotel Kiss next door. Then pass entrance street right to big public bathhouse. Come to the turnoff right to big hotel Ixtapan.

IF TO: Ixtapan hotel, turn right here and up slightly.

IF TO: Taxco, Iguala, Acapulco, etc., start Ixtapan de la Sal – Iguala Log.

Hope you have a real nice time here Ixtapan – they've got a dandy 9-hole golf course just across from the big hotel. The baths are very helpful and healthful.

End of Log 14

LOG 15 *START:* Ixtapan de la Sal, Mex *END:* Iguala, Gro

UD-017

66.5 MI or 106.4 KM
DRIVE TIME – 1,1/2 HOURS
SCENIC RATING – 3

0.0	0.0	Starting at entrance (right) to Hotel/Spa Ixtapan, Hotel Vista Hermosa, proceed ahead down parkway.
0.2	0.3	Pass Hotel Ideal at left.
0.5	0.8	**GAS**, right. Trees make lovely arch over road.
0.8	1.2	Another **GAS**, right at junction with road (right) to Coatepec and Zacualpan (about 1 km off the main highway, and an LP gas at left just before station). There's an AA hall across the street from **GAS** station.
1.8	2.9	Exit left for Rancho San Diego.
2.0	3.2	Hotel Tierra Blanca, left. Topes. **GAS**, left. **KM 84**.
2.8	4.5	Hotel Tonatico, left. Space for small RV's. Dry camping. VI, MC., then enter town of Tonatico, 6383 folks.

MI	KM	
3.0	4.8	White sign painted on side of building says "Desviación/Taxco/Cuernavaca" left. This is the bypass. TURN LEFT with long white wall on your right, and go 1/4 mile on dirt road. Then just past white building take first right. There will be two horses, one brown and one sorrel, left. Sign says TAXCO – CUERNAVACA. Very bumpy dirt road. Pavement starts after a block, but even it is bumpy.
3.2	5.1	Restaurant Ana Isabel, right.
3.4	5.5	AA hall, left.
3.6	6.5	Careful for topes. Come to "T" and turn left to rejoin highway.
6.5	10.4	Wind thru roadside village of Terrero.
8.1	13.0	Pass side road (right) to Grutas de la Estrella (Star Caves). Note majestic mountain ranges ahead. **KM 95**.
10.0	16.0	Cross state line – leave state of México and enter state of Guerrero. **KM 99**.
11.2	17.9	Topes. Enter village of Piedras Negras. Note Abraham Lincoln school ahead at left. The Mexican people are great admirers of Lincoln who was a good friend of Benito Juárez, but they never met as Lincoln was assassinated before Juárez won his revolution. Pass hotel Los Arcos, right. **KM 100**.
12.0	19.2	End tope zone. Curve left and out. **KM 102**.
14.6	23.4	Pass mirador, a nice lookout point on both sides of road where you can look down into deep Luluvar Canyon with Río Chontalcoatlán down in the bottom. **KM 104**.
16.6	26.5	Thru tile-making village of El Mogote. Tiles are made of slices of various shades of rocks set in cement. Topes. **KM 108**.
17.5	28.0	End tope zone. Leave metropolis of El Mogote. Careful for sharp curves and downshifting descents, ahead.
21.6	34.5	Wind down thru village of Cacahuamilpa.
22.2	35.5	Leave Cacahuamilpa and continue sharp curves.
23.1	37.0	Come to junction with Hwy #116 to Cuernavaca. Although you can get to the Cuernavaca/Acapulco toll road from here, we got lost. Instead continue ahead.. Cacahuamilpa caves and Taxco straight ahead. **KM 117**.
24.4	39.0	Pass turnoff left for famed Cacahuamilpa caves. These cave were discovered back in 1835 and still haven't been fully explored.
28.1	45.0	Pass side road (left) to Cuernavaca and Acapulco toll road. Right fork is for Taxco and Iguala (Hwy #95).

IF TO: Cuernavaca, turn left and join Taxco - Jct Hwy 95D Log (page 98) at mile 7.8.

29.7	47.5	Thru Axixintla, mostly to left. **KM 65**. Thru desert-looking rock forest.
34.1	54.5	Road divides briefly. Left fork also takes you to the Cuernavaca toll road. Straight is to Taxco. Road narrows to two lanes.
35.0	56.0	Village of Huajojutla over at left and down.
35.3	56.5	Sharp curve left and over narrow stone bridge and up thru village of La Azul.
36.8	59.0	Vendors along roadway sell quartz, rocks and other minerals.
38.8	62.0	Highway Patrol station at left.
40.3	64.5	Wind past village of Tehuilotepec down at left. Then wind down. Slow for sharp curves.
40.6	65.0	Come to entrance of Hotel Monte Taxco (previously Holiday Inn) at right. To get to hotel, stop and get visitor's pass, wind up right and then take left fork at top of hill.
41.5	66.4	Now under Taxco's aqueduct arches and into town on Av. J.F. Kennedy. For info on accommodations see Taxco Eat & Stray (page 126).
42.0	67.2	City's tourist office at left. **GAS**, left. Then Hotel De la Borda up lane at left. Street at right leads uptown to zócalo.
42.3	67.7	Very attractive Posada de la Misión at right – excellent! Don't hesitate to pull over to right into their parking area and make the place your headquarters while you look over town.
42.5	68.0	Pass Secretariat of Tourism office at left. Then OK Motel Loma Linda at left. Wind on down alongside hill on right.
43.0	68.8	Bus station at left. **GAS**, right. For uptown Taxco, Hotels Rancho Taxco, Victoria, Santa Prisca, Meléndez, etc. turn right here and start uphill.
43.5	68.8	Wind around and leave Taxco Then wind down rather sharply. Brake with your motor.
45.0	72.0	Pass side road (right) to Hacienda San Francisco Cuadra – fair inn built from ruins of an old mining village.
46.8	74.9	Thru village of Minas Viejas (Old Mines).
50.0	80.0	The village on yonder hill with big church is Tecapulco.
51.0	81.6	Slow and over bridge and thru edge of aforementioned Tecapulco.
52.0	83.2	Old Taxco off and up to left. Then follow little Río Ejido on winding road.
52.5	84.0	Pass side road (left) to Old Taxco, the forerunner of the present town of Taxco.
53.0	84.8	Spratling's famous silver factory at left – well worth a visit.
56.5	90.4	Lake Tuxpan dead ahead in the distance and on down.
60.0	96.0	Thru village of El Naranjo (The Orange Tree). Curve left at far end and over railroad (LOOK-&-LISTEN).
62.0	99.2	Slow for narrow bridge. Then curve left.
64.0	102.4	Over narrow bridge. Federal corn experimental station at left. School at right, then Pepsi plant. Historic city of Iguala over to right.

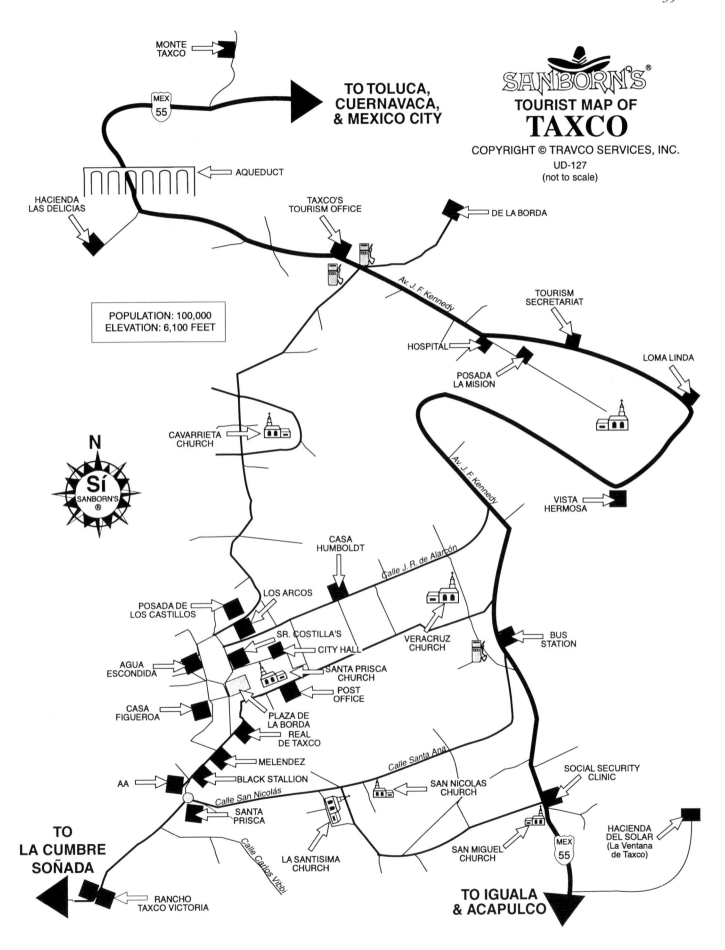

IGUALA is the "Philadelphia of Mexican Independence" –where Iturbide drafted his Plan of Three Guarantees and where independence was proclaimed on February 24, 1821. It was here that the Mexican flag was first hoisted over a government building. There are some good enough hotels here (downtown) – the Royalty and the Velasco, but the best in the area is La Cabaña Motel/Restaurant a short way beyond the junction ahead.

MI	KM	
66.0	105.6	Ahead here (don't take left fork) under highway overpass.
66.3	106.1	Come now to junction with Hwy #95. **GAS**, right.

IF TO: Acapulco via free road, straight ahead. You can't get to the toll road from here.

End of Log 15

LOG 16 *START:* Iguala, Gro *END:* Acapulco, Gro (Free)

UD-017

144.0 MI or 230.4 KM
DRIVE TIME 4 – 4 1/2 HOURS
SCENIC RATING – 2

This is a wonderful two-lane road with a good surface, generally adequate passing places (though when you are behind a truck on a long, blind curve, you may dispute this). Have patience, you will eventually be able to pass. Even RV's should be able to take this road as far as Chilpancingo. After that, the road is really curvy and takes a couple of hours longer than the toll road.

0.0	0.0	Having taken the left fork here at Iguala junction, proceed ahead past **GAS**, right.
0.7	1.1	Take leave of Iguala (population 300,000).
1.0	1.6	LP gas at right.
3.0	5.0	Pass side road (left) to Huitzuco. Iguala airport at left. **KM 129**.
12.7	20.3	Village of Sábana Grande on right. **GAS**, with so-so restaurant. Then some nice straight stretches for a change.
13.2	21.1	Curve left.
25.0	40.0	Note roadside stands at left. Stop and have a look at their pottery if you like. It's made in the village of Xalitla down at left on river.
34.5	55.2	Now up thru Zopilote (Vulture) Canyon for the next 17 miles and follow alongside Río Zopilote on left.
39.5	63.2	Pass Filo de Caballo archeological site. **KM 190**.
46.0	73.6	Note tunnel at right that was on the old road before they dug thru this cut.
53.5	85.6	Skirt Zumpango del Río over at left, better known just as Zumpango. **GAS** at left. AA, Then thru series of cuts. Watch for rocks on pavement.
64.5	103.2	Note military garrison at left. Then **GAS**, on left. Then ahead onto divided bypass around Chilpancingo (population 97,000, elevation 4,000 feet). Pass monument left to General Nicolás Bravo (1776-1854), leader of Mexican Independence and born in this town. Motel San Antonio at right. Speed limit 80 KPH.
65.0	104.0	Take leave of Chilpancingo. For Acapulco, get in left lane.
68..5	105.0	**GAS**, right.

IF TO: Acapulco, via Autopista del Sol toll road, go straight, following "cuota" signs. Join Iguala - Acapulco Log Toll (page 24) at mile 37.0. Although it is only seventy odd miles from here, it could take two hours on this road. Pay the bucks and go in style, unless you just want to see the country. **KM 278**.

68.7	109.9	Pass side road (left) to Mochitlán and Grutas (caves) De Juxtlahuaca.
70.5	112.8	Pass junk yard at right. Then slow for sharp right curve thru cut.
72.0	115.2	Summit (altitude about 4,400 feet).
74.0	118.4	Thru "green rock" cut (green because of copper content. Then pass side road (left) to Mazatlán.
75.0	120.0	Now thru scattered pine forest.
91.0	145.6	Thru community of Cajeles. Then Los Ches Restaurant.
94.0	150.4	Slow thru little town of El Ocotito. **GAS**, at right. Thru settlement of Mojoneras.
101.0	161.6	Note red papaya stands thru here. Then enter town of Tierra Colorada. Now it's really tropical (altitude 1,100 feet). Then **GAS** at right. Pass flock of open air restaurants at right.
108.0	172.8	Over Río Papagayo. Then slow for sharp right curve. Xolapa Canyon at left.
115.5	184.8	Over Río Xaltianguis.
117.7	188.3	Slow and stop for military "revisión," a checkpoint for drugs and firearms. The man might want to look in your trunk.

MI	KM	
129.0	206.4	Thru little town of El Treinta. These places with unusual "number" names used to be that many kilometers from Acapulco on the old road – hence the names.
132.0	211.2	Bypass (right) to Hwy #200 and Ixtapa-Zihuatanejo and Coyuca RV Park. Ahead for you.
134.0	214.4	Now alongside Río de la Sábana at right. Then thru stretched out community of Los Organos.
134.7	215.5	Thru community of El Quemado.
137.5	220.0	Here where the toll road joins us. Merge with traffic coming from left. Right fork goes to Zihuatanejo.
138.0	220.8	Orphanage at right – you are most welcome to visit. It is run by an American church. Don't hesitate to go and see the fine work they're doing down here with these less-fortunate children.
138.5	221.6	**GAS**, left.
139.5	223.2	Cemetery on left is where Johnny Weismuller (the original Tarzan) is buried. Note coconut stands thru here. Pass junction Hwy #200 (right) to Pinotepa Nacional. Then thru village of Las Cruces.
141.5	226.4	Top. Now beautiful Acapulco is in view and wind down.
142.2	227.5	Pass Hwy #200 to Pie de la Cuesta and Zihuatanejo. Then pass village of La Garita.

IF TO: Zihuatanejo, turn left and start Acapulco - Ixtapa Log (page 142).

142.7	228.3	Down and curve left. Careful for pedestrians.
144.0	230.4	Welcome to Acapulco. Pass **GAS** station (watch 'em!) at right. Come now to Diana Circle on Costera Miguel Alemán (named after the town's Number One citizen, Ex-president Miguel Alemán (street better known just as "Costera"), with a parking lot at left and commercial center at right.

Have a wonderful time in Acapulco, but WATCH THAT SUN – it's plenty hot!

IF TO: Pinotepa Nacional, Puerto Escondido, or Puerto Angel, go 3/4 way around glorieta and start Acapulco - Puerto Escondido Log (page 25).

End of Log 16

LOG 17 *START:* Mexico City, DF *END:* Puebla, Pue

UD-077

76.5 MI or 122.4 KM
DRIVE TIME 1 3/4 – 2 1/2 HOURS (except rush hour 7-9:30 AM, 2–4 PM, 5–7 PM)
SCENIC RATING - 3

Beautiful multi–lane expressway that climbs and goes through a forest. Well engineered. Some steep grades.

0.0	0.0	In Mexico City, starting at the Angel of Independence Monument, proceed ahead up Reforma, heading east, with Hotel Maria Isabel Sheraton and U.S. Embassy over at left. Mexicano and American airlines offices on right. Then stock exchange on left (glass dome).
0.2	0.3	Come to small circle with one big palm tree on it. TURN RIGHT onto Niza street. Chevy dealer on left.
0.3	0.5	Pass Sanborn's on Hamburgo. Go three blocks, passing Insurgentes.
0.5	0.8	Pass Suites Niza on right. In front of you is Cabero Refrigeración and Nieto signs. Come to Chapultepec/Río de la Loza. TURN LEFT following Clínica Londres sign.
0.7	1.1	Having turned left onto Río de la Loza, proceed ahead on lateral and merge left onto Chapultepec. Ahead is Corona sign on left.
1.1	1.8	Pass Cuauhtémoc metro station. VEER RIGHT just before giant radio/TV tower and cross EJE 1 PTE (Av. Cuauhtémoc). Baños on right. Follow airport signs onto Fray Servando.
1.7	2.7	Cross EJE CENTRAL Lázaro Cárdenas.
2.2	3.5	Pass Hotel Costa Azul, right. Then under overpass (Calz. Tlalpan).
2.5	4.0	**GAS**, right. Then cross EJE 1 OTE (Calz. La Viga) with fire station and La Merced market at right.
3.0	5.0	Go under subway and cross EJE 2 OTE (Av. Congreso de la Unión).
3.3	5.3	Pass city hall and Jardín Balbuena on right.
4.0	6.4	Vip's Restaurant on right. Then Banamex on right.
4.3	6.9	Get ready for turn as you cross Galindo y Villa. Left fork goes to airport. TAKE RIGHT FORK onto Av. Ocho (8). You'll cross many (ascending) numbered streets.
4.8	7.7	Pass Mercado Ignacio Allende at right.
5.0	8.0	Follow Calz. Zaragoza/Puebla signs. Get in left lane.
5.2	8.3	Pass Puebla Metro station. Then under Metro tranvia. You'll turn left as you merge onto Río de la Piedad.
5.4	8.6	Now merge onto 6 lane divided Río Churubusco.

MI	KM	
5.6	9.0	Move to right lane at first opportunity. Hardware store (Ferretería) at right. Then TURN RIGHT onto Zaragoza (which is also Hwys #150-190).
5.8	9.3	Work you way to center lanes for highway to Puebla.
6.7	22.6	Under pedestrian crossover. Banamex, right.
8.1	13.0	Huge ISSSTE hospital at right. Then federal radio monitoring station over to right. Gigante at left.
8.7	13.9	TOK'S restaurant, left. Sign: 150 – PUEBLA, STRAIGHT.
10.1	16.2	Pass **GAS**, right – hard to get to. (There's another station a mile ahead, but it's usually congested.) Burger Boy. Stoplight. EXIT HERE IF TO **GAS** AT 11.1.
11.1	17.8	Here's that other **GAS**. (Need to take exit right after going under pedestrian crossover at 12.1 to get to this **GAS** station.)
12.1	19.4	Pass **GAS**, right. Then UNDER OVERPASS AND TAKE RIGHT FORK (PUEBLA CUOTA) and up and around onto Toll Road Hwy #150D - follow PUEBLA CUOTA. Cross state line here – leave Federal District (DF) and enter state of Mexico. Now up gradually.
14.1	22.6	Curve left around mini-mountain. Then a straight stretch. On a clear day you can see famed snow-capped Mts. Popocatepetl "Popo" and Ixtaccihuatl "Ixty," or "sleeping Lady" off to right.
18.6	29.8	Slow for tope and pull up at green light slot at tollhouse and pay toll (car – $15, 2 axle – $30, 3 axle $45, extra axle – $8). Restrooms are at right – park at right just beyond tollhouse. **KM 32**.
30.1	48.2	"Mirador" at right, a place where you can stop and park and enjoy the lovely view. You're at 8,000 feet.
31.1	49.8	Now more curves and up into majestic pine forest. 9,200 feet. You'll see a sign that says "Caution with ice on road." Welcome to sunny Mexico. Farther on, you'll have to beware of fog as you descend this same mountain!
35.4	56.6	Up in here is the highest point on the road – 10,700 feet above sea level. This is the CONTINENTAL DIVIDE, the backbone of the North American continent. Then start winding down stretch – not too fast! You're in a National Park. Remember to shift to a lower gear if you want to have any brakes left at the bottom! Easy does it!
41.1	65.8	Careful here! Pass turnoff right to Río Frío rest area – **GAS**, food, arts-and-crafts, lodging, camping. Then under old road and cross state line again – leave state of Mexico and enter state of Puebla.
47.6	76.2	Village of Santa Rita de Tlahuapan, right. Then another "mirador" at right.
48.6	77.8	Over bridge over Río Emperador – go a little slow and note its deep, deep gorge.
58.9	94.2	Pull up at green light slot at tollhouse and pay remainder of Puebla toll (cars – $13, 2 axle – $26, 3 axle – $39, Extra axle – $7). Restrooms again at right.
60.4	96.6	Over bridge over railroad. Then wide curve right.
68.6	109.8	Big steel mill off to right. Then village of Xoxtla "shoaks-tla," right.
74.5	119.2	Pass huge Volkswagen factory at left.
75.5	120.8	Now down and over bridge over Río Atoyac.
76.5	122.4	Slow now as you approach junction Hwy #190. **GAS**, and self-serve snack restaurant at right (restrooms in restaurant cleaner than those in **GAS** station). If you need gas, this is a good spot for it, although there are OK **GAS** station in towns just off toll road.

IF TO: Puebla (or to Mesón del Angel Inn or Las Americas RV Park), Cholula, or Oaxaca, (via Hwy #190), bear right at exit and start Puebla - Izucar de Matamoros Log (page 88).

IF TO: Oaxaca, Tehuacán via toll road, continue ahead and start Puebla - Oaxaca Log (page 44).

IF TO: Orizaba, Fortín de las Flores, or Veracruz, continue ahead (following TLAXCALA/ORIZABA signs), under overpass, and start Puebla - Veracruz Log. See Mexico's Colonial heart book (page 20).

End of Log 17

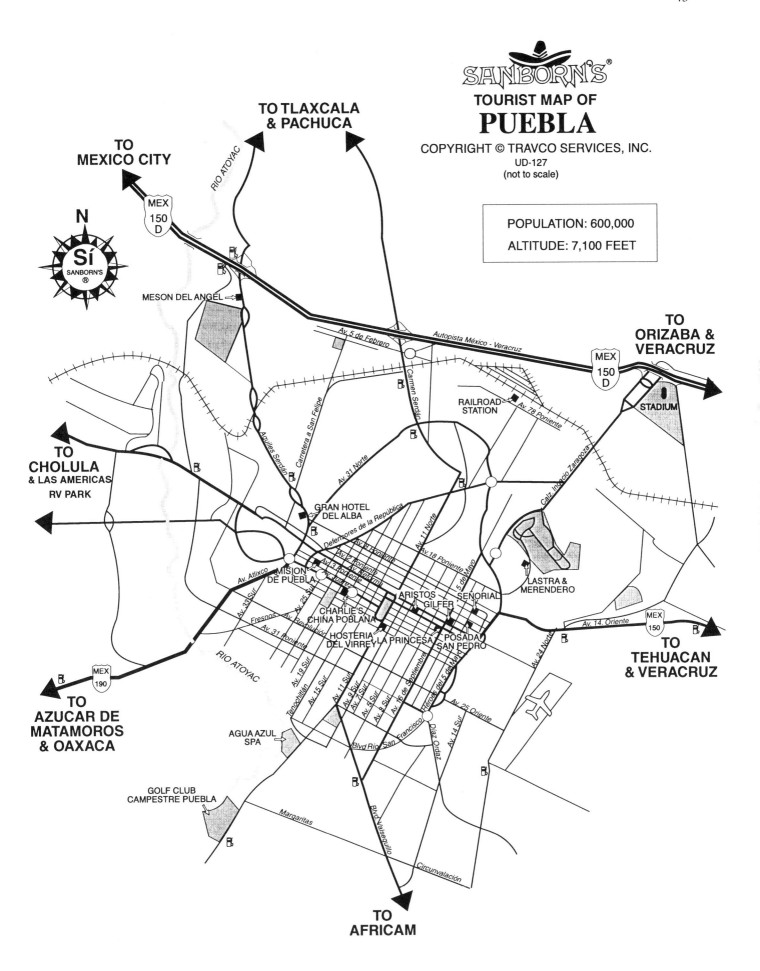

SANBORN'S®
TOURIST MAP OF
PUEBLA
COPYRIGHT © TRAVCO SERVICES, INC.
UD-127
(not to scale)

POPULATION: 600,000

ALTITUDE: 7,100 FEET

TO TLAXCALA
& PACHUCA

TO
MEXICO CITY

RIO ATOYAC

MEX
150
D

N

Sí
SANBORN'S
®

MESON DEL ANGEL

Av. 5 de Febrero

Autopista México - Veracruz

TO
ORIZABA &
VERACRUZ

MEX
150
D

Carmen Serdán

RAILROAD
STATION

Av. 78 Poniente

STADIUM

Aquiles Serdán

Carretera a San Felipe

Av. 31 Norte

Calz. Ignacio Zaragoza

TO
CHOLULA
& LAS AMERICAS
RV PARK

GRAN HOTEL
DEL ALBA

Defensores de la República

Av. 11 Norte

Av. 18 Poniente

LASTRA &
MERENDERO

Av. Atlixco

MISION
DE PUEBLA

Av. 3 Poniente

Av. 2 Poniente

Av. 3 Poniente

Av. Reforma

Av. Juárez

5 de Mayo

ARISTOS
GILFER

SEÑORIAL

Av. 33 Sur

Av. 25

CHARLIE'S
CHINA POBLANA

HOSTERIA
DEL VIRREY

LA PRINCESA

POSADA
SAN PEDRO

Fresnos

Av. Reública

Av. 31 Poniente

RIO ATOYAC

Av. 14. Oriente

MEX
150

TO
TEHUACAN
& VERACRUZ

Av. 24 Norte

MEX
190

TO
AZUCAR DE
MATAMOROS
& OAXACA

Av. 19 Sur

Av. 15 Sur

Av. 11 Sur

Av. 9 Sur

Av. 7 Sur

Av. 5 Sur

Av. 3 Sur

Av. 16 de Septiembre

Tlanchinol

Tepochitlan

Francisco

Diaz Ordaz

Av. 14 Sur

Franc. del 5 de Mayo

Av. 25 Oriente

AGUA AZUL
SPA

Blvd Rio San

GOLF CLUB
CAMPESTRE PUEBLA

Margaritas

Blvd Valsequillo

Circunvalación

TO
AFRICAM

LOG 18 *START:* **Puebla, Pue** *END:* **Oaxaca, Oax**

UD-086

216.5 MI or 346.4 KM
DRIVE TIME 3 1/2 HOURS
SCENIC RATING — 3

MI	KM	
0.0	0.0	Here at junction with Hwy #190 to Izucar de Matamoros and Oaxaca, continue ahead following 150D/ORIZABA signs.
1.5	2.4	Come to glorieta junction with Hwy #119 left to Tlaxcala and right into Puebla.

IF TO: Tlaxcala, Pachuca exit left and start Puebla - Pachuca Log at mile 2.

2.3	3.7	Stanly plant at right. SKF plant at left.
2.5	4.0	Over railroad (LOOK-&-LISTEN).
4.3	6.9	Puebla exit to right. Stadium, right. Orizaba free road exit right. Mexico exit left. Orizaba up the middle and straight ahead.

Now is a good time to tell you about General Zaragoza, the Texas-born hero of famed Cinco de Mayo (5th of May) Battle of Puebla when Mexico defeated the French on these plains. The good general wasn't really born in Texas but in Goliad in what is NOW Texas. In those days it was part of Mexico, so Mexico always takes a good-natured ribbing about having to come to Texas for its very best general.

5.1	8.2	Pemex refinery at right. Bimbo factory, left.
6.5	10.4	Little town of Nopaluca 'way over to right. Note mountain over at left — that's famous MT. LA MALINCHE ("The Wicked Woman"), Mexico's fifth highest mountain at 13,700 feet. The other four are Orizaba, Popo, Sleeping Lady, and Nevado Toluca, in that order.

"La Malinche" (really "Malintzi") was Cortés' Indian mistress, and has always been considered a traitor — hence the appellation "Wicked Woman."

8.6	13.8	**GAS**, at right and at left. **KM 134**.
13.3	21.3	Over bridge over railroad. Topes. Get in left lane (right lane for local traffic). Then SLOW for tollhouse ahead at Amozoc Interchange. Head for ORIZABA slot and pay toll (cars — $13; 2-axle — $26; 3-axle — $39).
15.3	24.5	Now over bridge over usually dry tributary of Río Atoyac.
17.3	27.7	Under overpass. Then past village of Magdalena Tetla, mostly to left.
21.0	33.6	At right is a spot to park and "stretch your legs."
24.5	39.3	Village of Tepeaca at right, with old abandoned hacienda.
26.3	42.1	Note majestic MT. ORIZABA ahead at left, Mexico's highest (more about this magnificent mountain further down pike).
28.6	61.8	Come now to Hwy #140 Interchange. Restaurant Peñafiel just ahead on right.

IF TO: Perote, Teziutlan, or Jalapa, exit here (also if to Tehuacán via old (free) Hwy #150) and start Hwy 150D - Jalapa Log (not incuded in this book).

IF TO: Tehuacán, Fortín, Orizaba, Veracruz, continue ahead on #150-D toll road.

29.5	47.2	Village of Acatzingo at left.
37.0	59.2	Pass exit (right) to Quecholac and Tecamachalco.
40.8	56.3	Through maguey fields and under a flock of overpasses.
43.0	68.8	Pass exit (right) to San Miguel Jaltepec.
44.3	70.9	Popular Oasis truck stop-restaurant, left. Then **GAS**, on both sides of highway. **KM 192**.
52.5	84.0	Come to exit for the toll road to Oaxaca. Straight goes to Veracruz

IF TO: Oaxaca, Tehuacán, EXIT RIGHT.

IF TO: Veracruz, continue straight and join Puebla - Veracruz Log. See Mexico's Colonial Heart book (page 20) at mile 52.5.

52.6	84.2	Having turned onto toll road to Oaxaca, continue ahead on wide 2-lane road.
53.2	85.1	Pass exit (right) to town of Cuacnopalan. **KM 2**.
53.6	85.8	Pass gravel pit mine on right.
54.6	87.4	Under sign that says "Welcome to the Cuacnopalan - Oaxaca Toll Road." Altitude just under 8,000 feet. Speed limit 110 km/hr.

MI	KM	
61.5	98.4	Begin descent into a large valley.
64.3	102.9	Cross Loma Colorado bridge over deep gully and begin climb up thru cuts and landslide area.
65.7	105.1	Top at 7,000 feet and start long downgrade. The cuts are covered sometimes with cement or maya (chicken coop wire) to help prevent landslides.
77.2	123.5	**GAS** and Los Arcos 24-hour Restaurant at left Then over puente Tehuacán.
77.9	124.6	Pass exit (right) to Tehuacán. Don't hesitate visit this city of thermal water spas. See our Tehuacán Eat & Stray (page 133). Then come to first tollhouse (cars - $24, 2-axle - $48. 3-axle - $72). Clean restrooms. Altitude just under 6,000 feet. We start climbing again for a stretch. You can see the tops of the houses of Tehuacán in the valley over to left. **KM 40.**
83.0	132.8	Pass exit (right) to Huajuapan (before overpass) and (after overpass) Tehuacán. Sign says, Oaxaca 189 km.

IF TO: Huajuapan, Exit here and join Tehuacán - Huajuapan de León Log (page 90) at mile 4.0.

IF TO: Tehuacán, exit right after overpass and join Huajuapan de León - Tehuacán Log (page 92) at mile 70.0.

85.5	136.8	Note the beautiful mountains in the distance as we head down into a valley.
91.4	146.2	Pass exit (right) to village of San Gabriel Xilac. Oaxaca 174 kilometers.
92.5	148.0	We have now dropped to an altitude level of 4,200 feet.
97.9	156.6	Pass exit (right) to Tetitlán and Miahuatlán. Come to second tollhouse and pay toll (cars $15, 2-axle $30, 3-axle $48). Then restrooms on right. Now we are entering what looks like an organ cactus and garambullo forest.
106.2	169.9	Cross long Calapa bridge curving to the right and a warning that a landslide area lies ahead. This is also the state line, leave state of Puebla and enter state of Oaxaca.
108.1	173.0	Cross Carizarillos bridge curving right over a deep canyon.
114.1	182.6	Careful for a short 1/2 mile detour to right due to recent landslides. There had been a tunnel but it caved in.
116.2	185.9	Over Santa Lucía bridge curving to right.
121.6	194.6	Over puente Otates curving to right. Altitude 6,900 feet.
125.3	200.5	Pull-off rest area to right.
128.1	205.0	Top at 7,400 feet and start down
130.4	208.6	Cross bridge over Río Chiquito. **KM 121**.
132.0	211.2	Pass exit (right) to Concepción Tepelmeme. Sign says "Oaxaca 115 km."
133.3	213.3	Over Río Grande bridge and pass exit (right) to Tepelmeme Tamazulapan. **KM 124**.
144.0	230.4	Come to tollhouse and pay toll (cars $38, 2-axle $74, 3-axle $95) Then exit (right) to Coixtlahuaca and Suchixtlahuaca. Restrooms and first aid station just past tollhouse. Sign says "Oaxaca 99 kilometers.
150.1	240.2	Pass exit (right) to Nativitas, Monteverde. **KM 152**. Then careful for landslide area ahead.
160.5	256.8	Start long downgrade. Altitude 7,200 feet.
165.2	264.3	Pass exit (right) to Huacuapan and Nochixtlan (Hwy 131). The Nochixtlan exit is under the overpass and to the right.
167.1	267.4	**GAS** at left.
182.7	292.3	Over Río Díaz. We are now going thru greener landscapes with tall trees.
194.0	310.4	Pass restrooms first aid station as you come to exit (right) to Huitzo and last tollhouse and pay toll (cars $46, 2-axle $95, 3-axle $110).
209.2	334.7	Curve right and merge with traffic coming from the right as we enter the outskirts of Oaxaca City. Then pass monument at left in center of divided. Sign says "Oaxaca 2 km."
209.8	335.7	**GAS** at left and right. **KM 243**.
210.2	336.3	Higueras Motel at right.
210.5	336.8	Road widens as you come to "Welcome to Oaxaca" sign. Then Restaurant El Nixtequito at left.
211.8	338.9	Hotel Loma Bonita at left.
212.0	339.2	Trailer park Rosa Isabel at right. Then Hotel Villas del Sol at right.
212.3	339.7	Tennis club next to Breñamiel Arboledas at right.
212.5	340.0	Topes and Hotel La Cabaña on the right.
213.0	340.8	Motel Bel Air on the right. Big market Sonal at left
213.9	342.2	There is a large monument in center. Main route thru town curves left. Straight takes you to exit (right) to Monte Albán or down Calle Madero to Hotels Los Olivos and Primavera. See Oaxaca Eat & Stray (page 134) for details on accommodations.

IF TO: Downtown, Tule and Tehuantepec turn left and on into town

IF TO: Monte Albán archeological ruins (a very interesting site about 7 miles from town), continue straight ahead 0.2 miles and turn right. There are two other roads that go to Monte Albán on the south side of town, but this is the best route.

46

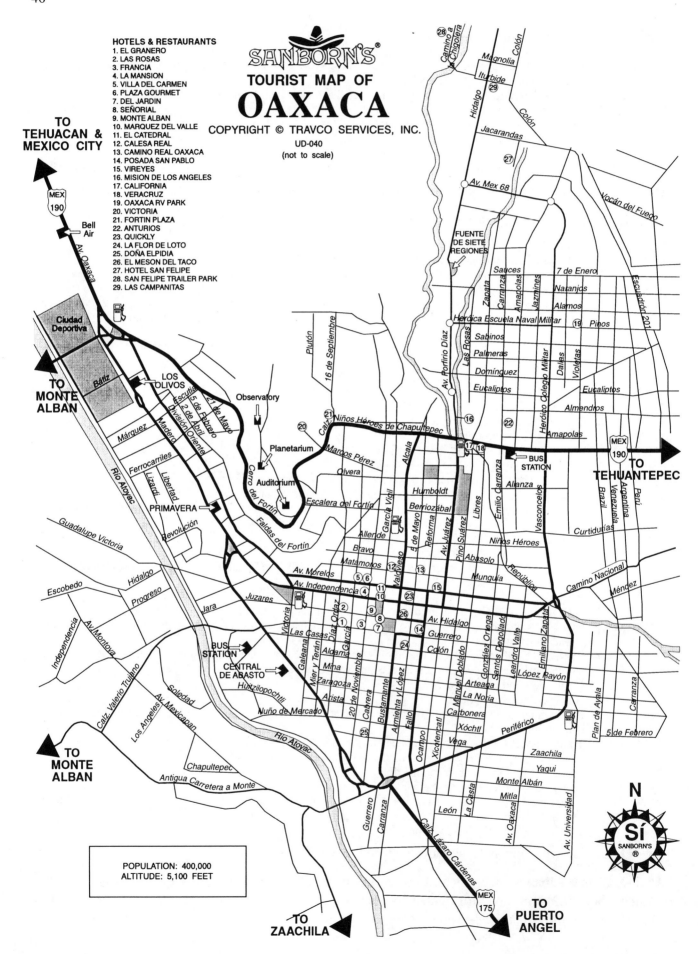

HOTELS & RESTAURANTS
1. EL GRANERO
2. LAS ROSAS
3. FRANCIA
4. LA MANSION
5. VILLA DEL CARMEN
6. PLAZA GOURMET
7. DEL JARDIN
8. SEÑORIAL
9. MONTE ALBAN
10. MARQUEZ DEL VALLE
11. EL CATEDRAL
12. CALESA REAL
13. CAMINO REAL OAXACA
14. POSADA SAN PABLO
15. VIREYES
16. MISION DE LOS ANGELES
17. CALIFORNIA
18. VERACRUZ
19. OAXACA RV PARK
20. VICTORIA
21. FORTIN PLAZA
22. ANTURIOS
23. QUICKLY
24. LA FLOR DE LOTO
25. DOÑA ELPIDIA
26. EL MESON DEL TACO
27. HOTEL SAN FELIPE
28. SAN FELIPE TRAILER PARK
29. LAS CAMPANITAS

SANBORN'S
TOURIST MAP OF
OAXACA
COPYRIGHT © TRAVCO SERVICES, INC.
UD-040
(not to scale)

TO
TEHUACAN &
MEXICO CITY

MEX
190

Bell
Air

Ciudad
Deportiva

TO
MONTE
ALBAN

Bátiz

LOS
OLIVOS

Observatory

Planetarium

Auditorium

PRIMAVERA

Escalera del Fortín

FUENTE
DE SIETE
REGIONES

Av. Mex 68

Heroica Escuela Naval Militar

BUS
STATION

MEX
190

TO
TEHUANTEPEC

Humboldt

Berriozábal

TO
MONTE
ALBAN

BUS
STATION

CENTRAL
DE ABASTO

POPULATION: 400,000
ALTITUDE: 5,100 FEET

TO
ZAACHILA

TO
PUERTO
ANGEL

MEX
175

N

Sí
SANBORN'S
®

MI   KM

214.0 342.4   Having veered left around glorieta, follow Tehuantepec sign. Pass sports stadium on right. Up hill and veer right past Hotel Huautla, left. Then wind up panoramic drive for a spell. Oaxaca is way down to the right.

215.2 344.3   Come to scenic overlook, right. Pass big Juárez Monument up at left. You can park and look over town if you wish. This is a nice view of Oaxaca City, the valley and Río Atoyac. Then Auditorio Guilguetza on left.

IF TO: Hotel Victoria, prepare to make a left turn ahead if the coast is clear. Otherwise turn right. Across from hotel is a little circle you go around and then facing the hotel, go straight when the coast is clear.

215.8 345.3   Pass Hotel Victoria, left. (If to there, turn sharp left - or to right and around little circle - and up steep driveway.) Continue ahead on curvy panoramic drive. Then pass Hotel Fortín Plaza, left. Then easy bend to right, then left.

216.1 345.8   Chrysler and Jeep dealer, left. Begin divided. Then Auto Servicio Solís on right.

IF TO: Hotel Parador Santo Domingo, turn right here.

216.4 346.2   Go uphill. Slow for topes at Social Security hospital, left.

216.5 346.4   Come to traffic light at Av. Juárez. **GAS** at right. Downtown is to your right. Left goes to Hotel Misión de Los Angeles, Misión Oaxaca, the medical school and IMSS hospital.

IF TO: Tule tree (a must visit place about 5 1/2 miles from town), Mitla, Tehuantepec, straight and start Oaxaca - Tehuantepec Log.

IF TO: Pochutla, Puerto Angel, continue straight and start Oaxaca - Pochutla Log (page 69). On this route about eight miles south of Oaxaca is the interesting town of San Bartolo Coyotepec, a famous place where you can find the best Oaxacan black pottery and artisans (well worth a visit).

End of Log 18

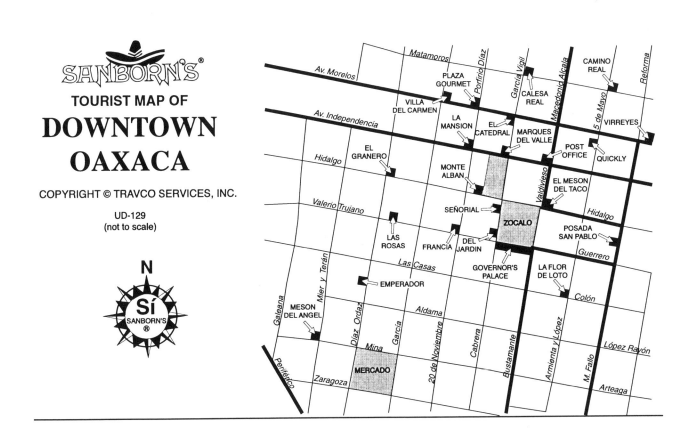

LOG 19 *START:* Oaxaca, Oax *END:* Tehuantepec, Oax

UD-087

152.0 MI or 243.2 KM
DRIVE TIME 4 1/2 – 5 HOURS
SCENIC RATING – 3

The highway from Oaxaca to Tehuantepec is quite winding, so don't plan to make a fast trip. Plan to get a reasonably early start from Oaxaca so you can stop off and see the famous Tule Tree, the Mitla Ruins, and Salina Cruz-on-the-Pacific. The only worthwhile accommodations or restaurant between here and Tehuantepec are at Mitla.

MI	KM	
0.0	0.0	Starting at junction of Hwy #190 and side street (Av. Juárez) to downtown (right), head east on divided parkway past **GAS** at right. Then Hotel California at right.
0.3	0.5	Pass Hotel Veracruz at right and bus station also at right.
0.5	0.8	Come to stoplight. Volkswagen at left and sports center at right. (If to Oaxaca RV Park turn left at next street – Violeta and go up about 1/2 mile.) Then Euzkadi dealer, left and downhill. Careful for tope.
1.0	1.6	Up thru Oaxaca's famous green rock quarries – many of their public buildings as well as fancy mansions have been constructed of this green stone.
1.2	1.9	Topes. Then **GAS**, right. Then pass campo militar at left.
1.4	2.2	Continue on divided. Hotel Del Bosque at right and more topes.
1.6	2.6	Cemetery at left. Then Goodyear, right. Post office, left.
2.7	4.3	Come to fancy mural monument to Benito Juárez at right. You can park at side of road if you want to take a photo. Pass Hwy #175 (left) to Guelatao (Juárez' birthplace) and on to Tuxtepec and Veracruz. Centro, right. Road narrows to two lanes.
3.5	5.6	Thru suburban village of San Sebastián. Posada Los Arcos at right.
5.6	9.0	Come to village of El Tule (population 6,000). To bypass town veer right. Straight to see Tule Tree up close. It's said that the base of this tree is of greater circumference than any other tree in the world, even including our giant Sequoias in California. It's said to be over 2,000 years old with a circumference of 160 feet and is an "Ahuehuete" which is a Cypress. Tradition holds that Cortés took a siesta under this tree when he came thru here. **KM 13**.
5.7	9.1	Over railroad crossing (LOOK & LISTEN). Then topes.
6.1	9.8	Over another railroad crossing (LOOK & LISTEN). End bypass of town.
7.4	11.8	Pemex storage plant at right. Then Agave plantation that grows Mezcal plants.
12.3	19.7	Pass side road (right) to DAINZU archeological zone, discovered in 1967 and opened to public in 1970. Of interest is a pair of stucco sculptures of "Cocijo," the rain god, one still in almost perfect condition including its brilliant color.
14.5	23.2	Pass side road (left) to Teotitlán del Valle.
15.0	24.0	Mezcal brewery plant on right.
17.6	28.2	Pass Red Cross as you skirt old town of Tlacolula (population 9,800) at right. Then **GAS** at right.

It's been said that the only place nowadays to buy Cochineal Dye is right here at Tlacolula's Sunday market. Cochineal is the famous old red color dye that was once the basis of the economy in this area. The magenta color of the uniforms of the British Red-coats that our colonists whipped back in 1776 came from Oaxaca's cochineal dye; likewise, the "liberty red" in the first tri-color of the French Republic. Since the development of synthetic dyes, however, there's not much demand for the genuine cochineal variety, except here and there where it is still preferred by the natives. (Cochineal is a little mite that attaches itself to the red bloom of the cactus which is where it absorbs its vivid coloring. The natives then gather millions of them, boil them and dry them in the sun and put them in packages. Fortunes were made on these tiny ticks in the olden days!)

MI	KM	
19.0	30.4	Mezcal access drinking place at left, where you can also get motor oil (perhaps the same stuff). **KM 35**.
20.0	32.0	Ruins of Zapotec-Mixtec YAGUL pyramid off to left on hillside, somewhat similar to Mitla but not quite as large nor as well restored.
24.5	39.2	Come to junction (left) with Hwy to Mitla (4 KM away). **GAS** at left.

IF TO: Mitla take left fork.

IF TO: Tehuantepec, Guatemala, take right fork.

MITLA, from the civilizations of the Zapotecas (first) and Mictecas (later) is well worth a short visit. Just wind along this side road thru the dusty little town of Mitla with its cactus fences to the end of the pavement, and go up and park in the compound (open daily, 9 - 5, admission charged).

Of prime interest at Mitla is the great mystery regarding Why it's the only archeological find in Mexico where there are no carvings or paintings of people and animals or symbols of mythology or the universe. In the big Hall of Monoliths, everything is geometric (lace like) and more like the fretwork of ancient Greece. And another mystery is how the huge 20-foot stone columns over the big doorways were lifted into place as some must weigh at least 15 tons!

There's an interesting little museum of Mixteca and Zapoteca items and artifacts on the left in the middle of town. An American, the late E.R. Frissell, did much of the early work and the museum, now run by Universidad de las Américas, was once part of his original collection.

Also at left in village adjacent to museum is Posada La Sorpresa, an 18th century hacienda converted to a delightful little inn. Its library is especially interesting, and its charming patio restaurant serves good American style specialties. Don't hesitate to overnight.

MI	KM	
27.5	44.0	Thru mezcal-brewing village of Matatlán (population 8,000). Topes (3) at entrance and exit of village (Mezcal is a low grade, powerful form of Tequila, for sale at stores thru here).
29.9	47.8	Watch for rocks on pavement. Pass Agua Santa and then careful on right horseshoe curve. **KM 52**.
42.5	68.0	Another right horseshoe curve here at La Ceiba ("The Five Leaf Silky Cotton Tree").
47.0	75.2	Thru riverside village of Totolapan. **GAS** at right. Then alongside Río Mijangos. **KM 80**.
50.0	80.0	Wind thru village of San Juan Guegoyache. **KM 85**.
59.0	94.4	Careful for very sharp curves.
60.0	96.0	Over one-lane bridge Las Catarinas (flash your lights for right-of-way).
64.8	103.7	Pass community of El Chacal. Watch for rocks on pavement ahead. Then San José de García. **KM 115**.
69.0	110.4	Thru spectacular Los Cantiles ("The Steep Rocks") Canyon with its sheer cuts.
72.0	115.2	Over little Río Camarón and down into Boquerón ("Big Hole") Canyon.
75.0	120.0	Pass village of Las Animas over to left. Then thru settlement of El Gramal, over bridge and pass side road (left) to little town of Nejapa.
80.0	128.0	Into village of El Camarón ("Shrimp"). **GAS** at right and over narrow Río Camarón bridge.
95.0	152.0	Road worker's settlement of El Coyul. Then community of Las Minas ("The Mines").
104.0	166.4	Thru settlement of Río Hondo and over little river of same name.
106.5	170.4	Over Puente Los Pilletes.
110.0	176.0	Thru village of La Reforma. Restaurant Reforma at left (not bad).
114.0	182.4	Thru village of Las Majadas. **KM 188**.
119.0	190.4	Thru village of Las Flautas. **KM 195**.
123.0	196.8	Pass Community of Marilú where there's a marble and onyx mill. Then down across one-lane bridge over Río Marilú. Then over Río Tequisistlán.
124.0	198.4	Look! A three mile straight stretch ahead! Well, Glory be!
130.0	208.0	Colonia San José at right. Then settlement of LLano Grande. *Vibradores* (speed bumps)
134.0	214.4	Big lake over to left was created when Mexico built Benito Juárez dam across Río Tehuantepec, sometimes called "Lake Marquez" or "Benito Juárez." Topes – *vibradores* and more.
137.0	219.2	Thru growing lake-side town of Jalapa El Marquez (population 23,000)
138.0	220.8	Pass side road (left) to Big Benito Juárez Dam – take a look if you wish. Dam is 88 meters high and has created Mexico's 12th largest artificial reservoir, capacity-wise, that is, with 942,000 cubic meters of water.
145.0	232.0	Pass community of Paso Alicia.
146.0	233.6	Note big Ricios Cave on mountain side at left. Then cross Puente Las Tejas.
147.0	235.2	Ruins of Guien Gola to left (7 km).
150.0	240.0	Cross twin bridges over Río Las Tortugas ("The Turtles"). Then penitentiary at right.
152.0	243.2	Pass **GAS**, at right and careful as you come to junction with Hwys #185 and #190-200 on outskirts of Tehuantepec (population 33,500).

IF TO: Jutitán and La Ventosa junction, take left fork, bend left slightly and start Tehuantepec - La Ventosa Jct Log (page 31).

IF TO: Salinas Cruz, Puerto Angel, etc. take right fork and start Tehuantepec - Pto. Escondido Log (page 138).

End of Log 19

LOG 20 *START:* Guadalajara, Jal *END:* Melaque Jct, Jal

UD-046

184.5 MI or 295.2 KM
DRIVE TIME 4 1/2 TO 5 HOURS
SCENIC RATING — 2

From Minerva Glorieta (Mile 0) to Mile 21 of this log, this highway is labeled #15-80 where it branches off (southeast) into Hwy # 15 and (west) into Hwy #80-54. Then, about a mile further west (Mile 23 1/4) you'll come to Hwy #54 (and the bypass around Acatlán) which branches off south while Hwy #80 continues westward to Melaque. (So don't become confused when you don't see any "Hwy #80" signs for the first 22 miles of this log.)

MI	KM	
0.0	0.0	Starting at Minerva with Fiesta Americana ahead on right and Danessa Ice Cream behind you on the left, Burger King ahead on the right and Tok's Restaurant on left, proceed ahead.
0.1	0.1	Palaclu's Chino Restaurant on the right, Columbo and the Super Flan Restaurant on the left.
0.2	0.3	Veer left and down on the divided freeway, under railroad thru Restaurant Row. El Caballo Restaurant will be on right along with Price Club. Firestone is on the left just before the traffic light.
0.5	0.8	You'll see a VW agency on left and after several stoplights, there will be a **GAS** station on the left.
0.7	1.2	Here you'll go under Lázaro Cárdenas Street.
1.0	1.6	Motel Campo is on left, Motel Chapalita beyond, and Posada Guadalajara on the right.
1.2	1.9	Gigante department store on the right.
1.3	2.0	There is a pretty fountain on the right.
2.0	3.2	Exit here for Holiday Inn Crown Plaza and pass statue of Mariano Otero at left. Plaza del Sol shopping center and Hotel Plaza del Sol are on the left.
2.3	3.7	You pass Holiday Inn at right and Motel Plaza del Sol at left.
2.5	4.0	Chrysler dealer is on the left and Ford on the right.
2.7	4.3	Guadalajara Grill at left.
2.9	4.6	Exit here for Hyatt Hotel.
3.3	5.3	Bolerama La Calma on right.
3.4	5.4	Holiday Suites del Real on right.
3.5	5.6	You pass thru impressive eagle road markers (which used to be the city limits of Guadalajara).
3.6	5.7	Administration Bldg. for Zapopan.
3.7	5.9	Gigante on right.
4.2	6.7	Restaurante Real Cazadores on right. Also **GAS** at right, but there's a better station 10 miles ahead.
4.4	7.0	Comercial Mexicana, left.
4.6	7.3	Coca Cola on right.
5.0	8.0	Careful now! Coming to junction with Periférico (There is usually a traffic cop here.) which goes to the Chapala road (Hwy #44) to the left (exit right after overpass) and to Tepic road (Hwy #15) to right. On left is a Mercedes Benz dealer; under Pedestrian crossing is Restaurant & Bar La Camarada.
6.0	9.6	Pass side road (right) to Ciudad Bugambilias and shopping center.
7.0	11.2	Pass side road (right) to El Palomar. Gigante is on right.
7.7	12.3	Pass side lane (right) to San José del Tajo Trailer Resort.
8.6	13.8	Good **GAS** on right.
9.4	15.0	Pass side road (right) to fabulous Santa Ana Golf Course and subdivision.
10.6	17.0	Pass Garden Hotel at right.
11.3	18.1	Fancy new Dunas Motel on right.
15.1	24.2	Town of Santa Cruz. **GAS** on both sides. Balneario Escondido and Vegetarian school at right.
16.6	26.6	Restaurant Mi Ranchito at right. Industrial park off to left.
18.0	28.8	Enter village of Buena Vista Take curve and wind on up.
19.1	30.6	Birriera Los Chavos at right.
22.0	33.6	Come to exit (right) to Morelia and Jocotepec. Right for Barra de Navidad also. Stay in left lane for Colima.

IF TO: Melaque and Barra de Navidad, EXIT RIGHT and Ahead on 2-lane road.

IF TO: Jocotepec, Morelia, turn right and follow Morelia Jocotepec signs. Join Guadalajara - Jocotepec Log. See Mexico's Colonial Heart book (page 54) at mile 22.

IF TO: Colima, straight ahead and join Guadalajara - Tecomán Jct Log (page 7) at mile 22.

26.0	41.6	Pass side road (left to Acatlán.
27.5	44.0	Slow for bumpy railroad crossing (LOOK-&-LISTEN). Then pass side road (right) to village of Bellavista.

MI	KM	
30.5	48.8	**GAS** at left and right. Then skirt edge of Villa Corona (population 12,000). Balneario (spa) Chimulco and RV park at left (50 spaces, all hookups, toilets, showers, restaurant, pool, open October - March).
31.4	50.2	At left, pass Balneario (spa) Agua Caliente with nice RV park (62 spaces, all hookups, showers, toilets, restaurant, pool, laundry, tennis).
43.3	69.3	**GAS** at right. Then wide curve right past Cocula.
46.0	73.6	Thru Santa María, Then pass side road (right) to San Martín Hidalgo.
49.5	79.2	Pass village of Los Parejos at right.
55.3	88.5	Pass side road (left) to Palo Alto. Then curve right thru community of El Mirador. Altitude 5,600 feet.
60.0	96.0	Thru settlement of Linda Vista.
63.0	100.8	Pass side road (left) to Ayotitalán. Then thru village of Ojo de Agua.
68.0	108.8	Thru Tecolotlán (population 15,000). Then over Río Tecolotlán.
77.0	123.2	Pass side cobblestone road (left) into Juchitlán (population 6,000) with pretty church domes. **GAS** at left. On a clear day you can see the two volcanoes Nevado de Colima (14,370 feet) and Fuego (12,000 feet) over to left.
80.0	128.0	Top, then down thru village of Colotitlán.
82.5	132.0	Pass village of Palo Blanco at right.
84.5	135.2	Pass reservoir at right with village of San Agustín on other side.
87.3	139.7	Pass side road (right) to San Clemente.
95.3	152.5	Skirt edge of Unión de Tula at right. **GAS** at right on far end of town.
96.5	154.4	Pass side road (left) to Ejutla. Then pass another side road (right) back into Unión de Tula.
103.0	164.8	Note Río San Pedro at bottom of chasm at right.
104.0	166.3	Commemorative road marker at right. If you park, be careful no one is coming when you get on highway again. This is called Puerto Manila (altitude 5,100 feet) where President López Mateos came to dedicate this highway.
109.3	174.9	Take right fork and over big steel bridge over Río San Pedro. (Left fork goes to El Grullo.) Then wind past village of El Corcovado.
113.5	181.6	Slow past side road (right) to famous San Francisco manganese mines - watch for trucks. Between here and Manzanillo you'll pass a lot of these big dump trucks that haul manganese ore from here to freighters at Manzanillo.
114.0	182.4	Curve right past Mezquitán at left.
117.5	188.0	Pass big Catholic Theological Seminary at left.
118.0	188.8	Cross Río El Cangrejo and veer left onto nice bypass of Autlán de Navarro. **GAS** at left. Then green house and packing sheds at left.
120.0	192.0	Come to end of bypass and turn left back onto highway, merging with traffic from town.
128.5	205.6	Thru Puerto Los Mazos summit (Altitude 4,600 feet).
135.5	216.8	Horseshoe bend of La Calera and continue along side river at right.
138.0	220.8	Another horseshoe curve called El Tigre. Note how tropical the scenery has become.
140.5	224.8	Sugar refinery at right and into village of Zapotillo.
143.5	229.6	**GAS** at left. Pass side road (right) to Purificación.
147.5	236.0	Pass side road (left) to Los Tecomates.
149.3	238.9	Thru Laguna El Rosario.
152.0	243.2	Thru settlement of Corte Colorado.
153.8	246.1	Pass side road (left) to La Concha.
158.8	254.1	Thru edge of La Huerta (population 15,000) at left. **GAS** at left.
168.0	268.8	Pass Ejido El Rincón at left.
172.5	276.0	Pass tropical village of La Palmita at left.
175.3	280.5	Now you can get your first glimpse of the Pacific. Watch for livestock thru here.
181.0	289.6	Pass settlement of La Paz at right.
184.5	295.2	Slow now! Come to junction with Hwy #200. Motel el Sol at left. Then **GAS** with restaurant at left.

IF TO: Puerto Vallarta, turn right and start Melaque - Pto. Vallarta Log (page 148).

IF TO: Barra de Navidad, Manzanillo, continue straight and start Melaque Jct - Tecomán Log (page 3).

End of Log 20

LOG 21 *START:* Melaque, Jal *END:* Guadalajara, Jal

UD-046

185.0 MI or 296.0 KM
DRIVE TIME 4 1/2 TO 5 HOURS
SCENIC RATING — 2

MI	KM	
0.0	0.0	At Melaque junction, head north up Hwy #80 on a nice straight stretch. **GAS** at right.
3.5	5.6	Pass settlement of La Paz at left.
5.0	8.0	Curve right and start winding up gradually.
6.3	10.1	Pass Ejido Lázaro Cárdenas over to right.
12.0	19.2	Pass tropical town of La Palmita at right.
16.5	26.4	Wide curve left past Ejido El Rincón at right. Then up.
19.5	31.2	Over Puente Lagunillas and wind down.
26.0	41.6	**GAS** at right and thru edge of La Huerta (population 15,000). Then some nice straight stretches.
31.3	50.1	Pass side road (right) to La Concha.
33.0	52.8	Thru settlement of Corte Colorado.
35.5	56.8	Thru Laguna El Rosario. Note sugar cane thru here.
37.5	60.0	Pass side road (right) to Los Tecomates.
40.8	65.3	Pass side road (left) to Purificación. Then **GAS** at right.
43.5	69.6	Thru village of Zapotillo. Note sugar mill at left.
44.0	70.4	Now start winding up.
56.3	90.1	Thru Puerto Los Mazos summit (Altitude 4,600 feet). Then wind down.
65.0	104.0	Veer right for bypass around Autlán de Navarro.
66.0	105.6	Packing sheds at left. Then pass **GAS** at left.
67.0	107.2	Cross bridge over Río El Cangrejo.
70.8	113.3	Curve left past Mezquitán at right. Then start winding up, over and down.
71.5	114.4	Pass side road (left) to famous San Francisco manganese mines.
75.0	120.0	Wind past village of El Corcovado. Then over steel bridge over Río San Pedro and curve left past side road (right) to El Grullo. Then up.
81.0	129.6	Puerto Manila (altitude 5,100 feet) where President López Mateos came to dedicate this highway. Commemorative road marker at left. If you park, be careful no one is coming when you get on highway again.
83.3	133.3	Now road straightens a bit thru pleasant little valley.
88.0	140.8	Wind around little town of Unión de Tula at left.
88.5	141.6	Pass side road (right) to Ejutla. Then **GAS** at left.
95.3	152.5	Pass community of San Cayetano at right.
97.8	156.5	Pass side road (left) to San Clemente.
100.5	160.8	Reservoir at left with village of San Agustín on other side.
102.5	164.0	Pass village of Palo Blanco at left.
104.0	166.4	Thru village of Colotitlán.
107.0	171.2	Pass cobblestone road (right) down into town of Juchitlán (population 6,000). **GAS** at right.
116.0	185.6	Curve right and over Río Tecolotlán. Then thru Tecolotlán (population 15,000).
121.3	194.1	Curve left thru village Ojo de Agua.
122.0	195.2	Pass side road (right) to Ayotitlán. Then up a stretch of winding road.
125.0	200.0	Thru settlement of Linda Vista.
129.5	207.2	Curve left thru community of El Mirador (Altitude 5,600 feet). Then curve right up past side road (right) to Palo Alto. Then start winding down.
135.5	216.8	Pass Village of Las Parejas at left.
139.5	223.2	Pass side road (right) to San Martín Hidalgo. Then thru Santa María.
143.0	228.8	Wide curve past Cocula. **GAS** at left.
154.8	247.7	At right, pass Balneario (spa) Agua Caliente with nice RV park (62 spaces, all hookups, showers, toilets, restaurant, pool, laundry, tennis).
155.5	248.8	Balneario (spa) Chimulco and RV park at right (50 spaces, all hookups, toilets, showers, restaurant, pool, open October - March). Then skirt edge of Villa Corona (population 12,000), **GAS** at left and right.
157.0	251.2	Pass side road (left) ti sugar mill village of Buenavista. Then slow for bumpy railroad crossing (LOOK-&-LISTEN).
158.0	252.8	Take left fork here past junction Hwy 54 (right) to Acatlán,
163.0	260.8	Come now to junction with Hwy #15. Begin nice divided road.
165.9	265.4	Birriera Los Chavos at left.

MI	KM	
167.0	267.2	Thru village of Buena Vista.
168.4	269.4	Industrial park on right. Then Restaurante Mi Ranchito on left.
169.9	271.8	Thru town of Santa Cruz. **GAS** on both sides. Balneario Escondido and Vegetarian school at left.
173.7	277.9	Fancy new Dunas Motel on left.
174.4	279.0	Pass Garden Hotel at left.
175.6	281.0	Pass exit (right and up overpass) to fabulous Santa Ana Golf Course and subdivision.
176.4	282.2	Good **GAS** on left.
177.3	283.7	Pass side road (left) to San José del Tajo Trailer Park.

IF TO: San José del Tajo Trailer Park, do not try to turn across traffic, continue straight ahead past the Siemans factory to the next overpass (El Palomar exit), exit right and up onto overpass and over highway. Continue to the opening which is the entrance to Gigante supermarket and make a U-turn and back to the highway and turn right. Retrace your steps past the Siemans plant, then pass Parrilla de Tajo restaurant on your right. Turn right at the entrance to San José del Tajo trailer park and follow the cobblestone road back to the office and turn right again.

178.0	284.8	Pass exit (right) to El Palomar. Gigante is over on left.
179.0	286.4	Pass exit (right) to Ciudad Bugambilias and shopping center.
180.0	288.0	On right before pedestrian crossing is Restaurant & Bar La Camarada and Mercedes Benz dealer. Careful now! Coming to junction with Periférico (There is usually a traffic cop here.) which goes to the Chapala road (Hwy #44) to the right and to Tepic road (Hwy #15) to left (exit right after overpass).
180.4	288.6	Pass Coca Cola plant on left.
180.7	289.1	Comercial Mexicana on right. Then **GAS** and Restaurante Real Cazadores on left.
181.3	290.1	Gigante on left. Then Administration building for Zapopan.
181.5	290.4	You pass thru impressive eagle road markers (which used to be the city limits of Guadalajara). Then Holiday Suites del Real on left.
181.7	290.7	Bolerama La Calma on left.
182.1	291.4	Exit here for Hyatt Hotel.
182.3	291.7	Guadalajara Grill at right.
182.5	292.0	Chrysler dealer is on right and Ford on the left.
182.7	292.3	Pass Holiday Inn at left and Motel Plaza del Sol at right. Exit here for Holiday Inn Crown Plaza and pass statue of Mariano Otero at right. Plaza del Sol shopping center and Hotel Plaza del Sol are on the right.
183.7	293.9	There's a pretty fountain on left. Then Gigante on left.
183.9	294.2	Motel Campo is on right, Motel Chapalita beyond, and Posada Guadalajara on the left.
184.2	294.7	Under Lázaro Cárdenas street. **GAS** on right.
184.7	295.5	Firestone is on the right. El Caballo Restaurant will be on left along with Price Club.
185.0	296.0	Come to Fiesta Americana on left and Danessa Ice Cream ahead of you on the right, Burger King on the left and Tok's Restaurant on right.

IF TO: Jalpa, Zacatecas continue straight and start Guadalajara - Zacatecas Log. See Mexico's Huasteca Potosina book (page 195).

IF TO: San Luis Potosí, Aguascalientes, turn right at circle and start Guadalajara -San Luis Potosí Log. See Mexico's Huasteca Potosina book (page 189).

IF TO: Querétaro, turn right at circle and start Guadalajara - Querétaro Log. See Mexico's Colonial Heart book (page 2).

IF TO: Mexico City or Morelia, Turn right and start Guadalajara - Morelia (toll) Log or Guadalajara - Jiquilpan. See Mexico's Colonial Heart book (page 39).

IF TO: Tepic or Pto. Vallarta turn left at circle and start Guadalajara - Tepic Log. See Mexico's Pacific Coast book (page 151).

End of Log 21

LOG 22 *START:* Tecomán, Col *END:* Jiquilpan, Mich

UD-085

163.5 MI OR 261.6 KM
DRIVE TIME 3 1/2 — 4 HOURS

MI	KM	
0.0	0.0	Here at Tecomán Junction, head north on 4-lane Hwy #110. Colima state ag college experiment fields on both sides of road with fruit-processing plant at left.
1.2	1.9	Note large Coca Cola bottling plant over on left.
3.3	5.3	Pass road left to Caleras and Madrid.
7.3	11.7	Pass village of Tecolapa at left.
9.5	15.2	Pass side road (right) to Ixtlahuacan. **KM 26**.
15.5	24.8	Pass side road (right) to Los Amoles
17.3	27.7	Pass another road (right) to Los Amoles. **KM 13**.
18.2	29.1	**GAS** at left.
21.5	34.4	Note famed twin volcanoes in distance ahead, NEVADO COLIMA and VOLCAN DE FUEGO.

VOLCAN DE FUEGO (fire) erupted during pre-Hispanic times, and since recorded time has erupted ten times. In May, 1957, it began spitting fire and smoke, and the red-glowing lava can still be seen in its crater. Fuego's elevation is 12,795 feet and Nevado's is 14,222 feet.

22.0	35.2	Pass side road (right) to Loma de Fátima.
23.5	37.6	Colima Golf course at left. Then **GAS** station at right
25.0	40.0	Careful now as you approach junction with Hwy #54 bypass at right but if you need food, **GAS**, or a place to stay, or if you'd just like to visit Colima, continue ahead a half-mile to the old junction and turn left into town; refer to Colima map (page 9) and Colima Eat & Stray (page 103). Then, when you're ready to continue ahead, retrace your steps to the junction.
25.1	40.2	Having turned right onto Hwy #54 bypass at yellow Bardahl building, proceed ahead. Then come to old junction with Hwy #110 and TURN RIGHT,

IF TO: Guadalajara, continue ahead on bypass of Colima and join Tecomán - Guadalajara Log (page 150) at mile 25.1

28.5	45.6	Cross Río Salado.
30.5	48.8	Alongside Río Salado gorge down at left.
32.5	52.0	Past side road right to Los Tepames.
33.5	53.6	Thru little ranching village of Tecuizitlán.
35.0	56.0	Pass side road left to hot springs deal.
37.5	60.0	Down over little Río Zarca. Then Ejido San Emigido to left.
42.0	67.2	Cross little bridge over Río Astillero.
44.0	70.4	Thru settlement of Trapichillos. Then side road (left) to Estación Alzada.
45.5	72.8	Cross state line. Leave state of Colima and enter state of Jalisco. Then cross Río de los Naranjos.
47.0	75.2	Slow for sharp hilltop horseshoe with red brick shrine on left. Thru Chula Vista.
51.5	82.4	Pass small community of company houses. Then under big aerial tramway for conveying iron ore from the mine (to right in mountains) over to railroad — quite a deal. This ultramodern conveying system is 13 miles long and is owned by a Monterrey steel mill. Note big gadget over to left that allows the line to make a little turn.
54.5	87.2	Slow for sharp turn. Then past settlement of Santa Cruz.
58.0	92.8	Down past little town of Pihuamo down at right. Then tile factory at right.
60.5	96.8	Social Security hospital at left. Then thru tropical forest.
63.0	100.8	Over Río del Tule.
63.3	101.3	Pass side road (right) to sugar town of San José del Tule.
68.0	108.8	Village of San Martín at right. Watch for rocks on pavement ahead.
75.3	120.5	Over Río San Pedro.
77.0	123.2	Now wind alongside Río San Pedro down at left.
77.3	123.7	Pass side road (left) to Atenquique and Tuxpan.
80.5	128.8	Over little Río Tecalitlán and into little town of Tecalitlán and pass plaza at right. Then up past church, also at right. **GAS** at left and on out.
81.5	130.4	Down and cross little fork of Río Tuxpan.
89.3	142.9	Pass village of Taximaxtla down at right.
91.5	146.4	Cross steel bridge over Río Tuxpan. Thru village of San Rafael.
94.5	151.2	Pass side road (left) to Tuxpan and Atenquique.

MI	KM	
95.5	152.8	Come to junction with Hwy #54 (Entronque Guzmán). A left here takes you to Cd. Guzmán (about 20 miles away).

IF TO: Jiquilpan and Hwy #15, straight ahead

97.5	156.0	Curve right past side road (left) to Santa Cruz.
98.5	157.6	Slow for bridge over Río Tuxpan tributary. Then thru village of Zapotiltic.
99.8	159.7	Thru village of Vista Hermosa.
101.0	161.6	Curve right thru village of Soyatlán. Then up past Río Tuxpan at right and along base of mountain.
103.0	164.8	Curve left and take LEFT FORK past side road right down into sugar refinery town of Tamazula. Then up and curve left past statue on right overlooking town. There's the big, big sugar refinery at right near end of town — one of Mexico's largest.
107.8	172.5	Thru hillside village of La Huacana and alongside nice valley.
110.5	175.8	Curve right over narrow bridge over Río Contla. Then thru old town of Contla.
115.0	184.0	Into La Garita and curve right past church at left.
116.0	185.6	Narrow bridge over little Río Garita. Then wind on up and up thru mountains. Watch for rocks on pavement!
119.0	190.4	Thru mountain top settlement of El Veladero. Elevation 4,400 feet.
122.3	195.7	Community of Puerto Zapatero.
123.0	196.8	Elevation 5,300 feet. Now along nice skyline drive and into pretty pine forest.
127.0	203.2	Magnificent view off to right. Nice and cool up here.
129.8	207.7	Now you're up to 6,500 feet. Then mountain top settlement of La Confradia.
133.0	212.8	Thru edge of mountain top town of Mazamitla (elevation 6,900 feet). Then turn LEFT a block before plaza and out and down.
138.0	220.8	Cross state line. Leave state of Jalisco and enter state of Michoacán.
139.5	223.2	Into San José de García. Curve right past church on left and down into town. Pass plaza on left and church on right and go one block and TURN LEFT (follow A MEXICO signs).
145.0	232.0	Pass side road (right) to Valle de Juárez.
146.0	233.6	Slow for sharp right. Presa (dam) Valle de Juárez down at right.
149.5	239.2	Slow for another sharp right and over little bridge.
152.8	244.5	Down thru village of Abadiano.
156.8	250.9	Thru village of El Fresno.
169.5	255.2	Now down winding road into Jiquilpan ahead.
162.5	260.0	Enter little city of Jiquilpan. **GAS** at right. Then bend left. Bear right onto divided palm parkway.
163.5	261.6	Come to junction with Hwy #15.

IF TO: Zamora, Carapán (Uruapan), Quiroga (Pátzcuaro), and Morelia, straight ahead and start Jiquilpan - Morelia Log. See Mexico's Colonial Heart book (page 40). Next worthwhile accommodations at Pátzcuaro- Uruapan-Morelia.

IF TO: Guadalajara or Lake Chapala, TURN LEFT and start Jiquilpan - Guadalajara Log. See Mexico's Colonial Heart book (page 198). Next worthwhile accommodations at Lake Chapala area and Guadalajara.

End of Log 22

LOG 23 *START:* Jiquilpan, Mich *END:* Tecomán, Col

UD-085

163.5 MI OR 261.6 KM
DRIVE TIME 3 1/2 — 4 HOURS

0.0	0.0	Starting at junction with Hwy #15 at west end of Jiquilpan, proceed ahead on divided parkway.
0.5	0.8	Divided parkway ends.
1.0	1.6	**GAS** up on left.
6.5	10.4	Pass side road (left) to Quitupan.
7.0	11.2	Thru village of El Fresno.
11.0	17.6	Thru community of El Sabino.
15.8	25.3	Thru village of Abadiano.
19.5	31.2	Pass side road (left) to Valle de Juárez.
23.5	37.6	Enter little town of San José de García.
24.5	39.2	TURN RIGHT (follow Manzanillo signs). Ahead one block. Then TURN LEFT with plaza on right. After a block TURN RIGHT and ahead thru town. Then curve left at church on right.

MI	KM	
26.5	42.4	Cross state line. Leave state of Michoacán and enter state of Jalisco.
31.0	49.6	Enter little mountain-top town of Mazamitla. Altitude 6,900 feet. Lumber is big business in these parts.
31.3	50.1	Straight here. Left fork leads to business district.
31.5	50.4	TURN RIGHT. Follow Manzanillo signs.
32.5	52.0	Slow for right hairpin curve. Los Cazos resort area entrance on left. Then thru lovely evergreen forest area and start down into fertile Tuxpan Valley, where sugar cane is the big crop. Careful for many sharp curves on the way down.
48.0	76.8	Cross bridge over little Río La Garita, with abandoned sugar mill on right and enter village of La Garita. Then at far end, curve left and out onto winding road.
54.0	86.4	Enter old town of Contla with its abandoned sugar refinery on left. Then over Río Contla.
60.0	96.0	Thermal springs and swimming pool on right — more for locals.
60.5	96.8	Enter town of Tamazula, with sugar refinery down on left — one of Mexico's biggest. Then curve right at end of town.
63.0	100.8	Thru Soyotlán and ahead on winding road thru fertile Río Tuxpan Valley. Note Mount Nevado de Colima ahead — one of Mexico's famous peaks reaching an altitude of 14,000 feet.
66.0	105.6	Pass side road (right) to Santa Cruz.
68.0	108.8	Come to junction with Hwy #54 (Entronque Guzmán). A right here takes you to Cd. Guzmán (about 20 miles away).
69.0	110.4	Pass side road (right) to Tuxpan. Ahead to Colima and Manzanillo.
71.3	114.1	Thru village of San Rafael and cross bridge over Río Tuxpan.
74.0	118.4	Pass village of Taximaxtla down at left.
81.5	130.4	GAS at right. Enter little town of Tecatitlán. Pass church and plaza on left and out over little Río Tecatitlán.
86.3	138.1	Pass side road (right) to Atenquique.
86.5	138.4	Watch for rocks on pavement as you wind alongside Río San Pedro down at right.
88.0	140.8	Curve right over Río San Pedro.
95.3	152.5	Pass village of San Martín at left.
100.0	160.0	Pass side road (left) to sugar town of San José Del Tule.
100.3	160.5	Curve right and over Río Del Tule. Then curve left and up.
105.0	168.0	Tile factory at left and up past little town of Pihuamo, mostly down at left.
108.5	173.6	Pass settlement of Santa Cruz.
111.3	178.1	Note little lake over at right. Then under big aerial tramway for conveying iron ore from the mine (to right in mountains) over to railroad — quite a deal. This ultramodern conveying system is 13 miles long and is owned by a Monterrey steel mill. Note big gadget over to left that allows the line to make a little turn. Then pass little community of company houses.
116.5	186.4	Pass red brick shrine on right in the settlement of Chula Vista.
118.5	189.6	Over Río de los Naranjos. Cross state line. Leave state of Jalisco and enter state of Colima.
121.3	194.1	Pass side road (right) to Alzada. Then thru settlement of Trapichillos.
123.0	196.8	Cross bridge over Río Astillero.
125.3	200.5	Ejido San Emigido at right and over little Río Zarca.
128.5	205.6	Pass side road (right) to hot springs deal.
129.5	207.2	Thru little village of Tecuizitlán.
131.0	209.6	Pass side road (left) to Tepames.
133.0	212.8	Now down alongside Río Salado gorge down at right.
134.5	215.2	Cross bridge over Río Salado.
138.0	220.8	Come to junction with (Hwy #54) bypass around and into state capital of Colima.

IF TO: Downtown Colima, continue straight. For accommodations, see Colima Eat & Stray (page 103).

IF TO: Guadalajara via toll road, turn right and join Tecomán Jct - Guadalajara Log (page 150) at mile 25.1.

IF TO: Manzanillo, turn left.

138.6	221.8	Pass exit (right) back into Colima.
139.2	222.7	Start down some dangerous curves.
139.5	223.2	Pass exit (right) to town of Coquimatlán. Restaurant Rancho Grande at right.
139.8	223.7	GAS on left, accessible at retorno. Then pass Colima golf course at right.
141.4	226.2	Pass retorno and side road (left) to Loma de Fátima.
145.1	232.2	GAS at right.
145.4	232.6	Sign says Manzanillo 85 km, Armeria 38 km. **KM 12**.
146.0	233.6	Pass side road (left) and left turn lane to Los Asmoles. **KM 13**.
147.8	236.5	Pass another road (left) into Los Asmoles.
150.2	240.3	Top and begin steep downgrade.

MI	KM	
154.3	246.9	Pass side road (left) to Ixtlahuacan. **KM 26**.
156.2	249.9	Pass town of Tecolapa over to right.
159.9	255.8	Pass road (right) to Caleras and Madrid. Then thru coconut palms.
162.1	259.4	Note large Coca Cola bottling plant on right.
163.5	261.6	Pass exit (right) to railroad station and to town of Tecomán. This is the junction with Hwy #200 that goes south to Acapulco. Then pass a retorno left also to Tecomán.

IF TO: Playa Azul, Acapulco, exit right, crossing over highway on overpass and into Tecomán. Start Tecomán - La Mira Jct Log (page 10).

IF TO: Manzanillo, continue ahead on toll road and start Tecomán - Melaque Log (page 147).

End of Log 23

LOG 24 START: La Mira Jct, Mich   END: Uruapan, Mich

UD-041

156.5 MI or 250.4 KM
DRIVE TIME 5 HOURS
SCENIC RATING — 3

NOTE: This is a very winding up-and-down road so don't expect to make much time.

MI	KM	
0.0	0.0	Here at La Mira junction Hwy #200, proceed ahead on Hwy #37.
9.3	14.9	Thru community of Los Coyotes.
11.3	18.1	Thru community of Los Amates.
17.5	28.0	Note red color of soil thru here. Start 37 miles of winding up-and-down road with a few sharp horseshoe curves.
21.3	34.1	Pass settlement of El Taguazal at right.
36.0	57.6	Slow for bumpy vados and enter town of Arteaga (population 14,000). Then **GAS** at left.
38.5	61.6	Fonda El Molino, a truck-stop restaurant at right.
45.8	73.3	Thru Las Juntas. Then over bridge Las Juntas and slow for sharp right curve.
47.3	75.7	Note ranch way down at right.
51.0	81.6	Pass community of La Lajita.
55.5	88.8	Truck stop of Hermanas Ramírez at right.
63.5	101.6	Pass community of Rancho Nuevo at right.
67.0	107.2	Wide spot of Palo Pintado at right.
68.3	109.3	Pass community of El Guayabito at left. Then down steep grade.
69.5	111.2	Over bridge and thru Paso del Chivo (Goat's Pass). Then pass El Reparito.
73.5	117.6	Pass side road (right) to Infiernillo dam.
76.0	121.6	Thru community of Las Cañas.
78.8	126.1	Thru La Vinata.
80.3	128.5	Pick up railroad at left.
83.0	132.8	Thru settlement of El Descansadero.
85.0	136.0	Thru Ejido Los Pocitos (a cattle co-op farm).
87.5	140.0	Pass community of Ciriancito, mostly at left.
89.0	142.4	Thru Los Ranchos.
91.3	146.1	Thru scattered community of Nuevo Centro. You can see part of Infiernillo Dam.
95.5	152.8	Thru riverside settlement of El Limoncito.
98.8	158.1	Down thru San Pedro Barajas. Railroad at right and up alongside valley on left.
104.0	166.4	Thru village of Cupuancillo and at far end curve left. Then over couple of bridges over tributaries of Río Tapalcatepec.
106.0	169.6	Pass village of El Chilar at right.
107.3	171.8	Pass side road (left) to Tumbiscatio, 77 Km.
108.5	173.6	Cross puente Capirio over Río Tepalcatepec. Then thru El Capirio.
111.0	177.6	Pass side road (right) to Carrera de Mata. Then long straight stretch thru nice countryside.
114.3	182.9	Pass village of Gambara at right.
116.8	185.9	Thru community of El Letrero.
119.0	190.4	**GAS** at left. Come now to cross roads with Hwy #120 at little circle monument to Emiliano Zapata on horseback. Go halfway around glorieta and ahead. Right is to Apatzingan where there's a big truck garden and also where the Mexican Constitution was signed in 1814. Left goes to Ario de Rosales and on to Pátzcuaro.

58

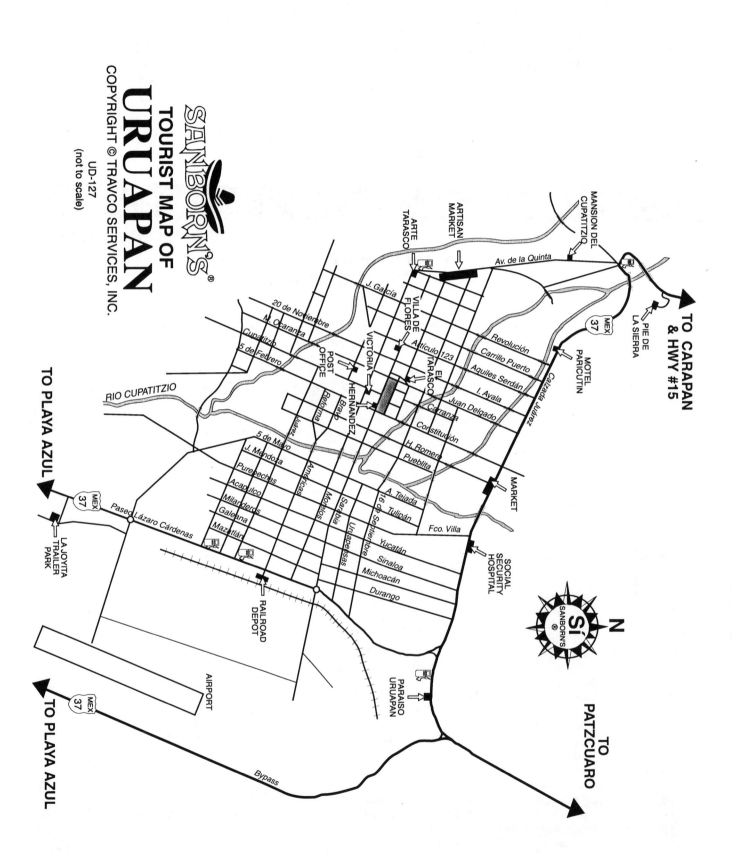

SANBORN'S®
TOURIST MAP OF
URUAPAN
COPYRIGHT © TRAVCO SERVICES, INC.

UD-127
(not to scale)

TO CARAPAN
& HWY #15

MANSION DEL
CUPATITZIO

PIE DE
LA SIERRA

ARTE
TARASCO

ARTISAN
MARKET

Av. de la Quinta

MEX
37

MOTEL
PARICUTIN

J. García

VILLA DE
FLORES

20 de Noviembre

N. Ocaranza

VICTORIA

Artículo 123

Revolución

Carrillo Puerto

Cupatitzio

POST
OFFICE

EL TARASCO

Aquiles Serdán

Calzada Juárez

5 de Febrero

RIO CUPATITZIO

HERNANDEZ

Bravo

Reforma

Carranza

Constitución

I. Ayala

Juan Delgado

TO PLAYA AZUL

5 de Mayo

Juárez

H. Romero

Pueblita

J. Mendoza

Américas

A. Tejada

MARKET

Purepechas

Morelos

16 de Septiembre

Tulipán

Acapulco

Sarabia

Fco. Villa

SOCIAL
SECURITY
HOSPITAL

MEX
37

Milanderos

Urapetisas

Yucatán

Galeana

Mazatlán

Sinaloa

Paseo Lázaro Cárdenas

Michoacán

LA JOYITA
TRAILER
PARK

Durango

N

Si
SANBORN'S®

RAILROAD
DEPOT

PARAISO
URUAPAN

TO
PATZCUARO

AIRPORT

MEX
37

Bypass

TO PLAYA AZUL

MI	KM	
120.0	192.0	Pass crop duster's airfield at right and **GAS** at left. Then Las Carretas Restaurant at left.
121.0	193.6	Bend right and thru town of Nueva Italia where a few descendants of an originally Italian colony reside.
124.0	198.4	Thru railroad station community of Estación Nueva Italia. Note vegetable sheds at left on railroad. This is a big shipping point for vegetables grown in this area such as onions, tomatoes, asparagus, mangos, limes etc., shipped mostly to the USA.
127.0	203.2	Cross El Marquez Bridge over Río Cupatitzio.
128.8	206.1	Pass side road (right) to El Huaco, 7.5 miles. Then community of La Laguna at right. Now over railroad crossing.
132.8	212.5	Thru edge of little town of Gabriel Zamora. **GAS** at left and onto short stretch of divided boulevard. Then pass side road (right) to El Cobano. Go halfway around monument glorieta and out.
133.8	214.1	Thru community of El Injerto.
137.0	219.2	Straight thru village of La Gallina (The Chicken).
138.0	220.8	Thru cut and curve right. Then over high bridge and into Barranca Honda and sharp right thru cut.
141.3	226.1	Pass community of Charapendo at left.
148.0	236.8	Pass side road (left) to Matanguaran and Presa Cupatitzio. Then wind alongside Tzararacua Canyon.
150.0	240.0	Pass side road (left) to La Tzararacua ("The Sieve" in Purepechan Indian). Here's where the Cupatitzio River forms a stupendous 90-foot waterfall.
151.5	242.4	Pass La Loma.
153.0	244.8	Up thru village of Zumpimito and curve right.
153.5	245.6	Thru suburban village of La Pinera and into city of Uruapan.
154.0	246.4	Come now to fountain glorieta. Go halfway around and ahead on divided boulevard. Then pass Pepsi plant at right.
154.8	247.7	Come to another fountain glorieta. Go halfway around and ahead. **GAS** at left.
156.0	249.6	Come to still another fountain glorieta. Go halfway around and continue straight ahead. Then Pemex storage tanks at right.
156.5	250.4	Come to junction with road to Pátzcuaro at right.

IF TO: Pátzcuaro, turn right and start Uruapan - Pátzcuaro Log. See Mexico's Colonial Heart book (page 86). **GAS** ahead at right.

IF TO: Carapán, continue straight and start Uruapan - Carapán Log. See Mexico's Colonial Heart book (page 88).

End of Log 24

LOG 25 *START:* Uruapan, Mich *END:* La Mira Jct, Mich

UD-041

156.0 MI or 249.6 KM
DRIVE TIME 5 HOURS
SCENIC RATING — 3

NOTE: This is a very winding up-and-down road so don't expect to make much time.

0.0	0.0	Here at junction Hwy #37 and Pátzcuaro road, having taken the left fork, proceed ahead on nice bypass of Uruapan.
0.5	0.8	Pemex storage tanks on left. Come to a fountain glorieta. Go halfway around and continue straight ahead.
1.7	2.7	Come to another fountain glorieta. Go halfway around and ahead. **GAS** at right.
2.5	4.0	Pass Pepsi plant at left. Come to still another fountain glorieta. Go halfway around and continue straight ahead and take leave of Uruapan.
3.0	4.8	Thru suburban village of La Pinera.
3.5	5.6	Curve left and down thru village of Zumpimito.
5.0	8.0	Pass La Loma
6.5	10.4	Pass side road (right) to La Tzararacua ("The Sieve" in Purepechan Indian). Here's where the Cupatitzio River forms a stupendous 90-foot waterfall.
8.5	13.6	Wind alongside Tzararacua canyon. Then pass side road (right) to Matanguaran and Presa Cupatitzio.
15.2	24.3	Pass community of Charapendo at right.
18.5	29.6	Sharo left curve thru cut and into Barranca Honda and over bridge. Then curve left and thru another cut.
19.5	31.2	Straight thru village of La Gallina (The Chicken).
22.5	36.0	Thru community of El Injerto.

MI	KM	
23.7	37.9	Thru edge of little town of Gabriel Zamora. Pass side road (left) to El Cobano. Go halfway around monument glorieta and out. Then **GAS** at right.
27.7	44.3	Over railroad crossing. Then community of La Laguna at left and pass side road (left) to El Huaco, 7.5 miles.
29.5	47.2	Cross El Marquez Bridge over Río Cupatitzio.
32.5	52.0	Thru railroad station community of Estación Nueva Italia. Note vegetable sheds at left on railroad. This is a big shipping point for vegetables grown in this area such as onions, tomatoes, asparagus, mangos, limes etc., shipped mostly to the USA.
35.5	56.8	Thru boom town of Nueva Italia where a few descendants of an originally Italian colony reside.
36.5	58.4	Las Carretas Restaurant at right. Then pass crop duster's airfield at left and **GAS** at right.
37.5	60.0	Come now to cross roads with Hwy #120 at little circle monument to Emiliano Zapata on horseback. Go halfway around glorieta and ahead. Left is to Apatzingan where there's a big truck garden and also where the Mexican Constitution was signed in 1814. Right goes to Ario de Rosales and on to Pátzcuaro. **GAS** at right.
39.5	63.2	Thru community of El Letrero. Then a long straight stretch thru nice fertile countryside.
42.0	67.2	Pass village of Gambara at right. Note mountains in the distance ahead. Watch for livestock thru here.
45.5	72.8	Pass side road (left) to Carrera de Mata. Then curve left and wind into mountains.
48.0	76.8	Pass community of El Capirio. Then cross bridge over Río Tepalcatepec.
49.2	78.7	Pass side road (right) to Taumbiscatio, 77 Km.
50.5	80.8	Pass village of El Chilar at left.
52.0	83.2	Cross a couple of bridges over tributaries of Río Tapalcatepec. Then curve left and thru village of Caupuancillo.
57.5	92.0	Down thru San Pedro Barajas. Railroad at left.
61.0	97.6	Thru riverside settlement of El Limoncito alongside huge Lake Infiernillos (Little Hell).
67.5	108.0	Thru Los Ranchos.
69.0	110.4	Pass community of Ciriancito, mostly at right.
71.5	114.4	Thru Ejido Los Pocitos (a cattle co-op farm).
73.5	117.6	Thru settlement of El Descansadero.
77.7	124.3	Thru La Vinata.
80.5	128.8	Thru community of Las Cañas.
83.0	132.8	TAKE RIGHT FORK. Left fork goes to Infiernillo dam.
87.0	139.2	Pass El Reparito. Then thru Paso del Chivo (Goat's Pass) and over bridge. Now start another steep grade.
88.2	141.1	Pass community of El Guayabito at right.
89.5	143.2	Wide spot of Palo Pintado at left.
101.0	161.6	Truck stop of Hermanas Ramírez at left. Then begin 37 miles of winding road with some sharp horseshoe curves.
105.5	168.8	Pass community of La Lajita.
109.2	174.7	Note ranch way down at left.
111.5	178.4	Sharp left curve and over Las Juntas Bridge and thru community of same name. Then alongside river.
118.0	188.8	Fonda El Molino, a truck-stop restaurant at left.
120.3	192.5	Enter town of Arteaga (population 14,000), biggest in these parts. Then **GAS** at right.
135.0	216.0	Pass settlement of El Taguazal at left.
136.3	218.1	Note red color of soil thru here and careful for rock slides during rainy season.
145.0	232.0	Thru community of Los Amates.
147.0	235.2	Thru community of Los Coyotes.
156.0	249.6	Straight thru town of La Mira (population 12,500).
156.5	250.4	Come to junction with Hwy #200.

IF TO: Ixtapa, Zihuatanejo, Acapulco, turn left and start La Mira - Ixtapa Log (page 12).

IF TO: Manzanillo, continue straight and start La Mira - Tecomán Log (page 145).

IF TO: Playa Azul, continue straight and follow stub log below.

TO PLAYA AZUL

0.0	0.0	Continue straight but careful for topes.
1.8	2.9	Curve left and straight thru palms.
4.0	6.4	Bend left and come to little circle. Pass **GAS** at left and enter village of Playa Azul. Bend left and continue ahead with Pacific on right.
4.5	7.2	Hotel Playa Azul at right (45 A/C rooms, restaurant, bar, pool, pets OK, MC, VI, and several RV spaces with hookups). Then Hotel María Teresa at left (60 rooms, restaurant, bar, pool, pets OK, parking, MC, VI). Then Military garrison at left.
4.8	7.7	Come to Hotel Loma (80 rooms, restaurant, bar, pool, parking, no pets, MC, VI).

End of Log 25

LOG 26 *START:* Ixtapa, Gro *END:* Cd. Altamirano, Mich

UD-077

118.3 MI or 189.3 KM
DRIVE TIME 3 1/2 - 4 HOURS
SCENIC RATING — 3

This portion of Hwy #134 was constructed piece by piece following the development of Ixtapa into a first class resort. It's a great time saver as it connects Hwy #200 with Toluca. There's virtually no heavy truck traffic; however, the next 118 miles are both a blessed and cursed! Although the road surface is excellent and the scenery (majestic rain forested mountain slopes) is exemplary, the constant curves and rocks on the pavement force a slow pace, so exercise extreme caution, especially on blind curves, and wind down leisurely. Be sure to gas up before you start.

MI	KM	
0.0	0.0	Here at and junction with Hwy #200, pass military inspection check point and proceed ahead up Hwy #134.
3.5	5.6	Cross Río Ixtapan and begin winding up.
5.0	8.0	Pass side road (right) to town of Calabazilito.
5.5	8.8	View Río Ixtapa valley to right and careful for rocks on roadway.
8.3	13.3	Cross Río Las Caramicius and thru bus stop of Las Olas (The Waves). Note the beautiful forested mountain slopes and the 150-foot trees. Wonder how long it will be before corn and pasture replace them?
14.0	22.4	Thru bus stop hamlet of María Isabel.
16.3	26.1	Pass side road (left) to Zumatlán.
17.0	27.2	Careful for possible rock slide thru here. Then over Río Montor.
23.5	37.6	Soda stop store at left.
26.5	42.2	Cross bridge over Río El Ciruelo and then over Río La Cuba.
27.3	43.7	Cross bridge over Río Aguatillo and then over Río Cedral.
31.0	49.6	Thru community of Villa de Zaragoza and over Río Verde.
35.0	56.0	Cross bridge over Río San Antonio. You can understand why it took so long to complete this stretch of highway after crossing so many bridges.
38.0	60.8	Thru village of San Antonio.
40.0	64.0	Zona de Nieba (Fog warning) sign. You'll see many more ahead.
42.0	67.2	Careful now for series of very sharp curves and rocks on road.
49.0	78.4	Summit, Now begin winding down leisurely.
55.3	88.5	Zihuaquillo truck stop at left - no need to stop.
61.5	98.4	Overlook Barranca de Los Machos.
63.0	100.8	Cross bridge over Río Aguacate and then over Río Ceiba Mocha
65.0	104.0	Cross Los Enfermos bridge.
66.3	106.1	Over Río Cunancito and then El Cedral.
67.5	108.0	Cross puente El Cuaisle and begin climbing sharply.
69.0	110.4	Another military inspection checkpoint.
70.5	112.8	View Barranca Honda (Deep Gorge) - aptly named!
72.5	116.0	Pass rock monument to Javier Llanderal Rueda and others who lost their lives constructing this road. (Don't let it scare you.)
76.3	122.1	Over Arroyo El Viejo.
83.5	133.6	Over puente Parado II.
95.5	152.8	Pass side road (right) to community of Pinzán. Highway finally straightens out a bit!
98.0	156.8	Pass side road (left) to Placeres Del Oro and over Río Del Oro.
105.5	168.8	Come to crossroads, but continue straight ahead.
115.0	184.0	Enter community of Coyuca de Catalán (population 10,000). Then **GAS** at right and cross Río Miguel Alemán. This is also the state line. Leave state of Guerrero and enter state of Michoacán.
118.0	188.8	Enter Cd. Altamirano (population 12,000), largest in these parts.
118.3	189.3	Come now to glorieta and junction Hwy #49. Right is to Iguala and left is to Morelia. **GAS** at right.

IF TO: Toluca, straight ahead and start Cd. Altamirano - Toluca Log.

End of Log 26

LOG 27 *START:* Cd. Altamirano, Mich *END:* Toluca, Mex

UD-077

134.0 MI or 214.4 KM
DRIVE TIME 3 1/2 - 4 HOURS
SCENIC RATING — 3

MI	KM	
0.0	0.0	Here at junction with Hwy #49 in Cd. Altamirano, proceed ahead on short stretch of divided highway.
0.5	0.8	Pass market at left and cross Miguel Alemán bridge over Río Temascaltepec and thru suburb of Riva Palacio.
1.0	1.6	Pass junction (left) with Hwy #49 to Zitácuaro and Morelia.
1.5	2.4	Restaurant Los Arcos at left has OK food and clean restrooms.
7.0	11.2	Come to state line. Leave state of Michoacán and enter state of Guerrero.
10.3	16.5	Enter Cutzmala (population 14,000). **GAS** at right, curve left and out.
13.0	20.8	Cross bridge over Río Cutzmala.
16.5	26.4	Pass side road (right) to Limón Grande.
20.5	32.8	Pass side road (right) to El Salitre.
25.5	40.8	Cross bridge over Río Alboreja.
31.5	50.4	Thru village of Balderama.
34.0	54.4	Thru village of El Pochote.
37.5	60.0	Note long narrow waterfall way up to left.
38.5	61.6	Thru settlement of La Cantina.
40.0	64.0	Come to another state line. Leave state of Guerrero and enter state of Mexico and start winding and climbing (for the next 80 miles, in fact).
45.0	72.0	Pass settlement of El Guayabal.
46.0	73.6	Thru Las Anonas. (Anonas are a fruit resembling a hand grenade, with sweet, yellow flesh inside.)
50.0	80.0	Pass side road (right) to Presa Vicente Guerrero.
51.0	81.6	Thru community of Los Cuervos. To left is a small dam but where's the river?
55.3	88.5	Pass side road (left) to Acamuchitlán
59.0	94.4	Pass another Salitre.
70.3	112.5	Veer left for bypass around Tejupilco.

The town of Tejupilco was the center for the Matlatzingo people in pre-Hispanic times and where much of the jade used by the Aztecs in Mexico City was produced. There are several unexplored ruin sites in the area and the pretty little town has a Franciscan church on its main plaza worth visiting.

72.3	115.7	**GAS** at left and curve right, left, up and out.
82.0	131.2	Pass side road (right) to Ocotepec.
91.3	146.1	Slow for sharp left at Toluca sign and careful for *vibradores* (traffic bumps) ahead. Straight is to the town of Temascaltepec (population 10,000) a mining town where Ríos Comunidad, Colorado and Temascaltepec meet. It's worth a look-see if you've got a minute as it is situated at he bottom of this valley and offers colorful vegetation, cobblestone streets and a nice central plaza.
92.3	147.7	Pass side road (left) to Valle de Bravo.
114.0	182.4	Note Mesón Viejo down to right.
122.0	195.2	Thru mountain town of Buena Vista (good view) as you near the summit here at 9,500 feet elevation.
123.0	196.8	Pass side road (right) to Nevado de Toluca National Park (14 miles to crater).

NEVADO DE TOLUCA (also called "xinatecatl") is a snow covered volcano whose altitude is a shade less than 15,000 feet (4,690 meters). It is surrounded by pine forests and contains two crystal-clear lakes, "Sol" and "Luna" where fishing and scuba diving are permitted. It is a nice spot for a picnic lunch, although at times (morning and late evening fog makes driving tedious. Incidentally, in pre-Hispanic times the volcano was a site for pilgrimages and religious offerings.

127.5	204.0	Pass side road (left) to Zinacantepec with interesting San Miguel Monastery built in the 16th century with its interesting wall and ceiling murals.
130.0	208.0	Fancy funeral home and cemetery at left. Note village of Santa Cruz off to right.
131.0	209.6	**GAS** at right.
134.0	214.4	Pass children's hospital at left and come to junction bypass Hwys #15-55. For info on accommodations see Toluca Eat & Stray (page 124).

IF TO: Mexico City, turn right and start Toluca - Mexico City Log.

IF TO: Ixtapa de la Sal, Iguala, Acapulco, turn right and start Toluca - Ixtapa de la Sal Log (page 35).

IF TO: Morelia, turn left and start Toluca - Morelia Free Log. See Mexico's Colonial Heart book (page 190).

IF TO: Querétaro, turn left and start Toluca - Palmillas Log (page 156).

IF TO: Downtown, straight ahead.

End of Log 27

LOG 28 *START:* Toluca, Mex *END:* Mexico City, DF

UD-035

36.1 MI or 57.8 KM
DRIVE TIME 1 – 1 1/2 HOURS
SCENIC RATING – 3

Before you leave Toluca, heading for Mexico City, think about when you will arrive and plan ahead. The best time to arrive in Mexico City is before 7 AM, but if that's not feasible, the second choice is between 10 AM – 12 PM or between 3 – 6 PM because traffic is less congested during these hours. The traffic on the Periférico is no worse that any big city in the U.S. In fact, the drivers are more polite, it's just pretty crowded. Read ahead in log and plan your exit. RV's should avoid the city entirely.

Day	Monday	Tuesday	Wednesday	Thursday	Friday
Color	Yellow	Pink	Red	Green	Blue
Last #	5 & 6	7 & 8	3 & 4	1 & 2	9 & 0
Sometimes	7 & 8	9 & 0	1 & 2	3 & 4	5 & 6

Warning: Pollution controls have been implemented in D.F. and they do apply to tourists. The fine for disregarding is U.S. $120.00. If your plate ends in the "right" number, it's wrong to drive that day. Subject to change, the "day without a car" will be extended if a smog emergency is declared. How to tell? Hopefully The News or local paper will advise. All you can do is ask at the tollbooth. If your plate ends with a letter you cannot circulate on Fridays.

Any time you think a cop is being too eager, We suggest you write the cop's badge # down. See "cops" section in the filler. Also you must have a fire extinguisher in your vehicle while in Mexico City. It's a good idea to carry one anywhere you go.

MI	KM	
0.0	0.0	Here at south junction with Hwy #55, proceed ahead on Paseo Tollocán pass **GAS** station at right.
0.5	0.8	Highrise Hotel Terminal at right. Then VIP's Restaurant also at right. Now bend right pass social security hospital at right.
1.3	2.1	Bend left and continue ahead pass high line towers at left.
1.5	2.4	Come now to important stop-street and then head for that tree-lined divided boulevard at left – pass yellow sign (MEXICO), but if to Hotel Del Rey Inn – take access street to right.
2.3	3.7	Note Pfizer Pharmaceutical plant over at left, then Nestle's plant also on left.
2.6	4.2	Cross very bumpy railroad (LOOK-&-LISTEN).
3.0	4.8	Huge Chrysler-Dodge plant over and lots of big factories over to left – Toluca is quite an industrial town.
5.6	9.0	Nissan at left. **KM 56**.
8.0	12.8	Huge Zapata-on-horseback monument at left.
8.5	13.6	Over bridge over the Río Lerma – just a trickle here, but it gets to be quite a river when it flows into Lake Chapala, over near Guadalajara.
9.0	14.4	**GAS**, at left.
10.2	16.3	Hotel Real Hacienda at right.
12.2	19.5	Restaurant El More at right with cabrito al horno (baked) or ahumado (smoked). Open 10 AM till 9 PM. MC, VI. Ph & Fax: (728) 285-1232. **KM 45**.
16.4	26.2	Climb up thru national park with small rest stops right and left.

MI	KM	
17.4	27.8	Top – 10,000 feet.
18.7	29.9	Pass Marquesa roadside picnic rest area.
19.7	31.5	Cross state line – leave state of México and enter D.F. (Distrito Federal). Altitude 9,800 feet. **KM 31**.
23.0	36.8	You are going thru mountainous old growth pines. This is called Parque Nacional Miguel Hidalgo Y Costilla. Beautiful and very relaxing. Now thru tunnel (under free road). **KM 26**.
24.0	38.4	Come to tollbooth and pay toll (car – $21, 2 axle – $42, 3 axle – $63). You can see free road over to left. Then pass exit (right) for Desierto de los Leones Park and Naucalpan.
25.0	40.0	Going thru El Desierto de los Leones.
26.5	42.4	Thru tunnel.
27.5	44.0	Palacio de Hierro with Sears and Liverpool stores at left.
28.1	45.0	Pyramid at right with radio tower on top. **KM 17**.
28.5	45.6	Green glass building at right. Pass suburb of Santa Fe.
30.0	48.0	This is where toll road joins free road.
30.6	49.0	TURN LEFT for Paseo de la Reforma. Straight takes you into Mexico City via Av. Constituyentes.
31.7	50.7	Curve right past intersection with Paseo de Las Palmas (left) which also goes to Periférico. Then pass statue of Penelope at right.
33.0	52.8	Come to junction with Periférico.

IF TO: Cuernavaca, turn right before overpass and start Mexico City Periférico North to South. See Mexico's Colonial Heart book (page 95).

IF TO: Querétaro, San Luis Potosí, turn right just after overpass and join Mexico City – Querétaro Log at mile 1.9. See Mexico's Colonial Heart book (page 175).

IF TO: Downtown and hotels, continue straight past Monument to Mexico's Petroleum Industry.

33.4	53.4	Hard Rock Café and Spire fountain on left.
34.0	54.4	Pass Anthropological museum at left and continue ahead thru Chapultepec Park.
35.0	56.0	Come to the Angel de Independencia monument with Hotel María Isabel Sheraton and American Embassy over to left.

End of Log 28

LOG 29 START: Mexico City, DF END: Toluca, Mex

UD-035

36.1 MI or 57.8 KM
DRIVE TIME 1 – 1 1/2 HOURS
SCENIC RATING – 3

0.0	0.0	Starting at the Angel de Independencia monument with Hotel María Isabel Sheraton and American Embassy over to right, proceed westward on Reforma through Chapultepec park.
1.0	1.6	Pass Anthropological museum at right.
1.3	2.1	Next right is for area hotels on Av. Arquimedes at Auditorio Metro station. Then pass Contemporary Art museum and National Auditorium at left.
1.6	2.6	Hard Rock Café and Spire fountain on right.
1.9	3.0	Continue straight on Reforma over Periférico past Monument to Mexico's Petroleum Industry. Exit to right goes to Querétaro.
2.1	3.4	Good little Loma Linda restaurant ahead at right. Then **GAS**, right. Stoplight.
3.3	5.3	Stay in left lane. Pass statue of Penelope at left. Come to intersection (right) with Paseo de Las Palmas which goes back to the Periférico. Curve left and ahead on Paseo de la Reforma.
4.4	7.0	For Toluca toll road stay in right lane.
5.0	8.0	Come to "Y." VEER LEFT for toll road. Toluca free road goes to right. Then Syntex plant at right. **KM 14**.
6.5	10.4	Green glass building at left. Pass suburb of Santa Fe.
6.9	11.0	Pyramid at left with radio tower on top. **KM 17**.
7.5	12.0	Palacio de Hierro with Sears and Liverpool stores at right.
8.5	13.6	Thru tunnel.
9.8	15.7	Going thru El Desierto de los Leones.
11.0	17.6	Pass exit (right) for Desierto de los Leones Park and Naucalpan. Come to tollbooth and pay toll (car – $21, 2 axle – $42, 3 axle – $63) After tollhouse you'll see free road over to right.

MI	KM	
12.4	19.8	Tunnel. **KM 26**. You are going thru mountainous old growth pines. Beautiful and very relaxing after the rat-race D.F. This is called Parque Nacional Miguel Hidalgo Y Costilla. It's hard to believe that the world's largest city is only 12 miles away.
15.3	24.5	Cross state line – leave D.F. and enter state of México. Altitude 9,800 feet. Begin downhill. **KM 31**.
16.3	26.1	Pass Marquesa roadside picnic rest area.
17.6	28.2	Thru national park with small rest stops right and left. Top –10,000 feet.
18.6	29.8	Begin down hill curves. Brake with motor.

REMEMBER: On downhill stretches, brake with your motor – not your brakes. A burning smell means you've used your brakes too much. If you can, pull over and let 'em cool for ten minutes or so.

22.8	36.5	Restaurant El More at right with cabrito al horno (baked) or ahumado (smoked). Open 10 AM till 9 PM. MC, VI. Ph & Fax: (728) 285-1232. A relaxing spot for a bite after Mexico City traffic. If you don't like nopalitos (nopal cactus leaves) because of their slimy texture before, you'll find them different here. They are crunchy and flavorful and high in vitamin C. **KM 45**.
24.8	39.7	Hotel Real Hacienda at left.
26.0	41.6	**GAS**, at right.
26.5	42.4	Cross over Río Lerma – it's just a trickle here but gets to be quite a river when it flows into Lake Chapala, over near Guadalajara.
27.0	43.2	Pass statue of Zapata-on-horseback.
28.5	45.6	Pass exit to airport at right just past **KM 54**.
29.0	46.4	Nissan at right. **KM 56**.
31.6	50.6	Huge Chrysler-Dodge plant over at right. Lots of big factories over to right – Toluca is quite an industrial town. **KM 60**.
32.5	52.0	Cross very bumpy railroad (LOOK-&-LISTEN). Merge right and pass giant bowling pin on right.
32.8	52.5	Pass Nestle's plant on right. Then Pfizer Pharmaceutical plant on right.
33.1	53.0	TURN RIGHT and then merge left onto bypass. Straight goes downtown. At left is modern sculpture. High lines in middle of parkway and Las Torres Ford dealer at left.

IF TO: Ixtapa, Zihuatanejo turn left onto bypass and start Toluca - Cd. Altamirano Log (page 66).

IF TO: Ixtapan de la Sal and Taxco, turn left onto bypass and start Toluca - Ixtapan de la Sal Log (page 35).

33.4	53.4	Mercedes dealer then **GAS**, at right.
33.7	53.9	Follow Atlacomulco signs.
34.2	54.7	Cement plant at right.
34.8	55.7	Stoplight. **GAS**, at right. Cross Av. López Portillo and bend left.
35.0	56.0	Pass auditorium at right.
35.3	56.5	Right lane is for free road to Querétaro. Left lane for toll road. Don't exit yet. Exit coming up.
35.6	57.0	Pass church at left. For Morelia (Free) be in left lane. For Querétaro be in right lane.

IF TO: Querétaro, Palmillas, stay in right lane, follow Querétaro signs and start Toluca – Palmillas Log (page 156).

IF TO: Morelia, the scenic route, exit right just before bypass. We like this scenic way because it passes thru some of the most beautiful parts of Mexico, but it is a winding tedious road, so some will prefer the toll road to Morelia. Start Toluca –Morelia Log (not include in this book).

36.0	57.6	All traffic turns right.
36.1	57.8	Take first left over railroad onto divided parkway. Now heading toward Querétaro – also the way to the Morelia toll road.

IF TO: Morelia, Guadalajara, – EXIT RIGHT and start Toluca – Morelia Toll Log. See Mexico's Colonial Heart book (page 193).

IF TO: Querétaro via Palmillas, exit right, start Toluca – Palmillas Log (page 156).

End of Log 29

LOG 30 *START:* Toluca, Mex *END:* Cd. Altamirano, Mich

UD-074

134.0 MI or 214.4 KM
DRIVE TIME – 3 HOURS
SCENIC RATING –3

This route to Ixtapa is a lonely, deserted highway with no services and tough driving, but if you insist on taking it, here it is.

MI	KM	
0.0	0.0	Starting here at bypass junctions #15-55, head south on bypass. Pass tall government building and then children's hospital, both at right.
1.0	1.6	Careful! Turn right here at Nevado de Toluca – Temascaltepec sign and ahead on Hwy #134.
5.0	8.0	Fancy funeral home and cemetery at right. Note village of Santa Cruz off to left.
6.5	10.4	Pass side road (right) to Zinacantepec with interesting San Miguel Monastery built in the 16th century with its interesting wall and ceiling murals.
12.0	19.2	Pass side road (left) to Nevado de Toluca National Park (14 miles to crater).

NEVADO DE TOLUCA (also called "xinatecatl") is a snow covered volcano whose altitude is a shade less than 15,000 feet (4,690 meters). It is surrounded by pine forests and contains two crystal-clear lakes, "Sol" and "Luna" where fishing and scuba diving are permitted. It is a nice spot for a picnic lunch, although at times (morning and late evening fog makes driving tedious. Incidentally, in pre-Hispanic times the volcano was a site for pilgrimages and religious offerings.

13.0	20.8	Thru mountain town of Buena Vista (good view) as you near the summit here at 9,500 feet elevation.
15.0	24.0	Careful for series of sharp curves.
25.0	40.0	Pass side road (right) to Valle de Bravo.
42.3	67.7	**GAS**, at right. Slow and you enter out skirts of Temascaltepec (population 10,000), a mining town where Ríos Comunidad, Colorado and Temascaltepec meet. It's worth a look-see if you've got a minute as it sits at the bottom of the valley and offers colorful vegetation, cobblestone streets and a nice central plaza.
43.0	68.8	Veer right and bypass town (left fork takes you thru white arches into town) then curve right and up.
62.5	100.0	Jog right for bypass around Tejupilco de Hidalgo and **GAS** ahead at left.

The town of Tejupilco was the center for the Matlatzingo" people in pre-Hispanic times and where much of the jade used by the Aztecs in Mexico City was produced. There are several unexplored ruin sites in the area and the pretty little town has a Franciscan church on its main plaza worth visiting.

76.0	121.6	Pass side road (left) to Acamuchitlán.
89.5	143.2	Thru El Guayabal.
93.0	148.8	Pass side road (left) to sleepy little town of Bejucos.
94.0	150.0	Cross Río Bejucos and cross state line – leave state of México and enter state of Guerrero.
118.3	189.3	Pass side road (left) to Limón Grande and over bridge.
123.5	197.6	Thru town of Cutzamala de Pinzón.
128.0	204.8	Cross state line – leave state of Guerrero and enter state of Michoacán.
133.3	213.3	Pass junction with Hwy #51 to Zitácuaro and Morelia.
133.5	213.6	Cross bridge over Río Balsas. This is the state line – leave state of Michoacán and enter state of Guerrero again. Then enter Ciudad Altamirano with market at right.
134.0	214.4	Come to glorieta and junction Hwy #49.

IF TO: Ixtapa, Zihuatanejo, continue around circle and start Cd. Altamirano - Ixtapa Log.

IF TO: Iguala, turn left onto Hwy #49 (not logged).

End of Log 30

LOG 31 *START:* Cd. Altamirano, Mich *END:* Ixtapa, Gro

UD-074

127.0 MI or 203.2 KM
DRIVE TIME – 3 HOURS
SCENIC RATING – 3

This portion of Hwy #134 was constructed piece by piece following the development of Ixtapa into a first-class resort. Although the road surface is excellent and the scenery (majestic rain forest-covered mountain slopes) exemplary, the constant curves and rocks on the pavement force a slow pace, so exercise extreme caution, especially on blind curves! There's virtually no heavy truck traffic so you can wind down leisurely at your own pace.

MI	KM	
0.0	0.0	Having gone around glorieta at junction with Hwy #51, continue straight ahead, leaving Cd. Altamirano behind.
3.3	5.3	Enter town of Coyuca de Catalán. Cross Río Miguel Alemán and then **GAS**, at left.
20.3	32.5	Over Río Del Oro. Then pass side road (right) to Placeres del Oro.
22.5	36.0	Pass side road (left) to Pinzán.
34.0	54.4	Cross Puente Parado II and begin winding up.
45.5	72.8	Rock monument to one Javier LLanderal Rueda and to all who lost their lives building this road (but don't let it scare you).
48.0	76.8	Now thru Barranca Honda (deep gorge) – aptly named!
57.0	91.2	Thru Barranca de Los Machos and climb to summit.
73.0	116.0	Note Zona de niebla signs thru here meaning careful for the fog.
76.3	122.1	Careful for series of very sharp curves and possibly rocks on road, especially during rainy season.
100.5	160.8	Cross bridge over Río Montor and careful again for possible rock slides.
102.0	163.2	Pass side road (right) to Zumatlán.
110.0	176.0	Thru community of Las Ollas and across Río Las Caramicius. Note the beautiful forested mountain sides with those 150-foot trees! How long will it be before corn and pasture will replace them?
113.0	180.8	Careful again for rocks thru here. Ixtapa river valley to left and begin winding down.
115.0	184.0	Cross Río La Laja and wind down some more.
118.0	188.8	Come to junction with Hwy #200.

IF TO: Lázaro Cárdenas, Playa Azul, turn right and start Ixtapa – La Mira Jct Log (page 144).

IF TO: Ixtapa, Zihuatanejo, turn left and ahead.

120.5	192.8	Pass side road (right) to Ixtapa, but a better, more scenic road is 2 1/2 miles ahead.
122.0	195.2	Pass side trail (left) to El Pozquelite, 2 kilometers.
124.3	198.9	Slow for dangerous curve to right. Then gradually wind up.
125.0	200.0	Nice view of Ixtapa and its sparkling bay at right. Pass mirador where you can pull off and enjoy the view. Then come to junction.

IF TO: Ixtapa, turn right and take this scenic road into town. See Ixtapa Eat & Stray (page 104) for accommodations.

126.0	201.6	Note cemetery down at left. Then past village of Agua de Correa at left.
127.0	203.2	Come to town of Zihuatanejo at right.

IF TO: Acapulco, continue straight and start Ixtapa – Acapulco Log (page 15).

IF TO: Downtown Zihuatanejo, turn right and into town. See Zihuatanejo Eat & Stray (page 107) for accommodations.

End of Log 31

LOG 32 *START:* Pochutla, Oax *END:* Oaxaca, Oax

UD-087

147.8 MI or 236.5 KM
DRIVE TIME 4 1/2 – 5 HOURS
SCENIC RATING – 3

First visualized by Benito Juárez in May, 1848, Hwy #175 had been the only link between the Pacific coast and Oaxaca. While the road in itself is a superb engineering achievement, it is not recommended if towing a trailer or driving an RV. With its highest point reaching 10,122 feet above sea level, it is narrow in many places, has steep grades and especially during the rainy season is subject to frequent landslides and there are no accommodations between Pochutla and Oaxaca.

MI	KM	
0.0	0.0	Starting at junction of Hwys #200 and #175, proceed north.
0.8	1.3	Enter tropical town of Pochutla (population 20,000). Careful for pedestrians and for topes. Pass market at right and thru town.
1.5	2.4	Curve right, then left with many more curves ahead. **GAS** at right.
2.3	3.8	Sign says "Oaxaca 237 Km" (or 147 miles).
8.0	12.8	Thru small village of Chacalapa and over puente El Azufre (Sulfur).
11.3	18.1	Curve right and over bridge and on up thru highland coffee plantations.
16.3	26.1	Over puente Chacalapilla. Note red earth, lush vegetation and many curves.
18.5	29.6	View waterfall at right.
19.0	30.4	Thru little town of Candelaria Loxicha. This is Zapoteca Indian country.
20.8	33.3	Over puente El Alacrán (Scorpion).
23.0	36.8	Careful for rocks on pavement thru this cut.
26.5	42.4	Pass side road (right) to Pluma Hidalgo.
28.8	46.1	Thru little village of La Galera (The Galley).
31.0	49.6	Sign says "Zona de Niebla" (fog zone) and on up.
33.3	53.3	Community of La Soledad (Solitude, aptly named) at left. Careful for rocks on pavement and wind down.
34.3	54.9	Wide spot of Zochilitla at right.
37.5	60.0	Over bridge and pass community of Jalatengo at left. Then pass side road (left) to San Bartolomé Loxicha.
45.0	72.0	Waterfall at left.
50.3	80.5	Thru wide spot of Portillo Santa Ana and down.
52.5	84.0	Cross bridge over Río Molino.
55.3	88.5	Enter town of San Miguel Suchixtepec.
57.3	91.7	Thru community of Zapotitlán.
59.8	95.7	Wide spot of El Manzanel.
64.5	103.2	Thru village of San José del Pacífico.
72.8	116.5	Thru wide spot of San Andrés.
82.0	131.2	Thru village of Santo Tomás Tamazulapan.
84.5	135.2	Cross bridge and curve left. Skirt edge of Miahuatlán (population 9,500).
86.5	138.4	**GAS** at left. Cemetery also at left and curve left.
88.5	141.6	Pass aserradero (sawmill) at right.
89.8	143.7	Over bridge and pass community of Las Monjas at right.
92.8	148.5	Thru community of San José Llano Grande.
99.3	158.9	Curve left and over bridge.
103.8	166.1	Thru wide spot of Barranca Larga.
108.0	172.8	Thru little settlement of La Soritana and over bridge. Then enter town of Ejutla, whose complete name is Ejutla de Crespo. Slow for topes and ahead thru town.
109.0	174.4	TURN LEFT and after two blocks TURN RIGHT.
109.5	175.2	TURN LEFT and note huge, shady poplar trees. Pass Cemetery at left, curve right and out. **GAS** at left.
114.0	182.4	Straight ahead but like a roller coaster.
120.3	192.5	Pass village called Magdalena at left.
123.3	197.3	Pass another little village of San Dionicio Ocotlán at right.
125.3	200.5	Pass factory at left where comercial trailers are built.
125.8	201.3	Railroad on left. Curve left and over bridge and enter Ocotán de Morelos where an interesting market is held every Friday. Curve right with plaza at left and follow "Oaxaca" sign.
127.5	204.0	Thru settlement of San Antonio **GAS** at left. This is where the best floral embroidered blouses and dresses with smocked yokes are made. They come in a wide range of colors in either short or long sleeves, with the most popular being the white poplin blouse with colored flowers.

MI	KM	
129.3	206.9	Thru village of San Juan Chilateca and curve left.
130.5	208.8	Thru Santo Tomás Jalieza.
135.5	216.8	Down at left you can finally see Oaxaca Valley.
137.3	219.7	Hwy #131 that goes to Pto Escondido, merges at left. Straight ahead to Oaxaca.
139.0	222.4	Thru village of San Bartolo Coyotepec with its many black pottery shops.
139.5	223.2	Alfarería Doña Rosa at right (Alfarería means pottery or potter's art) This is the famous place where the best black pottery of Oaxaca is made. (Doña Rosa is dead now, but her sons have continued the tradition and name.) Up the street to the right is the factory, don't hesitate to stop and visit. They'll be more than happy to show you around. Then thru village of Santa María Coyotepec.
142.5	228.0	Entrance to Oaxaca's airport at left. **GAS** also at left.
143.0	228.8	Thru suburb of San Agustín de las Juntas.
145.0	232.0	Enter city of Oaxaca, a colonial, classic, charming, colorful city. See Oaxaca Eat & Stray (page 134) for accommodations.
146.0	233.6	Come now to glorieta. Careful as you cross railroad. Sign indicates Mexico City and Centro (downtown) to left and Tehuantepec to right. TURN RIGHT here and proceed east on Periférico. Pass street at right to Benito Juárez University and **GAS** also at right.
146.5	234.4	Pass Av. Independencia that goes (left) to downtown. Pass school at right and at left and ahead on nice divided Calz. Eduardo Vasconcelos.
147.3	235.7	Careful now as you merge with Hwy #190. Sports center at right. When the coast is clear TURN LEFT.

IF TO: Tehuantepec, turn right and join Oaxaca - Tehuantepec Log (page 47) at mile 0.5.

147.5	236.0	Pass bus station and Hotel Veracruz at left.
147.8	236.5	Hotel California at left and come to junction with Av. Juárez (left) to downtown. **GAS** at left.

IF TO: Puebla, Mexico City, via toll road start Oaxaca - Puebla Log (page 161).

IF TO: Cuernavaca or Puebla via Huajuapan de León, start Oaxaca - Huajuapan de León Log (page 81).

IF TO: Tehuacán, Huautla via free road, start Oaxaca - Tehuacán Log (page 71).

End of Log 32

LOG 33 *START:* Oaxaca, Oax *END:* Pochutla, Oax

UD-087

147.8 MI or 236.5 KM
DRIVE TIME 4 1/2 – 5 HOURS
SCENIC RATING – 3

First visualized by Benito Juárez in May, 1848, Hwy #175 had been the only link between Oaxaca and the Pacific coast. While the road in itself is a superb engineering achievement, it is not recommended if towing a trailer or driving an RV. With its highest point reaching 10,122 feet above sea level, it is narrow in many places, has steep grades and especially during the rainy season is subject to frequent landslides and there are no accommodations between Oaxaca and Pochutla.

0.0	0.0	Starting at junction of Hwy #190 and side street (Av. Juárez) to downtown (right), head east on divided parkway past **GAS** at right. Then Hotel California at right.
0.3	0.5	Pass Hotel Veracruz at right and bus station also at right.
0.5	0.8	Come to stoplight and TURN RIGHT here onto Calz. Eduardo Vasconcelos. VW at right and sports center, left.
0.8	1.3	School at right and left. Then pass Av. Independencia that goes downtown.
1.3	2.1	Bend right and pass **GAS** at left and entrance to Benito Juárez University.
2.0	3.2	Careful as you approach glorieta. Cross railroad track and take left fork. Follow "Puerto Angel/Aeropuerto" signs.
4.8	7.7	Thru suburb of San Agustín de las Juntas.
5.3	8.5	**GAS** at right. Entrance to Oaxaca's airport also at right.
8.0	12.8	Thru village of Santa María Coyotepec.
8.5	13.6	Note sign at left that says "Alfarería Doña Rosa" (Alfarería means pottery or potter's art) as you enter village of San Bartolo Coyotepec with its many black pottery shops.

San Bartolo Coyotepec is the famous place where the best black pottery of Oaxaca is made. (Doña Rosa is dead now, but her sons have continued the tradition and name.) Up the street to the left is the factory, don't hesitate to stop and visit. They'll be more than happy to show you around.

MI	KM	
10.5	16.8	Take left fork here and follow "Puerto Angel" signs. Right fork is Hwy #131 to Puerto Escondido.
17.3	27.7	Begin gradual climb as you leave Oaxaca's valley behind. Then thru Santo Tomás Jalieza.
18.5	29.6	Curve right and thru village of San Juan Chilateca.
20.3	32.5	**GAS** at right and thru settlement of San Antonio. This is where the best floral embroidered blouses and dresses with smocked yokes are made. They come in a wide range of colors in either short or long sleeves, with the most popular being the white poplin blouse with colored flowers.
21.8	34.9	Thru Ocotán de Morelos where an interesting market is held every Friday. Pass plaza at right and then curve left. Just a few blocks from the plaza, you'll find the street bursting with chicken and sugar cane vendors.
22.0	35.2	Cross bridge, curve right and out with railroad on right.
22.5	36.0	Pass factory at right where comercial trailers are built.
24.5	39.2	Pass little village of San Dionicio Ocotlán at left.
27.5	44.0	Another village called Magdalena at right.
37.8	60.5	**GAS** at right and enter Ejutla, whose complete name is Ejutla de Crespo. TURN RIGHT at arch. Follow "Miahuatlán" sign. and down this one-way street. Then TURN LEFT.
38.3	61.3	Now merge with highway and TURN RIGHT and ahead.
44.0	70.4	Thru wide spot of Barranca Larga.
48.3	77.3	Cross bridge and thru community of San José Llano Grande.
57.5	92.0	Pass community of Las Monjas at left and over bridge.
59.3	94.9	Pass aserradero (sawmill) at left.
61.0	97.6	Curve right and pass cemetery at right. **GAS** also at right.
63.0	100.8	Skirt edge of Miahuatlán (population 9,500), curve right and over bridge.
65.5	104.8	Thru village of Santo Tomás Tamazulapan.
75.0	120.0	Thru wide spot of San Andrés.
83.0	132.8	Thru village of San José del Pacífico.
88.0	140.8	Wide spot of El Manzanel.
89.0	142.4	Thru community of Zapotitlán.
92.3	147.7	Enter town of San Miguel Suchixtepec.
95.3	152.5	Cross bridge over Río Molino.
97.3	155.7	Up and thru wide spot of Portillo Santa Ana.
103.0	164.8	Waterfall at right.
110.0	176.0	Pass side road (right) to San Bartolomé Loxicha. This is Zapoteca Indian country. Pass community of Jalatengo at right and cross bridge over river.
114.0	182.4	Wind up and careful for rocks on pavement. Then community of La Soledad at right.
118.0	188.8	Thru little village of La Galera (The Galley).
121.3	194.1	Pass side road (left) to Pluma Hidalgo.
124.0	198.4	Careful for rocks on pavement thru this cut.
126.8	202.9	Over puente El Alacrán (Scorpion).
128.5	205.6	Thru little town of Candelaria Loxicha. Then pass little waterfall on left.
131.3	210.1	Over puente Chacalapilla. Note red earth, lush vegetation and many curves.
136.0	217.6	Up and down thru highland coffee plantations.
139.0	222.4	Over puente El Azufre (Sulfur) and thru small village of Chacalapa.
146.0	233.6	**GAS** at left. Enter tropical town of Pochutla (population 20,000). Careful for many curves ahead, for pedestrians and for topes. Then pass market at left.
147.8	236.5	Come to junction with Hwy #200.

IF TO: Pto Escondido, turn right and join Tehuantepec - Pto Escondido Log (page 138) at mile 126.0.

IF TO: Tehuantepec, turn left and join Pto Escondido - Tehuantepec Log (page 28) at mile 44.0.

IF TO: Puerto Angel continue ahead. See Puerto Angel Eat & Stray (page 121) for accommodations.

PUERTO ANGEL, at the end of a winding stretch of 8 miles, is an unspoiled little village reflecting itself in the blue waters of a small bay where fishing boats and naval ships doze. Besides the naval base, a few seafood restaurants, and its colorful fishing market, Puerto Angel offers two swimming beaches – "Zipolite," long and easily accessible where everybody wears a swim suit and "Playa del Amor" (Love Beach), small and encircled by hills and reached only by a brisk walk, where only birthday suits are used, this being the first public nudist beach in Mexico!

End of Log 33

LOG 34 *START:* Oaxaca, Oax *END:* Tehuacán, Pue

148.0 MI or 236.8 KM
DRIVE TIME 3 HOURS
SCENIC RATING – 3

We recommend that you use the Oaxaca - Puebla toll road rather than this route unless your destination is Huautla. Inquire locally as to the condition of this road.

MI	KM	
0.0	0.0	Start at traffic light at junction Hwy #190 with Av. Juárez. **GAS**, left – Downtown is to your left. To your right) are Hotels Misión de Los Angeles, Misión Oaxaca and the medical school. Head west (more northwest) on divided palm-lined parkway.
0.1	0.2	Slow for "tope" at social security hospital, right. Then uphill.
0.3	0.5	Goodyear, right. Chrysler, right.
0.4	0.6	Hotel Fortín Plaza, right. Then easy bend to left, then right.
0.8	1.3	Pass Hotel Victoria, right. If to there, turn sharp right and up steep driveway. Continue straight on curvy panoramic drive.
1.1	1.8	Stadium, right. Pass big Juárez Monument up at right. In background is the amphitheater where "Guelaguetza"; Oaxaca's biggest festival, is held on the last two Mondays during July. You can park at mirador, left and look over the town if you wish as there's a nice view of Oaxaca, the valley, and the Río Atoyac.
1.5	2.4	CAREFUL FOR SERIES OF DANGEROUS CURVES.
2.3	3.7	Hotel Huautla at right. AA group 24 hours.
2.5	4.0	SIGN: MEXICO – CENTRO DEPORTIVO – STRAIGHT. Road divides. VEER RIGHT.
2.7	4.3	Intersection. "MEXICO – STRAIGHT." That's for you. If you want to turn around, follow "Oaxaca, left."
2.8	4.5	**GAS**, right. Then Pepsi bottling plant at left.
3.0	4.8	Bel-Air Motel at left. Then out past suburb of Santa Rosa. Divided boulevard ends.
3.4	5.4	"Retorno" or turnaround, left. Then TOPES.
3.6	5.8	Mercado Santa Rosa, right.
4.1	6.6	Hotel La Cabaña, left. Then Oaxaca's golf course, left. **KM 188**.
4.6	7.4	Villa del Sol, left. Then Rosa Isabel RV Park, left.
5.0	8.0	Suburb of Pueblo Nuevo (New Village) mostly to left. **KM 186**.
6.0	9.6	Pass side road (right) to "Ciudad de los Niños," an orphanage, and also to a seminary.
7.2	11.5	Coca Cola bottling plant, left.
7.4	11.8	Pass side road (right) to San Pablo Etla.
8.0	12.8	Come to junction with toll road.

IF TO: Huautla or Tehuacán via free road, take right fork and ahead on this log.

IF TO: Tehuacán, Puebla via toll road, stay in left lane and join Oaxaca - Puebla Log (page 161) at mile 8.0.

IF TO: Huajuapan de León, take right fork and join Oaxaca - Huajuapan de León Log (page 81) at mile 8.0

8.5	13.6	Village of Santiaguito over at left.
9.3	14.9	San Sebastián up at right. Then balneario.
12.0	19.2	Little town of Santa Cruz Etla at left with big old church. **GAS**, right.
15.3	24.5	Thru village of Magdalena.
17.5	28.0	Pass side road (left) to Suchilquitengo and Atayuco.
20.8	33.3	Skirt edge of little town of Huitzo down at left. Careful for brown & white cow in road.
22.0	35.2	Over railroad and then over bridge. Come to junction with Hwy #131 to Tehuacán (Veracruz, Puebla, etc.). ADO bus station, right.

IF TO: Tehuacán, Puebla or Veracruz etc., TURN RIGHT and continue ahead on this log.

IF TO: Mexico City, Puebla (or Tehuacán on Hwy #125) via Huajuapan continue straight and join Oaxaca - Huajuapan de León Log (page 81) at mile 22.0.

22.5	36.0	Begin zone of topes as you go thru village of Telixtlahuaca.
22.7	36.3	Come to "Y." Take left fork.
24.5	39.2	More topes. The next 40 miles is a beautiful mountain drive with a series of curves, ascents and descents.
72.0	115.2	Cross bridge over Río Grande.

MI	KM	
74.0	118.4	Thru village of Cuicatlán. Pass Hotel Oasis, will do in a pinch.
77.0	123.2	Over railroad crossing (LOOK-&-LISTEN).
78.0	124.8	Cross another bridge over Río Grande. **KM 115**.
80.0	128.0	Thru wide spot Los Obos.
83.0	132.8	Over bridge.
86.0	137.6	Very sharp left curve.
88.0	140.8	Spectacular view of cactus thru here.
91.0	145.6	Cross still another bridge over Río Grande.
98.0	156.8	Note lime tree orchards on both sides of road.
101.0	161.6	Careful for some very sharp curves.
102.0	163.2	Pass San Juan Los Cues to right. **KM 74**. Now thru tree-lined wood and many curves. Use care.
106.0	169.6	Two small local places to eat at right.
107.0	171.2	Sharp curve right.
108.0	172.8	Pass side road (right) to Huautla de Jiménez. **KM 68**.

IF TO: Huautla, follow stub log below.

STUB LOG TO HUAUTLA

0.0	0.0	Having turned east, pass nice buildings and out.
0.5	0.8	Sharp curve right.
0.7	1.1	Pass city limits. Road winds and climbs with many S curves.
3.8	6.1	Cross state line – leave state of Oaxaca and enter state of Puebla. Altitude 4,600 feet.
9.3	14.9	Altitude 6,300 feet. Pullout view to right.
11.0	17.6	Cross state line again – leave state of Puebla and enter state of Oaxaca.
16.8	26.9	Altitude 7,400 feet. Puerto Soledad.
24.0	38.4	Pass Restaurant Lupita.
29.0	46.4	Puerto San Serenio (population 15,000). Altitude 6,400 feet.
31.0	49.6	Thru Santa Catarina.
40.0	64.0	Enter Huautla – Home of Instituto Nacional de Café. Then up to left to town plaza and church. This town enjoys international fame due to cures experienced there with hallucinating fungus plants.

End of Stub Log to Huautla

109.5	175.2	"Welcome to Teotitlán" sign, right (population 6,710). Road veers left. There are 2 emergency hotels in Teotitlán del Camino, Mana Sabina on Hwy and Yvonne in town.
110.2	176.3	Cross over state line – leave state of Oaxaca and enter state of Puebla.
112.8	180.5	IMSS hospital and clinic, right. You will occasionally see men or kids filling in potholes with dirt. If you give then small change, they'll be grateful.
113.0	180.8	Smokestack to right belongs to a sugarcane refinery. Cross bridge over pretty river.
117.0	187.2	Thru village with basketball court at left.
118.6	189.8	Thru another village with two sets of "topes."
121.4	194.2	Come to village of Coxcatlán. VEER LEFT. Straight goes into town.
122.0	195.2	Road splits, veer right. **KM 38**.
123.2	197.1	Road from right merges with highway.
125.5	200.8	Sugarcane fields on both sides of road. Road splits, keep right.
126.0	201.6	Thru village of Calipán. Restaurant La Morena (the dark one). Then Hospital with clinic at left.
127.5	204.0	Down hill. Banana trees and sugarcane to left. Mountains with Saguaro cactus, right. Over bridge.
128.0	204.8	Pass exit left to stores and market.
131.6	210.6	Pass town of Zinacatepec with church.
131.9	211.0	Come to traffic light. Turn right at light.
133.0	212.8	Thru little town of San Sebastián.
133.4	213.4	Pass Bachoco plant, right.
135.0	216.0	Take left turn at pipe plant to Hwy #131 and on to Tehuacán.
135.4	216.6	Careful for unpaved ditch crossing. Turn left to Tehuacán by cemetery. AA in town meets at 7 PM.
135.9	217.4	Come to Ajalpan (population 3,000). Watch for sewer hole in street. Pass pretty church with blue dove and white stars, left. Topes. Pass Farmacia Coculco, left. More topes. Turn right at sign to Tehuacán.
138.0	220.8	Village with **GAS,** at left.
138.3	221.3	Over railroad crossing (LOOK-&-LISTEN).
140.9	225.4	Restaurant Mirador at right – first class busses stop here. Road makes a "Y," take right fork.
141.3	226.1	Thru wide spot Santa Cruz Acapa.

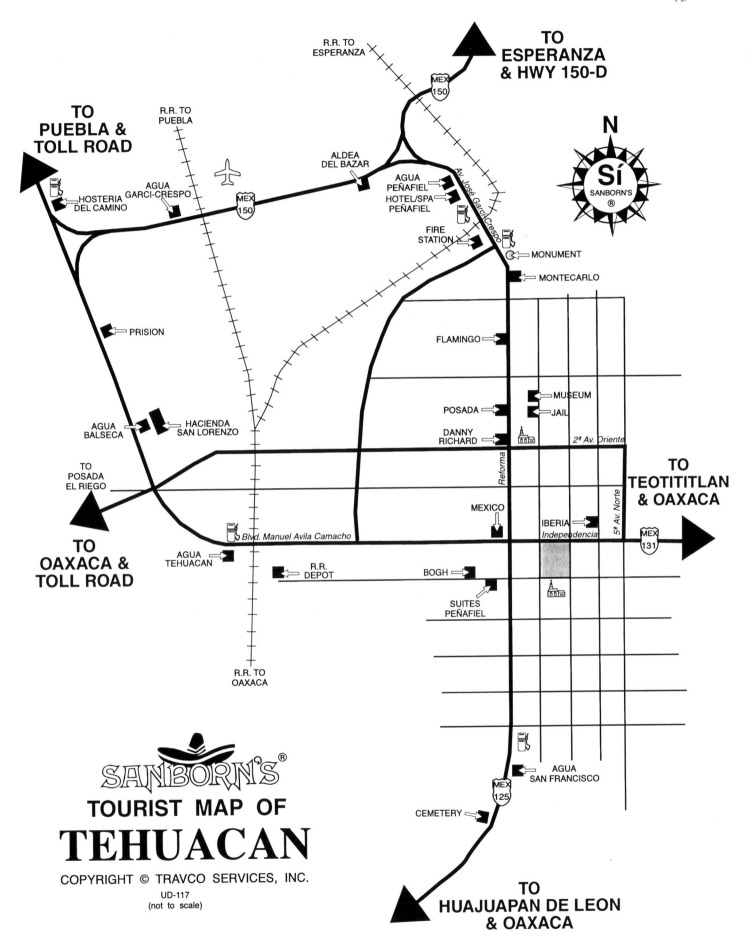

TO ESPERANZA & HWY 150-D

R.R. TO ESPERANZA

MEX 150

N

Sí SANBORN'S ®

TO PUEBLA & TOLL ROAD

R.R. TO PUEBLA

ALDEA DEL BAZAR

AGUA PEÑAFIEL

HOTEL/SPA PEÑAFIEL

Av. José Garci Crespo

AGUA GARCI-CRESPO

HOSTERIA DEL CAMINO

MEX 150

FIRE STATION

MONUMENT

MONTECARLO

PRISION

FLAMINGO

MUSEUM

POSADA

JAIL

DANNY RICHARD

2ª Av. Oriente

AGUA BALSECA

HACIENDA SAN LORENZO

Reforma

TO POSADA EL RIEGO

TO TEOTITITLAN & OAXACA

MEXICO

5ª Av. Norte

IBERIA

Independencia

MEX 131

TO OAXACA & TOLL ROAD

Blvd. Manuel Avila Camacho

AGUA TEHUACAN

R.R. DEPOT

BOGH

SUITES PEÑAFIEL

R.R. TO OAXACA

AGUA SAN FRANCISCO

MEX 125

CEMETERY

SANBORN'S ®

TOURIST MAP OF

TEHUACAN

COPYRIGHT © TRAVCO SERVICES, INC.

UD-117
(not to scale)

TO HUAJUAPAN DE LEON & OAXACA

MI	KM	
141.9	227.0	Over railroad crossing (LOOK-&-LISTEN).
143.0	228.8	"Egg Factory Equipment" to left. Thru lovely green valley of cornfields and small farms.
146.8	234.9	Enter Tehuacán city limits. See Tehuacán map (page 73) and Eat & Stray (page 133) for accommodations.
147.1	235.4	Cementos Veracruz, left.
148.0	236.8	Turn right at Calle 5 Norte, go two blocks and turn left onto Calle 2 Oriente. Careful for stoplights at each block. Then pass junction (right) with Hwy #125 to Huajuapan (Calle Reforma) with church on right. Altitude 5,800 feet. Hotel Mexico is two blocks to left on the right.

IF TO: Esperanza and Hwy #150D, turn right and start Tehuacán - Esperanza Log (page 93).

End of Log 34

LOG 35 *START:* Tehuacán, Pue *END:* Oaxaca, Oax

UD-103

148.0 MI or 236.8 KM
DRIVE TIME 3 – 3 1/4 HOURS
SCENIC RATING – 3

We recommend that you use the Puebla - Oaxaca toll road rather than this route unless your destination is Huautla. Inquire locally as to road conditions.

0.0	0.0	Starting here at tower with Hotel México at left, proceed ahead down one way street (Av. Independencia). Then pass junction (right) with Hwy #125 to Huajuapan. Head southeast. Careful for stoplights at each block, plaza right. Hotel Iberia, left. Altitude 5,800 feet.
0.5	0.8	Road narrows to 2 lanes.
0.9	1.4	Cementos Veracruz, right.
1.2	1.9	Pass city limits. Road narrow and rough here thru small suburban communities. Then thru lovely green valley of cornfields and small farms.
5.1	8.2	"Egg Factory Equipment" to right.
6.1	9.8	Over railroad crossing (LOOK-&-LISTEN).
6.7	10.7	Thru wide spot Santa Cruz Acapa.
7.1	11.4	Road makes a "Y," take left fork to Teotitlán. Restaurant Mirador at left – first class busses stop here.
9.7	15.5	Over railroad crossing (LOOK-&-LISTEN).
10.0	16.0	Village with **GAS**, at right.
12.1	19.4	Come to Ajalpan (population 3,000). Turn right at sign to Oaxaca. Topes. Pass Farmacia Coculco, right. More topes. Pass pretty church with blue dove and white stars, right. Watch for sewer hole in street.
12.6	20.2	Turn right to Oaxaca by cemetery. AA in town meets at 7 PM. Careful for unpaved ditch crossing.
13.0	20.8	Take right turn at pipe plant to Hwy #131 and on to Oaxaca.
13.5	21.6	"Hacienda" sign at right. (There's an IMSS hospital in town.)
14.6	23.4	Pass Bachoco plant, left.
15.0	24.0	Thru little town of San Sebastián.
16.1	25.8	Come to traffic light. Turn left at light.
16.4	26.2	Pass town of Zinacatepec with church.
20.0	32.0	Pass exit right to stores and market.
20.5	32.8	Over bridge. Mountains with Saguaro cactus, left. Banana trees and sugarcane to right. Road starts to climb.
22.0	35.2	Thru village of Calipán. Hospital with clinic at left. Then Restaurant La Morena (the dark one).
22.5	36.0	Road splits, keep right. Sugarcane fields on both sides of road.
24.8	39.7	Come to village of Coxcatlán. VEER RIGHT. Straight goes into town.
26.0	41.6	Road splits, veer left. **KM 38**.
26.6	42.6	Road from left merges with highway.
29.4	47.0	Thru village with two sets of "topes."
31.0	49.6	Thru another village with basketball court at right.
35.0	56.0	Cross bridge over pretty river. Smokestack to left belongs to a sugarcane refinery.
35.2	56.3	IMSS hospital and clinic, left. You will occasionally see men or kids filling in potholes with dirt. If you give then small change, they'll be grateful.
37.8	60.5	Cross over state line – leave state of Puebla and enter state of Oaxaca.
38.5	61.6	"Welcome to Teotitlán" sign, left (population 6,710). Road veers right. There are 2 emergency hotels in Teotitlán del Camino, Mana Sabina on Hwy and Yvonne in town.

MI   KM

40.0   64.0   Pass side road (left) to Huautla de Jiménez. **KM 68**.

IF TO: Huautla, follow stub log below.

STUB LOG TO HUAUTLA

0.0	0.0	Having turned east, pass nice buildings and out.
0.5	0.8	Sharp curve right.
0.7	1.1	Pass city limits. Road winds and climbs with many S curves.
3.8	6.1	Cross state line – leave state of Oaxaca and enter state of Puebla. Altitude 4,600 feet.
9.3	14.9	Altitude 6,300 feet. Pullout view to right.
11.0	17.6	Cross state line again – leave state of Puebla and enter state of Oaxaca.
16.8	26.9	Altitude 7,400 feet. Puerto Soledad.
24.0	38.4	Pass Restaurant Lupita.
29.0	46.4	Puerto San Serenio (population 15,000). Altitude 6,400 feet.
31.0	49.6	Thru Santa Catarina.
40.0	64.0	Enter Huautla – Home of Instituto Nacional de Café. Then up to left to town plaza and church. This town enjoys international fame due to cures experienced there with hallucinating fungus plants.

End Stub Log to Huautla

41.0	65.6	Sharp curve left.
42.0	67.2	Two small local places to eat at left. Now thru tree-lined wood and many curves.
46.0	73.6	Pass San Juan Los Cues to left. **KM 74**.
47.0	75.2	Careful for some very sharp curves.
50.0	80.0	Note lime tree orchards on both sides of road.
57.0	91.2	Cross bridge over Río Grande.
60.0	96.0	Spectacular view of cactus thru here.
62.0	99.2	Prepare for very sharp curve to right.
65.0	104.0	Over bridge.
70.0	112.0	Cross another bridge over Río Grande. **KM 115**.
71.0	113.6	Over railroad crossing (LOOK-&-LISTEN).
74.0	118.4	Thru village of Cuicatlán. Pass Hotel Oasis, will do in a pinch.
76.0	121.6	Cross still another bridge over Río Grande.
80.0	128.0	The next 40 miles is a beautiful mountain drive with a series of curves, ascents, and descents.
123.0	196.8	Now begin a zone of "topes," a series of 8 sets. **KM 200**.
124.8	199.7	Come to "Y," take right fork.
125.0	200.0	More topes and thru village of Telixtlahuaca.
125.6	201.0	Come now to junction with Hwy #190. Turn left to Oaxaca. Then over bridge.
127.5	204.0	Skirt edge of little town of Huitzo down at left. Careful for brown & white cow in road.
130.3	208.5	Pass side road (right) to Suchilquitengo and Atayuco. **KM 167**.
131.1	209.8	Pass side road (right) to Tlaltinango.
131.8	210.9	Village of Xochimilco to right.
132.5	212.0	Village of Magdalena to left.
133.5	213.6	Pass side road (right) to San Lázaro.
134.0	214.4	Rastro Avícola (fowl slaughterhouse) off to left.
135.8	217.3	Little town of Etla, right, with big old church.
138.6	221.7	San Sebastián and San Agustín to left.
139.1	222.6	Village of Santiaguito over at right. Oaxaca is the most "European" of Mexican cities.
139.6	223.4	Pass side road (left) to Santa Cruz Etla and San Pablo Etla.
140.0	224.0	Coca Cola bottling plant, right. Superior brewery, right.
141.0	225.6	Senicio "muelles" means "springs" at right. Begin divided. Here is where you join the toll road from Puebla.
141.5	226.4	Enter city of Oaxaca.
142.0	227.2	Pass side road (left) to "Ciudad de los Niños," an orphanage, and also to a seminary.
142.7	228.3	Rosa Isabela RV park at right.
143.0	228.8	Suburb of Pueblo Nuevo (New Village) mostly to left. Careful for next mile. **KM 186**.
144.0	230.4	Hotel Villa del Sol, right. Hotel Cabaña, right, then Oaxaca's golf course, right. **KM 188**.
145.0	232.0	Through suburb of Santa Rosa. Bel-Air Motel, right.
145.2	232.3	Pepsi plant, right. **GAS**, left. Come to junction with Hwy # 175 which goes to Ixtlán and Tuxtepec. Stay in middle lane to Oaxaca Centro and Puerto Angel. Get in left lane. Veer left around glorieta following Tehuantepec sign. Pass sports stadium, right. Uphill and veer right, past Hotel Huautla, left. You'll wind on a narrow panoramic drive for a spell.

MI   KM

146.9 235.0   Come to scenic overlook, right. Pass big Juárez Monument up at left. In background is the amphitheater where "Guelaguetza," Oaxaca's biggest festival, is held on the last two Mondays during July. Stadium, left. You can park at mirador, left and look over the town if you wish as there's a nice view of Oaxaca, the valley, and the Río Atoyac.

IF TO: Hotel Victoria – prepare to make a left turn ahead if the coast is clear. Otherwise turn right. Across from hotel is a little circle you go around and then facing the hotel, go straight when the coast is clear.

147.2 235.5   Pass Hotel Victoria, left. If to there, turn sharp left (or to right and around little circle) and up steep driveway. Continue straight on curvy panoramic drive.

147.6 236.2   Hotel Fortín Plaza, left. Then easy bend to right, then left.

147.7 236.3   Chrysler, left. Begin divided. Then Auto Servicio Solís, on right.

IF TO: Hotel Parador Santo Domingo, turn right here.

147.8 236.5   Go uphill. Slow for "topes" at social security hospital, left.

148.0 236.8   Stop at traffic light at junction Hwy #190 with Av. Juárez. **GAS**, right. Downtown is to your right. To your left) are Hotels Misión de Los Angeles, Misión Oaxaca, the medical school, and IMSS hospital. Head east (more southeast) on divided palm-lined parkway. For accommodations, see Oaxaca Eat & Stray (page 134).

IF TO: Tehuantepec, Tule tree, Mitla, straight and start Oaxaca - Tehuantepec Log (page 47).

IF TO: Pochutla, Puerto Angel, straight and start Oaxaca - Pochutla Log (page 69).

End of Log 35

LOG 36 *START:* Cuernavaca, Mor *END:* Izucar de M., Pue

UD-081

72.0 MI or 115.2 KM
DRIVE TIME 2 HOURS
SCENIC RATING — 3

Okay road, going through some very historic country. A little curvy, some 4 lane divided at the end with city traffic.

0.0   0.0   Starting at Hwy #95D interchange proceed east on road to Cuautla and Yautepec. At first stoplight is turn for Camino Real Sumiya Hotel.

IF TO: Sumiya Hotel, turn right at the first stoplight.

0.2   0.3   Pass statue of "Niños Héroes." This is a teenager at a cannon, commemorating the defense of Mexico City by military school cadets during the 1847 U.S. invasion.

0.7   1.1   Pemex tank farm, right.

1.1   1.8   Pass El Sol shopping center and Motel El Paso. Then Hotel Primavera, left.

1.7   2.7   **GAS**, left.

2.3   3.7   Over railroad crossing (LOOK-&-LISTEN).

2.7   4.3   Pass Nissan plant. Then Hotel Lofer, left.

3.1   5.0   Crossroads. Left goes to Tejalapa. Right goes to Juitepec.

5.2   8.3   Pass Versailes Trailer Park, right.

7.2   11.5 Pass GM plant. Then thru La Joya.

10.0 16.0 Down steep descending, winding road thru Cañon de Lobos (Wolf Canyon).

11.8 18.9 Curve left and pass side road (left) to Yautepec.

14.8 23.7 Pass cement factory, left.

16.5 26.4 Come to "T." Left goes into Yautepec. TURN RIGHT for Cuautla.

17.3 27.7 Under ancient aqueduct.

20.6 33.0 Pass side road (left) to Oaxtepec. Then pass gateway to Cocoyoc.

IF TO: Hacienda Cocoyoc Hotel, turn off here and then go right under toll road — it's a mile or so down the narrow paved road. This is one of the outstanding resort Inns of Mexico. This restored 400—year old sugar hacienda is really something to behold! It's really quite a magnificent layout, so don't hesitate to go there for lunch or for the night. For more info, see Cuautla Eat & Stray (page 132).

MI	KM	
21.2	33.9	Note Oaxtepec sports center at left, more or less exclusively for the use of government employees. See their fancy domed auditorium, a miniature Astrodome, no less. **GAS**, left. **KM 26**.
21.9	35.0	Pass side road (left) to Palo Verde and Calderón.
23.6	37.8	Begin divided highway.
23.9	38.2	Pass side road (left) to Casa Sano. Then McDonald's, left — where are the golden arches? Topes.
25.0	40.0	Enter suburb of Cuatlixco.
25.4	40.6	Hospital, right.
25.7	41.1	**GAS**, right and under gateway.
26.0	41.6	Coca Cola plant, left. Then under bridge and come to junction (left) with toll road from Cuernavaca. TURN RIGHT and into Cuautla.
26.6	42.6	Over railroad crossing. Then pass Benito Juárez monument in park at left.
27.6	44.2	**GAS**, right. Restaurant La Tía at left. Hotel Paraíso at left. Then pass side street (left) to Quinta Elena.
28.3	45.3	**GAS**, left. Hotel Vasco at left.
29.1	46.6	Pass Hotel Colonial on left. Little triangular plaza on right with cannon. Pass Hotel Linda Vista at left. Then over long bridge over Río San José or Río Cuautla as it's sometimes called. Then sports center on right.
29.6	47.4	Pass Hotel Asuriano at right. Then **GAS** left. Note: If to Agua Hedionda (Smelly Water), a popular thermal springs spa (no accommodations), take side road over at left. Hotel Varandero at right and Restaurant Retiro at left.
33.3	53.3	Over puente Guayabos. Then over puente Los Papayos.
39.8	63.7	**GAS**, left. Slow for junction (right) with old Hwy #115 to Izucar de Matamoros, via Atencingo (which we used to travel before the new highway ahead was built. If to La Lerma Spa, Hotel Atotonilco, turn right here and go 7.5 miles and then a short half mile to right.)
43.3	69.3	Over puente Amazinac. Note Cerro Gordo (Fat Hill) mountain over at left.
47.8	76.5	Pass side road (right) to water conservation project. Over Río La Laja which is the state line. Leave state of Morelos and enter state of Puebla.
50.6	81.0	Over puente Estulo. Then curve left thru little town of Tepexco. Then start climbing curvy mountain road with some dangerous curves.
61.6	98.6	Curve left past ruins of an old hacienda at right and over puente Ahuehueyo.
62.3	99.7	Over puente Atila. Then skirt edge of village of Rijo and pass another old hacienda at right.
65.3	104.5	Up thru village of Agua Dulce (Sweet Water).
66.3	106.1	Pass Balneario Amatitlanes, right, where home folks from these parts come to swim. Big pool but no food or overnight accommodations. In back of this neat little spa is an old abandoned sugar refinery that hasn't been in operation since the Revolution of 1910. Then Las Bungambilias, left.

By the way, the big hero of that revolution, Emiliano Zapata, did much of his fighting in this general neighborhood. The revolution was against the big landowners and also against the owners of the sugar haciendas. Many of the refineries were destroyed by the Zapatistas and were never rebuilt. Others fell to ruin when the owners abandoned them, no longer being able to compete against the huge refineries of the corporations. This is very fertile country particularly for raising cane — sugar cane, that is.

MI	KM	
67.3	107.7	Slow over railroad crossing (LOOK-&-LISTEN). (Left is to old "Free" Hwy #115 that goes back to Cuautla via Atencingo).
68.3	109.3	Pass truck—weighing station at right. Materiales del Fuerte and Restaurant Posada (looks okay), at left.
68.8	110.1	Thru village of Barrio Santa Cruz Cuautla. Then pass side road (right) to Putla.
69.6	111.4	Enter Izucar de Matamoros and come to junction with Hwy # 190.

IF TO: Puebla, turn left and start Izucar de Matamoros - Puebla Log (page 87).

IF TO: Huajuapan de León, Oaxaca, continue straight and start Izucar de Matamoros - Huajuapan de León Log.

End of Log 36

LOG 37 *START:* Izucar de M., Pue *END:* Huajuapan, Oax

UD-095

93.5 MI or 149.6 KM
DRIVE TIME -2 HOURS
SCENIC RATING — 2

MI	KM	
0.0	0.0	Starting at junction of Hwys #160 and #190, a mile south of Izucar de Matamoros, proceed south on Hwy #190.
1.0	1.6	Over bridge and thru little sugar town of Roboso, Start gradual winding up. Careful for rocks on pavement.
9.3	14.9	Thru community of El Tepene.
12.0	19.2	Pass side road (left) to Los Amates.
14.5	23.2	Thru village of El Pitayo which is the name of the cacti you see along the road.
16.8	26.9	Sharp left and right and thru village of Jualillos. Then wind up.
22.0	35.2	Sharp right and left and cross bridge over Río Atoyac. Then thru El Marquez.
24.0	38.4	Slow for another bridge and curve right.
26.5	42.4	Thru town of Tehuitzingo (population 8,000). **GAS** at left. Cross bridge over Río Tehuitzingo at other end of town.
33.3	53.3	Settlement of Tehuixtla over at left.
35.0	56.0	Pass side road (right) to Chinantla and Tecomatlán.
36.0	57.6	Pass community of Ahuehuetitla over on right.
38.5	61.6	Over bridge and wind thru Acateco Canyon.
42.5	68.0	Canyon community of El Papayo at left.
43.8	70.1	Hillside settlement of Nuevos Horizontes (New Horizons).
45.0	72.0	Thru community of San Bernardo (or as we choose to call it, "Sanborn Ardo.").
50.0	80.0	Cross bridge over Río de los Acuchiles and thru village of Amatitlán.
51.8	82.9	Pass cemetery at left and up into black pottery town of Acatlán de Osorio. Up cobblestone side street at left is a black Oaxacan pottery factory and kiln - interesting and worthwhile. It's behind house on left at top of hill at dead end.
52.0	83.2	Bend right and down thru town past interesting pottery shops. Hotel Romano Palace on left before plaza. Then turn right at far end of plaza and straight on thru.
52.3	83.7	LP gas at right. Slow for sharp left curve and cross bridge over Río de Los Acuchiles. Then **GAS** at right and over another bridge.
61.5	98.4	Pass side road (left) to Gabino Barrera.
66.8	106.9	Pass side road (left) to Petlalcingo over to left. Then cross bridge over Río Petlalcingo.
75.0	120.0	Thru community of Las Sidras.
76.5	122.4	Note little town of Chila down to left with yellow-domed church and another church up higher. Then wind for several miles.
81.8	130.9	Come to state line. Leave state of Puebla and enter state of Oaxaca.
84.3	134.9	Pass side road (left) to Zapotitlán. Thru here you may encounter local folks selling hats made of natural straw and synthetic fibers.
90.5	144.8	Pass monument to Lázaro Cárdenas at right. Now wind down into town of Huajuapan de León (population 60,000).
91.5	146.4	Truck inspection at right and curve left (left fork). **GAS** at left.
92.5	148.0	If to emergency Hotels García Peral and Laredo (see below), turn right here and go down to plaza. Straight ahead to Oaxaca. Bend left at far end of town and cross bridge over Río de las Granadas and out.
93.5	149.6	Come now to junction (left) with Hwy #125 that goes up to Tehuacán.

IF TO: Tehuacán, turn left and start Huajuapan de León - Tehuacán Log (page 92)

IF TO: Oaxaca, continue straight and start Huajuapan de León - Oaxaca Log.

Huajuapan de León offers two emergency hotels, García Peral (17 rooms, 2 stories on far side of plaza; restaurant; parking; pets OK; no credit cards) and Laredo (42 rooms, 2 stories beyond plaza a block or two; restaurant; bar; parking; pets OK; no credit cards).

End of Log 37

LOG 38 *START:* Huajuapan, Oax *END:* Oaxaca, Oax

UD-085

124.0 MI or 198.4 KM
DRIVE TIME 3 1/2 — 4 1/2 HOURS
SCENIC RATING — 3

Mostly two-lane. Mountainous. Curvy, but not so much so it'll make you sick, like Oaxaca — Pochutla.

MI	KM	
0.0	0.0	At junction (left) with Hwy #125. Leave Huajuapan de León. If you got a late start, think about staying here for the night, rather than drive at night. Remember, cows don't wear taillights. Over bridge.
1.0	1.6	VERY NICE Hotel Casa Blanca at left (65 rooms, restaurant-bar, disco, pool, enclosed parking, Children's playground, 4 RV spaces with water, (no ES, but nice) MC, VI, Phone 2-0779). Then community of Visa Hermosa. LP gas at left and **GAS**, also at left.
1.5	2.4	Over one-way bridge. Topes here are worse than in the north, so slow to a crawl.
2.7	4.3	TOPES. Thru village of El Molino. TOPES.
4.2	6.7	Down past side road (right) to Tezoatlán.
13.7	21.9	Pass scattered community of Reforma.
16.0	25.6	Top. Now wind down — elevation now about 6,400 feet.
17.5	28.0	Village of Tutla down to right. Watch for sheep crossing road all the way to Oaxaca.
20.0	32.0	Tamazulapan hydro-electric plant down at right.
22.7	36.3	Over steel bridge over dry Río de Oro.
24.0	38.4	TOPES. Then Restaurant El Comenal, right.
25.0	40.0	TOPES. Vanguardia Normal School at right. **GAS**, right and enter Tamazulapan (pop. 20,000) and straight on thru on blacktop. Big church at right and then plaza, also at right.
30.0	48.0	Community with exotic name of Yuyuza over to left.
31.0	49.6	Pass side road (left) to Teiupam.
36.9	59.0	Village of Morelos up at right. Thru Tierra Blanca. Sometimes there are axle-breaking pot holes in this stretch. Watch out and slow down.
38.7	61.9	Crossroads settlement of San Juan Teposcolula and pass junction (left) with Hwy #125 that runs down to Tlaxiaco and to Pinotepa Nacional near the Pacific on Hwy #200 (163 miles south of Acapulco), but don't tackle. We've talked to bus drivers who have been over it and they would rather not.
42.0	67.2	Road starts to get curvy. Pass community of Cieneguilla at left. Altitude 7,500 feet. Don't let the majestic red mountains surrounding you take all your attention. I did and nearly bought the farm through here. **KM 67**.
47.5	76.0	Slow and "take five" for a little SANBORN'S EXTRA. **KM 73**.

At left are the ruins of a huge Dominican convent built around 1550 and now rather nicely restored with several wood carvings and an embossed altar. The site is open from 10 AM till 6 PM daily (admission charged). Park at right in front and go on in. There's nobody around to tell you much about the place, but it's worth a brief stop — and anyhow, it's time to stretch your legs.

48.0	76.8	Into settlement of Yanhuitlán (population 14,000).
49.3	79.5	Village of Suchixtlán over at right.
52.0	83.2	Thru San Mateo Yucucuy. Pass old church at left. "YUCUCUY," spelled backwards is "Yucucuy!" If you say it forwards, it's pronounced "yoo-coo-kwee." Backwards, you'd pronounce it "yoo-coo-kwee" Yuk! Yuk! (Ol' Dan has to have his fun).
53.5	85.6	Thru village of Sinaxtla.
57.3	91.7	Into little town of Nochixtlán, whose real name is "Asunción." **GAS**, right, though sometimes out, clean restrooms. Also auto parts, fruit juices soft drinks in cans. ADO bus station. Nochixtlan is famous for its pottery and textiles. Population is about 20,000. Then one-lane bridge & bypass around town. Nice cemetery.
60.5	96.8	Pass side road (right) to Los Angeles. Did you take a "west" turn somewhere? Where's the smog?
62.5	100.0	Pass side road (right) to Zahuatlán. You'll see some Spanish moss growing in some trees now and again.
63.5	101.6	Note terraced land thru here at left.
64.0	102.4	Little chapel on yonder mini-mountain, at left, then Rancho 1810.
65.5	104.8	Community of El Paredón up at right. Really, watch for goats.
66.5	106.4	Community of La Cumbre. Altitude now approximately 7,000 feet. This region of Oaxaca state, home of the Mixtec Indians, is known as "Alta Mixteca."
68.0	108.8	Thru El Palmar, another mountain top settlement. Altitude now approximately 7,500 feet.
70.0	112.0	Skyline drive and community of Cuesta Blanca.
71.6	114.6	Mountain top community of Cortijo. Dan says: "Attitude is more important than altitude."

MI	KM	
74.2	118.7	Pass side road (right) to Unión Zaragoza, 5 kilometers away.
74.5	119.2	Thru mountain top settlement of Llano Verde.
83.7	133.9	What a good place for a church! There are no atheists on Mexican roads!

This country thru here brings to mind an old story told of many countries but one that fits Mexico best. The story goes that a Spanish king, impressed by the gold, silver and wealth pouring in from the far away land, ordered to appear before him a man who had just returned from "New Spain" (Mexico). "What does our new realm look like?" asked the king. The man picked up a sheet of paper and crushed and crumpled it until it resembled a complex of peaks, valleys and crests and placed it on the king's desk. "That, Your Majesty, is a map of New Spain."

86.0	137.6	Wind along mountain top and pass community of La Herradura with little shrine at right.
90.2	144.3	Hilltop community of El Tejocote and a half-mile later, come to microwave tower of El Tejocote to right. "Tejocote" is a tree bearing a fruit resembling a shoe.) Altitude 8,200 feet.
93.2	149.1	Thru little charcoal-burning community of La Carbonera. Finally, the road straightens a bit!
99.0	158.4	Thru community of Patio Escondido.
102.0	163.2	Into pretty valley and curve left over bridge. Pass side road (left) to Telixtlahuaca. Another bridge, then over railroad. Curve right. Come to junction with Hwy #135 to Tehuacán (or Veracruz, Puebla, etc.). ADO bus station, left.
103.0	164.8	Skirt edge of little town of Huitzo down at left. Careful for brown & white cow in road.
107.0	171.2	Pass side road (right) to Suchilquitengo and Atayuco.
109.0	174.4	Thru village of Magdalena.
112.0	179.2	Little town of Etla, right, with big old church. **GAS**, left.
115.0	184.0	Balneario. Then San Sebastián up at left. Balneario, by the way, means "spa."
115.5	184.8	Village of Santiaguito over at right. Oaxaca is the most "European" of Mexican cities.
116.0	185.6	Pass side road (left) to Santa Cruz Etla and San Pablo Etla.
117.5	188.0	Enter city of Oaxaca. See Oaxaca Eat & Stray (page 134) for accommodations.
118.0	188.8	Pass side road (left) to "Ciudad de los Niños," an orphanage, and also to a seminary.
118.7	189.9	Rosa Isabela RV park at right.
119.0	190.4	Suburb of Pueblo Nuevo (New Village) mostly to left. Careful for next mile. **KM 186**.
120.0	192.0	Hotel Villa del Sol, right. Hotel Cabaña, right, then Oaxaca's golf course, right. **KM 188**.
121.0	193.6	Through suburb of Santa Rosa. Bel-Air Motel, right. Take a look at Oaxaca map (page 46).
121.2	193.9	Pepsi plant, right. **GAS**, left. Come to junction with Hwy # 175 which goes to Ixtlán and Tuxtepec. Stay in middle lane to Oaxaca Centro and Puerto Angel. Get in left lane. Veer left around glorieta following Tehuantepec sign. Pass sports stadium, right. Uphill and veer right, past Hotel Huautla, left. Now road is 2-lane. You'll wind on a narrow panoramic drive for a spell.
122.9	196.6	Come to scenic overlook, right. Pass big Juárez Monument up at left. In background is the amphitheater where "Guelaguetza," Oaxaca's biggest festival, is held on the last two Mondays during July. Stadium, left. You can park at mirador, left and look over the town if you wish as there's a nice view of Oaxaca, the valley, and the Río Atoyac.

IF TO: Hotel Victoria — prepare to make a left turn ahead if the coast is clear. Otherwise turn right. Across from hotel is a little circle you go around and then facing the hotel, go straight when the coast is clear.

123.2	197.1	Pass Hotel Victoria, left. If to there, turn sharp left (or to right and around little circle) and up steep driveway. Continue straight on curvy panoramic drive.
123.6	197.8	Hotel Fortín Plaza, left (you can turn right and around here also). Then easy bend to right, then left.
123.7	197.9	Chrysler, left. Begin divided. Then Auto Servicio Solís, on right.

IF TO: Hotel Parador Santo Domingo, turn right here.

123.8	198.1	Go uphill. Slow for —topes— at social security hospital, left.
124.0	198.4	Stop at traffic light at junction Hwy #190 with Av. Juárez. **GAS**, right. Downtown is to your right. To your left) are Hotels Misión de Los Angeles, Misión Oaxaca, the medical school, and IMSS hospital. Head east (more southeast) on divided palm-lined parkway.

IF TO: Tehuahtepec, Tule tree, Mitla, straight and start Oaxaca - Tehuantepec Log (page 47).

IF TO: Pochutla, Puerto Angel, straight and start Oaxaca - Pochutla Log (page 69).

End of Log 38

LOG 39 *START:* Oaxaca, Oax *END:* Huajuapan, Oax

124 MI or 198 KM
DRIVE TIME 3 – 4 HOURS
SCENIC RATING — 2

Mostly two-lane. Mountainous. Curvy, but not so much so it'll make you sick, like Oaxaca – Pochutla.

MI	KM	
0.0	0.0	Start at traffic light at junction Hwy #190 with Av. Juárez. **GAS**, left. Downtown is to your left. To your right) are Hotels Misión de Los Angeles, Misión Oaxaca and the medical school. Head west (more northwest) on divided palm-lined parkway.
0.1	0.2	Slow for "tope" at social security hospital, right. Then uphill.
0.3	0.5	Goodyear, right. Chrysler, right.
0.4	0.6	Hotel Fortín Plaza, right. Then easy bend to left, then right.
0.8	1.3	Pass Hotel Victoria, right. If to there, turn sharp right and up steep driveway. Continue straight on curvy panoramic drive.
1.1	1.8	Stadium, right. Pass big Juárez Monument up at right. In background is the amphitheater where "Guelaguetza," Oaxaca's biggest festival, is held on the last two Mondays during July. You can park at mirador, left and look over the town if you wish as there's a nice view of Oaxaca, the valley, and the Río Atoyac.
1.5	2.4	CAREFUL FOR SERIES OF DANGEROUS CURVES.
2.3	3.7	Hotel Huautla at right. AA group 24 hours.
2.5	4.0	SIGN: MEXICO – CENTRO DEPORTIVO – STRAIGHT. Road divides. VEER RIGHT.
2.7	4.3	Intersection. "MEXICO – STRAIGHT." That's for you. If you want to turn around, follow "Oaxaca, left."
2.8	4.5	**GAS**, right. Then Pepsi bottling plant at left.
3.0	4.8	Bel-Air Motel at left. Then out past suburb of Santa Rosa. Divided boulevard ends.
3.4	5.4	"Retorno" or turnaround, left.
3.6	5.8	Mercado Santa Rosa, right.
4.1	6.6	Hotel La Cabaña, left. Then Oaxaca's golf course, left. **KM 188**.
4.6	7.4	Villa del Sol, left. Then Rosa Isabel RV Park, left.
5.0	8.0	Suburb of Pueblo Nuevo (New Village) mostly to left. **KM 186**.
6.0	9.6	Pass side road (right) to "Ciudad de los Niños," an orphanage, and also to a seminary.
7.2	11.5	Coca Cola bottling plant, left.
7.4	11.8	Pass side road (right) to San Pablo Etla.
8.0	12.8	Come to junction with toll road.

IF TO: Huajuapan de León, take right fork and ahead on this log.

IF TO: Huautla or Tehuacán via free road, take right fork and join Oaxaca - Tehuacán Log (page 71) at mile 8.0.

IF TO: Tehuacán, Puebla via toll road, stay in left lane and join Oaxaca - Puebla Log (page 161) at mile 8.0.

8.5	13.6	Village of Santiaguito over at left.
9.3	14.9	San Sebastián up at right. Then balneario.
12.0	19.2	Little town of Santa Cruz Etla at left with big old church. **GAS**, right.
15.3	24.5	Thru village of Magdalena.
17.5	28.0	Pass side road (left) to Suchilquitengo and Atayuco.
20.8	33.3	Skirt edge of little town of Huitzo down at left. Careful for brown and white cow in road.
22.0	35.2	Over railroad and then over bridge. Come to junction with Hwy #131 to Tehuacán (or Veracruz, Puebla, etc.). ADO bus station, right.

IF TO: Tehuacán, turn right and start Oaxaca - Tehuacán Log (page 71) at mile 22.0. If you're headed that direction, we've heard that this is an okay road, but lonely and curvy.

25.0	40.0	Thru community of Patio Escondido.
30.8	49.3	Thru little charcoal-burning community of La Carbonera. Now the curves begin!
33.8	54.1	Hilltop community of El Tejocote and a half-mile later, come to microwave tower of El Tejocote to left. ("Tejocote" is a tree bearing a fruit resembling a shoe.) Altitude 8,200 feet.
38.5	61.6	Wind along mountain top and pass community of La Herradura with little shrine at left.
40.3	64.5	What a good place for a church! There are no atheists on Mexican roads!

MI   KM
49.5   79.2   Thru mountain top settlement of Llano Verde.

This terrain brings to mind an old story told of many countries but one that fits Mexico best. The story goes that a Spanish king, impressed by the gold, silver and wealth pouring in from the far away land, ordered to appear before him a man who had just returned from "New Spain" (Mexico). "What does our new realm look like?" asked the king. The man picked up a sheet of paper and crushed and crumpled it until it resembled a complex of peaks, valleys and crests and placed it on the king's desk. "That, Your Majesty, is a map of New Spain."

49.8   79.7   Pass side road (left) to Unión Zaragoza, 5 kilometers away.
52.3   83.7   Mountain top community of Cortijo.
54.0   86.4   Skyline drive and community of Cuesta Blanca.
56.0   89.6   Thru El Palmar, another mountain top settlement. Altitude now approximately 7,500 feet.
57.5   92.0   Community of La Cumbre. Altitude has now dropped to approximately 7,000 feet. This region of Oaxaca state, home of the Mixtec Indians, is known as "Alta" (high) "Mixteca."
58.5   93.6   Community of El Paredón up at left. Really – watch for goats.
60.0   96.0   Rancho 1810 and little chapel on mountain top at right.
61.5   98.4   Note terraced land thru here at right.
62.5   100.0   Pass side road (left) to Zahuatlán.
64.5   103.2   Pass side road (right) to Los Angeles. Thru San Mateo.
66.1   105.8   Take LEFT FORK to bypass little town of Nochixtlán, whose real name is "Asunción." Nochixtlan is famous for its pottery and textiles. There are 20,000 souls here. **GAS**, though sometimes out.
66.8   106.9   Careful as you merge with road (right) coming from town. Then curve left over bridge. **GAS** clean restrooms, left. Also auto parts, fruit juices soft drinks in cans. ADO bus station. Then Pepsi depósito. Better gas up here. Huajuapan is sometimes out.
70.5   112.8   Thru village of Sinaxtla.
72.0   115.2   Thru San Mateo past old church at right.
74.3   118.9   Village of Suchixtlán over at left.
76.5   122.4   Into settlement of Yanhuitlán (population 3,000). Slow and "take five" for a little SANBORN'S EXTRA.

At right are the ruins of a huge Dominican convent built around 1550 and now rather nicely restored with several wood carvings and an embossed altar. The site is open from 10 AM till 6 PM daily (admission charged). Park at right in front and go on in. There's nobody around to tell you much about the place, but it's worth a brief stop – and anyhow, it's time to stretch your legs.

82.0   131.2   Pass community of Cieneguilla at right. Altitude 7,500 feet.
85.3   136.5   Crossroads settlement of San Juan Teposcolula and pass junction (left) with Hwy #125 that runs down to Tlaxiaco and to Pinotepa Nacional near the Pacific on Hwy #200 (163 miles south of Acapulco), but don't tackle. We've talked to bus drivers who have been over it and they would rather not.
87.1   139.4   Village of Morelos up at left. Then thru Tierra Blanca.
93.0   148.8   Pass side road (right) to Teiupam.
94.0   150.4   Community with exotic name of Yuyuza over to right.
99.0   158.4   Vanguardia Normal School at left. **GAS**, right and enter Tamazulapan (pop. 20,000) and straight on thru on blacktop. Big church at right and then plaza, also at right.
100.0 160.0   Topes and pass Restaurant "El Comenal," left.
101.3 162.1   Over steel bridge over dry Río de Oro.
104.0 166.4   Tamazulapan hydroelectric plant down at left.
106.5 170.4   Village of Tutla down to left.
108.0 172.8   Top. Now wind down – elevation now about 6,400 feet.
110.3 176.5   Pass scattered community of Reforma.
119.8 191.7   Down past side road (left) to Tezoatlán.
121.3 194.1   Topes. Thru village of El Molino.
123.0 196.8   Community of Vista Hermosa. LP gas at right and **GAS**, also at right. Then VERY NICE Hotel Casa Blanca at left (65 rooms, restaurant-bar, disco, pool, enclosed parking, Children's playground, 4 RV spaces with water, (no ES, but nice) MC, VI, Phone 2-0779). Into fringe of Huajuapan de León (population 100,000).
124.0 198.4   Over narrow bridge and come to junction (right) with Hwy #125.

IF TO: Izucar de Matamoros, Cuernavaca, Mexico City, etc., straight ahead and start Huajuapan de León - Izucar de Matamoros Log. There's **GAS** on the north edge of Huajuapan de León.

IF TO: Puebla and Mexico City via Tehuacán or to Fortín de las Flores and Veracruz, turn right onto Hwy #125 and start Huajuapan de León - Tehuacán Log (page 92).

End of Log 39

LOG 40 *START:* Huajuapan, Oax *END:* Izucar de M., Pue

UD-095

93.5 MI or 149.6 KM
DRIVE TIME - 2 HOURS
SCENIC RATING — 2

MI	KM	
0.0	0.0	Starting at junction of Hwys #190-125, head north on Hwy #190. Cross bridge over Río de las Granadas and into Huajuapan de León proper (population 60,000), mostly at left.
1.0	1.6	If to emergency Hotels García Peral and Laredo, turn left here and go down to plaza. **GAS** at right.
2.0	3.2	Pass truck inspection at left.
3.0	4.8	Note monument to Lázaro Cárdenas at left and curve right. Thru here you may encounter local folks selling hats made of natural straw and synthetic fibers.
9.0	14.4	Pass side road (right) to Zapotitlán.
11.7	18.7	Come to state line. Leave state of Oaxaca and enter state of Puebla. Then wind for several miles.
17.0	27.3	Note little town of Chila down to right with yellow-domed church and another church up higher.
18.5	29.6	Thru community of Las Sidras.
26.5	42.4	Cross bridge over Río Petlalcingo. Then pass side road (right) to Petlalcingo.
32.0	51.2	Pass side road (right) to Gabino Barrera.
40.0	64.0	Cross bridge over Río de Los Acuchiles. Then **GAS** at left. Then another bridge over same river. LP gas at left.
41.5	66.4	Enter black pottery town of Acatlán de Osorio. Pass plaza at left. TURN LEFT at dead end and ahead on 2-way street. Hotel Romano Palace at right and curve left and up past interesting pottery shops.
41.7	66.7	Up cobblestone side street at right is a black Oaxacan pottery factory and kiln - interesting and worthwhile. It's behind house on left at top of hill at dead end. Then pass cemetery at right.
43.5	69.6	Thru village of Amatitlán and cross bridge over Río de los Acuchiles.
48.5	77.6	Thru community of San Bernardo (or as we choose to call it, "Sanborn Ardo").
49.7	79.5	Hillside settlement of Nuevos Horizontes (New Horizons).
51.0	81.6	Canyon community of El Papayo at right.
57.5	92.0	Pass community of Ahuehuetitla over on left.
58.5	93.6	Pass side road (left) to Chinantla and Tecomatlán.
60.2	96.3	Settlement of Tehuixtla over at right.
67.0	107.2	Cross bridge over Río Tehuitzingo. Then thru town of Tehuitzingo (population 8,000). **GAS** at right.
71.5	114.4	Thru village of El Marquez. Then cross bridge over Río Atoyac.
75.0	120.0	Thru puerto Gato (about 3,600 feet). Slow for winding downgrade.
76.7	122.7	Wind thru village of Jualillos.
79.0	126.4	Thru village of El Pitayo which is the name of the cacti you see along the road.
81.5	130.4	Pass side road (right) to Los Amates.
84.2	134.7	Thru community of El Tepene. Start gradual winding down
92.5	148.0	Thru little sugar town of Roboso and over bridge.
93.5	149.6	Now come to junction with Hwy #160.

IF TO: Puebla or Mexico City via Hwy #190, take right fork and start Izucar de Matamoros - Puebla Log (page 87).

IF TO: Cuautla, Cuernavaca or Mexico City via Hwy #160, take left fork and start Izucar de Matamoros - Cuernavaca Log.

End of Log 40

LOG 41 *START:* Izucar de M., Pue *END:* Cuernavaca, Mor

72.0 MI or 115.2 KM
DRIVE TIME 2 HOURS
SCENIC RATING — 3

Okay road, going through some very historic country. A little curvy, some 4 lane divided at the end with city traffic. Special note: Plan your driving into Mexico City according to the following schedule. Fines are stiff.

MI	KM	
0.0	0.0	After taking the left fork, ahead toward Cuautla. Police station, right. SIGN: CUAUTLA — 67 KM.
0.8	1.3	Pass side road at left to Putla. Then thru village of Barrio Santa Cruz Cuautla.
1.3	2.1	Hotel Terraza, right. Materiales del Fuerte, restaurant Posada (looks okay), all right. Pass truck—weighing station at left.
2.3	3.7	Sign says: "Cuernavaca 106 Km." The other sign is telling you not to drive in D.F. if your plate ends in the wrong #. SEE ABOVE. (Left is to old "Free" Hwy #115 that goes thru Atencingo which we used to travel before the new highway ahead was built.) Then SLOW for railroad crossing (LOOK-&-LISTEN).
3.3	5.3	Las bugambilias, right. Then Balneario Amatitlanes, left, where home folks from these parts come to swim. Big pool but no food or overnight accommodations. In back of this neat little spa is an old abandoned sugar refinery that hasn't been in operation since the Revolution of 1910.

By the way, the big hero of that revolution, Emiliano Zapata, did much of his fighting in this general neighborhood. The revolution was against the big landowners and also against the owners of the sugar haciendas. Many of the refineries were destroyed by the Zapatistas and were never rebuilt. Others fell to ruin when the owners abandoned them, no longer being able to compete against the huge refineries of the corporations. This is very fertile country particularly for raising cane — sugar cane, that is.

MI	KM	
4.3	6.7	Down thru village of Agua Dulce (Sweet Water). Road straightens out.
7.3	11.7	Another hacienda at right, then skirt edge of town of Rijo. Then over Puente Atila.
8.0	12.8	Over Puente Ahuehueyo. Then curve right past ruins of still another old hacienda at left.
14.3	22.9	CAUTION! Curvy mountain road. Dangerous "S" curve, right then left. Slow as you wind down.
19.0	30.4	Curve right thru little town of Tepexco. Then over Puente Estulo.
21.8	35.5	Over Río La Laja. Leave state of Puebla and enter state of Morelos. Then pass side road (left) to water conservation project.
26.3	42.1	Mount Cerro Gordo (Fat Mountain) over at right. Then over Puente (bridge) Amazinac. **KM 97**.
29.8	47.7	Slow for junction (left) with old Hwy #115 back to Izucar de Matamoros. (If to La Lerma Spa — Hotel Atotonilco — turn left here and go 7.5 miles and then a short half—mile to right.) Then **GAS**, right.
36.3	58.1	Over Puente Los Papayos. Then down over Puente Guayabos.
40.0	64.0	Restaurant Retiro at right (not for you). Hotel Varadero, left. Then OK **GAS**, right. Note: If to Agua Hedionda (Smelly Water), a popular thermal springs spa (no accommodations), take side road back at right. Then pass Hotel Asuriano at left.
40.5	64.8	Enter city of Cuautla. Sports center at left. Then over long bridge over Río San Jose (or Río Cuautla, as it's sometimes called) past Hotel Linda Vista on right. Then little triangular plaza on left with cannon. Pass Hotel Colonial on left. See Cuautla Eat & Stray (page 132) for accommodations.
41.3	66.1	Hotel Vasco at right. Left goes to downtown. **GAS**, right (more ahead).
42.0	67.2	Pass side street (right) to Quinta Elena. Then Hotel Paraíso at right. Then restaurant La Tía, right. **GAS**, left.
43.0	68.8	Pass Benito Juárez statue in plaza at right. Over railroad crossing.
43.2	69.1	Curve right and merge with traffic from downtown. Sign says: "Mexico Cuota (toll), Right."
43.4	69.4	Come to fork in road. Sign says: Mexico Libre (free) left."

IF TO: Cuernavaca via toll road veer right. Follow "Cuernavaca, 95D" Signs. Skip stub log & resume toll log.

IF TO: Mexico city via toll road veer right. Follow "Mexico 95D" signs. Skip stub log & resume toll log.

IF TO: Cuernavaca via free road, Oaxtepec, Hacienda Cocoyoc, Trailer Park Versailles keep left. Follow stub log below.

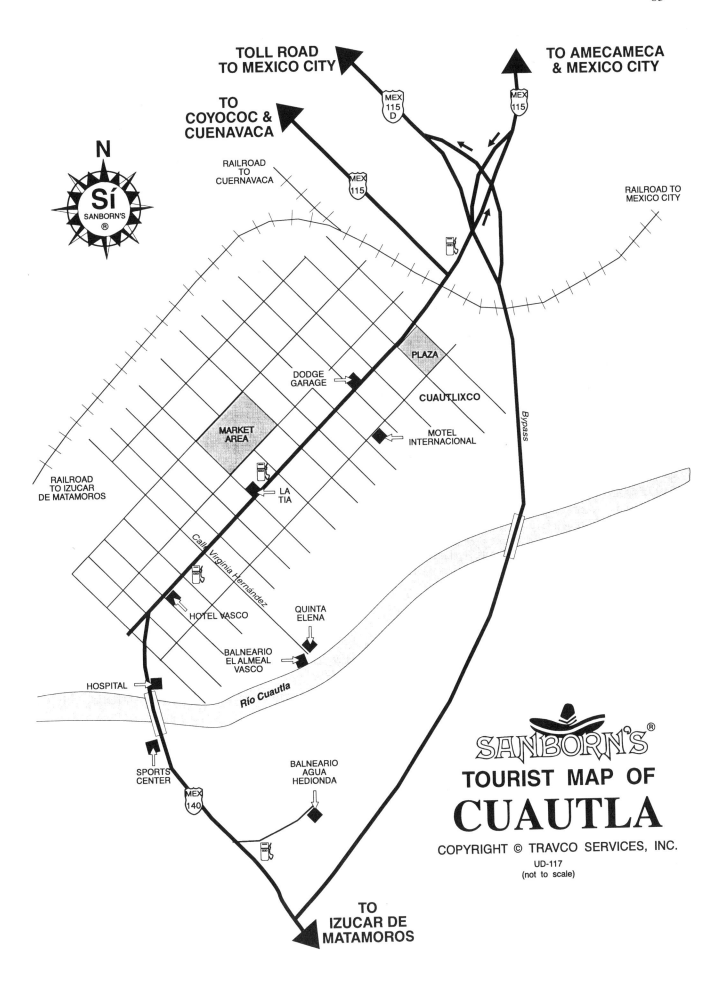

TOLL ROAD
TO MEXICO CITY

TO AMECAMECA
& MEXICO CITY

TO
COYOCOC &
CUENAVACA

MEX
115
D

MEX
115

RAILROAD
TO
CUERNAVACA

MEX
115

RAILROAD TO
MEXICO CITY

PLAZA

DODGE
GARAGE

CUAUTLIXCO

MARKET
AREA

MOTEL
INTERNACIONAL

Bypass

RAILROAD
TO IZUCAR
DE MATAMOROS

LA
TIA

Calle Virginia Hernández

QUINTA
ELENA

HOTEL VASCO

BALNEARIO
EL ALMEAL
VASCO

HOSPITAL

Río Cuautla

SPORTS
CENTER

BALNEARIO
AGUA
HEDIONDA

MEX
140

SANBORN'S®
TOURIST MAP OF
CUAUTLA

COPYRIGHT © TRAVCO SERVICES, INC.

UD-117
(not to scale)

TO
IZUCAR DE
MATAMOROS

N
Sí
SANBORN'S
®

STUB LOG "LIBRE" TO CUERNAVACA.

This route is not recommended for RV's unless to above mentioned trailer park.

MI	KM	
43.5	69.6	Having veered left at toll road, proceed ahead on 2 lane. Follow "Cuernavaca" signs.
43.6	69.8	Under bridge. Keep right. Coca-Cola, right.
43.9	70.2	Under gateway. **GAS**, left.
44.2	70.7	Hospital, left. Topes.
44.6	71.4	Now 4-lane. Then into suburb of Cuautlixco.
45.5	72.8	McDonald's, right — where are the golden arches? Topes.
45.7	73.1	Sign says: "Cuernavaca, straight; Casa Sano, right." Straight for you.
46.0	73.6	Divided ends. Still 4 lane.
47.7	76.3	Sign says: "Cuernavaca, straight; Palo Verde, Calderón, right."
48.4	77.4	Topes. Entering Cocoyoc. Note Oaxtepec sports center at right — more or less exclusively for the use of government employees. See their fancy domed auditorium — a miniature Astrodome, no less. **GAS**, right. **KM 26.**

IF TO: Hacienda Cocoyoc Hotel, turn off here and then go left under toll road — it's a mile or so down the narrow paved road. This is one of the outstanding resort Inns of Mexico. This terrific restored 400-year old sugar hacienda is really something to behold! It's really quite a magnificent layout, so don't hesitate to go there for lunch or refreshments or for the night. For more info, see Cuautla Eat & Stray (page 132).

49.0	78.4	Pass gateway to Cocoyoc. Pass side road (right) to Oaxtepec.
49.5	79.2	Road opens to 4 lane.
52.3	83.7	Under ancient aqueduct. Then, Guess What? Topes.
52.8	84.5	Then **GAS**, "Servicio Ullo," right. Then a Sign that says: "Cuernavaca — straight." Looks like George Washington Parkway in Maryland.
53.1	85.0	Come to fork. Sign says: "Cuernavaca, left; Yautepec, right. Divided highway again.
54.8	87.7	Pass cement factory, right.
57.8	92.5	Pass side road, right, to Yautepec. Then curve right.
59.0	94.4	Thru "Cañon de Lobos" (Wolf Canyon). Pass dump, right. Steep climb, winding road, divided 4-lane highway.
62.4	99.8	Through La Joya. Then GM plant.
64.4	103.0	Pass Versailes Trailer Park at left.
66.5	106.4	Pass side road (right) to Tejalapa. Pass side road (left) to Jiutepec.
66.9	107.0	Hotel Lofer, right. Then Nissan plant.
67.3	107.7	Over railroad crossing (LOOK-&-LISTEN).
67.9	108.6	**GAS**, right. Then traffic light.
68.5	109.6	Hotel Primavera, right. Then Motel El Paso. Then shopping center, "El Sol."
68.9	110.2	Pemex tank farm, left.
69.4	111.0	Sign says: Acapulco, Cuernavaca, straight; Mexico, right. Pass statue of "Niños Héroes." This is a teenager at a cannon, commemorating the defense of Mexico City by military school cadets during the 1847 U.S. invasion.

IF TO: Mexico City via toll road, turn right. Follow "Mexico" Signs and start Cuernavaca - Mexico City Log (page 158).

69.6	111.4	Sign says: Centro, straight; Acapulco, airport, right.

IF TO: Downtown Cuernavaca, straight ahead.

IF TO: Acapulco, turn right and start Cuernavaca - Iguala Log (page 23).

End of Stub Log

Continuation of main log:

47.5	76.0	This is 2-lane, though it is the autopista. **GAS**, right.
48.1	77.0	**KM 26.** Then emergency phone. Just like on U.S. freeways, you'll see these from now on.
49.1	78.6	Under pedestrian crossing. Then another in a mile. Then another. **KM 23.** Then phone.
51.5	82.4	Tollhouse. Clean rest rooms (usually). Phone. Pay the man (or woman). After paying your toll, proceed ahead past fertile Yautepec Valley down at left. Pretty country ahead. Still 2 lane.

MI	KM	
54.2	86.7	Under bridge. 4 lanes. Looks like George Washington Parkway, Maryland.
59.0	94.4	That's Tepoztlán in the valley over at right — a very interesting little place with a huge historical convent and worthwhile museum. It also has a picturesque inn, Posada Tepozteca. Note huge old church and convent looming above everything else. Then on ahead past Tepoztlan turnoff and on up to the next tollhouse.
60.5	96.8	SLOW now as you come to tollhouse — take a slot with green light. Pay toll. You may be asked to turn in your toll ticket (or receipt) that they gave you back at the last tollhouse (or pay another toll if you did not get a ticket) — clean restrooms here at this tollhouse. Then out and ahead down #115—D.
61.5	98.4	Under overpass. Then over railroad and highway becomes divided.
64.9	103.8	Sign says: Cuernavaca, Acapulco, straight; Mexico, right.

IF TO: Mexico City, exit right and join Cuernavaca - Mexico City Log (page 158) at mile 12.0.

IF TO: Cuernavaca, trailer park, straight.

IF TO: Acapulco, straight and follow Acapulco Cuota (toll) signs.

65.9	105.4	Having gone straight, go under old road to Tepoztlán. Get ready to exit for Cuernavaca Trailer Park. Follow signs. **KM 74.**
68.0	108.8	Rest area, right. Then Firestone plant, left. Then exit for Cuernavaca Trailer Park.
71.0	113.6	Subdivision and Club Lomas del Paraíso, left.
72.0	115.2	**GAS**, right. Then exit for Cuernavaca, right.

IF TO: Acapulco, follow Acapulco signs. Start Cuernavaca - Iguala Log (page 23).

IF TO: Cuernavaca, turn right.

End of Log 41

LOG 42 START: Izucar de M., Pue END: Puebla, Pue

UD-095

46.0 MI or 73.6 KM
DRIVE TIME -1 HOUR
SCENIC RATING — 2

0.0	0.0	Starting at junction of Hwys #160 and #190, proceed north on Hwy #190 and enter town of Izucar de Matamoros. Hospital at left and then curve left. Slow as you cross narrow bridge.
0.5	0.8	Ahead on 2-way street past church at left and market at right.
2.0	3.2	Come to stop sign at dead end. TURN RIGHT when coast is clear. **GAS** at right and curve right. Then over railroad crossing (LOOK-&-LISTEN).
2.3	3.7	Curve left past another **GAS** station at right.
3.3	5.3	Curve right and thru Alchichica.
6.0	9.6	Curve left and enter La Galarza. Slow past school at left.
11.0	17.6	Thru village of Tepojuma and **GAS** at right.
13.0	20.8	Enter little village of Teyuca with blue water tower at right.
16.0	25.6	Crossroads. Left is to Champusco and Huilulco to right.
20.3	32.5	Thru edge of La Trinidad, mostly over to left.
21.5	34.4	Down over bridge. Pass crossroads to San Diego (left) and La Libertad (right). Then curve right and onto bypass of Atlixco.
24.0	38.4	Over railroad crossing (LOOK-&-LISTEN).
25.5	40.8	Curve right and ahead.
26.5	42.4	Curve left and up thru Rancho San Gabriel.
27.3	43.7	Pass side road (left) to Tlamapa and over railroad crossing.
28.0	44.8	Down and curve left past irrigation canal. Then cross bridge over Río Nexapa.
32.0	51.2	Pass side road (right) to Chalchihuapan.
33.0	52.3	Down past side road (left) to Chilpilo. Then side road (right) to San Bernabé.
34.5	55.2	Pass another side road (left) back to Chilpio. Then thru outskirts of Acatepec.
35.5	56.8	Wide curve left past Acatepec proper off to left. Pass side road (left) to Tonanzintla, site of Santa María de Tonanzintla Church.

Santa María de Tonanzintla Church is a real jewel of Mexican architecture and popular art. Actually an Indian chapel, it is rather plain on the outside (as are many of Mexico's treasures), but the interior fairly explodes with brilliant crimsons, blues, greens and yellows. Vivid tones and imaginative sculptures highlight this gem which was completely financed and constructed by the local villagers. Plus, just outside the village is the national observatory, regarded as one of the most important and well-equipped in Latin America. It is said that 90% of the Milky Way, our galaxy, is visible from here.

MI	KM	
37.0	59.2	Pass side road (right) to Cacalotepec.
40.0	64.0	Pass side road (left) to Mexico City, the free road. It is recommended that you continue on this log to the toll road.
40.5	64.8	Take right fork onto wide divide boulevard. Over bridge and enter Puebla. Bend right and ahead.
42.0	67.2	Come to glorieta. Go 3/4-way around and continue on divided. Then come to Av. Reforma.

IF TO: Downtown Puebla, turn right.

42.2	67.5	Come to Av 2 Poniente. A left here takes you to Cholula and to Las Americas RV Park.
42.5	68.0	Bend left past Renault sign at right and then Ford at right. Pass tall monument at left. Chevy dealer at left.
43.5	69.6	Around water fountain monument. Then over railroad crossing. Then another fountain.
44.0	70.4	Around another monument at left.
45.0	72.0	Pass Mesón del Angel at left.
46.0	73.6	Come to junction with Hwy #150.

IF TO: Mexico City, get in left lane and follow Mexico signs. Up and over toll road and get into right lane and take right exit and around and onto toll road. Watch for merging traffic from left. Start Puebla - Mexico City Log (page 164). **GAS** at right just ahead.

IF TO: Veracruz or Tlaxcala, get into right lane and curve right onto toll road and start Puebla - Veracruz Log. See Mexico's Colonial Heart book (page 20).

End of Log 42

LOG 43 *START:* Puebla, Pue *END:* Izucar de M., Pue

UD-095

46.0 MI or 73.6 KM
DRIVE TIME -1 HOUR
SCENIC RATING — 2

0.0	0.0	Starting at interchange junction of Hwys #95 and #190, head south on divided Hwy #190. Pass Hotel Mesón del angel over at right.
1.0	1.6	Come to glorieta, around and ahead over railroad crossing (LOOK-&-LISTEN).
2.0	3.2	**GAS** at right.
4.0	6.4	Come to intersection. Left is to Veracruz via free road and to downtown Puebla.
5.0	8.0	Begin 2-lane road and careful for pedestrians.
6.0	9.6	**GAS** at right.
7.0	11.2	Ornate church at left, and on a clear day there's a good view of twin mountains, Popocatepetl (Mt. Popo) and Ixtaccihuatl (Sleeping Lady). Mt. Popo has an altitude of 14,955 feet, formed by volcanic action, and Ixtaccihuatl is actually an extension of the lava overflow of its twin, Popocatepetl.
9.0	14.4	Veer left at Atlixco sign. Right is to Cholula, the city with 365 churches, one for each day of the year.
10.0	16.0	Wide curve right past Acatepec proper off to right. Pass side road (right) to Tonanzintla, site of Santa María de Tonanzintla Church.

Santa María de Tonanzintla Church is a real jewel of Mexican architecture and popular art. Actually an Indian chapel, it is rather plain on the outside (as are many of Mexico's treasures) but the interior fairly explodes with brilliant crimsons, blues, greens and yellows. Vivid tones and imaginative sculptures highlight this gem which was completely financed and constructed by the local villagers. Plus, just outside the village is the national observatory, regarded as one of the most important and well-equipped in Latin America. It is said that 90% of the Milky Way, our galaxy, is visible from here.

| 10.5 | 16.8 | Pass side road (right) to Chipilo. |
| 13.0 | 20.8 | Here's another nice view of Mt. Popo. |

MI	KM	
14.0	22.4	Pass side road (right) to San Andrés Cholula.
18.0	28.8	Over railroad crossing (LOOK-&-LISTEN).
19.5	31.2	Curve left for bypass of town of Atlixco.
21.0	33.6	Thru flower fields and note Atlixco over to right.
23.0	36.8	Golf and country club at left.
24.0	38.4	Careful and stop for oncoming traffic from Atlixco and when clear, continue ahead thru fertile valley.
30.0	48.0	Pass side road (right) to La Venta.
35.0	56.0	**GAS** at left and thru sugar cane fields.
38.0	60.8	Thru village of La Galarza.
40.0	64.0	Thru village of Totetla.
43.0	68.8	Calcium plant at right and enter agricultural town of Izucar de Matamoros.
44.0	70.4	**GAS** at left and then curve right.
45.0	72.0	TURN LEFT at Oaxaca sign. Pass church on right and busy market on left.
46.0	73.6	Come to junction with Hwy #160.

IF TO: Cuautla, Cuernavaca or Mexico City, turn right and start Izucar de Matamoros - Cuernavaca Log (page 84).

IF TO: Oaxaca, continue ahead and curve left. Start Izucar de Matamoros - Huajuapan de León Log (page 78).

End of Log 43

LOG 44 *START:* Esperanza, Pue *END:* Tehuacán, Pue

UD-103

30.0 MI or 48.0 KM
DRIVE TIME 3/4 HOUR
SCENIC RATING - 2

This is a good route to get from Toll Road #150D to the famous resort town of Tehuacán where there is good Hotel México next door to the once famous Hotel Spa Peñafiel. Peñafiel, incidentally, is the big bottling plant where they put up Mexico's *Número Uno* bottled drinking water, "Agua Peñafiel." Likewise, this is a good route to Oaxaca. From Tehuacán, you can continue south on Hwy #125 till Huajuapan de León where it junctions with Hwy #190, or you can continue south on Hwy #131 until Telixtlahuaca where it junctions with Hwy #190, just 22 miles north of Oaxaca.

0.0	0.0	Having exited the toll road around to right, careful for 2-way traffic ahead, move to right lane. Careful for traffic behind and in front. At "T" junction take left turn and ahead. Right is to Cd. Serdán (not for you).
0.5	0.8	After crossing railroad (LOOK-&-LISTEN), take the right fork.
1.3	2.1	Pass side road (left) to Puente Negro.
4.3	6.9	Pass side road (left) to Puerta Cañada.
5.5	8.8	Scattered village of Barrio de la Soledad at left.
6.8	10.9	Pass side road (left) to San Antonio Soledad and up. Road narrows slightly ahead.
9.0	14.4	Bend left and down over railroad (LOOK-&-LISTEN) – careful, it's bumpy. Then pass side road (right) to Tecamachalco, but ahead for you.
13.0	20.8	Sharp, long hairpin turn curving down to right.
13.5	21.6	Under high stone overpass.
16.8	26.9	Skirt little town of Azumbilla over to right and proceed ahead to junction.
17.0	27.2	Slow now and take right fork (follow TEHUACAN sign) and stop at stop sign. Then proceed onto Hwy #150 and ahead with Azumbilla down to right.
19.0	30.4	Careful for "topes."
24.5	39.2	Thru village of Santa Ana.
27.0	43.2	Villa Alegría Spa (Happiness house) down on right is a bath and restaurant spot for the nearby home folks, and very popular on weekends and holidays.
29.0	46.4	Slow now over railroad (LOOK-&-LISTEN) and curve right. Then careful as you come to junction with free road to Puebla. Take left fork. Slow as you merge with other side of little highway triangle. Then ahead into town.

MI	KM	
29.8	47.7	Pass big ultramodern Peñafiel water bottling plant on right – this is where all those Peñafiel semitrailer trucks come from that you've probably noticed on Mexican highways hauling spring water to all corners of the country. It's big business hereabouts – and there are several other spring water bottling firms here in Tehuacán, such as, Garci-Crespo, Agua San Francisco, El Riego, San Lorenzo, etc.
30.0	48.0	Come now to former Hotel Spa Peñafiel, now a school, at right and end of log. For accommodations se Tehuacán Eat & Stray (page 133).

IF TO: Oaxaca via toll road, join Puebla - Oaxaca Log (page 44) at mile 77.9.

IF TO: Oaxaca, via Huajuapan de León, start Tehuacán - Huajuapan de León Log.

End of Log 44

LOG 45 *START:* Tehuacán, Pue *END:* Huajuapan, Oax

UD-103

74.0 MILES or 118.4 KM
DRIVE TIME – 3 – 4 HOURS.
SCENIC RATING — 3

This is a peaceful, two-lane with little traffic. A cacti lover's delight! Botanists from all over the States make field trips to this area beginning about 10 miles south of Tehuacán to study all the different types of desert flora. Also, you'll see onyx-crushing and screening plants. Then you'll pass salt-drying beds. If you get an early start, you can easily make Oaxaca today. Leave by noon and you'll still make it, though it'll be close to dark when you arrive. Better leave earlier.

MI	KM	
0.0	0.0	At junction of Hwy #125 and Hwy #150, in San Lorenzo, just after passing **GAS** , at left, veer left. Right would take you downtown Tehuacán.
0.3	0.5	Garci-Crespo, San Lorenzo bottling plant, right.

IF TO: Huajuapan, VEER RIGHT. Skip stub log.

IF TO: Downtown, straight. Careful for traffic at "Alto" sign! Follow stub log below.

STUB LOG TO DOWNTOWN HOTELS

MI	KM	
0.4	0.6	Road divides into 4 narrow lanes.
0.5	0.8	Hotel Aldea del Bazar, right. Fancy, Arab-style place.
0.8	1.3	Red multi-storied housing project, right. Left, cyclone fence. Passing behind water-bottling plant.
1.2	1.9	Modern shopping center, left, with "Magic-land," auditorium, cinema.
1.3	2.1	Nissan, left. Speed limit 60 Km/hr.
1.8	2.9	Careful for merging traffic from right. Curve left. Goodyear, Chrysler-Dodge, right. General Tires, Firestone, left. Road narrows to 3 lanes your way.
1.9	4.9	Road narrows to 2 lanes your way. Water tower for Etiqueta Azul, right.
2.0	3.2	**GAS**, left. Slow, bumpy, uneven railroad crossing. Traffic congests.
2.3	3.7	Stoplight! For Hotel Mexico, turn right onto Av. Independencia.

End of Stub Log

MI	KM	
0.3	0.5	Right, long brick wall. Left is backside of Hotel Aldea. Arab –looking structure.
0.5	0.8	Road 2 lanes, not divided. Pass behind factory "Asbestos Tehuacán."
1.0	1.6	Ahead, you can see water-tower (Etiqueta Azul) & red brick housing project.
1.3	2.1	Careful! Intersection with Blvd. Aldama.
1.8	2.9	Cross Ave. Baja California.
2.8	4.5	Careful for series of "S" curves. Nice view of Tehuacán, left.
3.3	5.3	Come to junction with Chazumba, right, Tehuacán, Hwy #150, left. Veer right. Come to stop sign. Turn right. Out and ahead on nice 2 lane road.
3.5	5.6	Slow (30 Km/hr) thru village of Coapam, mostly at left. Watch for rocks on road ahead. **KM 7**.
4.0	6.4	Come to junction with Puebla - Oaxaca toll road.

IF TO: Puebla via toll road, exit right and join Oaxaca - Puebla Log (page 161) at mile 133.4.

IF TO: Oaxaca via toll road, go up overpass and exit right. Pay toll. Join Puebla - Oaxaca Toll Log (page 44) at mile 83.0.

MI	KM	
4.5	7.2	Mitsa factory, right. Sharp curve left. Then Onix Mendosa quarry, right.
5.0	8.0	Begin climbing. Sharp left.
8.0	12.8	Downhill. Begin series of dangerous curves.
8.3	13.3	Over bridge and up past San Antonio Tlaxcala. Then old church at left. **KM 15**.

Note the many varieties of cacti thru here – this is where botanists come on their field trips and where many professors bring their classes to study.

10.6	16.7	Careful for truck entrance, left.
11.0	17.6	Pass blue shrine at left.
12.5	20.0	Thru growing little town of La Venta. Note onyx crushing and screening plants in this area – they turn out onyx chips which are used in the making of terrazzo floors, etc.
14.3	22.9	Note salt-drying beds at left. Then sign says you're entering a botanical garden. **KM 26**. It'll be curvy & hilly for a spell.
16.3	26.1	Down past village of Zapotitlán Salinas. **KM 27**.
18.5	29.6	We've got to get over yonder mountains – but how?
18.0	28.8	Over dry Río Acatlán.
20.0	32.0	Settlement of Teloxtoc over to right.
22.8	36.5	Pass settlement of Colonia San Martín at right.
28.3	45.3	Pass village of Santiago Acatapec, left. Then nice skyline drive.
31.8	50.9	Thru little unnamed mountain top community. Notice the kids wearing big hats walking along the road.
34.0	54.4	Come now to state line – leave state of Puebla and enter state of Oaxaca. Scenery changes. It's greener, less desert-like. You're entering a little valley.
35.0	56.0	Pass side road (right) down to Frontera.
38.3	61.3	Thru village of Chazumba, (population 7,000) mostly right.
42.3	67.7	Curve right and over bridge over Río Huapanapam, and thru little town of Huapanapam. Pass side road (right) to Acaquizapan. **KM 61**.
48.0	76.8	Community of Piedra Lisa (Smooth Stone), right. Downhill. Road straightens, for a bit.
51.8	82.9	Pass side road (right) to village of San Pedro y San Pablo Tequixtepec. Then shrine at left.
54.8	87.7	Now thru pleasant little valley with big trees.
56.5	90.4	TOPES! Down thru village of Miletepec with church at right with pretty tiled domes.
58.8	94.1	Still winding along edge of Río Cuyotepeji Valley. Cornfields!
60.8	97.3	Shrine at right. Down thru village of Cuyotepeji.
63.5	101.6	Pass side road (right) to little town of Santa María Camotlán. Valley gets bigger.
67.0	107.2	Thru scattered village of El Espinal.
68.5	109.6	Conasupo warehouse, right. Another scattered settlement of La Luz Nagure.
70.5	112.8	Now thru village of Huajolotitlán.
71.0	113.6	Hotel Mixteca resort.
72.8	116.5	Quinta Shangri-La, right. Then South Seas, thatched roof restaurant, left.
73.0	116.8	Cross curved bridge over little Río Salado.
74.0	118.4	Slow now, and come to junction Hwy #190 just south of town of Huajuapan de León. Federal police station in front of you.

IF TO: Oaxaca, turn left onto Hwy #190 when coast is clear and start Huajuapan de León - Oaxaca Log (page 79). It's 120 miles to city limits of Oaxaca, and the only accommodations here are Hotels Laredo and García-Peral.

IF TO: Izucar de Matamoros, Cuernavaca, or Puebla – turn right and start Huajuapan de León - Izucar de Matamoros Log (page 81).

End of Log 45

LOG 46 *START:* Huajuapan, Oax *END:* Tehuacán, Pue

UD-103

74.0 MILES or 118.4 KM
DRIVE TIME – 3 – 4 HOURS.
SCENIC RATING — 3

This is a peaceful, two-lane with little traffic. A cacti lover's delight! Botanists from all over the States make field trips to this area beginning about 10 miles south of Tehuacán to study all the different types of desert flora. You'll pass salt-drying beds and also you'll see onyx-crushing and screening plants.

MI	KM	
0.0	0.0	At junction of Hwy #125 and Hwy #190 just south of Huajuapan, proceed north on Hwy #125.
1.0	1.6	Cross curved bridge over little Río Salado.
1.2	1.9	Pass South Seas thatched roof restaurant, right. Then Quinta Shangri-La, left.
3.0	4.8	Hotel Mixteca resort.
3.5	5.6	Now thru village of Huajolotitlán.
5.5	8.8	Thru scattered settlement of La Luz Nagure. Then pass Conasupo warehouse, left.
7.0	11.2	Thru scattered village of El Espinal.
10.5	16.8	Pass side road (left) to little town of Santa Maria Camotlán.
13.2	21.1	Down thru village of Cuyotepeji. Shrine at left.
17.5	28.0	TOPES! Down thru village of Miletepec with church at left with pretty tiled domes.
19.2	30.7	Now thru pleasant little valley with big trees.
22.2	35.5	Pass side road (left) to village of San Pedro y San Pablo Tequixtepec.
26.0	41.6	Community of Piedra Lisa (Smooth Stone), left.
31.5	50.4	Pass side road (left) to Acaquizapan and thru little town of Huapanapam. Then cross bridge over Río Huapanapam. **KM 61**.
35.7	57.1	Thru village of Chazumba, (population 7,000) mostly left.
39.0	62.4	Pass side road (left) down to Frontera.
40.0	64.0	Come now to state line – leave state of Oaxaca and enter state of Puebla. Scenery changes. It's not as green, more desert-like.
42.2	67.5	Thru little unnamed mountain top community. Notice the kids wearing big hats walking along the road. Then nice skyline drive.
45.7	73.1	Pass village of Santiago Acatapec, right.
51.2	81.9	Pass settlement of Colonia San Martín at left.
56.0	89.6	Over dry Río Acatlán.
57.7	92.3	Down past village of Zapotitlán Salinas. **KM 27**.
59.7	95.5	Note salt-drying beds at right. **KM 26**.
61.5	98.4	Thru growing little town of La Venta. Note onyx crushing and screening plants in this area – they turn out onyx chips which are used in the making of terrazzo floors, etc.
63.0	100.8	Pass blue shrine at right.
63.4	101.4	Careful for truck entrance, right.

Note the many varieties of cacti thru here – this is where botanists come on their field trips and where many professors bring their classes to study.

65.7	105.1	Pass San Antonio Tlaxcala. Old church at right and over bridge. **KM 15**.
66.0	105.6	Up thru series of dangerous curves.
69.5	111.2	Onix Mendosa quarry, left. Sharp curve right. Then Mitsa factory, left.
70.0	112.0	Come to junction with Puebla - Oaxaca toll road.

IF TO: Oaxaca via toll road, exit right. Pay toll. Join Puebla - Oaxaca Toll Log (page 44) at mile 83.0.

IF TO: Puebla via toll road, go up over overpass, exit right, pay toll and join Oaxaca - Puebla Log (page 161) at mile 133.4.

70.5	112.8	Slow (30 Km/hr) thru village of Coapam, mostly at right. **KM 7**.
71.0	113.6	Come to stop sign. TURN LEFT. Then come to junction (left) to Chazumba, (right) to Tehuacán.
71.2	113.9	S curves and nice view of Tehuacán at right.
72.2	115.5	Cross Av. Baja California.
72.7	116.3	Careful! Intersection with Blvd. Aldama.
73.5	117.6	Pass behind factory "Asbestos Tehuacán."
73.7	117.9	Right is backside of Hotel Aldea. Arab -looking structure. Left, a long brick wall. Then Garci-Crespo, San Lorenzo bottling plant, left.

IF TO: Esperanza and Puebla - Veracruz toll road, continue straight 0.3 miles till you come to junction with Hwy #150. Start Tehuacán - Esperanza Log.

IF TO: Downtown, turn right. Careful for traffic at "Alto" sign! Follow stub log below.

STUB LOG TO DOWNTOWN HOTELS

MI	KM	
0.4	0.6	Road divides into 4 narrow lanes.
0.5	0.8	Hotel Aldea del Bazar, right. Fancy, Arab-style place.
0.8	1.3	Red multi-storied housing project, right. Left, cyclone fence. Passing behind water-bottling plant.
1.2	1.9	Modern shopping center, left, with "Magic-land," auditorium, cinema.
1.3	2.1	Nissan, left. Speed limit 60 Km/hr.
1.8	2.9	Careful for merging traffic from right. Curve left. Goodyear, Chrysler-Dodge, right. General Tires, Firestone, left. Road narrows to 3 lanes your way.
1.9	4.9	Road narrows to 2 lanes your way. Water tower for Etiqueta Azul, right.
2.0	3.2	**GAS**, left. Slow, bumpy, uneven railroad crossing. Traffic congests.
2.3	3.7	Stoplight! For Hotel Mexico, turn right onto Av. Independencia. See Tehuacán Eat & Stray (page 133) for accommodations.

End of Log 46

LOG 47 *START:* Tehuacán, Pue *END:* Esperanza, Pue

UD-103

30.0 MI or 48.0 KM
DRIVE TIME 3/4 HOUR
SCENIC RATING – 2

This is a good route to get from Tehuacán to Toll Road #150D, where you can decide to go either Puebla and Mexico City (Hwy #150D west) or Jalapa (Hwy #144 north) or Veracruz (Hwy #150D east).

0.0	0.0	Starting here in Tehuacán at entrance to former Hotel Spa Peñafiel, now a school, at left, proceed ahead.
0.2	0.3	Pass big ultramodern Peñafiel water bottling plant on left. It's big business hereabouts – and there are several other spring water bottling firms here in Tehuacán, such as Garci-Crespo, Agua San Francisco, El Riego, San Lorenzo, etc.
1.0	1.6	Careful as you come to junction with free road (Hwy #150) to Puebla. Take right fork. Slow as you merge with other side of little highway triangle. Slow now over railroad (LOOK-&-LISTEN) and curve left.
3.0	4.8	Villa Alegría Spa (Happiness house) down on left is a bath and restaurant spot for the nearby home folks, and very popular on weekends and holidays.
5.5	8.8	Thru village of Santa Ana.
13.0	20.8	Slow now and TAKE LEFT FORK. Right fork goes to Orizaba (old Hwy #150).
13.2	21.1	Skirt little town of Azumbilla over to left.
16.5	26.4	Under high stone overpass.
17.0	27.2	Up sharp, long hairpin curve to left.
21.0	33.6	Pass side road (left) to Tecamachalco, but ahead for you. Up over railroad (LOOK-&-LISTEN) – careful, it's bumpy. Then bend right.
23.2	37.1	Road widens slightly. Down and past side road (right) to San Antonio Soledad.
24.5	39.2	Scattered village of Barrio de la Soledad at right.
25.7	41.2	Pass side road (right) to Puerta Cañada.
28.7	45.9	Pass side road (right) to Puente Negro.
29.5	47.2	Take left fork and over railroad crossing (LOOK-&-LISTEN).
30.0	48.0	Come to junction with Hwy #150D (straight goes to Cd Serdán and on to Jalapa (Hwy #144).

IF TO: Orizaba, Veracruz, turn right onto toll road and join Puebla - Veracruz Log at mile 60. See Mexico's Colonial Heart book (page 20).

IF TO: Puebla, Mexico City, go under overpass and turn right curving up onto toll road and join Veracruz - Puebla Log at mile 95. See Mexico's Colonial Heart book (page 170).

End of Log 47

LOG 48 *START:* Toluca, Mex *END:* Tres Marías, Mor

UD-076

40.0 MI or 64.0 KM
DRIVE TIME 1 – 2 HOURS
SCENIC RATING — 4

Pretty, wooded, curvy road. This shortcut is highly recommended to avoid Mexico City for car, RV's, bicycles or burros. It is slow but safe. Some call it "The Tope Tour to Tres Marías." Go slow, topes are high here.

MI	KM	
0.0	0.0	Having exited left (SE) from Hwy #55 from Toluca, head south on a two lane road.
0.4	0.6	Entering Estado de Mexico Municipio de Mexicaltzingo. Sign above you says, "Here live distinguished Mexicans."
0.7	1.1	Pay attention! Not much in the way of landmarks. Topes. Then turn left. Vulcanizadora at right. You are on another 2 lane road. Topes. Pass a Vulcanizadora Abraham at right.
0.8	1.3	Huge 3 person shrine on right. TURN RIGHT to Santiago Tianguistengo. Road left goes to Mexicaltzingo and to Santa Atizapán. Taquería "La Salsa" (not recommended) to the left as you curve right. More topes. You are on Hwy #934.
1.7	2.7	Entering Municipio of Chapultepec.
2.1	3.4	Pretty red and white village.
2.5	4.0	School at left. Topes.
3.0	4.8	Topes. Texaco store and horse crossing. Sharp curve right. Watch the topes.
4.3	6.9	Sharp curve left.
5.3	8.5	Entering Santa Cruz de Atizapán. Look at that old tree on the right.
5.7	9.1	Hacienda Atenco at left. 3 sets of topes in town.
6.5	10.4	Tlaltizalpa to left.
7.0	11.2	Santa Atizapán to right. Restaurant La Palapa at left. Cabrito al horno (baked), but good. Open 9 AM till 7:30 PM. MC, VI. Interesting stuffed coyote eating bird inside. Seafood, soup, spaghetti and more. Garci-Crespo mineral water. **KM 11**.
7.4	11.8	Santiago straight ahead for you. Tenango to right.
8.3	13.3	Santiago Tianguistengo. (Population: 40,970.) Cementos Monterrey & Kompras market to left. 2 topes. IMSS hospital at right. Grave markers for sale.
8.6	13.8	Take a right but be very careful! Narrow street. If there's a car or truck already there, one of you will have to back up. I tried going thru town to find a better way and believe me – it's worse.
8.7	13.9	Go one long block then take a left by a playground and a grain storage place.
9.0	14.4	Turn right towards Chalma. Malinalco to left. A school, watch out! This is another tough turn. Topes immediately after turn. Restaurant La Tranca to left. Clínica San José and Freyssinet at right.
9.4	15.0	Statue of Benito Juárez to left.

IF TO: Tres Marías (also known as Tres Cumbres), straight ahead. Industrial park is on your right.

IF TO: Centro and Jalatlaco, turn left at "Y."

9.5	15.2	Veer right for Tres Marías. Having veered right at the statue of Benito Juárez, proceed ahead.
10.1	16.2	Leave Santiago Tianguistengo. (Population 40,971.) Factory "Hitchner" to the left.
10.4	16.6	Straight to Tres Marías. Tenango to the left. Under overpass. La Marquesa to the right.
13.0	20.8	School on right. Topes.
13.4	21.4	Dangerous curve right with a brown cow on the side of the road.
14.3	22.9	Right to Tres Marías. Left to Jalatlaco and La Marquesa. Also, careful topes are very high.
14.4	23.0	Topes. Church at right. Then sharp turn left. Topes.
15.0	24.0	Topes. Leaving Coatepec.
16.6	26.6	Church at right.
17.3	27.7	La Esperanza to right.
18.7	29.9	Horseshoe curve right. **KM 15**.
20.0	32.0	Topes. Coyotepec to left. **KM 17**.
20.7	33.1	Fedomex warehouse to right. Topes.
21.6	34.6	Crossroads: left to Tres Marías and right to Chalma. Topes. Curve left. School on left. Pass by Santa Maria church on right.
26.0	41.6	The worst of the curves begin. Next 12 miles are really slow.
28.8	46.1	Careful for rocks on road.
30.3	48.5	Lake Zempoala to right. Toluca to left.

MI	KM	
30.6	49.0	Lake to the right. **KM 14**. Altitude 9,200 feet.
32.0	51.2	National forest Lagunas de Zempoala.
33.4	53.4	A.A. sign on rock.
36.6	58.6	Down hill. Passing by Huitzila. Turn left. Stop sign. Pretty church on right.
37.1	59.4	Careful for sharp left turn.
37.7	60.3	Turn right onto bypass.
39.0	62.4	Cemetery "San Jose" at left.
39.4	63.0	School at right. Topes.
39.7	63.5	Ahead northeast to Tres Marías. Cross Hwy #95, Mexico-Cuernavaca. You can follow this free road if you like, or ahead to nice divided toll road. Turn right on "Y." Careful for oncoming traffic, but there's no other way. Church at right.
40.0	64.0	Down hill. Bumpy road. Pass Pollos Rostizados and then "Abarrotes Yadira" on right. Curve left. Come to concrete map and monument. Ahead of you is the toll road, Hwy #95D.

IF TO: Cuernavaca, Cuautla, Acapulco, turn right onto toll road and start Mexico City - Cuernavaca Log (page 18) at mile 40.3.

IF TO: Mexico, D.F., turn right onto toll road, go to next "retorno" and turn around, heading north. Join Cuernavaca - Mexico City Log (page 158).

Note: Be careful that your license plate is not prohibited from driving today. There may be additional "non-driving" days IF a pollution alert is declared. See schedule in Cuernavaca - Mexico City Log.

End of Log 48

LOG 49 START: Tres Marías, Mor END: Toluca, Mex

UD-076

40.0 MI or 64.0 KM
DRIVE TIME 2 1/2 – 3 HOURS
SCENIC RATING — 4

Pretty, wooded, curvy road. Folks, this route could be called "tope town tour" and is slow, but it's better than Mexico City madness! We recommend it for cars, RV's and bicycles. Go really slow, as topes are pretty high ones. The first 20 miles take the longest, then it's easy. Relax and enjoy the view! There's a good cabrito (al horno) down the road.

0.0	0.0	Having turned right (west) at concrete map and monument, proceed ahead on 2 lane road. Curve right and pass "Abarrotes Yadira" and then Pollos Rostizados on left. Bumpy road. Up hill.
0.3	0.5	Church at left. Turn left on "Y." Careful for oncoming traffic, but there's no other way. Cross Hwy #95, Mexico-Cuernavaca. Ahead southwest to Zempoala on Hwy #934.
0.6	1.0	Topes. School at left.
1.0	1.6	Cemetery "San Jose" at right.
2.3	3.6	Turn left onto bypass.
2.9	4.6	Careful for sharp right turn.
3.4	5.4	Pretty church on left. Stop sign. Turn right. Up hill. Passing by Huitzilac. Topes.
6.6	10.6	AA sign on rock.
8.0	12.8	Going thru national forest of Lagunas de Zempoala.
9.4	15.0	Lake to the left. Altitude 9,200 ft. **KM 14**.
9.7	15.5	Lake Zempoala to left. Right for Toluca.
11.2	17.9	Careful for rocks on road.
14.0	22.4	The worst of the curves are over.
18.4	29.4	Passing by Santa Maria church on left. School on right. Curve right. Topes. Crossroads: left to Chalma and right to Tianguistengo.
19.3	30.9	Topes. Fedomex warehouse to left.
20.0	32.0	Coyoltepec to right. Topes. **KM 17**.
21.3	34.1	Horseshoe curve left. **KM 15**.
22.7	36.3	La Esperanza to left.
23.2	37.1	Topes and more topes. Careful topes are very high.
23.4	37.4	Church at left.

MI	KM	
25.0	40.0	Entering Coatepec. Topes.
25.6	41.0	Topes, then sharp turn right. Church at left. Topes.
25.7	41.1	Left to Santiago Tianguistengo and Toluca. Right goes to Jálatlaco and La Marquesa.
26.6	42.6	Dangerous curve left with a brown cow on the side of the road.
27.0	43.2	Topes. School on left.
29.6	47.4	Straight to Santiago Tianguistengo. La Marquesa to the left. Under overpass. Tenango to the right.
29.9	47.8	Factory "Hitchner" to the right. Enter Santiago Tianguistengo (population 40,971).
30.5	48.8	Statue of Benito Juárez in front of you. Veer left for Toluca.

IF TO: Centro and Jalatlaco, turn right at "Y."

IF TO: Toluca (veer left), straight ahead.

MI	KM	
30.6	49.0	Having veered left at the statue of Benito Juárez, proceed ahead. Industrial park is on your left. Freyssinet plant, left.
30.8	49.3	Take a left at the school.
30.9	49.4	Regional Preparatory school.
31.0	49.6	Pass Conasupo cone-shaped silos at right.
31.2	49.9	Go one block and take a left. Topes and IMSS Hospital at left. Super Kompras at right. 1 KM from cabrito.
31.6	50.6	Cementos Monterrey at right.
32.4	51.8	Thru Santa Cruz de Atizapán. What a tree to left!
32.5	53.4	Restaurant La Palapa at left. Cabrito al horno (baked), but good. Open 9 AM till 7:30 PM. MC, VI. Interesting stuffed coyote eating bird inside. Seafood, soup, spaghetti and more. Garci-Crespo mineral water. **KM 11.**
32.9	52.6	Atizapán over to left.
33.8	54.1	Passing Hacienda Atenco. Topes. Veer RIGHT and thru town.
35.3	56.5	Nice view of Nevado de Toluca at left.
36.4	58.2	Entering Municipio de Chapultepec. Topes in town.
37.1	59.4	Cemetery at left.
37.4	59.8	Wedding Cake church and school at left. Topes. Going thru red and white town.
37.8	60.5	Left is to Ixtapan San Andrés. Come to "Y." Toluca straight ahead.
38.7	61.9	Escuela preparatory #45 at right. Topes. Town is to the right. Taquería "La Salsa," right (not recommended). TURN LEFT and ahead.
39.1	62.6	Three cross shrine on left. More topes.
39.4	63.0	Come to "T." Take a right. There is a Vulcanizadora and not much else.
39.5	63.2	Big cross monument at left.
40.0	64.0	Take a right ahead taking road to Toluca. You intersect Hwy #55, just south of Metepec. **KM 9.**

IF TO: Toluca, turn right onto busy divided Hwy #55. Join Ixtapan de la Sal - Toluca Log (page 154) at mile 45.3.

IF TO: Ixtapan de la Sal, turn left onto busy divided Hwy #55. Join Toluca - Ixtapan de la Sal Log (page 35) at mile 3.0.

End of Log 49

LOG 50 *START:* Cuernavaca, Mor *END:* Ixtapan / la Sal, Mex

UD-076

65.0 MI or 104.0 KM
DRIVE TIME 1 1/2 HOURS
SCENIC RATING – 3

MI	KM	
0.0	0.0	Starting here in Cuernavaca at east interchange at junction to old road to Cuautla and turn off to Sumiya Hotel, proceed southbound on Hwy #95 bypass. Hotel Cuernavaca at left. Sign says "Acapulco Via Corta – 268 km, free road – 340 km." **KM 92.**
1.7	2.7	Pass exit (right) to Tabachines. **KM 93.**
2.5	4.0	Come to south interchange. Acapulco cuota road is to left. Iguala free road is straight ahead. Downtown Cuernavaca on Av. Morelos is to right. Straight for you, under overpass.
2.8	4.5	Iguala free exits to right. Acapulco (Autopista del Sol) cuota veer left, go under overpass and curve right. The free road is for you. Several little stores and restaurants on right.
3.1	4.9	Topes. Two-way traffic. Then more topes. Then sign that says, Acapulco 335 km, Taxco 79 km and airport 16 km. Three lane traffic here, one lane going south and 2 going north.

MI	KM	
3.8	6.0	Downhill and begin series of sharp curves.
4.4	7.0	Pass exit (right) to town of Alta Palmira. Now just 2-lane road.
5.1	8.2	Begin undivided four lane.
5.5	8.8	Topes as you enter Village of Temixco off to right. More topes and big Hotel Principe at left.
6.3	10.0	Over topes. **GAS**, right and out.
7.4	11.8	Topes. Left fork takes you to downtown Acatlipa. Straight (toward Acapulco) for you. Congested traffic.
8.9	14.2	Airport to right. Topes. Straight for Taxco. Village at right is Xochitetec.
11.3	18.0	Congestion clears out. Two-lane winding road. Pass side road (right) to Xochitepec (19 km away).
15.0	24.0	Take left fork. **GAS**, left. Road (left) goes to Jojutla (19 km away) and Lake Tequesquitengo. Then more topes at small town Alpuyeca mostly to right.
15.3	24.5	Left fork for heavy truck traffic (goes back to freeway). Straight for you. Good enough Motel La Palapa at left.
16.3	26.0	Watch for cattle, especially a big brown and white cow on roadway.
17.2	27.5	Pass side road (right) to Miacatlán, Coatetelco and Xochicalco ruins. **KM 28**.
18.1	29.0	Highway now parallels the toll road at left. There are grutas in this area.
21.6	34.5	Slow for sharp curve then down.
22.3	35.6	Town of Zacatepec over to right.
23.8	38.0	**GAS**, right. Puente de Ixtla to right.
25.0	40.0	Then over bridge. Topes on both ends.
25.6	41.0	Another exit (right) for Puente de Ixtla. Over little bridge.
26.9	43.0	Pass side road (right) for grutas and Michapa. TAKE RIGHT HERE to go to Ixtapan de la Sal. Taxco is straight ahead (about a half hour ahead). Pass little community of Colonia El Paraíso.
27.9	44.6	Having turned right, pass LP gas on right.
30.0	48.0	Careful for cattle crossing.
37.2	59.5	Come to "T." TAKE LEFT FORK to grutas and Ixtapan de la Sal on Hwy 421. Right fork goes to Alpuyeca and Miacatlán. Topes in town of Michapa.
37.5	60.0	Over Río Amacuzac. Cross state line – Leave state of Morelos and enter state of Guerrero. Topes.
39.7	63.5	Slow for curves and thru electrifying town of El Transformador.
41.3	66.0	Slow for sharp curves. Entrance to Grutas de Cacahuamilpa off to left (cost $3 to park and $15 per person for hourly tour). Ixtapa de la Sal and Hwy #55, straight ahead.
41.9	67.0	Come to "T" (Hwy #55). Taxco (30 km) to left. TURN RIGHT to Toluca and Ixtapan de la Sal (36 km).

IF TO: Taxco, turn left and join Ixtapan de la Sal - Iguala Log (page 37) at mile 28.5.

43.1	69.0	Thru village of Cacahuamilpa.
47.8	76.5	Wake up! Topes. Thru tile making town of Mogote.
50.3	80.5	Topes as you go thru small town of Piedras Negras.
53.1	85.0	Cross state line – Leave state of Guerrero and enter state of Mexico.
55.3	88.5	Grutas La Estrella to left (3 km away). Then thru Puerta de Santiago.
56.3	90.0	Lots of topes as you skirt town of Terrero.
60.6	97.0	Thru town of Tonatico. Topes.
60.9	97.5	At second street into town, TURN RIGHT, following TOLUCA signs and on up thru town on Av. Matamoros. TURN LEFT after a couple of vibrators and end of pavement. A school on left after turn.
61.6	98.5	Rejoin highway. You're now on Calle Rodríguez
61.9	99.0	Municipal Balneario over to right, mostly for home folks.
62.2	99.5	Series of *vibradores* (speed bumps).
63.4	101.5	Curve right into town of Ixtapan de la Sal (population 13,000; altitude 6,312 feet) and slow for several topes.
63.8	102.0	Right fork goes to downtown, bus station and Hotel María Isabel. Pass Quinta Los Tecolotes at left. Pass side road (left) to Coatepec and Jardines. Right also goes to town. **GAS**, 200 meters to left.
64.4	103.0	**GAS**, left. Go thru arch of trees. San Román Nursery at right.
64.7	103.5	Pass Motel Ideal at right. Then begin divided. Take left to Hotel Ixtapan and Búngalos Vista Hermosa.
65.0	104.0	Come to statue of Diana and road to other hotels see Ixtapan de la Sal Eat & Stray (page 125) for accommodations.

IF TO: Toluca, straight ahead and start Ixtapan de la Sal - Toluca Log (page 154).

IF TO: Taxco, turn around and start Ixtapan de la Sal - Iguala Log (page 37).

End of Log 50

LOG 51 *START:* Taxco, Gro END: Jct Hwy 95D, Mor

UD-077

18.1 MI or 29.0 KM
DRIVE TIME 1/2 HOUR
SCENIC RATING — 2

This log takes you to toll road between Iguala and Cuernavaca.

MI	KM	
0.0	0.0	Starting in Taxco with Loma Linda Hotel at right.
1.0	1.6	State Tourism offices at right and under welcome arches.
1.9	3.1	LP gas at right.
3.0	5.0	Highway patrol station and tow trucks at right.
3.4	5.4	Pass side road (right) to Jelotepec.
7.8	12.5	Come to turnoff (right) to Cuernavaca via (old) toll road, Hwy #95. Amacuazac is straight ahead. Free road to Cuernavaca is a short stretch farther.

IF TO: Ixtapan de la Sal, Toluca, turn left and join Iguala - Ixtapan de la Sal Log (page152) at mile 32.9.

10.6	17.0	Long sharp left curve. Lookout point on left at end of curve. **KM 12.**
11.3	18.0	Another left curve.
12.0	19.2	Summit. Sharp right curve. KM 10. Then down.
17.4	27.8	Another sharp curve.
17.9	28.6	Come to tollbooth. Pay toll (car $7, 2-axle $13, 3-axle $19, extra axle $6). Clean restrooms at tollbooth. Straight ahead for Cuernavaca and Iguala. You're now on a short stretch of 2-lane divided.
18.1	29.0	Stay in left lane for Cuernavaca. Right lane goes to Iguala and Acapulco. Careful! There's a stop sign at end, where you turn left onto toll road.

IF TO: Cuernavaca, Mexico city, join Iguala - Cuernavaca Log (page 157) at mile 23.3.

IF TO: Acapulco, stay in right lane and join Cuernavaca - Iguala Log (page 23) at mile 27.7.

End of Log 51

Barra de Navidad

Area Code — 315

BARRA DE NAVIDAD lies between Puerto Vallarta and Acapulco on Mexico's "Costa de Bougainvillea," a coast of crushed shells, isolated capes, reefs with women's names, inlets with transparent waters and a surf that white-collars coconut palms.

Founded in 1533 by Spanish Captain Francisco de Hijar, Barra was shown on maps as "Xalisco" at that time. Five years later, on December 25th, Virrey Antonio de Mendoza disembarked here with his naval fleet to quell an insurrection of the Caxcanes and Tecos Indians. Because of his Christmas Day arrival, the town was christened "Puerto de Navidad" but was later renamed "Barra de Navidad."

In 1542 the first (but unsuccessful) expedition, headed by Ruy López de Villalobos, set sail from here in search of the Far East islands. In 1564, the Basque Miguel López de Legazpi weighed anchor from this port for the second crossing and, following an odyssey of several months, he eventually discovered what is today Manila in the Philippines. A monument erected in Barra de Navidad in 1964 commemorates the 400th anniversary of this maritime expedition. (Incidentally, Las Hadas' chic Legazpi Restaurant in Manzanillo features a mural by Fernando Calderón depicting the history of Barra; the fresco illustrates four ships in various states of construction as well as vessels sailing in the air toward the unknown.)

SLEEPING IN BARRA DE NAVIDAD

BARRA DE NAVIDAD – MOD – 60-room, 3-story hotel on beach at Legazpi #250. Restaurant. Pool. On-street parking. MC. Ph: 3324-4007 in Guadalajara.

BOGAVANTE – MOD – 22-room, 2-story beachfront hotel on Legazpi. No restaurant. On-street parking. Ph: 337-0384.

CABO BLANCO – MOD – Very nice 101-room, 3-story A/C hotel on beach. Restaurant. Bar. Disco. Nice pool and gardens. Marina. Tennis. Deep-sea fishing. Water sports. Shops. Parking. AE, MC, VI. Ph: 337-0022 or 337-0103.

DELPHIN – ECON – 24-room, 4-story hotel at Calle Morelos #23 across from Sands. Restaurant-bar. Pool. On-street parking. Ph: 337-0068.

EL MARQUEZ DE SANTANA – UPPER – Calle Filipinas #75. 30 rooms. Pool. Ph: 355-5304. Fax: 355-6300.

SANDS – ECON – 50-room, 3-story hotel across from Delfín at Calle Morelos #24. Seasonal restaurant. Bar. Club. Pool. Water sports. Parking. AE. Ph: 337-0018 or 337-0149.

TROPICAL – MOD – 42-room A/C hotel on beach downtown at Calle López de Legazpi #96. Restaurant. Bar. Pool. Boutique. On-street parking. AE, MC, VI. Ph: 337-0020 or 337-0149.

EATING IN BARRA DE NAVIDAD

CORALES – MOD – Good restaurant on López de Legazpi #146. Chicken, seafood. Orange tablecloth place. Polo de Puina special. Loud music. Converts to disco at night.

COLIMILLA – MOD – Island off coast a short way where there are two rustic restaurants specializing in seafood. Fish freshly caught, deliciously prepared, and good service.

MAR Y TIERRA – MOD – Excellent downtown restaurant on beach. Variety of seafood including shrimp and oysters, lobster, octopus, scallops, clams, bass, etc. Bar. Converts to disco at night. AE, MC.

MELANESA – MOD – Restaurant at M. López de Ligazpi, end of the street. Seafood, chicken, hamburger and oyster. Open 6 PM till 10 PM.

PANCHO – MOD – Popular, reasonably priced open-air seafood restaurant (palapa-style) near hotels on Legazpi #53.

PATY – ECON – VALUE. Popular restaurant at Calle Jalisco across from R. Chela. Same street as church. Very popular with home folks. Pollo, carne asada and pozole. Breakfast. Chamorro - pig hock stew. Open 8 AM till 11 PM.

PIZZERIA IVETTE – MOD – Av. Mazatlan #109 Altos. Pizza. Open 7 PM till 11 PM.

SLEEPING IN MELAQUE – SAN PATRICIO

BUNGALOWS PACIFICO – MOD – 47 one, two and three-bedroom kitchenettes on beach. No restaurant. Pool. Parking.

BUNGALOWS PUESTA DEL SOL – VALUE! – Gomez Farias # 202, S.P., PH: not yet. – Near Playa RV park. Really nice rooms (16 of 'em) set in 4 stories on beach. Nice and breezy, you can hear the pounding of the surf from every one. Kitchenettes. Owner Ignacio Gutierrez G. a very nice, helpful man. New and friendly. He may be set up for MC, VI when you get there, but maybe not. Ceiling fans. Nice balconies on some.

BUNGALOWS VILLA MAR – MOD – HIDALGO #1. Across from P. Las Gaviotas (no, the address isn't a misprint). 2 bedroom bungalows on beach. Rents by month only. Gardens. Balconies. B.B.Q. No credit cards. Ph: 337-0129.

CLUB NAUTICO MELAQUE – MOD – 38-room, 3-story hotel on beach at Francisco Madero #1. Rustic palapa-style restaurant. Bar. Pool. Parking. AE, MC, VI. Ph: 337-0239.

EL MARQUES – MOD – 4-bungalows at G. Farias #78. 2 parking spaces. Same owners as Hotel Melaque in Barra de Navidad. Ph: 337-0213, 337-0304, or 337-0082.

FLAMINGO – MOD – 40-room hotel downtown. 10 rooms A/C; 30 with fans. No restaurant. Parking. Ph: 337-0126.

LEGAZPI — MOD — Nice hotel located right on the beach at the north end of bay. Community kitchen. SATV. Pool. Ph: 335-5397.

POSADA LAS GAVIOTAS – ECON – 24-apartment like room motel at Hidalgo #1 on beach. Popular with families. Some with kitchens. Pool. Ceiling fans. Bunk beds. Garden. Patios. Ph: 337-0129.

POSADA PABLO DE TARSO – MOD – 20 bungalows, 2 bedrooms, near beach on G. Farias #49. Some with A/C. Ceiling fans. Stocked fridge comes with 2 cases of cokes and 2 six packs of beer. Covered Parking. Gardens. Clothes washing area. Discounts for long term. Long distance service. No kitchen. Pool. Ph: 352-1625, 337-0117, or 337-0268.

PUESTA DEL SOL – MOD – 47 rooms, 5 bungalows located at Juarez #162. Reasonably priced. Nice pool. Bungalows have kitchen. Music in rooms. TV. Ceiling fans. Ignacio Gutierrez owner.

VILLAMAR – MOD – Bungalows at Hidalgo #1. Rent by month. 2 bedroom, kitchen. Garden Balconies on beach. English spoken.

EATING IN MELAQUE – SAN PATRICIO

FONDA LOS PORTALES – ECON – Nice restaurant at G. Farías #68. Breakfast, Mexican food. Open 7 AM till 3 PM. Ph: 337-0268.

EL REY SOL – ECON – Funky restaurant with fountain in middle. Corner Reforma and Zapata.

POLLOS AL CARBON "MARIO" – ECON – Corner square and L. Mateos. Good roast chicken. Very popular with local folks.

RINCON TROPICAL – MOD – Good restaurant at Av. López Mateos #33. Good, plain food, seafood, Mexican food, liquados. Half a block towards ocean from square. Open 7 AM till 10 PM. Ph: 337-0214.

VIVA MARIA'S — MOD — A good restaurant with a friendly atmosphere and authentic Mexican food. It's run by the local town doctor, Roberto Pimienta. A local hangout for Americans and Canadians.

SLEEPING IN VICINITY (Between Melaque and Puerto Vallarta)

CHAMELA (44.5 miles north of Melaque Junction) – MOD – Small, Spartan 9-room hotel on Highway #200 in little community of Juan Pérez. No restaurant. Pool. Tennis. Beach 2 miles away. 5 RV spaces with all hookups. Parking.

EL TECUAN (20.3 miles north of Melaque Junction) – MOD – Nice 36-room, 2-story A/C hotel on another section of inviting beach. Good restaurant. Bar. Pool. Water sports. Canoeing. Deep-sea fishing. Horses. Hunting. Space for self-contained RV's (but walk to hotel is steep uphill grind). Parking. AE, MC, VI. Ph: 316-0085 in Guadalajara.

PLAZA DE CAREYES (33 miles north of Melaque Junction) – MOD – Good 100-villa, 3-story A/C complex styled after a Mediterranean village whose grounds cover 3700 acres with 8 miles of protected coastline. Restaurant. Bar. Disco. Pool. Movie. Tennis. Horses. Fishing. Jeep rental. Water sports. Boat ramp. Stores. Parking. AE, MC, VI.

CAMPING & RV PARKING

BOCA DE IGUANAS (10.5 miles north of Melaque Junction) – 30-space facility near Los Angeles de Tenacatita. Electrical and water hookups. Showers. Toilets. Pets OK. Phone 336-6735 in Guadalajara.
PLAYA – 45-space park on beach at Gómez Farías #250. All hookups. Showers. Toilets. Grocery. Ph: 337-0065.
VILLA POLINESIA (44.5 miles north of Melaque Junction) – Small, 8-space campground (camping permitted) off Hwy #200 in community of Juan Pérez. All hookups. Showers. Toilets. BBQ grills. Laundromat. Palapas. Ph: 22-3940 in Guadalajara.

End of Barra de Navidad Eat & Stray

Manzanillo

Area Code — 314

Manzanillo, with a population of 92,200, is a typical seaport - rather unattractive with little to offer except perhaps a zesty plaza with its treasured poinciana tree. The town is one of Mexico's old-time seaports with a good, deep harbor. As a matter of fact, as early as 1525 "Nueva España" was already constructing ships to explore the New World's unknown Pacific coast, and it was the Spanish who discovered that Manzanillo was an excellent location for a major seaport.

Manzanillo's north beach area is a very popular resort. There are hotels, motels and condos all along the shoreline to suit any budget. On Santiago Peninsula a little farther north stands Manzanillo's pride, Las Hadas (The Fairies), a luxurious jet-set resort styled after a Moroccan village.

There are several fine beaches to suit any taste, from calm and tranquil waters at Bahía Santiago to the surfing beaches of Cocos and Las Ventanas. Fishing is terrific: Marlin, sailfish, yellowtail, sea bass, red snapper, manta ray and dolphin abound. The best season is undoubtedly between November and February.

On Hwy #200, 26 miles north of Manzanillo and then 4 miles to the Pacific is the sleepy village of Cuyutlán where from February thru April you can catch a glimpse of the famous "Green Wave," nature's phosphorescent phenomenon, with its 45-foot crest rolling to shore.

FISHING - For deep-sea fishing arrangements, contact the personnel at any hotel.

SLEEPING IN MANZANILLO

ANGELICA – ECON – 14-bungalow beachfront complex, each unit consisting of 2 bedrooms, bath and kitchen. No A/C. Enclosed parking. Ph: 333-2982
ARCO IRIS (Rainbow) – MOD – 21-unit beachfront motel consisting of one- and two-bedroom kitchenettes. No A/C; ceiling fans only. No restaurant. Pool. Pets OK. Nice gardens. Enclosed parking. Ph: 333-0168.
CASA BLANCA ALAMAR – ECON –Av. Olas Altas #36. Economy 58-room, 2-story beachfront hotel consisting of 1-3 bedroom, 1-3 bath apartments. No A/C. No restaurant. Big salt-water pool. Parking. Ph: 333-0212 or 334-0397.
CLUB MAEVA – UPPER – All inclusive deal. Pay for meals, room and activities. A 514-unit, 2-story A/C blue-and-white villa complex, a village in itself, at north entrance to town (KM 25) on beach. Each unit with terrace, living-dining area, fully equipped kitchen, bath and one or two bedrooms. Bar. Disco. 2 pools (one large enough for water skiing). Tennis. Golf nearby. Mini-club for children; sports club for teenagers. Boutiques. Movie theater. Market. Art gallery. Transportation to beach. Beautiful landscaping. Parking. AE, MC, VI. Ph: 335-0595 Fax: 335-0395.
CLUB SANTIAGO – UPPER – Nice subdivision complex 11 miles north of downtown on Hwy #200. 48

condos, 28 small apartments and 30 houses (some with private pool). Restaurant. Bar. Pool. Golf course. Tennis. Parking. Beautiful landscaping. Ph: 335-0412 or 335-0415 Fax: 335-0400. In US call 303-371-5360.

CLUB VACACIONAL LAS BRISAS – MOD – 56-room, 2-story apartment complex at Av. Lazaro Cardenas #207. No A/C; ceiling fans only. No restaurant. Pool. Parking. Ph: 333-2075 or 333-1747 Fax: 333-4085.

CONDOMINIO EL FARO (Lighthouse) – MOD – Lovely development of deluxe one-and two-bedroom apartments named for beautiful large white replica of lighthouse atop hill in La Audiencia Subdivision. Restaurant. Bar. 2 pools. Parking.

FIESTA AMERICANA – UPPER – Blvd. Miguel de la Madrid KM 8.5. Restaurant. Disco. Ph: 333-1100, 333-2180.

LA POSADA – MOD – 2-story, 25-room beachfront hotel at Lázaro Cárdenas #201 near turning basin next to Roca del Mar. No A/C. Open-air dining room. Pool. Snack bar. Parking. Ph and Fax: 333-1899.

LAS HADAS (The Fairies) – UPPER – Top-flight 220-unit A/C beachfront on Peninsula Santiago, dazzling-white Moorish style luxury resort. 3 restaurants. 4 bars. Club. Disco. 2 pools. Movies shown. 18-hole golf course. Tennis. Stable. Infirmary. Marina. Boutiques. Water sports. Beautifully landscaped. Parking. AE, MC, VI. Ph: 334-0000 Fax: 334-1950.

MARBELLA – MOD – VALUE. 52-room, 4-story beachfront motel at KM 9.5 of Hwy #200. 12 with A/C; others with ceiling fans only. Good breeze. On beach. Plain, but good. Restaurant. Bar. Pool. Small pets OK. Parking. MC, VI. Ph: 333-1103 or 333-1105.

PLAYA DE SANTIAGO – MOD – 107-room, 6-story beachfront hotel. 20 rooms A/C. Restaurant. Bar. Pool. Tennis. Mini-golf. On-street parking. AE, MC. Ph: 333-0055, 333-0727 or 333-0270 Fax: 333-0344.

PLAZA LAS GLORIAS – UPPER – 86-suite A/C condo complex up on hill on Av. Del Tesoro. Good restaurant. Bar. Nice pool. Golf. Tennis. Beach club. Spectacular view. Parking. AE, MC, VI. Ph: 333-0812, 334-1054 Fax: 333-1530.

PLAZA LAS GLORIAS BEACH CLUB – MOD – Nice 17-apartment, 3-story A/C complex in Playa Azul Subdivision on Calle Del Mar next to Suites Nancy on beach. No restaurant. Pool. Parking. MC. Ph: 3-2510.

PLAYA GRANDE – MOD – 8-suite, 2-story complex at Miramar #33 on beach. No A/C. Kitchenettes. No restaurant. Pool. Parking. Ph and Fax: 335-0333.

POSADA SANTA CECILIA – MOD – 35-room, 2-story apartment complex on beach KM 8.5. No A/C. No restaurant. Pool. Parking. Pets OK. Ph: 333-1576 Fax: 334-1669.

ROSA MAR – MOD – 9-suite, 3-story complex at Av. Lazaro Cardenas #715. Some A/C. No restaurant. No pool. Parking. Good buy. Ph: 333-2959

RISCOS LA AUDIENCIA – MOD – 26 Villas on Calle de los Riscos. Ph: 334-1236.

SAN FRANCISCO – MOD – 28-kitchenette, 2-story complex with one-and two-bedroom units. No A/C; ceiling fans only. No restaurant. Pool. Parking.

SIERRA MANZANILLO RADISON PLAZA – UPPER – Av. La Audiencia #1, Peninsula Santiago. Restaurant. MC, VI. Ph: 333-2000

STAR – MOD – 9-suite, 2-story complex at Lázaro Cárdenas # 1313 on beach. Restaurant. Kitchenettes. Pool. Parking. MC, VI. Ph: 333-2560 or 333-1980.

VILLAS LA AUDIENCIA – MOD – 46 rooms at Av. La Audiencia and Las Palomas. Ph: 333-0861 Fax: 333-2653.

EATING IN MANZANILLO

COLIMA BAY CAFE – MOD – Another restaurant of the Anderson chain on main boulevard. Party hearty crowd. Drinking contests. All the usual entrees including shrimp, BBQ ribs, chicken, pork, etc. Popular with the younger crowd. Open 6 PM till midnight. Closed Sunday. MC, VI. Ph: 333-1150.

EL VAQUERO – UPPER – Restaurant on airport road near traffic circle and turnoff of Hwy #200. Steakhouse. Pricey, but quality. Open 1 PM till midnight. Ph: 333-1654.

GUADALUPE GRILL – MOD – Plaza Pacífico Peninsula Santiago. International cuisine. Ph: 334-0555.

JALAPEÑO – MOD – International restaurant next door to Arco Iris. Specialties include Chicken Kiev, onion soup and Cordon Bleu. Open 5 PM till 11 PM. Closed after Easter till November 1st.

L'RECIF – UPPER – Terrific seaside restaurant at tip of Juluapan Peninsula. Specialties include grilled seafood, Coq au Vin and Filete Pimienta. Breathtaking view. Lovely landscaping. Pool (with swim-up bar). Open 1

PM till 5 PM and from 7 PM till 11:30 PM. AE, MC, VI. Don't miss it! Ph: 333-0900.
MOUSTACHE'S BIGOTES – MOD – Calle Puesta del Sol #3. Open 1 PM till 8 PM. Ph: 333-1236
WILLY'S – MOD – International restaurant in Playa Azul Subdivision on beach at Calle Las Brillas. Wide variety of entrees. Open 6 PM till 11:30 PM (closed Mondays). AE, MC, VI. Ph: 333-1794.

CAMPING & RV PARKING

LA MARMOTA – MOD – At Playa La Audiencia. Spaces for 7 trailers. Water and electric. Ph: 332-5799, 333-0955 or 336-6248

End of Manzanillo Eat & Stray

Colima

Area Code — 312

Colima, population: 100,000, altitude: 1,600 feet, was founded in 1523 AD, The name is derived from the name of the Teco Indian leader and defender of this area Colímotl, king of Colimán. It was called Villa de Colima by Gonzalo de Sandoval after the Tecos were defeated. The territory of Colima became a free and sovereign state in 1857 and Colima the capital city. It is a very nice semitropical city with flat, well paved streets and boulevards that are easily negotiated.

Colima offers two rather interesting things to see:

1) A little short of fabulous, the Zaragoza Antique Automobile Collection is Sr. Francisco Zaragoza's private collection of 50 old-time (20's and 30's) American cars, all in beautiful condition and all operative. The most notable is a 1941 Packard that belonged to the wife of ex-president Manuel Avila Camacho, and the oldest model is a 1910 Willis Overland. Also among them you'll find a 1935 Cord, 1927 Essex, 1934 Oakland with a round thermometer on its radiator cap, 1926 Ford Model T with a coil box and self cranking starter and many other beauties. (In addition, he has about 350 more ancient autos out at huge old Hacienda del Carmen). The auto showroom downtown is open 9-1:30 and 4-7:30, seven days a week (admission charged).

2) The Anthropological Exhibit at the museum at the University of Colima is worthwhile if you are interested in this sort of thing. It's open 10-1 and 4-7 Mon-Fri and 10-1 Sat (admission charged).

About 6 miles north of Colima is the picturesque little town of Comala, worth a visit to enjoy its Spanish-style architecture and to tour the artisan center where wonderful exotic wood furniture is custom made, along with specialized paintings and iron works. It is open weekdays 9-1:30 and 4-7:30 Saturdays 9-2.

SLEEPING IN COLIMA

AMERICA — UPPER — Nice well-run downtown 75 room, 2-story A/C hotel at Morelos #162. Good restaurant. Steam baths and whirlpools (men only). Parking 2 blocks away. No pets. MC, VI. Ph: 312-9596 or 312-7488.
EL COSTEÑO — MOD — Comfortable 63-unit 2-story motel on Blvd., Carlos de la Madrid #1001 near south junction Hwy #110. 32 A/C rooms, rest with fans. Restaurant. Bar. Pool. Parking. No credit cards. Ph: 312-1925 or 312-1903.
GRAN HOTEL FLAMINGOS — MOD — Clean 49-room, 5-story hotel at Av. Rey Colimán #18 near main plaza. Restaurant. On street parking. No pets. No credit cards. Ph: 312-2525 or 312-2526.
LOS CANDILES — MOD — 77-unit, 2-story motel at Blvd. Camino Real #399 on northeast end of town on highway to Guadalajara. 31 A/C rooms, rest with fans. Restaurant. Pool. Parking. No pets. AE, MC. VI. Ph: 312-3212.
MARIA ISABEL — UPPER — 92-room A/C motel at Blvd. Camino Real #351 on northeast end of town. Restaurant. Bar. Night club. Pool. Parking. No pets. AE, CB, MC, VI. Ph: 312-6262 or 312-6464.
VILLA DEL REY — MOD — 56-unit, 2-story motel at Blvd. Camino Real KM 1. Some A/C rooms, rest with fans. Restaurant. Bar. Parking. No pets. AE, CB, MC, VI. Ph: 312-2917.

EATING IN COLIMA

CAMINO REAL DE COLIMA — Emiliano Carranza #306. Regional cuisine. Ph: 314-1589.
EL TABACHIN — Av. Del Trabajo #52. International cuisine. Ph: 312-1849.
LA CAVA — Av. Felipe Sevilla del Río #349. Charcoaled steaks.
LOS NARANJOS — Mexican-style short order restaurant at Gabino Barreda #34. Tacos, enchiladas, sandwiches, steaks, blue-plate specials. Ph: 312-0029, 312-7316.

End of Colima Eat & Stray

Ixtapa

Area Code — 755

IXTAPA, 4.4 miles (7 KM) northwest of Zihuatanejo and 150 miles northwest of Acapulco, is one of the new breed of resorts founded by computer. The two are far apart in character as they are in age. Zihua was around before Columbus. Ixtapa was born in a computer in the 1970's. Ixtapa is high-rise and fashionable. Zihua is more laid back. Each has its fans. Try 'em both.

In the 1970's, FONATUR, Mexico's private tourist development agency, fed the computer data on what a tourist most often seeks in a resort: i.e. climate, beach, vegetation, history, fishing, accessibility, etc., and out popped Ixtapa and Cancún. Later, Huatulco, Oax, on the southern Pacific coast was developed, using the same premise. Please don't call Ixtapa "another Cancún," if you don't want to start a ruckus with the nice folks who live here. Each resort has a different character, and Ixtapa is proud of the fact that it can never be overdeveloped. Only recently, with the advent of the marina have any new hotels been built. Ixtapa has white sand beaches, beautiful tropical vegetation, sparkling blue waters and delightful weather.

CLIMATE — The average annual temperature is 78.8° F (29° C). Summer temperature highs average in the low 90's, with nighttime lows in the high 70's. Winter highs reach the upper 80's and lows in the low 70's with balmy breezes year-round. During rainy season, June thru Sept., showers are usually brief and generally at night, so the sun shines almost 365 days a year.

GOLF and TENNIS — Most of the action is at del Palmar Beach where most of its hotels are located. Across from del Palmar Beach is the Ixtapa Golf Club (formerly the Palma Real) 18-hole golf course (6,910 yards) designed by Robert Trent Jones. The course, laid out among the coconut palms of an old coconut plantation, overlooks the bay and is surrounded by Ixtapa's residential area. The club house offers such facilities as a restaurant, pool, tennis courts and a playground for children. Open daily: 7 AM till 7 PM. For information and reservations Ph: 553-1062.

Major hotels in Ixtapa, the Ixtapa Golf Club and Hotel Villa del Sol in Zihuatanejo have tennis courts, lighted for nighttime playing. Big annual ATP International Tournament in Nov.

SHOPPING — Just beyond the golf course is the colonial-style La Puerta shopping center. In this self-contained center are a bank, nice restaurants, a supermarket, Turismo Caleta Travel Agency, real estate offices, bazaars, boutiques, an art gallery and a shop for renting bicycles and mopeds. Across from "hotel row" are several shopping centers.

NATURE — A 6-mile scenic road alongside the coastal lagoon connects Ixtapa to Playa Quieta (Quiet Beach) where the water is calm and transparent. At Playa Quieta there are showers, dressing rooms, plenty of parking and a good restaurant (Playa Quieta, specializing in charcoal fish Ixtapa style and red snapper a la Quieta).

DIVING — Over 30 fabulous sites range from easy reef dives to deep (100 feet) dives, plus shipwreck exploring. Run by NAVI instructor and marine biologist Juan Bernard Avila, the Zihuatanejo Scuba Center at Paseo del Pescador #4, Ph: 554-2147, offers it all. Night dives, instruction, certification and underwater photography (still and video) of your dives is also offered. Oliverio's, a well-known scuba gear shop and diving school, is also located on the beach.

FISHING — Deep-sea fishing here ranks among the best in the world. Marlin, sailfish, mahi-mahi (called dorado here) and roosterfish. Your hotel can book a boat or by contacting the boat cooperative. Cooperativa de

Lanchas de Recreo y Pesca Deportiva, Teniente José Azueta on the Zihuatanejo pier at Av. Ruis Cortines #40. Ph: 554-2056. Important International Sailfish Tournament is held on April 30.

In front of Playa Quieta stands Ixtapa Island, about a mile away. The island is a wildlife refuge and its principal inhabitants are deer, iguanas, raccoons, pelicans, sea gulls, parrots, badgers and armadillos. The water surrounding the island is perfect for skin diving, and there's a small restaurant-bar on the island.

HEALTH and EMERGENCY — 24-HOUR MEDICAL SERVICE – Emergency treatment, surgery, air-land ambulance service. Ph: 554-3823 or 554-3184, extension 2113 at Hotel Sheraton.

USEFUL INFORMATION — IXTAPA/ZIHUATANEJO HOTEL ASSOCIATION – Provides general information as well as assistance with special events and conventions. Individual and group reservations can be booked thru travel agents or directly with hotels. The office of the Hotel Association is in La Puerta Shopping Center, Local #2. P.O. Box 210, 40880 Ixtapa, GRO. Ph: 553-1566. Fax: 553-1543.

SECTUR (Mexican Tourism Secretariat) office is in La Puerta Shopping Center on Blvd. Ixtapa. P.O. Box 100, 40880 Ixtapa, GRO. Ph: 553-1967.

FONATUR sales office (for properties and investment) is in La Puerta Shopping Center. P.O. Box 180, 40880 Ixtapa, GRO. Ph: 553-0722. Fax: 553-0607.

BANK – Open from 9 AM till 1 PM, Mon thru Fri. Office hours are usually 9 AM till 2 PM and 4 till 7 PM, Mon thru Fri.

We hope you enjoy Ixtapa and if you tire of what it has to offer, don't hesitate to run over to nearby Zihuatanejo – you'll note the difference for sure.

SLEEPING IN IXTAPA

ARISTOS IXTAPA – UPPER – Blvd. Ixtapa – 225 room, 8 story hotel on the beach. Ixtapa's first deluxe hotel. 3 restaurants. Cafeteria. Bar. Disco. Pool. Shopping arcade. Gym. Beauty shop. Travel agency. Parking. AE, MC, VI. Ph: 553-0011. US: 800-527-4786. Fax: 553-2031.

DORADO PACIFICO – UPPER – Good 285 room, 14 story hotel on beach. 5 restaurants. Coffee shop. Bars. Club. 2 pools. Tennis. Boutiques. Drug store. Travel agency. Parking. AE, MC, VI. Ph: 553-2025. US: 800-448-8355. Fax: 553-0126.

DOUBLETREE RESORT — UPPER — Blvd. Ixtapa. 281 elegant rooms including 26 suites all with balcony and view of the ocean. 4 restaurants. Bar. SATV. Pool. Jacuzzi. Tennis. Gym. Water sports. Travel agency. Disco. AE, MC, VI. Ph: 553-0003 Fax: 553-1555.

FONTÁN – UPPER – 480 room, 8 story hotel on beach. Restaurants. Bars. Pool. Tennis. Parking. AE, MC, VI. Ph: 553-0033.

HOLIDAY INN SUNSPREE RESORT — UPPER — Blvd. Ixtapa. 195 plush rooms and suites with views of the ocean or the mountains. 5 junior suites. Electronic locks. SATV. 3 restaurants. Bar. Cafeteria. Pool. Water sports. Tennis. Gym. Horseback riding. Travel agency. Car rentals. Free parking. Wheelchair friendly. AE, DIN, MC, VI. Ph: 553-1066 Fax: 553-1991 US: 1-800-HOLIDAY, MEX: 91-800-00999.

KRYSTAL IXTAPA – UPPER – Blvd. Ixtapa – Lovely 254 room, 10 story hotel on beach. 5 restaurants. Bars. Disco. Pool. Tennis. Racquetball. In-room closed circuit movies. Servibars. Travel agency. Drugstore. Car rental. Shopping arcade. Parking. AE, MC, VI. Ph: 553-0333. US: 800-231-9860. Fax: 553-0216.

POSADA REAL – MOD – Good buy. 110 room, 4 story hotel on beach. SATV. Restaurant. Bar. Pool. Tennis. Curio shop. Travel agency. Parking. Small pets OK. AE, MC, VI. Ph: 553-1925, 553-1625. Fax: 553-1805. Mex: 91-5-669-4354.

QUALTON CLUB IXTAPA — UPPER — 160-room resort On the scenic highway just pas marina on beach. 2 restaurants. Bar. Pool. Jacuzzi. Tennis. Travel Agency. Disco. AE, MC, VI. Ph: 552-0080 Fax: 552-0070. MEX: 91-800-90496.

RIVIERA IXTAPA – MOD-UPPER – Blvd. Ixtapa – 138 room, 11 story hotel on beach. Restaurants. Disco. Pool. Tennis. Coffee shop. Boutique. Tobacco shop. Parking. AE, MC, VI. Ph: 553-1066. US: 800-343-7821. Fax: 553-1991. Mostly time share.

SHERATON RESORT IXTAPA – UPPER – Blvd. Ixtapa – Terrific 332 room, 12 story hotel on beach. 4 restaurants. Coffee shop. Piano bar. Pool. Shopping arcade. Tennis. Water sports. Travel agency. Barber and beauty shop. Parking. AE, MC, VI. Ph: 553-1858 Fax: 553-2438. US: 800-325-3535. MEX: 91-800-90325.

PRESIDENTE INTERCONTINENTAL – UPPER – Blvd. Ixtapa – Good 304 room, 11 story hotel on beach.

4 restaurants. Coffee shop. Bars. SATV. Multilevel pool. Tennis. Travel agency. Shopping arcade. Parking. AE, MC, VI. Ph: 553-0018 Fax: 553-2312. US: 800-468-3571 MEX: 91-800-90444.

VILLA DEL LAGO — UPPER — At Retorno de las Alondras #244. Bed and breakfast located at the Ixtapa golf course. 6 suites. SATV. Restaurant. Bar. Pool. AE, MC, VI. Ph: 553-1482 Fax: 553-1422.

WESTIN BRISAS IXTAPA – UPPER – Play Vista Hermosa – Luxurious 428 room, 14 story hotel on beach. 6 suites with private pool. 5 restaurants. 4 bars. 3 Pools. Servibars. Shops. Golf. Tennis. Parking. AE, MC, VI. Ph: 553-2121 Fax: 553-0751 US: 800-228-3000 MEX: 91-800-90223.

EATING IN IXTAPA

BECOFINO — MOD — Located in the Marina Ixtapa complex, overlooking the marina. Excellent Italian food: pastas, seafood and steaks. Desserts are out of this world. Open noon till 11 PM. AE, MC, VI. Ph: 3-1170

BOGART'S – MOD – Next to Krystal Hotel – International cuisine. Casablanca atmosphere. Ph: 553-0333.

BUCANEROS — MOD — Plaza Marina Ixtapa. The best international seafood. Ph: 553-0916.

CARLOS 'N' CHARLIE'S – MOD – Tropical restaurant next to Posada Real Hotel on beach. Barbeque ribs and seafood specialty. Open daily 1 PM till 1 AM (Closed Tuesdays). AE, MC, VI. Ph: 553-1085.

DA BAFFONE – MOD – Italian restaurant in La Puerta shopping center with terrace dining. All sorts of Italian specialties including Spaghetti Buoni. Also good soups, salads and BBQ ribs. Open 6 PM till midnight daily. AE, MC, VI. Ph: 553-1122.

EL SOMBRERO – UPPER – Los Patios shopping center – Excellent German and international food. Ph: 553-0439

EL TOKO TUCAN – MOD –Los Patios shopping center local #5. Good natural foods and burgers. Ph: 553-0717.

GOLDEN COLLUE – MOD – Los Patios shopping center – Inexpensive breakfast.

HACIENDA DE IXTAPA – MOD – Coffee shop in La Puerta shopping center. Mexican and American food. Open 8 AM till 10 PM daily. MC, VI. Ph: 553-0602.

LA OVEJA — MOD — Very good Mexican restaurant a few doors down from Sr. Frog's in the La Puerta shopping center. All dishes freshly prepared with real home-cooked flavor. Excellent soups and Mexican-style seafood and meat dishes. Open noon till 11 PM.

LA MISION — MOD — Los Patios shopping center Local #50. Mexican food.

LOS KAKTOS — MOD — Restaurant Club Bar 50 meters from the Airport. Pool. Billiards. Ping-pong. Dominoes. Ph: 554-7180.

LOS MANDILES — MOD — The best Mexican food and seafood. Open 2 PM till 11:30 PM.

MARINA CAFE — MOD — At Marina. Specialties are pizza sushi and mongol. Ph: 553-2288.

MC'S PRIME RIBE —MOD — Los Patios shopping center. Salad bar and prime rib. Ph: 553-0717.

MONTMARTRE – UPPER – Elegant restaurant in front of Fonatur office serving superb French cuisine as well as seafood. Open during winter season from 6 PM till 11:30 PM daily. AE, MC, VI. Ph: 553-0919.

PIZZERIA MAMA NORMA – MOD – Across from Presidente Intercontinental. Ph: 3-0274.

RAFAELLO'S PIZZA — MOD — Paseo Ixtapa #6. Pizza and pastas. Free delivery. Ph: 553-0092, 552-2386.

SR. FROG'S — MOD — Located in the La Puerta shopping center, it is part of the Carlos and Charlie chain. Imaginative soups, salads, Mexican food, seafood and steaks. Open 1 PM till midnight. AE, MC, VI.

SOLEIADO — MOD — In front of Double tree Resort. Mediterranean flavors. Ambiance and music. Canadian owners. Ph: 553-2101.

THE LIGHTHOUSE — MOD — Restaurant and bar next to Posada Real Hotel. Sensational and creative international cuisine. Full salad bar. Open daily 6 PM till Midnight. Ph: 553-1190, 553-1625.

VILLA DE LA SELVA – UPPER – Good restaurant near the Westin Resort Ixtapa. International and Mexican specialties plus seafood. Fabulous video of sunsets from cliff top settings. Open daily from 6 PM till 1 AM. AE, MC, VI. Ph: 553-0362.

VILLA SAKURA – UPPER – Great Japanese restaurant on hotel strip with lovely oriental gardens. Japanese specialties including Tempura, Sashimi, Yakitori, Tepanyaki, Yakimeshi and Shabu-Shabu. Good service. Open noon till 1 AM. AE, MC, VI. Ph: 553-0272.

DISCOS

Local night life can be found at Cristine, Visage, Euforia and Magic Circus and of course, Sr. Frog's.

End of Ixtapa Eat & Stray

Zihuatanejo

Area Code — 755

ZIHUATANEJO, (sometimes nicknamed: "Zihua" – Airport code: Zih) once a little port known for its lumber and ore shipments to the Orient, has awakened from its ageless lethargy, although it still remains a peaceful and relaxing town. From a village of a few thousand in the 1960's, it's grown to a town of 25,000 today – and still counting. Zihuatanejo was once called "Cihuatlán" (meaning land of women in Nahuatl, the Aztecs' language), so named because of a then-existent strong matriarchate.

Unlike its nearby neighbor, Ixtapa, Zihua is laid-back and quiet. Folks who come here are less into glamour and glitz than tucked away places and "getting away from it all." You'll probably fall in love with one or the other of them. Each has its own charm.

"Zihua" is famous for its many beautiful and secluded beaches. While Playa Principal, the downtown beach starting at the foot of the pier, lined by economy hotels and open-air seafood restaurants, is the most crowded and the least attractive, there are several other tropical and unspoiled beaches. Like Playa Madera (wood) just a short walk from downtown, so named because of the valuable wood and lumber (as well as silks and clothes) which were shipped the world over from there. It is the smallest of Zihuatanejo's beaches. Then in the middle of Zihuatanejo's bay is La Ropa Beach. Its name means "The Clothes" because according to local legend, a Chinese ship wrecked off the bay centuries ago and the crew's clothes drifted ashore. La Ropa, a little over a mile long is the beach most preferred by tourists because of its soft, white sand. And finally there is La Gatas Beach, looking more like a South Sea lagoon. Many guidebooks will tell you it means "the cats," but it isn't necessarily so. Thanks to the erudite authority on the area, Frank "Pancho" Shiell, we can give you the straight scoop. It's really named for the docile nurse-sharks that live in the neighborhood. Their whiskers are pretty long, so you could confuse them with a cat if ....

This beautiful beach was the "swimming pool" that Caltzontzin, the last of the Tarascan kings, built for his daughter, which was a wall of stones serving as a "breaker" to provide calm water and to keep out sea predators. This "breakwater" still remains, challenging times. Las Gatas is the scuba diver's and snorkeler's paradise, edged by palms and unspoiled with its crystalline water and coral reef. There are many little restaurants on the beach, selling live clams etc.

FISHING — Arrangements can be made at the "muelle" (pier) for half-day (4 hours) or full-day (8 hours) trips. Both large and small boats are available and carry a maximum of 8 persons. Prices quoted usually include tackle, bait and license.

EXCURSION BOATS — Boats are available over to Ixtapa Island and to Las Gatas Beach where sailboats, rowboats and surfboards can be rented. Sailboats and water-skiing boats are also for rent at La Ropa Beach and in front of Sotavento Hotel. The Catamaran "Tequila" departs daily at 11 AM from the municipal pier on a sightseeing and snorkeling cruise (cold drinks and lunch included, Ph: 554-2056).

DIVING — SCUBA DIVING GEAR can be acquired at Duran's and Oliverio's, both on Las Gatas Beach. Scuba diving instruction is also available.

SHOPPING — El Embarcadero is an interesting shop located in the downtown beachfront Hotel Casa Marina next to the plaza and features curios, crafts and clothing. Also worthwhile are the flea market at Ejido and 5 de Mayo, featuring Mexican arts and crafts and the handicrafts market near the port of entry on the principal public beach. Ruby's on Cuauhtémoc #7 has fine jewelry and sculpture.

IXTAPA AA — Go on the canal road towards Playa Madero. Pass La Boquita bakery. Turn towards Hotel Solimar. On one side of plaza is Spanish AA. Across the plaza is the English-speaking group. Thurs. 6 PM. Alanon and AA contact (7) 534-3767.

SLEEPING IN ZIHUATANEJO

AMUEBLADOS ISABEL – MOD – Located at Pedro Ascencio #11. 6 bungalows. A/C. Restaurant. Parking. Ph: 554-3661 Fax: 554-2669.

AVILA — MOD — 27-room A/C beachside hotel at Juan Alvarez #8. Restaurant. Bar. Parking. Ph and Fax: 554-2010.

BUNGALOWS ALLEC – MOD – Playa Madera – 12 bungalows. Ceiling fans. Some for 2 people, most for 4. Parking. Ph: 554-2002.

BUNGALOWS SOTELO — MOD — 10 A/C beachside bungalows on Playa La Madera. Restaurant. Bar. Parking.

CLUB DE PLAYA LAS GATAS – MOD – Rustic beach front "Polynesian" layout with 6 thatched-roof bungalows on Las Gatas Beach, reached only by boat. Restaurant (breakfast and dinner only). No pool. Parking. Pets OK.

FIESTA MEXICANA – MOD – La Ropa Beach – 60 A/C rooms. 2 restaurants. Bar. Pool. Palapa. Parking. AE, MC, VI. Ph: 554-3636 or 554-3776. Fax: 554-3738.

IMELDA – MOD – Catalina Gonzáles #11 – Center of town. Look at room first. Ph: 554-3199

IRMA – MOD – 80 room inn on cliff above La Madera Beach overlooking bay (separated from beach by outcropping rock). Some A/C. Restaurant. Bar. 2 pools. Parking. AE, MC, VI. Ph: 554-2025 or 554-2105. Fax: 554-3738.

LARIS – MOD – VALUE! At Altamirano #4 next to Peppers. 14 rooms. Parking. Ph: 554-3767.

OMAR – ECON – La Ropa Beach – 14 rooms and 1 bungalow. Budget. MC, VI. Ph: 554-3873.

PALACIOS – MOD – 20 room, 3 story hotel on Playa Madera. Restaurant. Small pool. On-street parking. Ph: 554-2055. Well kept.

PASEO DEL HUJAL – MOD – Paseo del Hujal #168 at corner of Oyamel. 35 A/C rooms. CATV. Cafeteria. Pool. Ph: 554-2071. Fax: 554-6289. E-mail: hpaseo@cdnet.com.mx

POSADA CARACOL – MOD – 57 room A/C hotel above Play Madera. Open-air restaurant. Bar. Disco. Pool. Parking. AE, MC, VI. Ph: 554-2035 or 554-2446.

RAUL TRES MARÍAS – MOD – Center of town at Juan Alvarez #52. 17 A/C rooms. Restaurant. Bar. Parking. Ph: 4-2977. There is another one also at Noria #48. 25 rooms. No A/C fans only. Ph: 554-2191.

SOLIMAR INN – MOD – Center of town on Plaza Los Faroles. 12 A/C suites. Pool. Travel agency. Ph: 554-3692.

SOTAVENTO-CATALINA – MOD – Actually two hotels under same management atop hill above La Ropa Beach. Sotavento offers 80 rooms with fans. Catalina also offers 40 rooms. Restaurant with open-air dining terrace. 3 bars. No pool. Parking. AE, MC, VI. Ph: 554-2032, 554-2074, 554-2033, 554-2034 or 554-2137. Fax: 554-2975.

VILLA DEL SOL – UPPER – 36 A/C suite complex on Playa La Ropa. One of the nicest, most romantic hotels in Mexico! Huge cabañas with pedestal beds. Hammocks on the front porch. NO children under 14. Sophisticated "villa in a jungle" atmosphere. Private balconies. Restaurant. Bar. Pool. Jacuzzi. Tennis. Parking. MC, VI. Ph: 554-2239 or 554-3239 Fax: 554-2758 US: 800-223-6510 MEX: 91-800-09340.

VILLAS MIRAMAR – MOD – Secluded, very nice A/C 18 room, 2 story hotel on Playa de la Madera. Restaurant. Bar. 2 Pools. Parking. A good buy! MC, VI. Ph: 554-2106 Fax: 554-2149 MEX: 91-800-90223.

EATING IN ZIHUATANEJO

BAY CLUB – MOD - On the road to Playa La Ropa – View of bay is lovely. Live jazz. Mesquite grill. Ph: 554-4844.

CANAIMA – MOD – Paseo del Pescador and Juan Alvarez – Popular open-air/enclosed restaurant downtown. Specializes in seafood. Open 1 PM till 11 PM. MC, VI. Ph: 554-2003.

CASA ELVIRA – MOD – Paseo del Pescador #16 – Mexican food. Ph: 554-2061.

COCONUTS – UPPER – Av. Agustín Ramírez #1 – Popular gathering spot, especially the bar. Specializes in seafood and Mexican dishes. Open noon till 1 AM. Ph: 554-2518. Closed Sept. and Oct.

DELI — ECON — A couple of blocks down from the tourist mercado, downtown at Cuauhtémoc #12. This restaurant is as simple as its name, but oh what good home cooking! Excellent soups and guacamole. Tortas, tacos and fish. Expresso and capuchino coffee. Open 8 AM till midnight.

EL MARLIN – MOD – Isla Ixtapa and La Ropa Beach – Seafood restaurant. Ph: 554-3766.

EL PICCOLO – MOD – Nicolás Bravo #29 – Small, neat restaurant. International cuisine offering several unusual specialties.

GARROBOS – MOD – Juan Alvarez #52 – Clean, plain restaurant downtown. Seafood specialties plus steaks and Mexican dishes. MC, VI. Ph: 554-2977.

LA CASA VIEJA — MOD — On La Madera Beach at Josefa Ortiz de Domínguez #7. American run with excellent seafood and Mexican food. Fresh handmade tortillas. Open 2 PM till midnight.

LA GAVIOTA – MOD – Informal palapa-style restaurant on La Ropa Beach. Terrific seafood! Ph: 554-3816.

LA MESA DEL CAPITÁN – MOD – Nicolás Bravo #18 – Popular restaurant resembling an old ship downtown. Traditional seafood plus all sorts of other dishes and famous Irish coffee. Close Sunday. MC, VI. Ph: 554-2027.

LA PERLA – MOD – Rustic style, palapa, open air restaurant right on the beach Play la Ropa – Freshest seafood in town. Open 9 AM till 10 PM. MC, VI. Ph: 554-2700.

LA SIRENA GORDA – MOD – Paseo del Pescador #20-A – Seafood, tacos and breakfast. Ph: 554-2687.

NUEVA ZELANDA – ECON – In center of town at Cuauhtémoc #23 – Juices, fruits and hamburgers. Popular with locals. Ph: 553-2340.

PEPPER'S GARDEN – MOD – Ignacio Altamirano #46 – VALUE! 6 blocks east from beach at the beginning of town. Patio dining. Bright and cheery. Tamales. Chicken in banana leaves. Authentic Mexican food. Ph: 554-3767.

TABOGA – MOD – Juan Alvarez and 5 de Mayo – Restaurant in front of Aero-Mexico. Various meats and seafood. Closed Sunday. Ph: 554-2637.

CAMPING & RV PARKING

The Playa Linda bit the dust, but an enterprising fellow is building one near Playa La Ropa. Check it out. Give him a try.

DISCOS

Local night life can be found at Bay Club-Samba Cafe. It offers dancing to live jazz and salsa under the stars.

End of Zihua Eat & Stray

Acapulco

Area Code — 744

Acapulco has a population of 1,500,000. Climate is warm sub-humid, the average annual temperature is 27° C or 80° F. with rainfall during Summer and the beginning of Autumn. The vegetation is tropical forest.

ACCOMMODATIONS — Expensive: in the "Golden Zone" or "Zona Dorada" between the airport and the zócalo. CHEAP: around the zócalo (main square). INTERESTING: in the old section, called "Romantic Acapulco," "Traditional Acapulco" or "Caleta section." Boarding houses and apartments abound. Like Mazatlán, those who call this a "rich man's" city just don't know what they're talking about! There's a Mexican saying that you can come to Acapulco with a dollar in your pocket or a hundred dollars (before inflation) and still have a good time. I've done both. Hotel rates during the off season (May-November) usually run from 15-30% less.

AA — English speaking group meets at Horacio Nelson #250. Turn (away from water) off Costera at traffic light down from Days Inn at intersection with Oceanic 2000 and Sanborn's on beachside and with 100% Natural and Banca Confía across street on corners. Go one block to Calle Horacio Nelson and turn right. AA Club is about mid-block at #250 on beachside of street across from Euzkadi tires/Splash Car Wash. Wed, Fri, 5 PM. Call Richard. Ph: (74) 484-1022 or 484-6854 Fax: 484-6854.

CLIFF DIVERS — Evening performances (at 7:15, 8:15, 9:15, 10:15) are held at La Quebrada below Hotel EL Mirador. 3-4 dives per show. Ph: 482-1111 or 483-1155.

CRUISES — Glass-bottomed boats depart daily at 11:00 AM and 12:45 PM from the ski club on the Costera (Ph: 2-4313) or from Caleta Beach (below Hotel Caleta). You'll see the underwater world with its many varieties of tropical fish plus the famous underwater Guadalupe Shrine. YACHTS — The "Fiesta" and "Bonanza" (Ph: 82-6262 or 82-2055) or the "Sea Cloud" (Ph: 482-0785 or 482-1217) offer 2.5 hour cruises daily. Morning cruises sail at 10:30 AM, afternoon cruises at 4:30 PM and moonlight cruises ("lunadas") at 10:30 PM. Tickets sold at the pier, at most hotels and on the street. All three vessels have open bars and live music, and the "Bonanza" boasts a swimming pool.

DIVING ("Buceo") — Ask about the safety record of each from the tourist office. They vary greatly. Some dive shops are Divers de México (82-1398), the Agua-Mundo (82-1041) with two offices on the Costera (one by the Ski Club and another near the Bali Hai), the Arnold Brothers (have a good reputation, Ph: 82-0788) or the Perro Largo ("long dog"), also on the Costera. Check your equipment carefully — (particularly regulators) not well cared for.

FOLKLORIC BALLET OF GUERRERO — Folkloric dancing from the Mexican states of Jalisco, Michoacán, Yucatán, Veracruz and Guerrero is featured each Wednesday and Sunday at 9:00 PM at Netzahualcoyotl Theater at the convention center. Reservations and tickets are available at Turismo Caleta.

GOLF — The Hotels Acapulco Princess (Ph: 484-3100) and Pierre Marques (Ph: 484-2000) have 18-hole golf courses, and the city of Acapulco's Club de Golf is located along the Costera opposite the Elcano (Ph: 484-0781).

HORSE-DRAWN CARRIAGES ("Calesas" or "Calandrias" — they're like "Pulmonias" in Mazatlán) — This interesting means of transportation is packed up and down the Costera. Agree on a set rice before going.

KIDS — CiCi, a giant water-park on the Costera in the Gold Zone, across from the Embassy. Fish and animals, rides, shows, different ways to get wet. Ph: 484-1970. Recommended. Papagayo Park — 60 acres of rides and tropical scenery. At the old Papagayo Hotel site, on Costera at Hornos Beach. Acapulco Aquarium, Mágico Mundo Marino on the Caleta Beach Pier, displays more than 35 types of marine life native to the Mexican Riviera, fish from all over the world and other aquatic sea life. It also has a pool for the kids to play in, a museum, lookout deck and a miniature beach club. Open daily 9 AM till 5 PM, closed Tues. Admission charged. Acapulco Zoo — Roqueta Island — Small boat ride to Island (small charge). Displays some animals in their natural habitat. Also has a playground for the kids. In the future, they have plans to build an auditorium. Admission charged.

SAILBOATS, PARACHUTE RIDES and WATER SKIING — These are available at most beachfront hotels on the Costera. Be sure to set your price in advance. Remember — parachute at your own risk.

SPORT FISHING — Fishing is usually excellent year round for sailfish, marlin, dolphin, bonito, pompano, mackerel, red snapper, barracuda, etc. Make arrangements with a travel agency, or directly with the fishermen's union at the wharf. Prices vary depending on size of boat and number of persons fishing (including bait and tackle; food and refreshments extra). Freshwater fishing is available at Coyuca Lagoon at Pie de la Cuesta. Be sure to see your boat before you pay.

TENNIS — Public courts at Av. Prado off the Costera (Ph: 484-0004). A few private tennis clubs are open to the public such as Club del Mar a block off the Costera behind Hotel Arabela (Ph: 484-5260) and the Villa Vera Racket Club on the hill across from Hotel El Presidente (Ph: 484-0333). Some of the deluxe hotels including the Acapulco Princess, Pierre Marques, Hyatt Regency, El Matador and Hyatt Continental have rental tennis courts (but guests are first preference).

TOURISM OFFICE — State — Centro Internacional Acapulco, Ph: 484-750 or Costera # 54 Ph: 484-1014. Federal — Costera #187, Ph: 485-1041. Acapulco Tourist office — Priv. Roca Sola, Ph: 484-7621 or 484-7630 Fax: 484-8134.

CONSULATES — AUSTRIA — J. R. Escudero #1-2, Centro — 482-5551, 482-2166. CANADA — Diane McClean, Club del Sol Hotel, local #7 — 485-6600, 485-6621. FEDERAL REPUBLIC OF GERMANY — Mario Wichtendahl, Antón de Alaminos #46, Fracc. Costa Azul — 484-7437, 484-1860. FINLAND — Costera Miguel Alemán #500 — 484-7641, 484-0986. FRANCE — Vidal Mendoza Bravo, Av. Costa Grande #235 — 482-3394. GREAT BRITAIN — Derek Gore, Las Brisas Hotel — 485-1650, 484-6605. ITALY — Giussepe Cavagna, Gran Vía Tropical #615-B Fracc. Las Playas — 483-3875, 484-7050 Ext. 116-17. HOLLAND — Angel Díaz Acosta, El Presidente Hotel — 484-1700, 484-1800. NORWAY — Maralisa Hotel, Enrique El Esclavo s/n — 484-3525. PANAMA — Ignacio de la LLave #2, Centro Edificio Oviedo — 482-3259. SPAIN — Tomás Lagar, Av. Cuauhtémoc y Universidad #2 — 485-7500, 485-7049. SWEDEN — Av. Insurgentes #2, Fracc. Hornos Insurgentes — 485-2935. UNITES STATES OF AMERICA — Bon Urbanek, Club del Sol Hotel — 485-6600, 485-6621.

ESA COSA NO SE DICE — Barra de Coyuca, Gro. At end of Pie de la Cuesta road. Ask for Timo's boat Araceli. Good ride.

MISCELLANEOUS — Pharmacy — Farmacia Americana located at Horacio Nelson #40 directly across from Days Inn and Baby O's. Owner Tom Alexander speaks English and is a great guy.

SLEEPING IN ACAPULCO

ACAPULCO DAYS INN – MOD – Costera #2310 – (Formerly Romano's Le Club) NICE. 328-room, 20-story hotel across from Baby O's disco. Restaurant. Bar. Disco. Club. Pool. Boutique. Jeep rentals. Limited parking garage and more on-street parking. AE, MC, VI. Ph: 484-5332.

ACAPULCO IMPERIAL – MOD – Costera west of Diana Circle – 100-room, 10-story midtown hotel across street from beach. No restaurant (except for breakfast). Pool. Servibars. Curio and tobacco shop. Beauty shop. Parking. AE, MC, VI. Ph: 482-4768, 482-2861. Fax: 483-0575. Mex: 01-800-710-9333. E-mail: imperial@hamacas.com.mx

ACAPULCO MALIBU – MOD – Av. Alemán #20 – Octagon-shaped 80-large-room, 7-story beachfront hotel east of Diana Circle. Restaurants. Pool. Servibars. Parking. AE, MC, VI. Ph: 484-1070, 484-0369 or 484-0320. Fax: 484-0475.

ACAPULCO PARK – UPPER – A family hotel at Av. Costera Miguel Alemán 127. 88 A/C rooms. CATV. Pool. Tennis. Secure parking. AE, MC, VI. Fax: 485-5489. E-Mail: hotel@parkhotel-acapulco.com

ACAPULCO PLAZA – UPPER – Costera #123 – Deluxe 28-story, 1008-room beachfront hotel. 5 restaurants. 5 bars. Pools. Servibars. Tennis. Jacuzzi. Shops. Health club. Golf nearby. AE, MC, VI. Ph: 485-9050. US: 800-HOLIDAY. Fax: 485-5493. Holiday Inn.

ACAPULCO PRINCESS – UPPER – Revolcadero Beach – Fabulous 1019-room, 15-story resort hotel out near airport. Restaurants. Coffee shop. Clubs. Huge lobby bar. Discos. Salt- and fresh- water pools. Sauna. Tennis (indoor-outdoor). 18-hole, par-72 golf course. Shopping arcade. Health club. Valet parking. AE, MC, VI. Ph: 484-3100, 469-1000, 469-1015 Fax: 469-1016. US: 800-223-1818.

ACAPULCO TORREBLANCA – MOD – Majahua #25 – 250-room, 16-story condo hotel. Restaurant. Pool. Parking. AE, MC, VI.

ACAPULCO TORTUGA – MOD – Costera #132 – 8-story, 252-room hotel a block down and across from Condesa del Mar. Restaurants. Bars. Pool. Sauna. Massage. Parking. AE, MC, VI. Ph: 484-8889. Fax: 484-7385. E-Mail: tortugaaca@webtelmex.net.mx

ALBA – See Suites Alba de Acapulco.

ARBELA DEL PACIFICO – MOD – Costera #55, east of Diana Circle –50-room, 9-story hotel near convention center. Restaurant. Club. Pool. Travel agency. Drugstore. Silver shop. Parking. MC, VI. Ph: 484-2164.

AREKA SUITES – MOD – Small, 13-unit hotel on cliffside in older part of town behind Boca Chica. No restaurant. Pool. Kitchenettes. Parking. AE, MC. Ph: 482-2066.

BALI-HAI – MOD – Costera #186 – 121-unit, 2-story motor hotel west of Diana Circle across street from beach. Restaurant. Pool. Parking. AE, MC, VI. Ph: 485-6622, 485-7045. Fax: 485-7972.

BARCELÓ PANORAMIC – MOD – Condesa – 200-room hotel downtown. 2 restaurants. Bar. Pool. Tennis. Parking. AE, MC, VI. Ph: 484-0724, 484-0709, Fax: 484-8639. Marvelous view of Calesa Beach and downtown. E-Mail: informes@barcelo-panoramic.com

BAY CLUB ACAPULCO – M0D – Costera Miguel Alemán #266, Fracc. Hornos. 118 A/C rooms. Restaurant. Pool with bar. Parking. Travel Agency. 485-4545, 485-4364, 485-4602, 482-8228. Fax: 485-0774.

BELMAR – MOD – Gran Vía Tropical y Cumbres s/n, Frac. Las Playas, 1/2 block from Caleta Beach. 77 rooms (A/C or fan). Restaurant. Pool. Parking. MC, VI. Ph: 483-8098, 483-8098. Fax: 483-8098.

BOCA CHICA – MOD – Caleta Beach – 3-story, 45-room hotel. Restaurant. Pool. Water sports. Parking. AE, MC, VI. Ph: 483-6388, 483-9515. Fax: 483-9513. US: 1-800-346-3942. E-Mail: bocach@acabtu.com.mx

CALETA – UPPER – At the end of the Costera, (actually Gran Via Tropical) across from Roquetta Island – Old-time favorite. This is a truly fine old hotel with character, charm and luxury. The rates are reasonable for its caliber. 260 rooms, 9 stories of elegance. Huge suites. Parking. Restaurants. AE, MC, VI. Ph: 483-9940, 483-9334.

CALINDA BEACH ACAPULCO – MOD – Costera #1260 – 358-room, 28-story motor inn in round tower east of Diana Circle. Restaurants. Coffee shop. 4 lounges. Disco. Pools. Shopping arcade. Parking. AE, MC, VI. Ph: 484-0410. Fax: 484-4676. E-Mail: calinda@acabtu.com.mx

CAMINO REAL ACAPULCO DIAMANTE – UPPER – In the new Diamante area, fringing Pichilingue Beach on Puerto Marquez Bay. 155 rooms. Pools. All the amenities. MC, VI. Ph: 481-2010. Reservations in US or Canada: 1-800-7-CAMINO.

CASA LE MAR – MOD – Lomas del Mar #32-B – Bed and Breakfast in private home. Mostly gay male clientele "with women genuinely welcome" as owner Richard Dean says. Vegetarian meals available with one day advance notice. Pool and 1 minute walk to beach. To get there, turn right off Costera by Denney's onto Lomas del Mar. At top of hill, turn right, then immediately left. Ph: 484-1022, 484-6854. Fax: 484-6854.

CLUB DEL SOL – MOD – Costera – 300-room, 4-story hotel across street from beach. Restaurant. Bar. Pool. Shopping arcade. Travel agency. Beauty shop. Parking. AE, MC, VI. Ph: 485-6600.

CLUB DORADOS – MOD – Av. Universidad y Dr. Ignacio Chávez, Fracc. La Bocana. 57 A/C rooms. Restaurant. Bar. Pool. Ph: 487-4600, 487-4646. Fax: 487-4624.

CLUB VERANO BEAT – ECON – Costera #482 – Nice 82-suite hotel, accross from Marina and yacht club. Restaurant. Bar. Pool. Servibars. Tennis. Squash. Baby sitting. Parking. AE, MC, VI. Ph: 482-5790. Fax: 482-5793.

CONTINENTAL PLAZA – UPPER – Costera – Nice 435-room, 11-story hotel at Diana Circle. Restaurant. 24-hour coffee shop. Disco. Huge pool. Shopping arcade. Tennis. Parking. AE, MC, VI. Ph: 484-0909 Fax: 484-2021.

COPACABANA – UPPER – Costera Miguel Alemán #130 Tabachines #2 – Nice 18-story, 422-room A/C beachfront hotel a couple of blocks from convention center. Restaurant. Bar. Pool. Tennis and golf across street. Parking. AE, MC, VI. Ph: 484-3260 or 484-3155. Fax: 484-6268. Romano chain.

COSTA CLUB – UPPER – Costera Miguel Alemán #123. 506 Deluxe A/C rooms including 28 Junior Suites, 48 Bay Suites, 2 Governor Suites and one Presidential Suite. SATV. Tub and shower. 4 restaurants. Bars. 4 pools. Tennis. Health club. AE, MC, VI. Ph: 485-9050. Fax: 485-5493. Mex: 01-800-093-4900. US: 1-800-53SUITE. e-mail: costclub@webtelmex.net.mx

COSTA LINDA – MOD – Costera Miguel Alemán 1008. 44 A/C rooms. Pool. Tennis. Parking. Ph: 482-5277, 482-2549. Fax: 483-4017.

DALIAS ACAPULCO – ECON – Calzada Caletilla #20, Las Playas. 30 A/C rooms. Pool. Parking. Ph: 483-0518, 483-0446. Fax: 482-6308.

DORAL PLAYA – MOD – Costera #265 – 150-room, 10-story hotel west of Diana Circle across from beach. Restaurant. Coffee shop. Club. Pool. Parking. AE, MC, VI. Rather noisy. Romano chain. Ph: 485-0232, 485-0103. Fax: 485-7065.

DORAL SUITES – MOD – 19-apartment, 8-story complex east of Diana Circle not far from beach. One- and two-bedroom units. No restaurant. Small pool. Private terraces. Kitchens. AE, MC. Ph: 84-1575.

EL CANO – UPPER – Av. Costera Miguel Aleman 75. Really nice, quiet and recently remodeled, 140-room, 9-story hotel a block east of Diana Circle on beach. Open-air restaurant. Pool. Gym. Shops. Parking. AE, MC, VI. Ph: 435-1500 Fax: 484-2230. E-Mail: elcano@hotel-elcano.com.mx

EL CID – MOD – Costera #248 – 140-room, 6-story hotel west of Diana Circle across street from beach. Restaurant. Bar. Pool. On-street parking. AE, MC, VI. Ph: 485-1312. Fax: 485-1387. Reasonable. E-Mail: 104164.30@compuserve.com

EL DORADO – MOD – 20-room, 22-story hotel on side street near convention center. No restaurant. Pool. On-street parking. AE, MC, VI.

EL PRESIDENTE – UPPER – Costera #89 – 400-room, 15-story twin-tower beachfront hotel east of Diana Circle. 3 restaurants. Pools. Boutiques. Drugstore. Tobacco shop. Travel agency. Arts and crafts shop. Parking. AE, MC, VI. Ph: 484-1700 or 484-1800. US: 800-777-1700. Fax: 484-1376. E-Mail: hotpresi@infosel.net.mx

FIESTA AMERICANA CONDESA – UPPER – Costera Miguel Alemán #1220 east of Diana Circle on Condesa Beach – Luxurious 500-room, 17-story hotel. 5 restaurants including rooftop supper club. Lobby bar. SATV. Disco. Pools. Parking. AE, MC, VI. Ph: 484-2828 Fax: 484-1828. US: 800-345-5094.

HOLIDAY INN ACAPULCO – UPPER – Costera M. Alemán #123 – 1,008 rooms. Restaurant. Bar. Pool. Tennis. Health club. Gift shop. AE, MC, VI. Ph: 485-8050 Fax: 485-5285

HOWARD JOHNSON MARALISA – MOD – Calle Alemania s/n, just off Costera – 89-room, 4-story beachfront west of Diana Circle. Restaurant. Disco. Pools (one therapeutic). Newsstand. Parking. AE, MC, VI. Ph: 485-6677 or 485-6730. Fax: 485-9228. US: 1-800-I-GO-HOJO. E-mail: maralisa@aca-novenet.com.mx

HYATT REGENCY ACAPULCO – UPPER – Costera #1 – Very nice 640-room, 24-story hotel on east end. CATV. 3 restaurants. 24-hour coffee shop. Club. Disco. Pool. Tennis. Shopping. Sauna. Parking. AE, MC, VI. Ph: 469-1234 or 484-2888. Fax: 484-1513, 484-5509. US: 800-233-1234. E-mail: mespinosa@acabtu.com.mx

LA JOLLA – MOD – 74-unit, 3-story motel across from Yacht Club near Caleta Beach. Restaurant. Pool. Parking. MC, VI. Ph: 482-5862, 482-5858.

LA PALAPA – MOD – Fragata Yucatán #210 – 340-suite, 30-story hotel a long block off Costera in area behind Posada del Sol. Restaurants. Bar. Night club. Pools. Shopping arcade. AE, MC, VI. Ph: 484-5363 or 484-5730. US: 800-334-7234. Fax: 484-8399. Best Western chain.

LAS BRISAS – UPPER – Costera, Carretera Mejía #5255 – Unique 300-pink-and-white "casita" layout sprawled on hillside east of town on road to airport. Restaurants. Club. Private beach club. Pool (plus additional private or share pools with each "casita"). Tennis. Stocked refrigerators. Boutique. Rental pink-and-white jeeps. Parking. AE, MC, VI. Ph: 484-1733, 483-1580, 484-1650. US: 800-228-3000. Fax: 484-2269. Westin chain.

LAS HAMACAS – MOD – Costera #23 – Very nice grounds and some character, 160-room, reasonably priced 5-story motor inn near downtown. Restaurant. Club. Pool. MC, VI. Ph: 483-7746, 483-7709 Fax: 483-0575. US: 800-421-0767.

LOS FLAMINGOS – MOD – Av. López Mateos and Los Flamingos – 47-room, 3-story hotel above ocean in older part of town. Some A/C. Restaurant. Pool. Parking. MC, VI. Ph: 482-0690, 482-0691 or 482-0692. Fax: 483-9806.

LOS PERICOS – MOD – Costera – 65-room hotel near downtown at Costera #465. Restaurant. Pool. Parking. AE, MC, VI. Ph: 482-0301, 482-4078. Budget only. Noisy.

MAJESTIC – MOD – Av. Pozo del Rey #73 – Marvelous place. It's an old favorite. 200-room old hotel in old part of town – just down from the Acapulco Children's Home. Restaurant. Bar. SATV. Large pool. Parking. AE, MC, VI. Ph: 483-2713 or 483-3710. Fax: 483-2032.

MARIS – MOD – Hornos Beach – 84-room, 12-story hotel. Restaurant. Pool. Club. Parking. AE, MC, VI. Ph: 485-3440, 485-8440.

MARSEY – MOD – Bargain! Just past Princess. 20 kitchenettes. Pool. Fairly quiet garden. MC, VI. Ph: 484-

3218.

MISION – ECON – Bargain value. Quiet hotel by zócalo, by old tree. At Felipe Valle #12, just off La Paz. Women traveling alone will feel perfectly safe here. Nice courtyard. Restaurant serves Pozole every Thursday and buffet every day. Ph: 482-3643.

MONTE ALEGRE – MOD – San Marcos #51 – 15-unit apartment complex in older part of town. 1- and 2-bedroom units. Kitchens. Parking. MC, VI. Ph: 482-0428.

MOZIMBA DE ACAPULCO – MOD – Playa La Angosta – 37 rooms. Restaurant. Bar. AE, MC, VI. Ph: 482-1629 or 482-2785.

PIERRE MARQUEZ – UPPER – Revolcadero Beach – Posh 341-room hotel adjacent to Acapulco Princess (same management). Restaurants. Bars. Dancing. Pools. Tennis. 18-hole, par-72 golf course. Shops. Parking. AE, MC, VI. Ph: 484-2000. Fax: 484-8554. US: 800-223-1818, US Fax: 212-371-2723. Built by late J. Paul Getty.

PLAYA HERMOSA – MOD – One block off Costera behind El Cid and across from tourist office. 20 rooms and bungalows. A writer's-type place with nice tropical gardens, sitting room and A/C library. Full breakfast included in price. Pool. No credit cards. Ph: 485-1491.

PLAYA SUITES ACAPULCO – UPPER – Av. Costera Miguel Alemán No.123. A/C Guest Rooms: 502 Suites including 408 with 2 double beds, 60 Bay Suites and 24 Penthouse with 2 double bedrooms. CATV. Bathrooms with tub & shower. Restaurant. Bar. Pool. Parking. AE, MC, VI. Ph: 485-8050. Fax: 485-8731. USA: 1-800-53 SUITE E-mail: ventas@playasuites.com.mx

PLAZA LAS GLORIAS EL MIRADOR – MOD – La Quebrada #74 – 133-room multilevel cliffside hotel. Open-air restaurant (from which you can watch famous cliff divers). Coffee shop. Pools. Shops. Parking. AE, MC, VI. Ph: 483-1155 or 483-1221. US: 800-342-AMIGO. Fax: 482-0638.

PLAZA LAS GLORIAS PARAISO – MOD-UPPER – Costera #163 – 420-room, 20-story hotel west of Diana Circle on Condesa Beach. Restaurants. Bars. Pool. Newsstand. Barber shop. Beauty shop. Parking. AE, MC, VI. Ph: 485-5050 or 485-5596. US: 800-333-3333. Fax: 485-5543.

POSADA JACARANDAS – MOD – Río Atoyac #15 – Small 10-unit apartment hotel a mile north on Hwy #95 in quiet residential area. No A/C. No restaurant. Pool. Parking. Ph: 485-5207.

ROMANCE INN ACAPULCO – UPPER – St. Vista de Brisamar No. 6, Fracc. Joyas de Brisamar. 50 A/C rooms. Restaurant. Pool. Parking. AE, MC, VI. Ph: 481-2176, 481-2180, 481-2252, 481-2200. Fax: 481-2102. Mex: 01-800-715-4812 E-Mail: informes@romanceinn-acapulco.com

SANDS – MOD – Costera #178 and Juan de la Cosa – 60-room, 5-story hotel with 34 bungalows, practically across from Continental. No restaurant. Pool. Boutique. Jeep rentals. On-street parking. AE, MC, VI. Ph: 484-2260. US: 800-422-6078. Fax: 484-1053. E-mail: sands@sands.com.mx

SHERATON ACAPULCO – UPPER – Costera Guitarrón #110 – 220-room hotel on beach. Restaurant. Bar. Pool. Health club. Water sports. Gift shop. MC, VI. Ph: 481-2222 Fax: 484-3760.

SOL-I-MAR – MOD – Cañonero Bravo #5, behind Days Inn – 80-apartment, 2-story complex a half-block from beach. 2-bedroom units. No restaurant. Pool. Parking. Ph: 484-1356.

SUITES ALBA DE ACAPULCO – MOD – Gran Via Tropical #35 – VALUE. Reasonably priced in "Romantic" zone. 200 rooms in 6 buildings and bungalows, 2 pools, restaurant, bar, roof garden with stunning view, kitchenettes. Coffee shop. Mini-supermarket. Tennis. Beach club (it's high above the beach itself, but they have transportation there), shuttle service. Ph: in D.F. 522-2374, 522-0696, ACA – 83-0073. FAX 83-8378.

VILIA – ECON – Roqueta #54 – 60-room, 5-story hotel in older part of town. Restaurant. Bar. Salt-water pool. Parking. AE, MC, VI. Ph: 483-3311.

VILLA D'ALMA – MOD – Costa Grande #111 – Private 10-room apartment hotel in older part of town below Coyuca 22 Restaurant. No restaurant. Pool. Parking. AE, MC, VI. Ph: 482-1716.

VILLA LINDA – ECON – 23 La Nao St. – Furnished apartments right behind Universidad Ave., 3 blocks from main beaches and major hotels. Kitchenettes. Pool. Garden. Off-street parking. English. Ph: 487-4412.

VILLA LOS ARCOS – MOD – Av. Monterrey #195 and Venados – 130-room hotel behind golf course. Restaurant. Pool. Limited parking. AE, MC, VI. Ph: 484-2280, 484-2295, 484-8421 or 484-2258.

VILLA VERA RACQUET CLUB – UPPER – Lomas del Mar #35 – 80-room racket club high on hill across from El Presidente. Excellent restaurant. Bar. Disco. Pool plus private pools. Jacuzzi. Tennis. Parking. AE, MC, VI. Ph: 484-0333. US: 800-223-6510. Fax: 484-7377. Where the celebrities used to put up.

BUDGET PLACES

These guest houses are put in here for the more adventurous traveler, who's on a limited budget. While they don't have the quality and standards of our recommendations, many folks have traveled all over Mexico staying at budget hotels. You look and decide for yourself. They'll often be noisier (though not always), and you're more likely to meet younger bus travellers, Mexican tourists and Europeans.

There are some less expensive places in the Gold Zone, away from the beach, towards the hill.

The inexpensive but acceptable places are around the zócalo, in the direction of Caleta and a block or two west – on and around LA PAZ and QUEBRADA streets. There are several here with prices from a few dollars to about 50% less than anywhere else. Ask to see your room first.

CALIFORNIA – La Paz #12. 25 rooms. Ph: 482-2893.

CORAL – Quebrada #56.

ISABEL – ECON – On La Paz. Nice. Ph: 482-5024

MARIE ANTONIETA – Teniente Azuelta #17. Restaurant.

PIE DE LA CUESTA

PUERTA DEL SOL – MOD – Before you get to Ukae Kim. A cut above budget, but not fancy. Strange place. Pool, but ?. Ask to see room.

UKAE KIM – MOD – Pie de la Cuesta del Sol #356 – CHARMING, ROMANTIC hideaway 22 rooms, 1 with jacuzzi, gauze-curtained double beds and most with a view. On ocean. Pool, 4 palapas, bar, restaurant, parking. Stay there with someone you love. MC, VI. Ph: 460-2187, Fax: 460-2188.

EATING IN ACAPULCO

AMIGO MIGUEL – MOD – Calle Azueta and corner of Benito Juárez. Excellent seafood including oyster and shark. Open 11 AM till 9 PM. Ph: 482-5195.

BETO'S – MOD – Costera at Condesa Beach – Tropical beachside restaurant between Presidente and Continental. Jungle-like atmosphere on beach, next to Blackbeard's. Nice view. Go down 3 flights of stairs. Mexican food, seafood, lobster and steak. Specialties include giant shrimp, steak-lobster combo, red snapper and spring chicken. Spectacular view of bay. Dancing waters. Open 10 AM till Midnight daily. VI, MC. Ph: 484-0473.

CARLOS'N'CHARLIE'S – MOD – Costera #999 – Popular second-story bar-grill practically across from El Presidente, another member of the Anderson chain of noisy, "party-hearty" attitude restaurants. Popular with younger set. International cuisine including shrimp brochette, BBQ ribs, bass, steak with mushrooms, etc. Holds drinking contests, which can be pretty rowdy. Open daily from 6:30 PM till midnight (closed Tuesdays). AE, MC, VI. Ph: 484-0039.

COCULA – MOD – Costera Alemán #497 – Open-air grill serving spare ribs, chicken, pork chops and cheese fondue as well as Cocula watercress salad. Open 6 PM till 1 AM. Ph: 484-5079.

COYUCA 22 – UPPER – Coyuca #22 – Attractive Roman-decor open-air restaurant in older part of town overlooking Pacific on one side and bay on other. International cuisine. Open 7 PM till 10:30 PM. Reservations suggested. AE, MC, VI. Ph: 482-3468 or 483-5030. Open November 1 – April 30.

DINO'S – UPPER – Costera #137 – Nice second-floor restaurant resembling an Italian villa west of Diana Circle across from Condesa Beach. Italian and continental cuisine. Open 5 PM till midnight. AE, MC, VI. Ph: 484-0037.

EL CABRITO – MOD – Costera #1480 – VALUE! OK, cabrito lover's –here's your place in the sun! REAL "cabrito al pastor" (cooked over coals). (Way up 2 long blocks from the convention center – towards Colón circle – next to Hard Rock Cafe and CiCi waterpark). Longtime favorite, owned by Galeana family, used to be located under tree at Papagallo park. Also has seafood and Mexican dishes (good, too), like "birra" (broth), "frijoles a la jarra or charra" (beans with broth), tacos, etc. Open-air or enclosed dining. Open 2 PM till 2 AM Mon – Sat Sun, till 11 PM. VI, MC. Ph: 484-7711.

EL CAMPANARIO – Just up the street from Panoramic. International cuisine. Open daily from 6:30 PM till 1 AM. Ph: 484-8831

LA LANGOSTA LOCA ("The Crazy Lobster") – MOD – Condesa Beach –Open-air seafood restaurant across from Fiesta Tortuga. Good for lunch and dinner. Open 10 AM till midnight. Live entertainment. MC, VI. Ph: 484-5974.

LA PINZONA – MOD – Pinzona #65 – Superb Mexican food restaurant overlooking Acapulco Bay. Owners speak English. Ph: 483-0388 or 483-9905. Open only during the high seasons. Thanks to Ray St. Sauveur of Toronto, Ont. Canada.

LAS DELICIAS – ECON – Pto. Marquez – Turn left at Pie de la Cuesta. Left at dead end after 1/2-mile. It's at a row of seaside palapa restaurant on your right. Strictly seafood.

LE BISTROQUET – MOD – Andrea Doris # 5. Turn right at 100% Natural across from Oceanic 2000. Go one block. It's on the left. French cuisine and paella specialties. Not for the party-hearty crowd, but for those who appreciate a quiet romantic atmosphere. Open-air dining in a lush garden. Open 6 PM till midnight. Owner, Roberto Rodríguez and Chef, José Luis, came here from New York. Ph: 484-6860.

MARINA CLUB – MOD – A family-run restaurant in Caleta section. Great seafood. Eat under palm frond palapas. Japanese sushi bar. 4 pages of sushi choices. Tempore also hamburger. Open 2 PM till midnight. Ph: 483-6601

McDONALDS – MOD – Right on the water behind CiCi's. Your favorite fast food restaurant. Open from 8 AM till 12 PM. Ph: 481-0362, 485-5593

NACHO'S – On Teniente Azueta at corner with Benito Juárez. Across from Amigo Miguel. Seafood.

PARADISE – MOD – Condesa Beach – Popular, expensive beachfront thatched-roof open-air restaurant. Seafood specialties including grilled shrimp and red snapper. Open noon till midnight. Dancing to informal combo. AE, MC, VI. Ph: 484-5988 or 484-7064.

PIPO – ECON-MOD – Costera #105 – VALUE! Next to El Cabrito. Seafood in laid-back open air atmosphere. Reasonable prices. Open 1:00 PM till 9:30 PM. VI, MC. Ph: 484-0165. Also in Pto Marquez on Playa Majahua. Ph: 466-0098.

SANBORN'S – MOD-UPPER – More of the Sanborn's restaurants located throughout Mexico, one next to Condesa del Mar and another downtown near zócalo, on Costera #1226 (Ph: 484-4465). Mexican and international food, newsstand, pharmacy, curios, etc. Popular with local businessmen for breakfast and lunch. Open daily. AE, MC, VI. Also on near AA and Days Inn on Costera.

SUNTORY – UPPER – Costera #36 – Exquisite Japanese restaurant. Sushi, tepanyaki, shabushabu and sashini incomparable! Remarkable wine list. Reservations a must. Open daily 2 PM till midnight. (Closed Sundays). AE, MC, VI. Ph: 484-8088 or 484-8766.

INEXPENSIVE RESTAURANTS

You'll find several off the zócalo, near the budget hotels.

100% NATURAL – ECON – VALUE. An oasis of calm in the middle of the frenzied hedonism of the strip! Semi-vegetarian natural foods, sandwiches, licuados. Across from Hyatt. Go just to see their names of the licuados – "Toro" (7 fruits and orange juice), "Maniaco" (bananas, strawberries, granola, milk), "Hercules," "Vampiro." Licuados, by the way, are a great, inexpensive meal (particularly for breakfast). Garden-like setting. No credit cards.

ASTORIA – ECON – End of zócalo. Outdoor/indoor. Good horchata. No coffee.

TACOS TUMRAS — On the Costera across from Days Inn. Great tacos from spit-roasted beef. Open 7:30 PM till 1 AM.

PIE DE LA CUESTA

STEVE'S HIDEAWAY – MOD – Eat ON the lagoon, floating on pontoons! As you enter town, across from Puerta del Sol hotel, on the lagoon side. Turn right down dirt drive. Owner Steve a character and all-around nice guy who served in the South Seas with the U.S. armed forces and brought some of it home with him. Open when Steve feels like it (which is most of the time).

UKAE KIM – MOD – Pie de la Cuesta #356 – Elegantly informal patio dining by the pools. At hotel by same name. Classical music. Open 10 till 9, 7 days. Ph: (55) 5649-4892 Mexico. Sra. Rebecca Sánchez.

DISCOS & NIGHT CLUBS

ALL THE LARGER HOTELS in Acapulco have night clubs and discos that rate high for those who want to disco. All discos/clubs listed below have a cover charge, though you can usually get "discount" tickets from many sources – especially time-share hustlers. Popular now is a "pay-one-price" for all you can drink deal. Expect to dress up for the fancy ones. They aren't cheap. For more "typical" night life, try one of the "Tropical" bars on the Costera, closer to the zócalo. Some are on the beach and all are crowded with local folks and budget tourists.

ATRIUM – Costera #30 – Used to be BOCCACCIO Continental disco next to El Tropicano. Open 10:30 PM till 5 AM. For "beautiful people" (who enjoy dressing with imagination). Big moment arrives at 2 AM when the tambourine, champagne and candle party begins. Ph: 484-1900, 484-7018.

BABY'O – Costera #22 – Very nice disco east of Diana Circle. Open 10:30 PM till dawn daily. Special party nightly. Magnificent acoustics. Also barber shop, whirlpool and breakfast room to send you home relaxed and fed. Ph: 484-7474, 484-7018.

LE DOME – Costera #4175 – Disco east of Diana Circle across from Holiday Inn. Open 10:30 till 5 AM. Sound vibrates in rhythm with flashing lights. AE, MC, VI. Ph: 484-1190, 484-1191.

CAMPING & RV PARKING

ACAPULCO – MOD – 60-space park 8 miles up coast on Hwy #200 at Pie de la Cuesta on beach in nice tropical setting. All hookups. Toilets. Showers. Dump station. Shaded concrete patios. Store (in season). Boat launch on nearby lake. Security. No phone. Friendly. English.

CORCES SUNSET – UPPER – 1 mile down road to Coyuca. 48 spaces with all hookups. 37 large spaces. 11 small spaces. On beach. Restaurant. Bar. TV. Pool. Volleyball. Basketball. Security. No loud radios, etc. AE, MC, VI. Ph: 482-3452. Fax: 483-7830.

DIAMANTE ACAPULCO RV PARK – MOD – Part of Diamante chain (Cuernavaca) at Copacabaña #8, just east of Princess (towards airport). 80 spaces. All hookups. Pool. Showers. Toilets. Ice. Security ("guarantee security, tranquility and good service"). Beach in front of Vidafel, 500 meters away. Concrete pads. Mechanic. Ph: 481-2829, 466-0200, 466-0900.

EL COLOSO – MOD – 150-space facility in suburban village of La Sábana, east of Acapulco. Turn north off Hwy #95 at Puerto Marques turnoff (5,1/2 miles from airport [turn left at "Y" after 2 miles from #200], 3,1/2 miles from La Roca RV park), following La Sabana signs. Go 4,1/2 miles to "T," turn left. Go 1,1/2 miles. Park is on your right (In summer, more for locals with salón de fiestas with wedding parties). All hookups. Toilets. Showers. Laundry. Pool. Restaurant. Rec. hall. Brick patios. Ph: 441-8497 in La Sabana.

EL VECINITO – MOD – On road to lagoon after Coyuca. Go 3 km north of town, turn left at topes. Then about 5 km toward Gulf. No hookups. Rustic.

LA ROCA – MOD – 8-space unkempt park 9.5 miles east of town on Hwy #200, 5 kilometers south of El Coloso. All hookups. Showers. Toilets. Pool. Concrete patios. No security. Ph: 482-0827.

PLAYA SUAVE – UPPER – Just off Costera – 38-space park west of Diana Circle near midtown, between De Gante and ACA Imperial. All hookups. Showers. Toilets. Concrete patios. Ph: 485-1885. Make sure you get a receipt when entering.

QUINTA DORA – MOD – Pie de la Cuesta – 30-space park 8 miles up coast on Hwy #200 across from Acapulco Park on Laguna Perla de Coyuca in coconut grove. All hookups. Showers. Restrooms. Boat launch. Restaurant. Bar. Washing facility. No phone.

OTHER SERVICES

LAUNDRY – On La Paz near Teniente Azuete. Good service. English spoken.
TOURIST ASSISTANCE – 484-6163, 484-7050.
RED CROSS – 485-4100, 485-4101 Ext. 165.
FIRE STATION – 484-4122, 484-4123.
HIGHWAY PATROL – 485-0647. HIGHWAY EMERGENCY SERVICE – 485-1022, 485-1595.
EMERGENCY HOSPITAL IMSS – 483-5550. EMERGENCY HOSPITAL ISSSTE – 485-3312.

LEAVE SOMETHING OF YOURSELF BEHIND

We all take something with us when we leave Acapulco: romantic memories of moonlit beaches, truly fantastic gourmet meals, lazy days of sun-baked indolence or just a fun time. Here's an opportunity to do something to repay this great city for all it has given us. Consider it a living legacy.

Acapulco is people. People make or break your visit. Some you never see, but they see you. Some of the residents of Acapulco live on the beach where you shared a few romantic memories. Some people fight over the garbage cans behind your fancy restaurants. They aren't bums, or lazy people — they're just kids abandoned by families that just couldn't afford another mouth to feed or runaways from intolerable home situations. The story's the same the world over. In Mexico, it's just tougher. Given a chance, these kids will be the friendly and warm hotel, restaurant workers, doctors, cops and government officials that your children will meet when they come to the town you love. Without help, at best, they'll be tough, suspicious and resentful. At the worst, without education or skills, they'll turn to dishonest means to survive.

There IS a place that makes a difference. No one can save the whole world or take care of all the orphans. Each one of us can do what we can — or we can be too self-centered to care.

THE ACAPULCO CHILDREN'S HOME ("CASA HOGAR DEL NIÑO de ACAPULCO A.C.") is located in the old "Pozo del Rey" hotel on Av. Gran Tropical, corner Av. Las Américas, is in the Caleta section of town. Founded in 1978, over 50 boys (depending on funds) are given a chance to live with dignity. That's all. No coddling. They learn that to stay, they must obey certain rules: 1. Treat each other and everyone they meet with respect. 2. Be honest — respect private property. 3. Study — learn to read and write — English and Spanish. 4. Work — they have a cooperative restaurant-ice-cream-parlor which they operate. It's located at the Original Acapulco Fat Farm, Calle Juárez #10 (2 blocks west of the zócalo) Ph: 483-5339. Do they change for the better? It depends on how soon they get the kid off the street. Not all make it. Those who can't abide by the rules are given a choice — shape up or ship out. Those who do (shape up), make good citizens any country could be proud of. A few go on to professional studies, but some don't. Nevertheless, they all have a better hand to play than they were dealt at birth.

This is a nonprofit, NONDENOMINATIONAL, tax deductible (in Mexico and Canada, and perhaps soon, the U.S.), charitable organization. The ACH gets NO HELP from ANY government, church or organized charity. YOU are its only hope. SEE how the boys live and how you can help. CALL 482-2203 or 482-2639. The director, Jack, will show you around and give you a good cup of coffee. Bring what you can — food, clothes (Don't you have more than you need?), medical supplies, toys or ask Jack what they need. Cash is appreciated — they have to pay electricity and phone bills. You can send donations to the following folks:

Debora Green
1650 Oak Knoll
Dallas, TX 75208
(214) 942-5447

Lino Darchun
3100 N. Sheridan Rd.
Chicago Il 60657
(312) 477-9242

Brian Leslie
Canadian Foundation for Children of Acapulco
251-Cambell St. N7T2H2
Sarnia, Ont Canada

End of Acapulco Eat & Stray

Puerto Escondido

Area Code — 954

PUERTO ESCONDIDO, Paradise of Ecoturism, is on Mexico's Pacific Coast, 249 miles from Acapulco and 70 miles north of Huatulco. Take a few days to explore all its wonders: for example, the Chacahua Lagoons, an ecological reserve 38 miles away - with its wildlife sanctuary of tropical birds called "Stork Island" and fascinating biological Crocodile farm. At Zicatela beach, incredible waves make surfing a year round attraction, and you can also go horseback riding. Carrizalillo Bay offers sensational snorkeling and mysterious underwater caves you can explore.

SLEEPING IN PUERTO ESCONDIDO

ACAURIO – ECON – Bungalows on beach. Very friendly owner, practices home medicine. Vegetarian restaurant. Ph: 582-0357, 582-1027.

ALDEA DEL BAZAR – UPPER – 48 rooms. Restaurant. Pool. Pre-Hispanic Spa. Massages. Secure parking. Hard beds. Ph and Fax: 582-0508.

BARLOVENTO — ECON — Bungalows on the road to the lighthouse. Ph : 582-0220.

BEN-ZAA — ECON — On the road to Carrizalillo. Experience the real world class fishing. Contact Steve or Del Posing, 4023 Rt. 113 Kankakee, IL 60901 Ph: (815) 932-9039, 932-5213 Fax: (815) 932-5414. E-mail: paleale@colint.com Website: www.eden.com/~tomzap/ For flight information call Tompson Travel: (815) 468-9445. Phone in Mexico: 582-0523 Fax: 582-0553.

CASTILLO DE REYES — ECON — Av. Pérez Gasca s/n. 582-0442

CAMINO DEL SOL – MOD – 30-room A/C hotel. Laundry service. Restaurant. Ph: 582-0243.

JARDIN REAL – MOD – At corner of Tlacochahuaya and Guelatao. 16 rooms. Quiet. Hard beds. BBQ pits Restaurant. Pool. Secure parking. Ph: 582-0736, 582-0687.

LAS GAVIOTAS – MOD – 21-room hotel on Car. Costera 2nd north. Parking. No A/C. Restaurant. Bar. Pool. AE, MC, VI. Ph: 582-0245, 582-0948.

LAS PALMAS – ECON – 40-room hotel on Pérez Gasga downtown on Principal Beach. Restaurant. Bar. Parking. Ph: 582-0230, 582-0303.

LOREN – ECON – 16-room hotel downtown at Pérez Gasga #507. Restaurant. Parking. VI. Ph: 582-0057.

NAYAR – ECON – 37-room hotel downtown at Pérez Gasga #407. Restaurant. Parking. Ph: 582-0319, 582-0113.

PARAISO ESCONDIDO – MOD – Value! Nice 20-room A/C hotel near downtown at Calle Union 10. Turn right by travel agency. Restaurant. Bar. Pool. Parking. Ph: 582-0444.

POSADA REAL – UPPER – Nice rambling 100-room A/C hotel on Bacocha Beach at west end of town. Restaurant. Bar. Pool. Parking. AE, MC, VI. Ph: 582-0133, 582-0185.

RANCHO EL PESCADOR – MOD – 38-room A/C hotel on Hwy #200 at west end of town. Restaurant. Pool. Tennis. Parking. AE, MC, VI. Ph: 582-0495, 582-0443.

ROCAMAR – ECON – 16-room hotel downtown at Pérez Gasga #601 overlooking bay. Restaurant. Bar. Street parking. Ph: 582-0339, 582-0381.

SANTA FE – MOD – Very nice 44-room and 8 bungalow hotel on Marinero Beach off Hwy #200. Restaurant. Bar. 2 Pools. Parking. MC, VI. Ph: 2-0170. American Management. Selective. Does not use travel agents. 30-rooms and garage. Old world hospitality. One of my favorite hotels in Mexico. Ph: 582-0170 Fax: 582-0266

SUITES VILLA SOL – UPPER – Nice, spacious 108-room A/C hotel on Bacocho beach west entrance to Puerto Escondido at Loma Bonita #2. Pool. Restaurant. Motorcycle rental. AE, MC, VI. Ph: 582-0061, 582-0314, 582-0038, or 582-0308 Fax: 582-0451. DF Ph: 5-517-1117; Fax: 5-569-2979.

VILLA BAY – ECON – 12-rooms. Beach side of road. Nice.

VILLA DE LAS BRISAS – MOD – 12-rooms. On Hwy #200 .8 miles before town. Nice sea breeze. Balconies. Fridge. Restaurant. Bar. Parking. Pool table. Pool. Good deal. Reservation Oaxaca Ph: 951-6-8459, 956-3415.

VILLA ESCONDIDO – UPPER – 12-unit villa with ceiling fans only. MC, VI.

VILLA LOS DELFINES – MOD – Bungalows located at Cerro de la Iguana Playa Zikatela. Gorgeous place "Honeymoon type." Very helpful. Ph: 582-0785, 582-0467. FAX: 585-0546 or 586-8878.

VILLA MARINERO – MOD – Bungalows located at Costera del Pacífico S/N Col. Marinero. For reservations call Ph: 2-0180. Dr. Manuel Quijas López, gerente.

VILLA RELAX – MOD – Near Bacocho beach. Carretera Costera, Hwy #200, on left side coming fom Acapulco, just before the ice plant. Quiet. 10 units with 2 double beds. Hammocks. Terraces with sea view. Parking. Night security. 2 pools. Tennis. Shady grounds. Great restaurant next door. Ph: 582-0819.

VILLAS SANTIAGO – MOD – 5 casas. Long term. Write Pedro Santiago Apdo. #76 Pto Escondido OAX Mexico. No parking.

EATING IN PUERTO ESCONDIDO

ALICIA – ECON – Inexpensive but not as good as El Fogón across the street. Next to Exchange on beach. Popular with backpackers. Serve licuados and Mexican food. VI.

BANANAS – MOD – Popular open-air thatched roof restaurant on Pérez Gasga. Open 7 AM till 3 AM daily. Short orders, light meals, etc.

CAFE CAPUCCINO – MOD – Great breakfasts and seafood.

CARMEN'S PASTERLERIA – MOD – Bakery just off Playa marinero, up the road past the new Flores de Maria. For folks tired of tortillas and Bimbo bread (Mexico's tasteless factory baked bread). Bakes whole wheat bread, croissants, carrot cake, banana bread, peanut butter cookies. Birthday cakes on request.

COCO – MOD – Restaurant/Bar serving seafood, meats and chicken. 3 for 1 happy hour. Lively music (Sometimes live). Open 4 PM till 11 PM.

EL POSADA D'LOREN – MOD – Restaurant on Av. Gasga near the end of the Ped Mall. Char grilled seafood and steaks. Rowdy atmosphere. Tables on the beach. Open noon till 1 AM.

HERMAN'S BEST – ECON – Tacos, seafood and Mexican food just before pedestrian mall. Open 12 Noon till 2 AM.

IL VIADANTE DE HUGO – MOD – On Garza Gasca. Pizza. Pasta. Fish. MC, VI.

LA GOTA DE VIDA – MOD – Vegetarian food near west end of pedestrian walking mall, near Nayar hotel.

LA PERGOTA MEXICANA – MOD – Restaurant down from Abel. Same food. Humble. Open 6 AM till 9 AM and 10 AM till 5 PM. Variable.

LA PERLA ILAMENTE – MOD – Restaurant on Av. Pérez Gasga. Great food, music and atmosphere. (Thanks to Mr. and Mrs. M. Wickware, Stittsville, Ontario)

LA SARDINA DE PLATA – MOD – Open-air seafood restaurant below Castel Puerto Escondido overlooking sea. Well-prepared seafood, steaks and drinks. Open noon till 11 PM daily. AE, MC, VI. Ph: 582-0328.

LAS PALMAS – MOD – Restaurant in hotel. Serves soups, seafood, meats and chicken. Open 8 AM till 9 PM. MC, VI. Ph: 582-0230.

MARIO'S PIZZALAND – MOD – Pizza place by parking area. Found they use 11 eggs per kilo of dough. Impeccably clean. Vegetarian pizzas. Pasta Salads. Run by Mario. Handmade thatched roof (Took 8 days to make) Open 2 PM till 11 PM. MC, VI. Ph: 582-0575.

MIRAMAR – ECON – Small, 10 tables. Breakfast, lunch and dinner. Open 7 AM till 10 PM. Cash only.

NORMA'S – ECON – 3 tables. Cash only. Hours vary.

OSTERIA DEL VIANDANTE – ECON – Seafood, pasta and chicken. Open 3 PM till 11 PM. AE, MC, VI. Ph: 582-0671.

PERLA FLAMEANTE – MOD – Seafood, shark, pompano, Cajun styles and teriaki restaurant at Av. Pérez Gasga #100, corner Marina Nacional. Money exchange and bookstore. Huge tape collection. English speaking. Open 8 AM till 1 AM. Ph: 582-0203.

RINCON DEL PACIFICO – MOD – Beachfront restaurant part of hotel. Enter from street or beach. Open 7 AM till 10 PM. AM, MC, VI. Ph: 582-0056.

SPAGHETTI HOUSE – MOD – Italian food off Pérez Gasga downtown towards beach. Turn at Bananas. All sorts of Italian dishes. Open noon till 11 PM daily. MC, VI.

CAMPING & RV PARKING

LA ALEJANDRIA – MOD – Camp located at kilometer 125 Carretera Pto. Escondido-Acapulco. Located right on fresh water lake. Fishing permitted. Boat trips to ocean. Visit Lake Manialtepec with exotic vegetation, rare birds, rare water animals and islands covered with aquatic flowers. Restaurant.

PALMAS DE CORTES – MOD – very basic 31-space facility in town on beach. 10 with (EW). 21 spaces with electricity only. Cold showers. Toilets. Store. For VW Vans and tents only!

PUERTO ESCONDIDO – MOD – 153-space facility on Carizalillo Beach. 113 spaces with all hookups. EWS. Cold showers. Toilets. Dump station. Pool. Ice. Ph: 582-0077 in Pto. Escondido or 955-3252 in Oaxaca.

VILLA RELAX – ECON – Carretera Costera, Hwy #200, on left side coming from Acapulco, just before ice plant. 10 RV spaces. 110/120 EWS. Toilets. Showers. Covered patio with chairs and tables. Snack bar. 2 pools. Tennis.Shady walled grounds. Night security. Great restaurant next door at Hotel Camino del Sol. Ph: 582-0819.

OTHER

MASSAGE – Patricia Heuze and Alejandro Villanueva at Av. Infraganti # 28, Col. Lázaro Cárdenas. They also rent 2-bedroom apartments on monthly, weekly, daily basis.– for a select clientele. They do meditation and healing workshops and would like to fill their place with like-minded people. Ph: 582-09-08.

REPAIRS – If you need major (or minor) repairs to your camper or anything involving a drill, solder, cast-iron etc. BALCONERA ROJAS is the place. Sr. Rojas is friendly and adept at figuring out what you want. Turn toward beach at "new" municipal building. Go three blocks. Turn right. His shop is 3/4 of a long block down on left. There's also a welder one block over on right (go to en of block, turn right, then right again). He's on left.

End of Pto. Escondido Eat & Stray!

Puerto Angel

Area Code — 958

SLEEPING IN PUERTO ANGEL

BUENA VISTA – ECON – 13-rooms with ceiling fans and mosquito netting. Restaurant. Owner a woman from California. Charming. Good beds. Beautiful view.

LA CABAÑA – ECON – Nice, 23 rooms. Fans. Decent beds. Nice garden overlooking ocean.

POSADA CAÑON DEVATA – ECON-MOD – 10-room hotel just up from the Playa Panteón 1/4 mile from turnoff into town. Run by Suzanne and Mateo López. It's a unique place for special people. Hidden away in a tropical rain-forest-like setting, it features vegetarian family-style dining, little cottages and a mediation chapel. New age kind of crowd. Closed during May and June. Ph: 584-0397.

POSADA RINCON SABROSO – ECON – Uphill. Megan and Agustín. Ceiling fans. Clean hammocks or patio with view of your own.

SORAYA – MOD – 32-room hotel located on the hill above the pier, Domicilio Conocido. It is the first you'll see, facing the bay. It's nice, modern and reasonable. Very good view. 5 rooms with air-con. Some rooms have sea view and balconies. Good restaurant. Parking. SATV. May, June, September, October and November discounts.

EATING IN PUERTO ANGEL

All beachfront restaurants' hygiene may vary, so ask locally how things are currently.

BETO'S – ECON – Up hill past the creek. Very popular with foreigners.

CAPPY – ECON – Located at the beginning of track that descends to Playa del Panteón.

CORDELIA'S – ECON – Restaurant on the beach, halfway around La Playa Zacatela. Cheap, friendly. Parking. Lobster, shrimp, fish.

EL TIBURON – MOD – Same owner as King Creole. Excellent food. Varied menu. Live music.

KING CREOLE – MOD – Last one on the beach. Seafood, Italian food, steaks. Food washed with purified water. Owner John J. Reilhac speaks English and French.

TAI-PAN – MOD – Last restaurant in town, just down past King Creole.

SUSY – MOD – On Playa del Panteón at turnoff to Posada Cañon Devata

VILLA FLORENCIA – MOD – Italian cuisine. Best coffee in town. Capuchino. Great atmosphere.

CAMPING & RV PARKING

LOS TAMARINDOS – ECON – At KM 246, 2.6 miles before town. They also have 5 one-room bungalows with ceiling fans and parking.

OTHER

UNIVERSIDAD DEL MAR – Has tourism classes as well as aquaculture.

MAZUNTE – Sea turtle museum on site of old sea turtle slaughter house.

End of Pto. Angel Eat & Stray!

Huatulco

Area code — 958

Another of the "new" mega-resorts, Huatulco is supposed to be different. There are nine bays in the 22 mile stretch that make up the area. The development calls for a respect for the ecology and careful planning. The development was formally opened Nov. 1988. By 1990, there were two water treatment plants and a third one planned. By 2018 or so, the government projects that more than 300,000 folks will live here to support the tourism industry. That's a bit larger than Cancún. As always, there are some who believe that the land and the people who live there would have been better off left alone, but there is no doubt that the standard of living has improved dramatically.

In 900 B.C., it was the seat of the Zapotec culture. Then the Mixtecas took a shine to it. The Spaniards dropped in when they arrived. It became an important port, like San Blas and Acapulco. Then, in 1575, the Englishman, Sir Francis Drake stated shooting the place up. A few years later (depending on which history book you read), another Englishman, Thomas Cavendish, attacked the place. He was pretty upset because there was little to loot, so he decided to steal the huge wooden cross that stood over the town. They couldn't chop or saw it, and it wouldn't burn. I guess he really got mad then! Supposedly, he tried to drag it down with a line attached to one of his galleons, but no go! This sacred cross (hence the name Santa Cruz de Huatulco) was later taken to Oaxaca by the Catholic Church. The Church managed to chop it up and a silver sliver of it went to the Vatican. True story? Anyway, it's legend.

The next happening of historical significance was the betrayal of Revolutionary hero Vicente Guerrero on the beach in 1831, although another story has it happening in Acapulco. Then the place quieted down.

Regardless, with an average temperature of 82° you may agree with a Fonatur brochure that states, "... nothing matches the intimacy of our bays." From west to east, the 9 bays are: San Agustín, Chachacual, Cacaluta, Maguey, Oregano, Santa Cruz, Chahue, Tangolunda, Conejos.

Fishing, diving, snorkeling and hedonism are the main activities. Enjoy.

SLEEPING IN HUATULCO

BUSANNI – MOD – Calle Carrisal, Lote 11, Manzana 10, La Crucesita, 12 rooms. Ceiling fans.

CASA ROBERT – MOD – Calle 11, Lote 4, Sec. E, Santa Cruz, PH: no –Nice, homey place off main drag (B. Juárez) at end (for now) of hotel district. Turn right 1/4 mile past Hotel Posada Binniguenda. 5 rooms, ceiling fans. Set in a natural setting, flush against a hill, surrounded by lush vegetation.

CLUB MED – UPPER – Paseo de Tangolunda S/N – On right, just before turn to Sheraton. The largest Med in Western Hemisphere. Very limited parking. All inclusive, planned social activities, fixed dining hours etc. Tennis, health club (limited), no jacuzzi, no steam room, no sauna. Ph: 584-0069 US 800 - CLUB MED

CONDOTEL – MOD – On west side of road from highway, just before crossroads and across from gas station. It has only suites. Supposed to be reasonably-priced.

GRIFER – MOD – Av. Guamuchi, corner Carrizal, La Crucesita, Ph: 587-0048 – 20 rooms, ceiling fans.

LA CASITA – MOD – Chacah Manzana #14, Lote 3, La Crucesita, 4 rooms. A/C, some with view. Very pleasant, homey atmosphere.

MARLIN – Next to Magic Circus disco – Big highrise that is probably noisy. We didn't get to see any rooms.

POSADA BINNIGUENDA – MOD to UPPER – #5 Paseo Benito Juárez, Santa Cruz, An OK colonial style, 74 nice big rooms, A/C, SATV, pool, bar, restaurant. PH: 587-0077, 587-0379, or 587-0078, FAX: 587-0284 (D.F. (5) 660-4222 ext. 1811)

ROYAL MAEVA – UPPER – APDO. 227 – All-inclusive deal. That means you pay for room, food and planned social activities upon check-in. Small rooms. Suites have jacuzzis, but none for the rest of us. Pools. Tennis. Golf. Restaurants. SATV. Disco. Ph: 581-0000 or 581-0048, Fax: 581-0220.

SHERATON – UPPER – Paseo de Tangolunda S/N – Everything you'd expect in this highrise, 346 rooms. A/C. SATV. Pools. Tennis. Golf. Health club. Sauna. Ph: 581-0055, 581-0065, 581-0039 D.F. (91-5) 207-3933, 514-5981, US: 800 - 325-3535, Fax: 581-0113, 581-0335, D.F., (915) 514-5981.

SUITES BUGAMBILIAS – MOD – Calle Carrisal La Crucesita, 3 stories, 10 A/C suites.

EATING IN HUATULCO

CACTUS – ECON – On square. Mexican food.

DON WILLO – On the square, La Crucesita – Very good, Italian food. Nice courtyard. English-speaking. Nice place.

El OASIS – ECON – On square. Good sandwiches. Shrimp tacos and Comida Típica. MC, VI. Open daily 8 AM till 12 Midnight.

There are several inexpensive places in La Crucesita and a few moderate ones in Santa Cruz.

CAMPING & RV PARKING

LOS MANGOS – MOD – Santa Cruz – Av. Benito Juárez S/N – Turn right at crossroads, go uphill 200 meters or 1/4 mile. 30 spaces (EWS). Showers. Nice trees. Family-run.

OTHER PLACES

ENGLISH SPEAKING DOCTOR – Dr. Balbeno Cano, Pochutla, Oax. near post office.

CRAFTS – Santa Cruz – There's a nice little market by the marina. Prices are all subject to bargaining, so have at it. Lots of English and a little aggressive.

MAGIC CIRCUS – Santa Cruz – Disco near end of B. Juárez, below market. Wild, loud and popular.

SAVAGE – Huatulco – Disco across the street from Sheraton.

TOURISM OFFICE – Blvd. Shahue Next to IMSS clinic. Ph: 584-0030, 584-0262, 584-0246, ext 124.

End of Huatulco Eat & Stray.

Salina Cruz

Area Code — 971

SALINA CRUZ is a little old Pacific seaport with a population of 40,000. It's not what you might call really untidy and probably worth a visit if you have the time, especially if you've never seen the Pacific. Their somewhat pothole streets are wide and divided, not unlike those in some of our own western towns. You'll not need a map to get around, but here's one anyhow, so you won't worry about getting lost. You may well find several ocean going freighters in port.

Salinas Cruz is the southern terminal of the famous Trans-Isthmus Railroad that runs the shortest distance (north of Panamá, that is) between the Atlantic and Pacific Oceans — from Coatzacoalcos to Salina Cruz. Several attempts have been made to build a canal across this narrow isthmus, but they never got much beyond the talking stage. One time a New Orleans out fit ran a Mississippi river boat from Coatzacoalcos up the Río Coatzacoalcos to Suchilpan and then took their passengers on to Salinas Cruz by horseback and carriages — and believe it or not, hundreds of gold seekers cut across the continent in this manner en route to the California '49 Gold Rush. It might not have been very comfortable, but it sure beat going all the way around Cape Horn.

Then, nobody but Captain Eads, the man who built Eads Bridge across the Mississippi River at St. Louis, tried to work up a triple track railroad that would carry complete freighters across the isthmus — but his big deal never jellied. Finally, a regular railroad was finished in 1907, and it did a fantastic land-office business running a dozen trains a day until... you guessed it, a few years later the Panamá Canal opened and that was curtains for the Trans-Isthmus Railroad. However, the railroad somehow survived and still operates.

If it's getting late, here are some hotels and restaurants that Mexican Tourism recommends but we haven't checked them out. See Map (page 30) for location.

SLEEPING IN SALINA CRUZ

ALTAGRACIA - Ph: 714-0627
CALENDAS - Ph: 714-4574
COSTA REAL - Ph: 714-0239
FIESTA ISTMO - Ph: 714-3972
LEÑA REAL - Ph: 714-0085

EATING IN SALINAS CRUZ

CAMPESTRE - Ph: 714-2974
CLUB DE LA SALSA - 714-3207
EL LUGAR - Ph: 714-0863
LA PARRILLA - Ph: 714-5335
LA PASADITA - Ph: 714-2848

End of Salina Cruz Eat & Stray

Toluca

Area Code — 722

TOLUCA, capital of the state of Mexico, is a fast-growing mountain city of 500,000 inhabitants and, although located in a valley, it is one of Mexico's highest cities at 8,792 feet. Surrounded by tall mountains, pine forests, lakes and rivers, Toluca, nevertheless, is better known as an industrial center than a vacationer's paradise. "Toluca" is derived from the Matlatzinca words "dios tolo" which mean "god." The Matlatzincas were the pre-Hispanic founders of Toluca and many of their ruins are scattered throughout the state. One fairly-well restored site is CALIXTLAHUACA, located about 6 miles outside Toluca. A larger site, TEOTENANGO, is located 13 miles from Toluca on Highway #55 to Ixtapan de la Sal.

The city offers shopping and restaurants in LOS PORTALES, a large, multi-portico building a block off the main plaza and is the social center of Toluca. Worth seeing are the BOTANICAL GARDENS adjacent to the Governor's Palace. The building is adorned with countless murals of stained glass and more than 1,000 species of plants can be found inside. If in town on a Friday, don't miss "TIANGUIS" (market day). One of the largest in Mexico, it offers a good cross-section of items produced in the area, especially baskets. A visit to the volcano NEVADO DE TOLUCA 29 miles southwest off Highway #134 is a good day's outing. The snow-covered peaks, pine forests and two crater lakes are a great setting for hiking and picture-taking. Then farther south on the same highway are the interesting TEJUPILCO archeological ruins (see Toluca - Cd. Altamirano Log, page). In all, a worthwhile side trip.

Spend a day or so in the area en-route to your destination - you'll enjoy it! In addition to being a lovely section of Mexico, the climate is exhilarating.

SLEEPING IN TOLUCA

CASTEL PLAZA LAS FUENTES – 4 miles east of Toluca on Hwy #15. 152 rooms. Good restaurant. Bar with live music. Heated enclosed pool. SATV. Secure parking. No pets. AE, MC, VI. Ph: 216-4666 or 216-4769.

COLONIAL – Hidalgo Ote. #103. 40 rooms. Restaurant. Bar. Ph: 215-9700 or 214-7066.

DEL REY – On parkway leading into Toluca. 150 rooms. Restaurant. Bar. Pool. SATV. Parking. No pets. AE, MC, VI. Ph: 214-9888.

FIESTA MEXICANA – Hotel and Spa 40 miles north on Hwy #55 – Quite a deal! 44 rooms. 6 suites with jacuzzi. They have a real spa with Swedish showers, jacuzzi, steam, massage, facials, weight reduction etc. Restaurant. Tennis courts. Pool. Gym. AE, MC, VI. Ph: 212-2236, 212-2238 Fax: 212-2337.

PASEO – On parkway leading into Toluca. 87 rooms. Restaurant. Bar. SATV. Parking. No pets. AE, MC, VI. 6 RV spaces with electricity and water.

EATING IN TOLUCA

LA CABAÑA SUIZA – On parkway leading into Toluca. Very good food and service. Swiss and Mexican dishes, steaks, seafood plus delicious coffee and desserts. Open 1 PM till midnight daily. AE, MC, VI. Ph: 216-1885.

End of Toluca Eat & Stray

Ixtapan de la Sal

Area Code — 721

IXTAPAN de la Sal is Mexico's best "SPA" town. Accommodations vary from inexpensive to elegant. It's a flower-filled delight and a great place to rid yourself of the "miseries." It's apt to be crowded on weekends, though. If nothing else, take the "Roman Baths" at the public balneario with your significant other to relax your nerves from Mexico City traffic. Enjoy.

Most places will quote you prices based on 3 meals.

SLEEPING IN IXTAPAN DE LA SAL

AVENIDA – MOD – Av. Benito Juárez #614. Hotel with gardens. Restaurant. Bar. Pool. 4 baths. Parking. Ph: 413-1029.

BELISANA – MOD – Av. Juárez # 64. 49 Rooms. Restaurant. Pool. Parking. Ph: 413-0013, 413-0040.

BUNGALOWS LOLITA – MOD – Clean, comfy 60-unit layout a block from Diana Square. Restaurant. Bar. Pool. Tennis. Playground. Parking. MC, VI. Ph: 413-0016 Fax: 413-0230.

DORANTES – MOD – 26 Rooms. Very nice, cozy. Ecología s/n. Friendly. Family owned. Owner, Horacio Dorantes, is a very interesting fellow and a fountain of knowledge. If you are on a budget, you can't do better. Nice restaurant. Pool. Parking. MC, VI. Ph: 413-0734, 413-1060.

IDEAL – MOD – 26-room, 2-story south highway layout. Restaurant. Bar. Pool. Parking. MC, VI. Ph: 413-0194.

IXTAPAN – UPPER – A true "SPA" with exercise and diet programs, massages, reflexology, facials, body wraps, mud wraps, etc. Big 250-room, 10 suites, 5-story hotel as nice as anything in Mexico (compares favorably with our own French Lick, Hot Springs, White Sulphur, etc.). Restaurant. Bar. Pools with thermal (105° F.) and fresh water. Club surrounded by 12 dancing, multicolored fountains. 9-hole golf course. Tennis. Bowling. Billiards. Shuffleboard. Theatre. Health club. Horses. Enclosed covered parking. AE, MC, VI. DF: 264-6392, 264-2613 or 264-2673. Ph: 413-0021 or 413-0304. US: 800-223-9832 (E and M Assoc.). NY: 212-599-8280 Fax: 212-599-1755.

KISS – MOD-UPPER – 3-story, 66-room, 2 suite, 1 Jr. suite hotel in front of Diana statue on main boulevard. Restaurant. Bar. Pool. Beauty shop. Hydromassage (Jacuzzi). Sauna. Tours. Reflexology. Enclosed parking. MC, VI. Ph: 413-0349 or 413-0901 Fax: 413-0842.

SARA ISABEL – MOD – Older 40-room, 2-story hotel next to Kiss. Restaurant. Bar. Bar Chateau Maguey. Aquabar. Pool. Parking. MC, VI. Ph: 413-0245 or 413-0197. Fax: 413-0084.

VISTA HERMOSA – MOD – Blvd. Arturo – Hotel across from Ixtapan. Pool. Parking. MC, VI. Ph: 413-2383, 413-2140.

The "Balneario" next door to the Hotel Ixtapan (also owned by the Romano Family) is open to the public, with two large thermal pools and a wading pool for the children. The "Baños Romanos" are private rooms with large marble jacuzzis. Each room has 2 cots and a dressing area, piped in music and Roman motif. Quite a deal. Romantic as all get-out. Opens 7 AM. Admission charged. Reservations suggested. Regardless of which hotel you're staying in, you can "take the baths" inexpensively.

EATING IN IXTAPAN DE LA SAL

LUGAR SIN NOMBRE – ECON – Av. Juárez s/n across from Belisana. Good comida. Open 10 AM till 7 PM.

End of Ixtapan de la Sal Eat & Stray

Taxco

Area Code — 762

TAXCO – The Silver City – This is the most famous of the historical colonial towns of Mexico, declared a national monument by the Mexican government in 1928. It sits on a hill among hills and almost anywhere you walk in the city there are fantastic views. Taxco was founded in 1522 by Cortés for the purpose of mining silver and reached the height of its prosperity in the 18th Century. Today its fame and economy depend largely on the more than 200 silver art and craft shops that line the cobblestone streets.

If you take Autopista del Sol, get off at Chilpancingo exit, then look for (IGUALA) sign to get to Taxco.

There is a museum dedicated to William Spratling, the American silversmith responsible for reviving Taxco's silver industry through craftsmanship. It is located just behind Santa Prisca and is open Tuesday thru Saturday 10 AM till 5 PM; Sunday 9 AM till 3 PM. Admission fee is charged.

SLEEPING IN TAXCO

AGUA ESCONDIDA – MOD – Rather good, clean 50-room hotel just off zócalo at Calle Guillermo Spratling #4. Restaurant. Bar. Pool Parking. Pets OK. AE, MC, VI. Ph: 622-0726

DE LA BORDA – MOD – Good 95-room hotel just off highway near north end at Cerro del Pedregal #2. 2 restaurants. Bar. Pool. Boutique. Arts and crafts shop. Parking. Pets OK. AE, DIN, MC, VI. Ph: 622-0025, 622-0225.

EL TAXQUEÑITO – MOD – Av. de los Plateros. Ph: 622-0623, Fax: 622-5737.

ESTCLAR – ECON – 2ª de Reforma s/n, Ph: 622-1341, Fax: 622-1768.

HACIENDA DEL SOLAR – UPPER – Quiet, cozy 13 cottage-style facility off Hwy #95 on Calle del Solar at south end of town situated on an 85-acre ranch. Famous La Ventana de Taxco Restaurant. Bar. Heated pool. Tennis. Boutique. Horses. Parking. No Pets. All units split-level. MC, VI. Ph: 622-0323, 622-0587.

LOMA LINDA – MOD – Nice and friendly cliffside 70-unit hotel on Av. de los Plateros #52. Restaurant. Bar. Pool. Parking. Pets OK. Space for 5 RV's (water and electricity hookups). AE, MC, VI. Ph: 622-0206, 622-0753 Fax: 622-5125. E-mail: gerencia@hotellomalinda.com

LOS ARCOS – MOD – Beautifully renovated 30-room inn, once a 17th-century monastery, near main plaza at Juan Ruiz Alarcón #12 across from Posada de los Castillo. Restaurant. Parking. No pets. AE, MC, VI. Ph: 622-1836 Fax: 622-3211.

MELENDEZ – ECON – Older 41-room hotel near zócalo at Cuauhtémoc #2. Restaurant (good breakfast). Bar. Parking. Pets OK. AE, MC, VI. Ph: 622-0006.

MONTE TAXCO – UPPER – Very good remodeled 3-story 153-room hotel, once a Holiday Inn at far north end on Hwy #95 atop La Cantera Mountain (Careful for steep but spectacular cobblestone entry climbing 800 feet from the highway). Restaurant. Bar. Club. Steam bath and gym. Jacuzzi. Massage. Pool. 9-hole golf course ("9 Holes in the Sky"). Tennis. Boutique. Curio shop. Horses. Very secure parking (get badge at entry). No pets. AE, CB, DIN, MC, VI. Ph: 622-1300 Fax: 622-1428. Mex: 01-800-980-0000. E-mail: montetaxco@silver.net.mx

POSADA DE LA MISION – MOD – Attractive 150-room inn conveniently located on highway near north end on Av. Cerro de la Misión #32. Restaurant. Bar. Pool with famous O'Gorman mural. Tennis. Silver shop. Travel agency. Parking. Pets OK. AE, CB, DIN, MC, VI. Ph: 622--5519, 622-0063, 622-0563, Fax: 622-2198. E-mail: lamision@taxco.net

POSADA DE LOS CASTILLO – ECON – Small, pleasing 15-room inn, owned by a renowned family of silversmiths, at Calle Juan Ruiz de Alarcón # 7, a block from plaza and across from Los Arcos. Cafeteria. Parking. Pets OK. AE, CB, DIN, MC, VI. Ph: 622-1396 Fax: 622-2935.

SANTA PRISCA – MOD – 38-room hotel at Cena Oscura #1, a favorite with tourists a couple of blocks from Plaza de San Juan. Good restaurant. Bar. Small enclosed parking area. No pets. AE, MC, VI. Ph: 622-0080, 622-0980 Fax: 262-2938.

VICTORIA – MOD – Nice older 174-unit colonial-style apartment-hotel (actually a two-hotel complex) perched atop a hill overlooking Santa Prisca Church at Carlos J Nibbi #57. Good restaurant. Bar. Pool. Parking. Pets OK. AE, CB, DIN, MC, VI. Ph: 622-0210, 622-1014, 622-0010.

EATING IN TAXCO

BONANZA – MOD – Steak house on Highway to Mexico City serving various cuts of meat as well as roast beef. Open daily 11 AM till 5 PM. No credit cards.

CIELITO LINDO – MOD – Long-time institution between Santa Prisca and Meléndez Hotel serving typical Mexican dishes and regional and international cuisine. Open daily 9 AM till 10 PM. No credit cards. Ph: 622-0603.

EL CAMPANARIO – MOD – Av. Benito Juárez #45-Altos. Agentina-style beef. Ph: 622-6966.

EL CARRUSEL – ECON – Good restaurant on Calle Cuauhtémoc next to Hotel Meléndez. Used to be called Caballo Negro.

DEL ANGEL – UPPER – Celso Muñoz #3, near church of Santa Prisca. Ph: 622-5525.

LA CASONA – MOD – Celso Muñoz #4. National and International cuisine. Ph: 622-1071.

LA ESTACIÓN – ECON – Cuauhtémoc #8, Centro. Restaurant and snack bar. Ph: 622-6351.

LA VENTANA DE TAXCO – UPPER – Excellent Italian gourmet restaurant in conjunction with Hacienda del Solar at far south end of town off Hwy #95. Terrific terrace dining with superb view of town. Open daily 8 AM till 11 PM. AE, MC, VI. Cited for gourmet cuisine by Bon Apetit magazine. Ph: 622-0587.

PACO'S BAR – MOD – Famous second story "watering hole" overlooking Santa Basilica Plaza. No credit cards.

SANTA FE – ECON – Across and down from Hotel Santa Prisca. Great typical Mexican food and comida corrida. Open 7:30 AM till 11 PM.

SOTARENTO GALERY– MOD – Av. Benito Juárez #12, Mexican and Internationa cuisine.

SR. COSTILLA (Mr. Rib) – MOD – Located at Plaza Borda #1. Spare ribs specialty and International cuisine. Open 1 PM till midnight. Ph: 622-3215.

CAMPING & RV PARKING

RV'S – While there is no RV park in town, if you are self-sufficient, ask at Loma Linda for Roberto Flores. He will guide you to a spot where you can park. If he is not there, call 622-1411 or 622-0776 or ask at front desk.

OTHER

GUIDE – Roberto Flores, Miguel Hidalgo #21, Ph: 622-1411, 622-0776, can often be found at Loma Linda 9 AM till 11 AM, very knowledgeable of many areas of Mexico, speaks English and shares Sanborn's philosophy. FILM – Slide film and 1 hour Photo development at Velvi's, across from Restaurant El Carrusel and Hotel Meléndez.

End of Taxco Eat & Stray

Cuernavaca

Area Code — 777

CUERNAVACA is the capital of the state of Morelos with a population of about 1,009,000 and an altitude of 5,000 feet above sea level. The town's chief claim to fame is its pleasant climate. Since it's a couple of thousand feet lower than Mexico City's 7,000 foot elevation, it's not as chilly during the winter, yet it's plenty balmy in summer. Since the days of the ancient Aztecs, Cuernavaca has been a summer retreat. Cortés, the conqueror, had a summer home here as well as Maximilian and Carlota years later, followed by practically all of Mexico's presidents, top government officials, foreign ambassadors and embassy people. On the popular holidays, hotel accommodations are hard to come by.

It's a shame you folks are not able to come along with us when we check out the fabulous places to stay here so that you can see firsthand all the absolutely lovely layouts! It's hard to go wrong here because there are a dozen or more beautiful inns in this delightful charming little city of Cuernavaca.

Cuernavaca also has some out-of-this-world private homes. Some of the richest people in Mexico maintain weekend homes down here — and some very wealthy Americans and Canadians as well. You might never know what luxuriant beauty lurks behind the flowered walls on the winding streets. Several of the better inns (posadas or hosterías) are former mansions.

You'll like Cuernavaca — if only you con get in those iron gates and behind those high walls, you would like it even more.

SLEEPING IN CUERNAVACA

BUNGALOWS LA ROSA – MOD – Emiliano Zapata #117 – Small 8 room motel at north end across from Posada Tlaltenango. Restaurant. 2 pools. Parking. Small pets OK. AE, MC, VI. Ph: 313-1100.

CAMINO REAL SUMIYA – UPPER – 163-unit hotel off 10 de Abril in secluded, tranquil Sumiya subdivision. This was Barbara Hutton's former summer home (heiress to the Woolworth fortune when she died with only $4,000 to her name). A Japanese-style getaway built in 1957 at the cost of $3,500,000. It is like walking into a Japanese retreat. There is a kabuki theater and behind the theater is a meditation garden, an authentic replica of a Japanese garden with lots of plants from Asia. It has 15 rocks buried 7/8 in the sand. You cannot see all 15 rocks except from one certain spot. (This is from Zen paradox that we can never see the whole truth, only part.) 2 Pools. Tennis. Golf. Ph: 320-9199 Fax: 320-9155. U.S.: 1-800-722-6466, Mex: 91-800-90-123.

CASINO DE LA SELVA – MOD-UPPER – Large, renovated 180-room northeast-end hotel on Av. Vicente Guerrero, formerly a gambling casino. 30 cottages. Terrace dining room. 2 clubs. Olympic-size pool with artificial beach. Art gallery. Tennis. Mini-golf. Bowling. Billiards. Horses. Movie. Playground. Parking. Pets OK. A, MC, VI. Popular with home folks. Ph: 318-0025. Fax: 318-9624.

CLARION CUERNAVACA RACQUET CLUB – UPPER – Fco. Villa #100 –Ritzy, secluded 23-acre resort with 52 plush suites including terrace and fireplace. 2 restaurants, one with lovely outdoor veranda. Disco-club. Olympic-size pool encircled by over-flowering shrubs. 9 flexi-paved all-weather tennis courts. Clubhouse. Tennis pro. Privileges to 2 nearby golf courses (Santa Fe and Los Tabachines). Parking. AE, MC, VI. Ph: 313-6122. Fax: 317-5483. Reservations a must.

DIANA INN – MOD – Peaceful 13-room inn perched atop a hill overlooking Cuernavaca (Kilometer 12.5 Exit on old highway to Cuautla and follow signs). Restaurant. Bar. Pool. Parking. MC, VI.

DEL PRADO INN CUERNAVACA – MOD-UPPER – Nardo #58 – Nice 200-room hotel in Rancho de Cortés Subdivision overlooking entire valley of Cuernavaca. 2 restaurants. Bars. Pool. Solarium. Tennis. Tropical gardens. Parking. AE, MC, VI. Ph: 17-4004. Fax: 17-4155.

HACIENDA DE CORTÉS – MOD – Plaza Kennedy #9 – 22-room restored hacienda in nearby Atlacomulco a mile south of Hwy #95 and Cuautla junction, originally owned by Martín Cortés son of Hernán Cortés, conqueror of Mexico. It was Cortés' getaway built in 1530. Unique house with art work and character. Each unit deluxe with living-dining room combo, bedroom and terrace. Exceptional restaurant. Bar. Pool. Whirlpool. Romantic gardens. Jacuzzi. Parking. AE, MC, VI. Ph: 315-8844, 316-0867 Fax: 315-0035. In D.F.: (5) 564-5998 Reservations suggested.

HACIENDA VISTA HERMOSA – UPPER – Rambling 225-room hotel 20 miles southeast of Cuernavaca off Hwy #95D at village of San Jose built in 1529 as a sugar mill and operated until 1910 when its owners were evicted by the revolution and the place was left in ruins. Rooms decorated in beautiful antiques. Restaurant. Big pool fed by ancient aqueduct. Carriage display dating back to Maximilian's era in lobby. Parking. MC, VI. Ph: 315-2374, 315-3049.

HORTENCIAS – ECON – Av. Hidalgo #22 – Quiet, super place. Nearby parking. Ph: 318-1575.

HOSTERIA LAS QUINTAS – MOD-UPPER – Av. Díaz Ordaz #107 –Beautiful inn (one of Mexico's loveliest) and full-service, world-class spa with 49 suites, some furnished in modern decor and some in Old Spanish-colonial style. Excellent restaurant overlooking picturesque gardens. Cozy lounge. 2 pools. Jacuzzi suites. Parking. AE, MC, VI. Ph: 318-3949. Fax: 318-3895. US: 1-800-321-4622. Advance reservations required.

IBERIA – ECON – Calle Rayón #9 – 26 rooms. Small parking lot inside courtyard. No trucks. Ph: 312-6040

LE CHATEAU RENE – MOD – Calzada De Los Reyes #11 – Cozy 12-suite inn in European decor at north entrance to town, a long block from Emiliano Zapata Monument. Top-notch restaurant specializing in European cuisine. Bar. Pool. Parking. AE, MC, VI. Attractive grounds and pleasant atmosphere. Ph: 317-2300.

ILEBAL – MOD – Chula Vista #7 – 35 rooms located in the historical district. Restaurant. Bar. Jacuzzi. Pool.

Parking. MC, VI. Ph: 318-2725, 318-2755, or 318-2749. Fax: 314-3820.

LA POSADA VALE DE CUERNAVACA – MOD – Río Panuco and Río Papaloapan – Delightful 7-suite inn in Vista Hermosa Subdivision. Restaurant specializing in Argentine cuisine. Bar. Pool. Parking. AE, MC, VI. Ph: 315-3049. Reservations a must.

LAS MAÑANITAS – UPPER – Ricardo Linares #107 – A landmark. Nice 22-room layout a half-block east off Hwy #95. Each room decorated in different Spanish-colonial decor. Outstanding restaurant serving international cuisine. Cocktail lounge with live music and dancing. Heated pool hidden by colorful walled garden. Valet parking. AE, MC, VI. Ph: 314-1466 or 314-1423. Fax: 318-3672.

LOS AMATES – ECON – Los Actores #112 – Good budget 21-room hotel. Family-style dining room. Pool. Parking. Popular with summer students.

LOS CANARIOS – ECON – Morelos #713 Nte. – Large, older 132-room economy-emergency motel on old Hwy #95-South. Restaurant. Bar. Pool. Parking. Pets OK.

MISÍON DEL SOL – UPPER – Av. Gral. Diego Díaz González, 31 Col. Parres – Near the Sumiya on the west side of the freeway. This is a beautiful resort and world-class spa and spiritual retreat. The grounds are 32,000 square meters of Southern California style landscaping. 40 rooms and a meeting room. Open air restaurant with vegetarian and meat and fish dishes. Spa services include temascal (sweat lodge), a very large outdoor jacuzzi, steam and sauna, as well as excellent massages etc. Pool is the prettiest I have ever seen with a large mosaic sun in the middle. Very ecologically aware management has installed a water treatment plant on the premises. Elegant. Ph: 321-0909, Fax: 321-1195. Mex. Toll free: 91-800-999-91, Mexico City: 91-5-616-3727, 616-0213, US: 1-800-321-4622.

PAPAGAYO – MOD – Motolinia #17 – 79-room midtown economy-emergency hotel just off old Hwy #95-North. Restaurant. Pool. Playground. Parking. Ph: 314-1711, 314-1924.

POSADA PRIMAVERA (formerly AROCENA HOLIDAY) – MOD – Paseo del Conquistador s/n – Nice 27 room motor hotel in Lomas de Cortés Subdivision not far from toll road interchange. Especially nice 8-room split-level section (bedroom-living room combos). Restaurant. Pool. Parking. MC, VI. Ph: 313-8383 Fax: 313-1938.

POSADA DE XOCHIQUETZAL – MOD – Francisco Leyva #200 – Nice downtown 14-room colonial inn converted from 17th-century mansion a block south of Cortés Palace. Dining room serving good American cuisine. Piano bar. Pool. Parking. AE, MC, VI. Ph: 318-5767, 318-6984. Fax: 312-9126.

POSADA JACARANDA – MOD – Cuauhtémoc #805 – Lovely 88-unit east-side inn on beautiful grounds. Romantic "love nest" suite in trees. Good restaurant. Cavern-style bar. Cave-style pool. Tennis. Jai-Alai. Mini-golf. Parking. AE, MC, VI. Ph: 315-7777, 315-7533, 315-7643 Fax: 315-7888.

POSADA SAN ANGELO – UPPER – Privada de la Selva #100 – Delightful 17-room inn converted from old mansion. Dining room. Bar. Pool. Parking. MC, VI. Ph: 312-6604 Fax: 312-7504.

RANCHO CUERNAVACA – VERY UPPER – Callejón del Arastradero s/n, Colonia Cahmpila (northeast of the city, see map) – This is the most elegant hotel in Mexico. The owner bills it as a bed and breakfast, and it is that and much more. You do get breakfast, but it is served by a butler! There are only 16 bedrooms, all different, all furnished with antiques. Lord Montagu of Great Britain stayed there, as well as other rich and famous celebrities. Some of the rooms have private jacuzzis. The grounds are extensive and landscaped. There is a pool. The entire place is furnished with $5,000,000 worth of European and Mexican antiques from the era of Maximilian. The owner William Markley Nixon III is a former Los Angeleno who was an architectural designer. He renovated and designed houses where many of Hollywood's stars lived before moving to Mexico and building his dream. He is a very cultured person, and it shows in the way the resort is designed. If elegance and romance are what you are looking for, this is your place. Bring lots of money, however. There is one "cheap" room for $150 for one, but most are in the $300 – $500 range. On weekends he hosts wedding parties, so you could see a real upper-class Mexican wedding if he has room. During the week, you should have no problem getting a room. Ph: 313-3962, Fax: 313-7828. US: 1-800-321-4622. VI, MC, AMEX.

VILLA DEL CONQUISTADOR – MOD – Paseo del Conquistador #134 – 54-room hotel. Restaurant. Bar. Pool. Parking. AE, MC, VI. Ph and Fax: 313-1055.

VILLA VEGETARIANA HEALTH SPA — UPPER — Mexico's Rejuvenation Resort. 38 guest units, heated swimming pool. Sauna. Steam baths. Squash, racket and tennis courts, Outdoor gymnasium. Organic gardens. Fruit trees. Private solariums for nude sun bathing. Fresh fruits and vegetables. Supervised fasting, nutritional and exercise programs. Weight reduction and other health related problems. Although they do accept guest for shorter stays, a minimum of 2 weeks is recommended. P.O. Box 1228, Cuernavaca, Morelos. AE, MC, VI. Ph: 313-1044.

EATING IN CUERNAVACA

HARRY'S GRILL – MOD – Gutenberg #3 – (Carlos 'N Charlie type) Popular turn-of-the-century decor bar-and-grill downtown at northeast corner of main plaza. International cuisine, but best are BBQ chicken and meat. Entertainment. Open 6 PM till 12:30 AM weekdays; 1:30 PM till 3:30 AM weekends. AE, MC, VI. Ph: 312-7679.

LA ADELITA – ECON – In front of Plaza Heroes and across from Palacio de Cortés – Sidewalk café with regional food including sopa de nopal, huixtlachotle, tacos, enchiladas, etc. Ph: 318-5697.

LA BUFA – ECON – Calle Comonfort #6-B – Near La Borda. Mexican food. Comida corrida. Open 9 AM till 6 PM daily.

LAS MAÑANITAS – UPPER – Ricardo Linares #107 – A absolute must. Everyone will ask if you ate there. One of Mexico's best dining places. Dine indoors or out in a beautiful garden where peacocks and other rare birds roam. Mexican and international cuisine (leaning toward French). Food superb and service excellent. Lunch from 1 PM till 5 PM; dinner from 7 PM till 11 PM. AE, MC, VI. Reservations a must (and be sure to arrive a half-hour in advance). Ph: 312-4646.

LA UNIVERSAL – MOD – Sandwiches. On plaza, next to McDonald's.

LOS ARCOS – MOD – Jardín de los Heroes # 4 – On the main plaza. Mexican food. Cappuccino. Patio dining.

MARCO POLO PIZZERIA – MOD – Across from cathedral on Calle Hidalgo #26. artisan exhibits. Serves Italian food. Home delivery. Open 1 PM till 9 PM daily. AE, MC, VI. Ph: 312-3484.

MOBY DICK – MOD – Plan de Ayala #383 – Small, unpretentious restaurant. Hamburgers, seafood, Hereford beef and international dishes are excellent. Open Noon till 10 PM; closed Mondays.

POZOLERIA EL BARCO – ECON – On Rayón #5 – Pozole all day, tacos etc. Open 11 Am till Midnight.

SUMIYA – UPPER – Japanese and international restaurant in hotel by same name 15 minutes from downtown Cuernavaca. International cuisine. Excellent service. Serves langostino (crayfish), duck and sushi. Beautiful atmosphere. Open for lunch and dinner. This is Barbara Hutton's legendary Japanese palace whose furnishings were imported from the Orient.

VEGETARIANO – MOD – Miguel Hidalgo #208 – Pleasant, quiet organ music. Warm atmosphere. Open 8 AM till 8 PM daily.

VIENA – MOD – Calle Guerrero #104 – Popular pastry (best in town) and coffee house downtown in arcade near plaza. Open 9 AM till 10 PM. Good Espresso and Cappuccino.

CAMPING & RV PARKING

DIAMANTE CUERNAVACA TRAILER PARK AND CLUB – UPPER – Just off Hwy 95-D on west side. Exit off Hwy 95 past Firestone plant and K-Mart on Ave. Diana. See directions in log. . 150 spaces, mostly filled with permanents but has an area for daily rentals and caravans. Electrical, water and sewer. Restrooms. Showers. Dump station. 2 heated pools. Rec. hall. Handball. Gym. Restaurant. Laundry. Concrete pads. Tennis. Store. Bar. Tours. English. Acre for field sports. Landscaped spaces with flowers. Space is limited. Ph and Fax: 316-0761.

EL PARAISO – MOD – South of the city, 11.4 miles off Hwy 95-D, take the Xochitepec exit. If coming from Acapulco, take the Airport exit and double back. See log for exact directions. This is a beautiful and serene location to camp. Spic and span facilities. 150 spaces, 65 with EWS. Pool. Hot water. Very clean bathrooms, showers. Good security. Highly recommended. Ph: 313-454, 313-455, Fax: 313-456.

OAXTEPEC VACATION CENTER – See below.

NEARBY HOTELS THAT ARE WORTH THE DRIVE

HACIENDA COCOYOC – UPPER – Charming, elegant hotel and world-class spa. Worth the money and less expensive than some nearby hotels. A restored 16th-century hacienda about 30 minutes from downtown Cuernavaca on the Cuautla Hwy – 260 rooms, 25 master suites with private pools. The spa is the only one in Mexico with an Alpha Jet capsule, which simulates a sensory deprivation chamber and puts you into an alpha level of sleep. It is the most elegant spa in the area and very highly recommended. Excellent masseuses. Restaurant. 2

large pools. Tennis. 9-hole golf course. Horses. Popular for meetings and conventions. Ph: 356-2211, 356-1211. Fax: 356-1212 In Mexico City: 5-550-6480. US 1-800-321-4622.

LAS ESTACAS – ECON – 20 miles southeast of Yautepec and Hacienda Cocoyoc in Tlaltizapán. This swimming resort has a hotel, 12 bungalows that are handicapped accessible and over 50 spaces for RV's with 15 EWS. Quiet, country setting. Special. Restrooms, restaurant, mini-super (the proceeds from which are given directly to the employees), tent camping. The crystal clear river (23° Centigrade) that flows through it is excellent for swimming. Many movies were shot using this location, including the last James Bond movie. I can think of no more beautiful place to stay. Ph: 342-1444.

OAXTEPEC VACATION CENTER – Once a favorite retreat of Montezuma. Pleasant vacation and convention center located about 25 miles from the turnoff at Hwy #95D. It has hotels that accommodate up to 2,000 people. Odorless (almost), cool sulfur pools as well as regular swimming pools. Playgrounds. Athletic fields. Restaurants. Lots of Mexican families come out on the weekends. Quite a deal. Pools are drained on Monday and filled on Tuesday, so you can swim Wednesday to Sunday. It also has 10 spaces for RV parking (water and electricity only). It's worth a visit. Ph: 352-1960.

STUB LOG TO OAXTEPEC, CUAUTLA

MI	KM	
0.0	0.0	After leaving freeway at junction of Hwys #95-D and #115-D, continue ahead (east) on Hwy #115, over railroad tracks. Lots of topes ahead.
0.6	0.7	Straight onto divided at intersection unless to Rancho Cuernavaca. Do not take left fork. (If to Rancho Cuernavaca, go 1/4 mile, take left at intersection. You'll see a sign for it. One-tenth of a mile after turn, it is on your right. Big blue gate. Announce yourself into the speaker, and they'll let you in, if you are good).
0.9	1.4	Curve left at cemetery. Right at "T." Topes.
2.4	3.8	Pass Benedictine monastery, left. KM 4.
6.7	10.7	At GAS, get onto toll road here at Tepoztlán, population 13,000 souls.
7.2	12.0	Toll booth. Cars $11. Extra axles $6. Las Estacas, exit just after toll booth towards Yautepec. KM 12.
21.6	34.5	Exit right for Cocoyoc, Oaxtepec. Then, left for Oaxtepec, right for Cocoyoc. Topes.
21.9	35.0	Gas, right. Hacienda Del Río, left.
22.7	36.3	Enter metropolis of Cocoyoc, population 8,000.
22.9	36.6	Come to "T." Left for Cocoyoc, Agua Hedionda. Right for Oaxaca and Las Estacas.

End of Cuernavaca Eat & Stray

Cuautla

Area Code — 735

CUAUTLA (whose original name, "Cuauhtlán", means "the place of the eagles") is a rather interesting place. For centuries it has been a popular spa, even back in the Aztec days and later with the Spaniards. (It is the burial place of the revolutionary hero and leader of agrarian reform, Emiliano Zapata.) Its altitude is 4,295 feet above sea level and has a population of around 70,000. Cuautla is becoming increasingly popular with tourists now that it is more easily accessible with the completion of the toll road. Oaxtepec, a little village 20 miles north of Cuautla (just north of toll road), is where Moctezuma developed the first botanical garden in America. With the exception of fabulous Hacienda Cocoyoc some four miles west of Cuautla, the various hotels and inns in Cuautla and vicinity are, shall we say, adequate.

SLEEPING IN CUAUTLA

BALNEARIO AGUA HEDIONDA — Popular thermal springs resort a couple of miles southeast of Cuautla on blacktop road. No accommodations or restaurant, only dressing cabanas. ("Agua Hedionda" means "stinky water" and that's what it is, but it's said to have curative powers.) Apt to be jam-packed on weekends and holidays.

BALNEARIO EL ALMEAL — Popular thermal springs spa at end of side street beyond Quinta Elena. No accommodations. Restaurant. Thermal pools.

BALNEARIO LAS TERMAS (ATOTONILCO) — 60-room, 2-story hotel next to Atotonilco thermal springs on hillside overlooking stream a half-kilometer off old Hwy #115. Restaurant. Several pools plus small lake. No credit cards. (Hot springs are claimed to be helpful for arthritis and rheumatism.)

HACIENDA COCOYOC — Marvelous 325-room, 400-year old restored sugar hacienda, one of Mexico's top resorts. 4 restaurants. Disco. Pool spanned by old aqueduct. Some suites with private pool. 9-hole golf course nearby (green and caddy fees). Tennis. Horses. Buggy rides. Ping-pong. Trap shooting. AE, CB, DI, MC, VI. Ph: 352-2000. Apt to be crowded on Mexican holidays or when booked for convention.

INTERNACIONAL — 24-unit hotel on street parallel to road thru town. Restaurant. Pool. Some kitchenettes. MC, VI.

OAXTEPEC CENTRO VACACIONAL ("Vacation Center") — 124-bungalow, 12-cottage layout in nearby Oaxtepec developed by the IMSS ("Instituto Mexicano del Seguro Social") as a vacation spot for its members (but it's open to the public on weekends). 3 restaurants. Bar. Coffee shop. 25 spring-fed pools. Movie theater. No credit cards. Ph: 352-1085.

QUINTA ELENA — Pleasant 11-kitchenette layout on Calle Virginia Hernández. No restaurant. Pool. Balneario ("spa") All meals next door. No credit cards. Ph: 352-0341.

VASCO — 102-room, 2-story hotel in midtown, Cuautla's largest. Restaurant. Pool (sulfurous water). Solarium. Squash. Billiards. Disco. MC, VI. Ph: 352-1400.

EATING IN CUAUTLA

LA TIA — OK place on Cuautla's main street. Specializes in broiled chicken, Mexican dishes and short orders. No credit cards. ("La Tia" means "the aunt," and in the States we would probably call this place "Aunty's.")

End of Cuautla Eat & Stray

Tehuacán

Area Code - 238

TEHUACAN is a nice little city with a population of about 125,000 – clean and prosperous. Everybody seems to be going places – busy and happy. It's 5500 feet above sea level with a pleasant dry climate. In addition to being Mexico's #1 mineral water town, Tehuacán is also a center for the manufacture of onyx products like book ends, ash trays, little animals, Aztec calendar plaques, etc. There's also a leather factory in town across the street from the Hotel Montecarlo where several rather interesting leather items are made - like floppy hats, Daniel Boone fringed jackets, etc. The mineral water (the good stuff) has lithium in it. Honest, it says so on the bottle. Maybe that's why we all mellow out a little bit when we come here.

Tehuacán's market (Saturday) is interesting. It's a couple of blocks east of the main downtown intersection. Also, the town has a museum "Museo Valle de Tehuacán" at Calle 1 North #209. Its 12-room exhibition features interesting items such as corn cobs dating back 10,000 years. It's open from 9 till noon and from 3 till 5 (closed Monday). Legend has it that the first corn was cultivated in these parts.

You can also visit the mineral springs water bottling plants - inquire at your hotel. The largest are "Peñafiel," "Garci-Crespo," "San Lorenzo," and "El Riego."

Casa de Cambio, "Inter Solaris" – Reforma #311. Ph: 372-0308. Open 9:00 – 1:30 and 4:30 – 6:00 – Monday thru Friday ONLY!

SLEEPING IN TEHUACAN

ALDEA DEL BAZAR – MOD – At northeast edge of town near San Lorenzo. On the bypass around town from the Puebla highway. Interesting 32 cottage hotel done in Arabian motif, but alas, no jacuzzis or harem dancers. Pleasant surroundings, park in front of room. Hard beds. Pool. Restaurant. MC, VI. Ph: 372-2550 Ph and Fax: 372-2558

BOGH SUITES – MOD – 0.5 blocks off zócalo – All suites, 17 altogether. 0.5 blocks off main square. Pleasant place, discount for cash. Parking at log 1 block away. MC, VI. Ph: 372-3879.

HOSTERIA DEL CAMINO – ECON – Morelos #7 – Colonial-style 23-room, 2-story hotel on Hwy #150 at far end of town. Restaurant. Pool. Parking. Ph: 372-3612.

IBERIA – MOD – VALUE! – 217 Insurgentes Ote. (Corner 3rd) – Oldest hotel in town, has seen its ups and downs. Now on an up. Remodeled, it's a garden paradise when you enter. 2 stories and lots of potted plants. 25 BIG rooms. Still, it's more like fancy budget than middle-class, but some of us prefer that. Manager, Leticia Cortés, is a nice person who speaks English. Parking 1/2 block away. Restaurant Iberia. Ph: 373-1500, 373-1511, 373-1507.

MEXICO – MOD – Reforma y Independencia – Very good 90-room, 2-story hotel built around pretty patio in midtown at junction of town's two main streets. Some suites. 3 TUBS! Excellent dining room. Pool. Parking (with security – but you'll pay a few pesos for it). Replica of Granada, Spain's Alhambra Fountain in courtyard. Rotary Club meets and eats here. AE, MC, VI. Traveler's checks cashed with passport only. Ph: 372-0019, 372-1319, 372-2419, 372-0340, 372-0067. Fax: 372-2519.

MONTE CARLO – ECON – Av. Avila Camacho S/N – Big old 85-room, 2-story hotel on main north-south street at north end. No restaurant. Pool. Parking. Ph: 2-0700.

POSADA MONROY – ECON – Reforma 211 – Really nice. 22-room hotel built around patio on main north-south street. Parking. Ph: 372-0491.

EATING IN TEHUACAN

CAFETERIA LA GRANJA – MOD – North side of zócalo. Outside tables. Opens early for breakfast – 7 AM. Mexican food. Open 7 AM till 11 PM.

DANNY RICHARD – MOD – Reforma Nte. 205 – Pizza and Mexican food. Nice. Piano bar. Looks like a popular spot with all sorts of tourists. Nice. Ph: 372-0433.

FLAMINGO – MOD – 231 Reforma Nte. – My favorite cheap breakfast –licuados, ice cream, sandwiches. Good. Open 8 AM till 10 PM.

IBERIA – MOD – In hotel by same name. Spanish cuisine, paella, etc. Good, reasonable comida corrida.

PEÑAFIEL – MOD – South side of zócalo. Mexican and international food. Seafood. Good breakfasts. Dine inside or outside. Of all the places to feed on the zócalo, this is the classiest one. The others are more beer and sandwich-type restaurants.

End of Tehuacán Eat & Stray

Oaxaca

Area Code — 951

OAXACA is absolutely one of the nicest towns in Mexico – a personal favorite of ours. Only two things wrong – it's just too far from anywhere, and it takes too long to get here. But once you've made it way down to this Zapotec country, you'll be well rewarded for your time and effort. One of the nicer things about Oaxaca is the ease with which you can move around on the flat, wide one-way streets. And one of the really nice things about Oaxaca is the friendliness of its people. What's more, there are many interesting things to see – archeological, historical and cultural. And Oaxaca has a big variety of good accommodations. All in all, this is a terrific town. It's suggested you take a sight-seeing trip of the town itself (very worthwhile). The Museo (museum) Rufino Tamayo at Morelos #503 is a colonial-style mansion containing a collection of antiques donated by Tamayo. Also, the state museum (in the old convent section of the Santo Domingo Church) houses many interesting exhibits – plus some treasures from Monte Albán. You might want to spend the morning taking the tour up to the fabulous scraped off mountain top archeological ruins of MONTE ALBAN – the road up is good blacktop but slightly narrow, very winding and a bit squeamish. In the afternoon take the city tour. You'll enjoy the local sights. You really don't need a guide to drive you to see the ancient TULE TREE (right next to Hwy #190 which is 6 miles south of town) or the famous MITLA archaeological ruins (24 miles south of here just off Hwy #190 on a paved road) – the next log, Oaxaca - Tehuantepec, provides info on these places. You can see them on the morning you take off for Tehuantepec and La Ventosa.

Here in Oaxaca the CENTROAMERICANA DE VIAJES TRAVEL AGENCY is recommended for sight-seeing services (downtown at Portal de Flores #8). The owner, Senor JORGE ("hor-hay") GONZALEZ, is a good Rotarian who has built up a nice business from scratch on good service and fair dealing.

One of the most interesting things to see here in Oaxaca is CASA ARAGÓN at J.P. García #503 (near market). This is the firm that makes the famous Oaxaca machetes, swords and knives for home and hunting. Eight generations of Aragons have been making quality cutlery since 1750 – they've made machetes for ex-Presidente Nixon, Charles DeGaulle, Porfirio Díaz (currently in a museum in France) and many other dignitaries. Tourists are very welcome to visit the factory where the knives are made – it's a little dirty, but aren't all forges and foundries? Of course, one of the most interesting features about the knives and machetes made by the Aragon family are the pithy sayings and proverbs engraved on every blade. CASA ARAGÓN is a most interesting place – don't miss it!

If you want BLACK OAXACAN POTTERY, it is suggested that you drive down to the village of San Bartolo Coyotepec a short way south of town on Hwy #175, where the peasants who make the pottery have set up a "union" or "co-op" shop-and-sales agency. The first village you come to will be Santa Maria Coyotepec – but this is not what you're looking for, even though the last names are similar. Keep going to the next village, San Bartolo Coyotepec. Then at a pottery sign turn left onto a dirt street, go a few yards and stop in front of the walled yard at left. Lock your car and walk on into the yard – the display of pottery is in the little building just beyond the clearing – someone there will speak English. Better just buy what you want and take it along in your car – don't attempt to have it shipped as the pottery is very fragile. The men will wrap your purchases reasonably well so that it should make it home all right in the trunk of your car.

While you're driving around town be sure to go up Porfirio Díaz Street to the north end (up past Misión de los Angeles) and see the statues of the women of Oaxaca state gathered around a pretty fountain. Also, you'll see the beautiful main building of the medical school, once the hacienda of a rich rancher. There's quite a school complex on behind it toward the suburb of San Felipe.

Two very nice customers, A. Pérez and J. Pierson of Long beach CA, gave us these tips. Careful of street vendors selling rugs. Many are machine-made. Try art galleries for the real thing. Lo Mano Mágico on Alcala ped. mall has good stuff. Teotilán del Valle is a good spot for rugs. The whole town makes 'em, or so it seems. They found good cloth and dresses behind Mitla ruins.

OTHER USEFUL INFO

AA – English – Inquire at lending library or leave note in mailbox #414 at post office. Ph: 515-3728 or 515-1989.

LAUNDRY – Lavandería Automática "Clin" – 20 de Noviembre #605-B. Ph: 516-2342.

LIBRARY – Alcala #305 – Open 10 till 1, 4 till 6, M-F. – Books in English. Loan privileges to members. Please inquire about fees. Even if you're not staying long, a donation for their building fund would be appreciated by ol' Dan.

POST OFFICE – Corner of Independencia and the Alemeda Park.

TOURIST OFFICE – 5 de Mayo #200. Really helpful folks.

SLEEPING IN OAXACA

ANTURIOS — MOD — Priv. Emilio Carranza #202, Col. Reforma close to the ADO bus terminal. 26 rooms. Restaurant. Parking. Ph: 513-0122, Fax: 513-0075.

BEL-AIR — ECON — On Hwy at the north edge of town, KM 542. 44 rooms. Ph: 512-6744.

CALESA REAL – MOD – García Vigil #306 – 77-unit, 2-story hotel near downtown. Ceiling fans. Restaurant. Bar. Pool. Parking nearby. MC, VI. Ph: 516-5795, 516-5544, 516-5995 Fax: 516-7232.

CALIFORNIA – MOD – Calzada Héroes de Chapultepec #822 – 2-story, 33-room hotel on Hwy #190. Small restaurant. MC, VI. Ph: 515-9500, 515-3628 Fax: 513-1771.

CAMINO REAL OAXACA – UPPER – Located on 5 de Mayo #300 in the heart of Oaxaca City, the former Convent of Santa Catalina. 91 rooms/suites. Restaurant. Bar. Pool. Curio shop. Gardens. Car rental. Travel agency. AE, MC, VI. Ph: 516-0611 Fax: 516-0732. For Reservations (US and Canada) call 1-800-7-CAMINO Mex: 91-800-9-0123.

FIESTA INN OAXACA – UPPER – Av. Universidad #140 Ex-hacienda de Candiani. 119 rooms. Restaurant. Bar. Pool. Free transportation to downtown. AE, MC, VI. Ph: 514-7905 Mex: 91-800-5-0450.

FORTÍN PLAZA – MOD-UPPER – Av. Venus #118, Col Estrella – Very attractive 96-unit, 6-story A/C hotel on Hwy #199 at north entrance to city. 2 restaurants. 2 bars. Coffee shop. Nicely landscaped pool. Parking. AE, MC, VI. Ph: 515-7777. Fax: 515-1328.

FRANCIA – ECON – 20 de Noviembre #212. 46-room downtown hotel. Ph: 516-4811, 516-4251.

GALA OAXACA – MOD – Hotel at Bustamante #103. 36-room downtown hotel. Noisy. Parking. Ceiling fans. CATV. MC, VI. Ph: 514-2251, 514-1305 Fax: 516-3660.

LA CABAÑA – MOD – Motel on Carretera Internacional (Hwy to Mexico) KM 539, Fracc. Bugambilias. 40 rooms. Jacuzzi. Parking. MC, VI. Parking. Ph: 512-5288, 512-6000.

LAS ROSAS – ECON – Trujano #112 – 19 rooms around a courtyard. Pretty good for budget. Ph: 514-2217.

LOS OLIVOS – MOD – Calz. Madero #1254 – 2-story, 70-unit motel near northwest entry to town. Restaurant. Bar. Pool. Parking. Ph: 514-1946, 514-2074. Fax: 514-2225.

MARQUES DEL VALLE – MOD – Portal de Claveria – Older 95 room, 5-story downtown hotel next door to cathedral. Elevator. Reasonable prices. Dining room. Sidewalk cafe. On-street parking. AE, MC, VI. Ph: 516-3677, 516-3474, or 516-3295. Fax: 516-9961.

MISIÓN DE LOS ANGELES – MOD-UPPER – 102 Calz. Porfirio Díaz – Restful, tranquil gardens surrounding 175 suites, just off Hwy #190 at north end of town. Near intersection with Calz. Niños Héroes and Porfirio Díaz. Tubs in master suites only. Tennis. 4 excellent restaurants. Bar. Pool. Tennis. Carports. Nicely landscaped. AE, MC, VI. Ph: 515-1000, 515-1500, 515-8727, 515-1222. US: 800-221-6509. Fax: 515-1680.

MONTE ALBAN – MOD – Alameda de León #1 – Attractive old 18-room, 2-story hotel, once a 17th-century bishop's palace, kitty-corner from main plaza. Patio dining room. Famous "Guelaguetza" Indian dancers on Wednesday and Saturday evenings. On-street parking. AE, MC, VI. Ph: 516-2777 Fax: 516-3265.

PARADOR PLAZA – MOD – Av. Munguía #104. 59 rooms. Restaurant. Lobby bar. Travel agency. Ph: 516-4900, 514-2027 Fax: 514-2037.

PARADOR SANTO DOMINGO DE GUZMAN – MOD – Very nice 18 suites at M. Alcalca # 804. Kitchens. Hard beds. CATV. Parking. MC, VI. Ph: 514-2171 Fax: 514-1019.

POSADA SAN PABLO – MOD – Seallo #102 – VALUE! – 22 rooms around a courtyard. QUIET. Clean. All different. No parking, sadly. It's upscale budget with friendly management. Each room has a little kitchenette set-up. Cute. Ph: 516-4914.

PRIMAVERA – MOD – Calz. Madero #438 – Nice enough 18 room place run by friendly folks. Parking. MC, VI. Ph: 516-1376, 516-4508, 514-5312.

SAN FELIPE OAXACA – MOD – Jalisco #15, San Felipe del Agua (Follow signs but turn right at "T" onto one-way, right after one block, left after one more block and right at major intersection) – Pretty, 160-room, 2-story hotel on rolling hillside overlooking city at San Felipe del Agua, with rooms decorated in regional arts and crafts. Indoor and outdoor restaurants. Disco. Pool and pool bar. Lobby bar. Tennis. Parking. AE, MC, VI. Ph: 513-5050, 513-5090. Fax: 513-5744 Mex: 286-0550 Fax: 51211-8496

SEÑORIAL – MOD – Portal de Flores #6 – VALUE! – 127-room, 3-story downtown hotel on west side of zócalo. Restaurant. Cafeteria. Bar. Pool. Parking, 1/2 block away. Ph: 516-3933. Fax: 516-3668.

VERACRUZ – MOD – Calz. Héroes de Chapultepec #1020 – 55-unit, 3-story hotel on Hwy #190 next to bus station near east edge of town. Restaurant. Enclosed parking. MC, VI. Ph: 515-0611 Fax: 515-0511

VICTORIA – MOD – Carr. Panamericana KM 545, LOMAS DEL FORTÍN #1 – VALUE! – Very nice 150-room, 3-story hotel plus 34 cottage units on Hwy #199 near Juárez Monument. Advertises itself as "the best hotel in Oaxaca." QUIET. Tubs in cottages. One of our favorites. Restaurant. Bar. Disco. Pool. Tennis. Ample parking, though driveway is steep. AE, CB, DI, MC, VI. Ph: 515-2633, Fax: 515-2411. In D.F.: 280-1870, Fax: 280-0498. US: 800-448-8355.

VILLAS DEL SOL – MOD – Bargain! Next to Breñamiel tennis club. 32 villas all with kitchen, living room and local TV. MC, VI. Ph: 512-6331.

XANDU – MOD – Hotel at KM 6,1/2 Carretera Aeropuerto. Bungalows. Monthly rentals. Very quiet. Pool. Gardens. Ph: 511-5080.

EATING IN OAXACA

DEL JARDÍN – MOD – On zócalo, below "Vasco" – Of all the sidewalk cafes, this seems to be the most popular with the widest variety of people. Food is consistently good and cappuccino is good. Service, well ... don't expect to be overwhelmed by it. If you knit, you'll have a good chance to get caught up. If not, make friends with someone at a nearby table. It's the thing to do.

DOÑA ELPIDIA – MOD – Oaxacan institution at Miguel Cabrera #413 (6 blocks south of zócalo) which has catered to local clientele for over 40 years. Serves best homemade regional specialties in beautiful courtyard filled with plants and birds. Open for lunch only from 1-5 PM daily.

EL ASADOR VASCO – MOD-UPPER – Portal de Flores #11 – Excellent, elegant (though not stuffy) upstairs restaurant on zócalo next to Señorial. International, regional and Basque (hence name) dishes. Winner of Travel-Holiday award 1980-1988. Strolling musicians. Terrific terrace overlooking plaza as well as indoor dining. Not cheap. Open daily from 5:30 PM till midnight. AE, MC, VI. Ph: 516-9719.

EL CATEDRAL – MOD – Colonial-style restaurant at García Vigil and Morelos, about 1,1/2 blocks from zócalo. Indoor cafeteria and "formal" dining as well as patio. Regional cuisine plus sandwiches and steaks. Open 8 AM till 1 AM daily. Street parking. MC, VI.

EL GRANERO – ECON – Av. Hidalgo #908-A – Natural food, Inexpensive seafood, 1 block off square.

EL MESÓN DEL TACO – ECON – Hidalgo #531 – Good tacos, good prices.

LA FLOR DE LOTO – ECON – Armenta y López #915 – Around corner from "Gourmet" and "Carmen" (in fact shares bathroom with "Carmen"). Vegetarian fare. Inexpensive comida corrida. Vegetarian crepes, quesadillas. Inexpensive breakfasts. Try "Aguas Revitalizantes" – alfalfa and pineapple with lime. It's good, really! Posters advertising courses in yoga and other metaphysical, holistic and mystical stuff. These are real people.

LA MANSIÓN – MOD – Colonial restaurant at corner of Díaz Ordaz Crespo and Independencia, once an interesting old home. Oaxacan specialties. "Guelaguetza" Indian dancers perform on Saturday evenings. Open noon till midnight. MC, VI.

PLAZA GOURMET – MOD – 509 Morelos – Comida corrida, licuados de yogurt, typical food in nice flowered courtyard setting. Upstairs section, too. Open 7 AM till 11 PM. Ph: 516-9146.

QUICKLY – ECON – Macedonio Alcala #100 – Absolutely one of the best bargains in town. Backpacker's headquarters, you'll likely meet students from around the world as you share long wooden tables, dormitory style. Mexican food, vegetarian food, licuados, fruits. Good, inexpensive breakfasts. Open 8 AM till 11 PM, M-S. Sun 11 AM till 11 PM. Ph: 516-0313.

VILLA DEL CARMEN – MOD – 511 Morelos – Next to "Gourmet." Similar, but they have seafood. 8 AM till 10 PM.

CAMPING & RV PARKING

OAXACA – MOD – Nice 175-space facility at Violetas #900. All hookups. Showers. Toilets. Pets OK. Laundromat. Rec hall. Night security. Doctor. Enclosed by high wall. Ph: 515-2796.

ROSA ISABEL – MOD – 55-space park at far north end on Hwy #190 (in suburban Loma de Pueblo Nuevo). All hookups. Bungalows. Showers. Toilets. Rec hall. Pool. Laundry. Sports club and golf course nearby. Bus service to town. Ph: 516-0770.

SAN FELIPE DEL AGUA – MOD – A new trailer park and campground located on a 5-acre horse ranch in the foothills of the Sierra Madre at the base of the San Felipe del Agua National Park. 15 minutes from downtown with panoramic views overlooking the city of Oaxaca. There are presently 4 sites with EWS and another 30 sites for units not requiring EWS (and plan to develope 50 sites with EWS). Fenced in on private property for security. Plenty of fresh mountain water plus space for walking, jogging, mountain biking or horseback riding. Reasonable rates – FIRST NIGHT FREE! To get there: Follow the signs to Hotel San Felipe, past the University at the Fuentes de Las 7 Regiones on Hidalgo to the only church in San Felipe. Turn left at the church onto Iturbide. Go down to bridge over the creek and up the hill on paved road to #10 Camino de la Chigolera. It is on the left hand side at the cyclone fence gate. English spoken. Owner: Douglas French. E-mail: french@Antequera.com Ph: 516-0654 Fax: 516-4239.

End of Oaxaca Eat & Stray!

LOG 52 START: La Ventosa, Oax END: Tehuantepec, Oax

UD-087

26.6 MI or 42.6 KM
DRIVE TIME 1/2 – 1 HOUR
SCENIC RATING –2

Between La Ventosa and Tehuantepec, the road is flat and wide, straight and fast. However, November thru March there are very stiff north winds in the La Ventosa area that can blow even the largest trailers and motorhomes off the road as they can reach almost hurricane force: So, if you're an RV'er, exercise caution!

MI	KM	
0.0	0.0	Starting at La Ventosa at junction with Hwy #185, proceed ahead past **GAS**, over at left. Sign says "Tehuantepec 40 KM."
1.0	1.6	Agricultural experiment station at left.
2.5	4.0	Electrical power station at left.
8.1	13.0	LP gas at left.
9.0	14.4	Over railroad bridge and cement factory on right.
9.5	15.2	Skirt edge of Juchitán (population 66,530). Pass side road (right) to Ixtepec. Then **GAS** station at left.

Here, as in Tehuantepec, just 16 miles ahead, you'll see the dark and statuesque women, in the colorful market areas, wearing handsomely embroidered dresses with starched ruffles and white-lace blouses called "huipiles." Incidentally, Zapotec is still widely spoken here.

9.7	15.5	Pass Coca Cola bottling plant at left with nice Colón Restaurant (bus stop for Colón bus line) next door, best in these parts and a real lifesaver (air-conditioned; clean; accommodating; tidy restrooms). Then cross Río Los Perros and take leave of Juchitán.
10.0	16.0	Pass Hotel Del Río at right.
10.5	16.8	Pass road (right) to Santa Almería Xadani.
13.8	22.1	Pass road right to air base.
24.7	39.5	Pass Hotel Calli at right (3-story, 80-room layout; restaurant; pool; pets OK; MC, VI; best around). Then exit right to Mixtequilla.
25.3	49.5	Pass entrance to Tehuantepec at left. Up and over railroad overpass and pass Tehuantepec proper at left (population 142,000).
26.1	41.8	Cross steel frame bridge over Río Tehuantepec and thru suburb of Barrio Santa María.
26.6	42.6	Come to junction with Hwy #190. **GAS**, at left.

IF TO: Oaxaca, take right fork and start Tehuantepec - Oaxaca Log (page 159).

IF TO: Puerto Escondido Salina Cruz, Pochutla, and on to Acapulco, take left fork and start Tehuantepec - Puerto Escondido Log.

End of Log 52

LOG 53 START: Tehuantepec END: Pto Escondido, Oax

UD-087

170.0 MI or 272.0 KM
DRIVE TIME 2 1/2 – 3 HOURS
SCENIC RATING – 3

Nice flat road, a little curvy. Skirts Pacific with some nice views. Careful for rocks on road – it's a landslide area. The bridges on this route are all badly surfaced and dangerous at higher speeds. Also, during rainy season, some bridges may be out. Pretty red-rock country.

0.0	0.0	Here at junction of Hwy #185 and #190. **GAS** on right. **KM 250**.
2.4	3.8	Hospital at left.
3.9	6.2	Motel El Encanto with air conditioning on left.
4.3	6.9	Big Hotel Cid del mar on left.
5.1	8.2	Pass Hotel El Pescador on left. Then Chrysler/Dodge dealer on left.

MI	KM	
5.9	9.4	Restaurant Dos Oceanos and **GAS** at left.
6.8	10.9	Entrance right to Pemex refinery, one of Mexico's largest. Ford dealer, left. **KM 295**.
7.2	11.5	Pass Restaurant El Parador on left.
8.0	12.8	Slow for TOPES. **GAS** station at left.
8.2	13.1	Budget Rent-A-Car at right.
9.0	14.4	TURN RIGHT when coast is clear. Straight goes into Salina Cruz (population 61,760), Red Cross at left. See Salina Cruz map (page 30) and Eat & Stray (page 123) for accommodations. **KM 393**.
9.2	14.7	Careful and cross Trans-Isthmus Railroad (LOOK-&-LISTEN). You are now on Hwy #200. TOPES (3 or more). Restaurant Hawaii 03 at right –very good seafood.
10.5	16.8	Come to "Y." Take right fork. Then wind on down. Up and thru a couple of cuts and then nice view of Salina Cruz Bay, its naval base and Pemex storage dock.
11.5	18.4	Hotel-Restaurant Playa del Marquez, left.
17.5	28.0	Wide spot of Guellaghiche at left.
18.9	30.2	Over puente Corralito.
21.0	33.6	Great view of bay to left.
26.0	41.6	Thru little village of El Morro Mazatán. Restaurant Mari at right has a good breakfast. Now you'll enter the red-rock country. **KM 365**.
28.4	45.4	Pass side road (right) to Aguascalientes (8 km away). We drove the 8 km so you wouldn't have to. We asked a resident if there was hot water – He replied, "No, no más el nombre" with a big grin.
30.4	48.6	Settlement of Santa Gertrudis Miramar at left.
32.0	51.2	Potential rock slides and wash-outs – inquire locally in rainy season (summer and late fall).
34.5	55.2	Pass side road (left) to Concepción on Bamba beach. Then thru village of Rincón Bamba down at right and over three bridges.
36.0	57.6	Note beautiful beach down to left – what a terrific spot for a resort. (Venerable Dan wrote that, back in the 1960's. I reckon he knew a good thing when he saw it!)
48.4	77.4	Salt drying beds, left. **KM 332**.
54.0	86.4	Cross bridge over Río Huamelula. Then pass side road (right) to San Pedro Huamelula.
55.5	88.8	Thru village of Santiago Astata (population 2,200) at left.
57.2	91.5	Cross bridge curving to left over Río Huamelula. Thru village of Santa María Huamelula and out. **KM 317**.
60.0	96.0	Cross bridge over Río Tapanala. Thru little village of Tapanala and out. Careful for pigs, really.
64.0	102.4	Over two small bridges then over a big bridge. Curve right.
66.2	105.9	Thru settlement of El Coyol. Over Río Coyol. Topes (several). Nice little humble restaurant Los Arcos for snacks and soft drinks. **KM 299**.
71.0	113.6	Small bridge over Río Ayuta then big bridge.
78.7	125.9	Pass huge rock on left called Piedra del Rosario. Then pass side road (right) to village of Chacalapa.
84.3	134.9	Cross bridge that curves to left over Río Zimatán.
91.6	146.6	Wide spot of Copalita at left then cross bridge over Río Copalita.
97.4	155.8	Pass side road (left) to Tangolunda. Then over another river, this one named Río Tangolunda. Sometimes (depending on the time of year) any or all of these bridges will have bad surfaces. Keep alert.
98.5	157.6	Pass side road (left) that takes you to Club Med and Tangolunda, Sheraton and other Huatulco hotels.
100.0	160.0	Pass side road (left) to Bahía Santa Cruz de Huatulco, 3 1/2 miles. This exit is for the resort hotel only – RV park and inexpensive hotels take the next turnoff. It's maybe one of the prettiest places around. See Huatulco Eat & Stray (page 122) for info on accommodations. There's **GAS** in town.
105.2	168.3	Over Río del Xuchil.
108.0	172.8	Huatulco's airport, right. **GAS** at left. **KM 238**.
108.3	173.3	Over Río Cuajiniquil (the pronunciation could kill you). Thru wide spot of Agua el Zapote.
109.0	174.4	Another crossroads. This is not your exit for Huatulco, the resort. Side road (right) is to big village of Sta. María Huatulco (but there is an RV park and economic hotels) while (left) is to village of El Arenal (sandy ground) and on to San Augustín. The latter is perched on a nice bay, but unless you drive a four-wheel vehicle, those 5 miles separating the highway from the bay are treacherous.
111.4	178.2	Over bridge over Río Coyula curving to right. Goat crossing. **KM 233**.
116.0	185.6	Pass side road (left) to village of Coyula, 4 kilometers, and (right) to settlement of El Limón, 5 kilometers.
121.5	194.4	Pass side road (left) to village of Zapotengo, 2 miles away. Then cross bridge over Río El Aguacate (The Avocado). Careful for rocks on road – this is a landslide area "zona de derrumbes."
122.2	195.5	Rancho Tres Lunas (Three Moons), right.
126.0	201.6	Come to junction Hwy 175 right to Pochutla (where there is **GAS** in town). **KM 210**.

IF TO: Puerto Escondido, straight ahead on this log.

IF TO: Oaxaca, turn right and start Pochutla - Oaxaca Log (page 68).

IF TO: Puerto Angel turn left and see Puerto Angel Eat & Stray (page 121) for info on accommodations.

PUERTO ANGEL, at the end of a winding stretch of 8 miles, is an unspoiled little village reflecting itself in the blue waters of a small bay where fishing boats and naval ships doze. Besides the naval base, a few seafood restaurants and its colorful fishing market (at mid-morning on the dock upon the fishing boats' arrival), Puerto Angel offers two swimming beaches – "Zipolite," long and easily accessible where everybody wears a swim suit and "Playa del Amor" (Love Beach), small and encircled by hills and reached only by a brisk walk, where only birthday suits are used, this being the first public nudist beach in Mexico!

MI	KM	
131.5	210.4	Thru village of San Antonio. **KM 198**.
136.2	217.9	Pass wide spot of El Venado (The Deer) at left. Over big bridge and curve left thru village of San Isidro.
140.8	225.3	Over Puente La Gartero.
144.5	231.2	Over bridge and thru settlement of Escobilla.
146.5	234.4	Over Río Cozoaltepec and another view of beach at left.
149.7	239.5	Curve right, then straight, with view of Pacific at left.
151.2	241.9	Villages of San Bernardino and Cozoaltepec at right. Then thru settlement of Santa Elena at left.
154.2	246.7	Thru settlement of Valdeflores and over Río Valdeflores.
158.0	252.8	Thru village of El Tomatal.
166.2	265.9	Cross bridge over Río Barra de Colotepec and curve right and thru village of same name. Road is straight with some ups and downs.
166.7	266.7	**GAS** at left.
167.0	267.2	Las Tortugas Ecological area at left.
167.3	267.7	Zicatelo beach to left.
167.5	268.0	Villa Las Brisas at left.
168.1	269.0	Pass exit (left) to Hotel Villa Bay
168.4	269.4	Villas del Mar, left
168.6	269.8	Hotel Il Villandante at right.
168.8	270.1	First dirt road to right leads to good massage and healing place 3/4 mile on left.
169.3	270.9	Another side road (left) to Zicatelo, Búngalos Villa Marinero, Marinero beach and Santa Fe Hotel, and vegetarian restaurant downhill to left (Calle de la Morro).
169.5	271.2	Over puente Regadillo. Military garrison at right where the 54th Infantry Battalion is stationed.
169.7	271.5	Bilingual cultural institute at right.
170.0	272.0	Come to junction with Hwy #131 to Oaxaca and side road (left) into idyllic tropical town of Puerto Escondido (population 8,200). See Pto. Escondido Eat & Stray (page 119) for info on accommodations. Careful for topes and curve right with white sandy beach down at left.

IF TO: Oaxaca, turn right. This road has not been logged, but the people at tourism say it has been recently paved but ask again to make sure it's safe. Otherwise, go back the 44 miles to Pochutla.

IF TO: Acapulco and to hotels El Mirador, Rancho El Pescador and Castel Bugambilias or to Puerto Escondido RV Park, continue straight ahead and start Pto Escondido - Acapulco Log.

End of Log 53

LOG 54 START: Pto. Escondido, Oax END: Acapulco, Gro

UD-087

261.4 MI or 418.2 KM
DRIVE TIME 6 – HOURS
SCENIC RATING – 3

Careful for livestock in right-of-way. Along this highway in Coajinicuilapa and surrounding area resides Mexico's only Black population. Also, along this route you may encounter military check-points, part of Mexico's campaign against arms and drug smuggling.

0.0	0.0	Here at junction with side road (left) into Puerto Escondido and Hwy #131 to Oaxaca, proceed ahead on Hwy #200. Nice view of Puerto Escondido Bay at left.
0.3	0.5	Big Coca Cola sign on building at right. Agencia Municipal, left. For Puerto Escondido Trailer Park on beach, turn left here, go one block, then turn right and on down partially paved road. Then Restaurant Tolteca, right. Puerto Angelito – Carrizalillo beach and tourist office at left.
0.5	0.8	Hotel Rancho El Pescador at right.

MI	KM	
1.0	1.6	Hotel Camino del Sol, right. Then pass side road (left) to Fraccionamiento ("subdivision") Bachocho at left and to Castel Puerto Escondido and also Hotel Jardín Real.
1.3	2.1	Tourist information house about 1/2 block down on right. Then **GAS** at right.
1.8	2.8	Puerto Escondido's airport at right.
5.6	9.0	Cross big bridge over Río Chila.
10.0	16.0	Thru Aguaje el Zapote and pass Instituto Bíblico Genesaret on left.
10.2	16.3	Pass La Isla del Gayo (Rooster Island).
26.2	41.9	Cross bridge over big river Hidalgo and thru village of Hidalgo.
30.8	49.3	Pass Hotel Paraíso Río Grande, curve left, over bridge and thru town of Río Grande (population 12,000).
46.6	74.6	**GAS** at left. Thru village of Santa Rosa de Lima.
51.1	81.8	Laguna de Chicahua Bird Refuge toward Pacific at left. Pass Industrial Citrícola ("citrus industry") de Oaxaca at left.
52.1	83.4	Thru wide spot of San José del Progreso.
61.9	99.0	Cross twin bridges over Río Verde. **KM 50**.
70.8	113.3	**GAS** at left.
71.1	113.8	Now thru village of Jamiltepec.
79.1	126.6	Thru village of Huaxpaltepec.
82.4	131.8	Thru Rancho Viejo.
87.4	139.8	Over bridge and curve right.
89.6	143.4	Into Pinotepa Nacional, a tropical town of 40,000 and a busy farm center for the Amusgo Indians with their colorful Sunday market. Pass plaza and note stalls on both sides of highway. **GAS** at left and right and LP gas at right.
90.8	145.3	Pass nice Restaurant and Club Campestre (enter thru white arches at left; good sandwiches and meals; pool; nice setting). Then Motel Carmona on left.
91.5	146.4	Pepe's hotel and restaurant on right. Then Motel Las Gaviotas also on right.
92.6	148.2	**GAS** at right. Then military garrison at left housing the 47th Infantry Battalion.
94.8	151.7	Pass road (right) to Cacahatepec and Tlaxiaco (Hwy #125).
95.3	152.5	LP gas on left.
96.4	154.2	Thru village of Mancuernas ("Pair of Thongs" or "Thongs for Throwing a Steer").
106.6	170.6	Thru settlement of Lagunillas.
108.6	173.8	Pass side road (left) to El Ciruelo (The Plum).
109.9	175.8	Cemetery at right and thru La Estancia ("The Stay").
119.0	190.4	Come now to state line – leave state of Oaxaca and enter state of Guerrero.
123.1	197.0	Pass side road (left) to Punta Maldonado. Then enter little town of Coajinicuilapa. If you're ready for a breather, Restaurant Lucy at right is OK; clean restrooms; friendly; interesting paintings. **GAS** at right.

Here in Coajinicuilapa dwells Mexico's only Black population, some of whom are descendants of African Bantu tribesmen while others trace their origin back to Zanzibar, where Ambrosio González, a Spanish noble (and once owner of these lands) brought them to replace the Indians who worked the mines and sugar plantations. The town was founded in 1562 by 40 families of African slaves who were freed in these parts; today this capitol of Afro-Mexico has grown to a population of 4,500. Many old customs still survive and are evidenced by the round huts, the long tunics worn by the older women, the young women carrying their infants on one hip and their peculiar Spanish accent (similar to the Castilian spoken by Cuban Blacks).

128.6	205.8	Thru Barajillas and over bridge of same name.
134.3	214.9	Over Río Santa Catarina with village of Milpillas at left.
141.1	225.6	Pass side road (right) to Ometepec, once a gold-mining center and still-very-charming town. Medical missionaries of the Southern Presbyterian Church operate a small "Hospital de la Amistad" ("friendship") here – visitors welcome. Then cross bridge over Río Quetzale.
151.8	242.9	Thru wide spot of Juchitán.
165.5	264.8	**GAS** at left and thru little sea-level village of Marquelia. The Pacific Ocean is just a few miles to left. Then cross Río Marquelia.
177.1	283.4	Pass town of Copala at right. Next 13 miles are rolling hills.
178.2	285.1	Over Río Copala. Then curve left and right.
186.6	298.6	Over Puente Jalapa.
190.0	304.0	Thru settlement of Ayutla and **GAS** at right.
190.6	305.0	Pass the 48th infantry battalion garrison at left. Then thru village of Cruz Grande. Pass side road (right) to La Unión.
198.6	317.8	Thru little hamlet of El Porvenir ("The Future") and over Puente Nexpa. Then thru village of Las Lomitas.
201.2	321.9	Over Puente Las Vigas and thru village of Las Vigas ("The Beams").
208.3	333.3	Acamiel honey processing plant on left.

142

MI	KM	
214.9	343.8	Enter village of San Marcos. Cemetery at right. Emergency Hotel and Restaurant Lecarma at left.
220.4	352.6	Over La Estancia bridge and thru La Estancia ("The Stay").
224.5	359.2	Thru settlement of El Cortés and over bridge.
228.6	365.8	Thru little hamlets of San Juan Chico first and San Juan Grande following.
232.5	372.0	Cross bridge over Río Papagayo ("Parrot River").
237.2	379.5	Thru village of San Antonio.
241.9	387.0	Thru settlement of El Bejuco ("The Rattan").
246.4	394.2	Thru another settlement, this one called Tres Palos.
248.4	397.4	Thru village of Tunzingo. Coca Cola bottling plant on right.
249.2	398.7	Thru settlement of El Cayaco. Restaurant Entre Amigos (among friends) on left.
251.4	402.2	Pass Motel Paraíso on left.
253.9	406.2	Slow as you approach junction with road to Puerto Marquez and short cut to Hwy #95 and on to Mexico City. This exit also takes you to Acapulco's airport, famous Acapulco Princess Hotel and Pierre Marquez Hotel.) Start wind up alongside bay down at left.
255.7	409.1	Nice view of Puerto Marquez down at left. In the olden days pirates who sailed the Pacific anchored on this sparkling bay for provisions and protection from enemies and storms.
257.4	411.8	Pass entrance (right) to unique Hotel Las Brisas.
259.1	414.6	Come now to glorieta (circle) – Follow COSTERA sign, bend right and start divided.
259.4	415.0	Pass Romano's Le Club Hotel at left.
260.1	416.2	Convention center at right housing restaurants, cafes, bars, theaters, folkloric ballets, movies and more.
260.4	416.6	Acapulco's sports center at right.
260.5	416.8	Holiday Inn at left. Then Fiesta Americana Hotel at left on beach.
260.8	417.3	Hotel El Presidente at left and then Sanborn's Restaurant, also at left. Then on thru concrete jungle of Hotels – Condesa del Mar, Fiesta Tortuga and Romano Palace.
261.4	418.2	Come now to Diana Circle and end of Log. GAS, at right. See Acapulco map (page 17) and Acapulco Eat & Stray (page 110) for accommodations.

IF TO: Acapulco downtown, proceed ahead on Costera (waterfront boulevard) Miguel Alemán.

IF TO: Iguala, Taxco, Cuernavaca, Mexico City, etc., TURN RIGHT onto Paseo del Farallón (Hwy #95) and head north and start Acapulco - Iguala Log (page 152).

IF TO: Zihuatanejo, Ixtapa and Playa Azul, TURN RIGHT onto Paseo del Farallón. Head north past GAS station at left and start Acapulco - Ixtapa Log.

End of Log 54

LOG 55 START: Acapulco, Gro END: Ixtapa, Gro

UD-077

162.0 MI or 259.2 KM
DRIVE TIME 3 1/2 - 4 HOURS
SCENIC RATING — 3

MI	KM	
0.0	0.0	Starting here at the Diana monument glorieta with GAS at left, proceed ahead up Farallón and pass Gigante shopping center on right.
1.8	2.9	Thru suburb of la Garita. Slow as you come to junction with Hwy #200. TURN LEFT onto Calz. Ruiz Cortines when the coast is clear and wind on thru the edge of Acapulco. (Straight goes to Mexico City.) Nice view of bay off to left.
2.4	3.8	Pass nice park at right. Then GAS at left.
3.1	5.0	IMSS and general hospital at left.
5.0	8.0	Come to stoplight. TURN RIGHT onto Av. Ejido and careful for topes.
5.5	8.8	BEND RIGHT onto Calz. Pie de la Cuesta. (Left fork takes you back into downtown Acapulco.) Careful as street narrows into a palm-lined lane.
8.5	13.6	Balcones del Mar at left.
9.5	15.2	Thru edge of village of Tabachines.
10.5	16.8	Thru edge of Barra de Coyuca and then Pie de la Cuesta, both suburbs of Acapulco.
16.0	25.6	Thru village of Bajos del Ejido and come to a PGR inspection station. Your car may be checked. Then pass road (right) that is a shortcut back to Hwy #95 to Iguala and bypasses Acapulco.
16.7	26.7	Over puente Guerrero and thru community of El Embarcadero.

MI	KM	
21.5	34.4	Aserradero Las Salinas (Salinas Sawmill) at right. Then series of curves.
22.7	36.3	Government coconut oil extracting plant at left.
24.7	39.5	**GAS** at left and enter town of Coyuca (population 50,000). Then cross big bridge over Río Coyuca.
26.5	42.4	El Carrizal with bungalows at left.
30.7	49.1	Thru El Zapotillo and on thru Las Tranquitas.
37.7	60.3	Cross bridge over Río Cayaco and thru village of same name.
40.0	64.0	Thru Vicente Guerrero (Vicente Guerrero, 1783-1831, was an independence fighter born in Tixtla, Guerrero, and the state is named in his honor. Like many a Mexican hero, he died by execution.)
43.0	68.8	Thru village of Zacualpan and over bridge.
44.0	70.4	Thru Colonia Cuauhtémoc.
45.7	73.1	Over bridge and thru village of Cacalutla.
49.0	78.4	Pass side road (right) to Ixtla, 3 kilometers.
50.5	80.8	Thru village of alcholoa. Then over another bridge and thru little community of Buenos Aires.
52.0	83.2	Thru community of El Ciruelar. Then over bridge and skirt edge of Atoyac de Alvarez to right.
54.0	86.4	**GAS** at right. Then pass side road (left) to Hacienda de Cabañas, 8 kilometers.
55.0	88.0	Cross long bridge over Río Atoyac and past settlement of Ticul at right. Then pass village of San Jerónimo and school at left.
64.0	102.4	Pass truck stop restaurant La Posta at right. Then pass side road (left) to Tetitlán and beach.
69.0	110.4	Enter town of Tecpan de Galeana (population 75,000) and school at left. **GAS** and cemetery, left. Then pass fancy church and take leave of town.
71.0	113.6	Thru villages of Colonia Ramos and El Cuchil. Careful for topes.
73.0	116.8	Pass settlement of Tenexpa at left.
76.0	121.6	Thru village of Rodecia.
78.2	125.1	Cross bridge over Río Nuxco. Then take right fork to bypass town of Nuxco.
82.9	132.6	Pass side road (right) to Guayabillo, 6 kilometers.
86.3	138.1	Thru village of San Luis San Pedro. **GAS** at left.
87.5	140.0	Cross bridge over Río Grande and up thru village of San Luis La Loma.
89.5	143.2	Over puente El Trapiche.
90.3	144.5	Pass Motel/Balneario La Cabaña at left.
91.4	146.2	Thru stretched-out village of El Llano, more properly referred to as "El Llano Rancho Alegre."
98.6	157.8	Pass side road (left) to Puerto Vicente Guerrero.
100.5	160.8	Thru village of Cayaquitos with Hotel Club Papanoa and Balneario Cayaquitos at left.
101.6	162.6	Sawmill and lumber yard at right.
102.7	164.3	Thru little town of Papanoa (population 3,500) with **GAS** at right.
104.3	166.9	Thru Los Laureles and village of Coyuquilla Sur at left.
106.6	170.6	Cross bridge over Río Coyuquilla and thru village of Coyuquilla Norte.
111.0	177.6	Thru Arroyo Seco.
114.0	182.4	Pass "mirador" at left - pull off for a breather if you like.
115.0	184.0	Nice drive alongside Pacific and past whistle-stop restaurant at left.
115.6	185.0	Thru tropical coconut groves past El Cayacal.
119.4	191.0	Thru settlement of Loma Bonita.
120.8	193.3	Thru village of Las Salinas, with its coconut palms. Then pass sea water evaporation plant at left.
123.5	197.6	Thru village of Juluchuca and cross bridge over Río Juluchuca. **KM 195.**
125.2	200.3	Over puente El Tuzal.
129.6	207.4	**GAS** at right.
130.5	208.8	Cross small then big bridge over Río Petatlán.
131.0	209.6	Thru town of Petatlán (population 18,000).
131.8	210.9	**GAS** at right. Then pass Guerrero State College at left.
135.3	216.5	Thru Palos Blancos and over Río Cueros.
136.8	218.9	Thru village of San Jerónimo and pass little cemetery up at right.
142.0	227.2	Pass side road (right) to El Zorco. Then cross puente Los Acohotes and up thru village of Los Achotes.
145.2	232.3	**GAS** at left. Then pass exit (left) to Ixtapa-Zihuatanejo International Airport.
147.7	236.3	Pass Motel Reyes on left.
151.3	242.1	**GAS** at right. Note monument made of blue blocks at left.
152.0	243.2	Come to large monument glorieta and into outskirts of Zihuatanejo.
153.0	244.8	Come to junction with main entrance into Zihuatanejo.

IF TO: Zihuatanejo, take left fork into town, see map (page 14). For accommodations see Zihuatanejo Eat & Stray (page 107).

154.0	246.4	Pass apartment complex village of Agua de Correa at right. Then come to entrance to Ixtapa.

IF TO: Ixtapa, turn left onto this "scenic" road which will take you into town, see map (page 13). For accommodations, see Ixtapa Eat & Stray (page 104).

MI	KM	
154.3	246.9	Pass "mirador" at left, where you can pull off and stop and enjoy the view.
154.6	247.4	Nice view of Ixtapa and its sparkling bay at left.
155.5	248.8	Pass side trail (right) to El Pozquelite, 2 kilometers.
157.0	251.2	Pass another road (left) into Ixtapa.
161.4	258.2	Thru village of Salitrera. Then over Río Salitrera.
162.0	259.2	Come to junction with Hwy #134.

IF TO: Cd Altamirano, Toluca, turn right and start Ixtapa - Altamirano Log (page 61).

IF TO: Playa Azul, Manzanillo, continue straight and start Ixtapa - La Mira Jct. Log.

End of Log 55

LOG 56 *START:* Ixtapa, Gro   *END:* La Mira, Mich

UD-077

68.0 MI or 108.8 KM
DRIVING TIME 1 1/2 HOURS
SCENIC RATING — 3

Although overall this is a fair stretch of highway, there are sections of rough, chuck-holed pavement so exercise caution in these areas.

0.0	0.0	Starting at junction (right) with Hwy #135 to Altamirano and Toluca, proceed ahead on Hwy #200 thru village of Salitrera.
0.3	0.5	Pass side trail (left) to Barrio Nuevo.
2.3	3.6	Thru village of Pantla and over Río Pantla.
5.5	8.8	Thru community of Buena Vista. Restaurant Compadres on right.
8.5	13.6	Pass side road (left) to Troncones. At this little town is an RV park and a restaurant on the beach called Burro Borracho (Drunken Donkey). They have beach bungalows. Ph: (755) 553-0809 Fax: 553-2417.
10.8	17.3	Cross bridge over Río Lagunillas and thru village of Lagunillas.
14.3	22.9	Over Río Los Llanos and thru settlement of Los Llanos.
19.3	30.9	Over Río Chutla and pass side road (right) to village of Chutla, 4 kilometers.
22.6	36.2	Pass side road (right) to La Unión.
24.0	38.4	Cross bridge over Río La Unión.
27.5	44.0	Thru settlement of El Chico and over Río El Chico.
30.1	48.2	Over Río Joluta. Pass side trail (left) to El Atracadero. Then thru village of Joluta.
34.0	54.4	Over Río Feliciano. Then pass rural road (left) to Feliciano.
37.4	59.8	Over Río Coyucuila and pass community of Coyucuila.
42.0	67.2	Thru village of Zorcua. Then cross big bridge over Río Zorcua.
45.8	73.3	Over Río Petacalco and thru village of Petacalco. School at left.
46.3	74.1	Over Canal de Llamada. Then pass side road (right) to village of Elías Calles.
51.7	82.7	Pass side road (left) to Zacatula.
52.8	84.5	Thru settlement of Tamacuas.
54.5	87.2	Come to state line. Leave state of Guerrero and enter state of Michoacán.
55.0	88.0	Note powerhouse at left and gates of Jose Maria Morelos Dam (Presa Villita).
57.0	91.2	Pass road (right) into Guacamayas. Begin 4-lane divided highway.
57.9	92.6	Cross twin bridges over Río Guacamayas and topes.
58.6	93.8	Come to junction with another road (right) into Guacamayas. Veer left. Then pass airport and subdivision of La Orilla at left.
60.2	96.3	Come to junction with road into Lázaro Cárdenas. Exit right just before overpass.

IF TO: Lázaro Cárdenas, continue up over overpass curving right, down and around and head into town.

LAZARO CARDENAS is the location of one of Latin America's largest steel mills, called "Las Truches" or "Sicartsa," owned by the government. During its construction the town's population swelled to over 100,000! Today, however, only a mere 20,000 reside here. The nicest hotel in the area is CASTEL HACIENDA JACARANDAS (120 a/c rooms; restaurant-bar; pool; AE, MC, VI; Phone 2-3555).

MI	KM	
60.7	97.1	Pass side road (left) to Sicartsa.
65.0	104.0	Careful for topes.
66.3	106.1	**GAS** at right and more topes.
68.0	108.8	Enter town of La Mira and come to junction with Hwy # 37.

IF TO: Uruapan, turn right and start La Mira - Uruapan Log (page 57).

IF TO: Playa Azul (3 miles ahead), Manzanillo, Colima, turn left and start La Mira - Tecomán Log.

End of Log 56

LOG 57 *START:* La Mira Jct, Mich *END:* Tecomán Jct, Col

UD-077

172.0 MI or 275.2 KM
DRIVE TIME 5 HOURS
SCENIC RATING - 3

0.0	0.0	Starting at La Mira junction with Hwy #37, proceed ahead on Hwy #200.
1.5	2.4	Careful as you approach exit (left) to Playa Azul.

IF TO: If to Playa Azul (and Playa Azul Hotel and RV Park Ph: (753) 536-0024 and 536-0001 and nice Hotel María Teresa Jericó, Independencia #626. Restaurant. Pool. MC, VI. Ph: (753) 536-0005 Fax: 536-0055), turn right; there's **GAS** at Playa Azul down road at left past topes.

2.4	3.8	Over El Bordón bridge. Thru wide spot of Acalpican and over Acalpican bridge. From this point, you'll encounter many, many bridges. (You can now readily understand why it took so long to complete this section of Hwy #200!)
6.0	9.6	Curve right and thru hamlet of El Habillal.
9.9	15.8	Thru little community of El Cayaco surrounded by palms and papayas. Then curve right.
13.6	21.7	Thru little fishing village of Las Peñas at left with several primitive restaurants and a secluded cove just right for camping. Then over puente Rangel.
14.2	22.7	Over puente El Bejuco and thru wide spot.
18.1	29.0	Over two bridges, Popayutla and Fallado Then thru settlement of Chuta and cross Chuta bridge over Río Carrizal.
22.2	35.5	Over puente Chuquiapan and pass settlement of Chuquiapan at left.
26.6	42.6	Over La Soledad bridge with magnificent view of La Soledad Beach at left. Then pass village of Mexcalhuacan at left and over Mexcalhuacan bridge.
28.7	45.9	Cross Playas Cuates, La Manzanilla I and Majahua bridges. **KM 42**.
32.3	51.7	Curve to left over puente Teolán.
34.6	55.4	Pass little village of Caleta de Campos at left on beach. Then down thru cut, curve left and over puente Bica de Campos. **KM 50**.
37.4	59.8	Over Hornos bridge and note beautiful beach at left with coconut palms. Then over long bridge over Río Nexpa.
41.9	67.0	Thru a handful of houses forming settlement of El Salado. Then over puentes El Salado, Bejuco I and Bejuco II.
45.7	73.1	Over puente El Chico and thru papaya groves and settlement of El Chico mostly at right.
49.8	79.7	Over Tupitina bridge curving left.
51.5	82.4	Cross El Tanque ("The Tank") bridge.
55.0	88.0	Over Manzanilla II bridge. **KM 81**.
56.2	89.9	Cross El Mezquite bridge and then over Tinaja bridge.
57.5	92.0	Thru village of Huahua (population 500). Then over long Huahua bridge.
60.4	96.6	Note palapa and mirador overlooking the ocean at left.
61.3	98.1	Over El Aguijote bridge.
64.6	103.4	Over Cuilala bridge.
70.7	113.1	Cross Tizupa bridge. Then thru little village of Tizupa.
76.8	122.9	Curve left and over Río Chocola.
83.5	133.6	Thru cut. Careful for rocks on pavement.
88.0	140.8	Down and curve left and cross big bridge over Río Cachán then thru village of Cachán.

MI	KM	
94.8	151.7	Cross Paso de Noria bridge and settlement of Paso de Noria, a handful of houses at left. Now enter zone where marine turtles are protected – this area has become a refuge because in recent years fishermen have mercilessly slaughtered them, creating a worldwide reaction.
98.8	158.1	Pass settlement of Maraota at left with paved airstrip near beach. Then over Río Maraota.
104.0	166.4	Over San Isidro bridge and thru village of Colola, mostly at left.
105.8	169.3	Over another pair of bridges and curve left.
107.4	171.8	Down and curve left. Then up steep grade thru Chinapa on beach.
109.8	175.7	Cross twin bridges over Río Motín. Then thru little village of Motín de Oro down at left.
113.7	181.9	Over bridge and curve left. Then pass side trail (left) to El Faro ("The Lighthouse").
116.3	186.1	Over bridge and curve right. Pass side road (left) to settlement of El Zapote. ("Zapote" is Spanish for sapodilla, a tropical evergreen bearing an edible fruit and yielding chicle.)
118.6	189.8	Over another bridge and curve left. Then cross bridge over Río Ixtapilla and thru village of Ixtapilla.
122.6	196.2	Cross bridge over Río Ostula, curve right and pass side road (right) to village of Ostula.
128.0	204.8	Now up and catch a glimpse of the beautiful Pacific. Curve left and down. Start winding section ("tramo sinuoso").
128.5	205.6	Cross triple set of bridges.
129.9	207.8	Over another bridge and enter little town of La Placita (population 8,500). **GAS** on right. Then Hotel de la Costa on left.
130.2	208.3	Hotel Rosales on left. Then cross bridge over Río Aquila.
133.6	213.8	Pass side trail (right) to villages of Aquila and Maquili. Stop for Army inspection checkpoint.
135.5	216.8	"El Mirador" at left (where you can pull off and soak up the panorama).
138.5	221.6	Pass village of Jan Juan de Alma at left with huge white sand beach.
146.2	233.9	Thru lush banana groves and over Río Ticuiz. Then pass side road (right) to El Ranchito. **GAS** at left.
149.1	238.6	Come to crossroads: Left is to Boca de Apiza and San Vicente and right is to village of Coahuayana.
149.9	239.8	Cross Río Coahuayana which is also the state line. Leave state of Michoacán and enter state of Colima (Mexico's third smallest state).
151.3	242.2	Pass another side road (left) to Boca de Apiza.
153.2	245.1	TAKE LEFT FORK here. Right goes to town of Cerro de Ortega (population 4,000).
157.8	252.5	Over Arroyo Zanja Prieta and curve right.
161.0	257.6	Pass Rancho 19 on left and side road (right) to Valle Nuevo.
161.4	258.2	Microwave relay station La Primavera ("The Spring") on right. **KM 256**.
163.3	261.3	Pass road (left) to Cerro de Aguilar, (3 Km). **KM 260**.
164.7	263.5	Thru Cofradia de Morelos, mostly at right.
166.7	266.7	Pass road (left) to Tecuanillo, 10 Km. (6.2 Mi.) on Pacific Coast.
168.0	268.8	TAKE LEFT FORK to bypass. Right fork goes to downtown Tecomán. **GAS** at left.

Incidently during the pre-Cortés era, Tecomán was known as "Caxitlán" and it was the capital of this region; in 1523, Captain Gonzalo de Sandoval conquered it under Cortés' orders and called it "San Sebastián."

168.9	270.2	TURN RIGHT and follow signs that say Colima y Manzanillo.
169.5	271.2	TAKE LEFT FORK onto Hwy #200 and ahead. Right goes back into Tecomán.
170.0	272.0	Pass Hotel Plaza on right. Then on left is Motel Real, A/C, Restaurant, pool, parking, Ph: (313) 134-0100 Fax: 134-1581.
170.5	272.8	**GAS** on right.
172.0	275.2	Come to junction Hwys #110 and #200.

IF TO: Colima, Guadalajara, exit right and start Tecomán - Guadalajara Log (page 150).

IF TO: Jiquilpan, Morelia, Mexico City, exit right and start Tecomán - Jiquilpan Log (page 54).

IF TO: Manzanillo, Puerto Vallarta, continue up overpass, curve around to right and merge with Hwy #200 toll road. Start Tecomán - Melaque Jct. Log.

End of Log 57

LOG 58 *START:* Tecomán, Col *END:* Melaque Jct, Jal

UD-077

72.3 MI or 115.7 KM
DRIVE TIME 1 1/2 - 2 1/2 HOURS

MI	KM	
0.0	0.0	Starting at junction of Hwys #110 and #200, proceed ahead on 4-lane highway toward Manzanillo.
3.7	5.9	**GAS** on right.
4.3	6.8	Pass Hotel Cascada, right.
5.4	8.6	Pass exit right to Armeria (population 27,572).
6.2	9.9	Over puente Armeria I.
7.7	15.4	Pass another exit (right) to Armeria, El Paraíso and to Hwy #200 (free road) to Manzanillo. Straight is to Manzanillo via toll road.
12.0	19.2	Over puente La Tilapía.
13.0	20.8	Over puente Palo Verde I.
13.5	21.6	Now over puente Palo Verde II. **KM 56**.
15.9	25.4	Thru lime growing area. Then Cross bridge over railroad curving down to left. **KM 50**.
16.2	25.9	Pass exit (right, after overpass) to Cuyutlán on coast, 7 kilometers. This is the place where late in April and in early May the famous "green wave" is supposed to roll in, a magnificent natural phenomenon.
16.5	26.4	Come to tollhouse and pay toll (Car $40, 2-axle $80, 3-axle $100). Restrooms at right.
28.5	45.6	Pass exit (right) to Campos and over bridge that curves to right.
29.5	47.2	Road narrows to 2 lanes as you cross puente Tepalcates and cross inlet to Cuyutlán lagoon.
29.9	47.8	Road widens again to 4 lanes.
31.7	50.7	Note beautiful view of bay over to left.
35.7	57.1	Pass exit (right and onto overpass) to downtown Manzanillo (population 93,000). Hotel zone straight ahead.

IF TO: Downtown Manzanillo, exit right and onto overpass curving to left. See Manzanillo Eat & Stray (page 101) for accommodation in the area.

IF TO: Hotel zone, Barra de Navidad, Puerto Vallarta, continue straight.

36.0	57.6	Come to monument junction. **GAS** at left. A left goes to downtown. Straight to Pto. Vallarta.

IF TO: La Marmota RV Park, turn right here. This road also goes to Minatitlán.

37.0	59.2	Come to junction with large auditorium on right.
37.8	60.5	Come to glorieta of sail boat. **GAS** at left. Military garrison at right.

IF TO: Star Hotel, Roca del Mar, popular La Posada Inn and other hotels, turn left here.

IF TO: Pto Vallarta, turn right and thru hotel zone.

39.0	62.4	Sports center and school at right. Then pass Condominium Mar y Mar at left.
39.3	62.9	Pass Posada del Sol at left, a condominium.
39.5	63.2	Motel Marbella at left on beach.
39.8	63.7	Arco Iris Motel at left. (Arco Iris is Spanish for rainbow.)
40.5	64.8	Pass village of Salahua mostly at right.
40.8	65.3	**GAS**, right and come to side road (left) to fabulous Moorish-style Hotel Las Hadas, complete with golf course. Incidentally, it's very expensive.
41.0	65.6	Pass side road (left) that leads down to Hotel Playa de Santiago. Then over Santiago bridge.
42.0	67.2	Thru village of Santiago (population 7,000).
43.0	68.8	Restaurant El Dorado at left. Then pass side street (left) that goes to Hotel Casablanca Alamar.
43.5	69.6	Club Maeva at right, a Mediterranean-style village consisting of 440 white-and-blue villas.
44.0	70.4	Cross overpass and sharp right curve past ruins of our U.S. World War II infirmary and convalescent camp on left. Our Allied warships and freighters used to transfer their sick, mostly those suffering from tropical disease, to Manzanillo. **KM 18**.
44.5	71.2	Settlement of Miramar at right and pass Vida del Mar Condominium resort and club Bahia de Santiago resort development and golf club at left. Then up over Río Miramar and take leave of Manzanillo.
46.3	74.1	Pass village of Naranjo at right.
48.0	76.8	Bear left thru Ejido La Central.
52.3	83.7	Cobblestone road (left) to Playa de Oro, 7 kilometers.
54.5	87.2	Thru La Cienega. Ejido Emiliano Zapata at left. Goat crossing. **KM 34**.
56.8	90.9	Straight here past side road (left) to Manzanillo's airport.
57.5	92.0	Thru village of Chavarín.

MI	KM	
60.0	96.0	Pass community of Río Marabasco at right. Tiered, flat leaf tree is almond.
61.0	97.6	Pass Goodyear left. Then up and over wide Río Marabasco on big Cihuatlán bridge. Crossing Río Marabasco, you also cross state line – leave Colima and enter Jalisco.
62.3	99.7	Enter town of Cihuatlán (population 24,500). **GAS** at left. Plaza at right with pretty white church behind. Technological School at right. Then cemetery and LP gas at left.
65.8	105.3	At left is a huge coconut palm forest – what a terrific view! Pass side road (left) to La Culebra (The Snake). **KM 5**.
67.0	107.2	Cross a couple of bridges over Arroyo Seco.
67.5	108.0	Thru banana plantation, coconut palms and village of El Aguacate (The Avocado).
70.0	112.0	**GAS** at left and thru little village of Jaluco. Then pass side road (right) to seashore village of Barra de Navidad (population 10,000). If you'd like to drive down for a look at this rather interesting place, hop to it – it's 2 miles and offers nice Hotel Cabo Blanco plus some other hotels, and you can usually buy nice big clusters of coral in the little shop on main corner. See Barra de Navidad Eat & Stray (page 99) for a listing of accommodations in the area.
70.5	112.8	Cross pair of bridges over little Río Jaluco
71.3	114.1	Pass seaside village of San Patricio at left. At junction TURN RIGHT. Side road (left) is to Hotel Melaque, Vista Hermosa, etc.

IF TO: Hotels Melaque, Vista Hermosa, etc., turn left.

72.3	115.7	Come to Melaque junction with Hwy #80. **GAS** at left.

IF TO: Guadalajara, proceed ahead and start Melaque Jct - Guadalajara Log (page 52).

IF TO: Puerto Vallarta, turn left and start Melaque - Pto. Vallarta Log.

End of Log 58

LOG 59 *START:* Melaque, Jal *END:* Puerto Vallarta, Jal

UD-016

131.8 MI or 210.9 KM
DRIVE TIME 3 – 4 HOURS
SCENIC RATING – 3

This very important coastal highway is a great shortcut and has contributed much to the growth of the Tenacatita-Melaque-Santiago-Manzanillo resort areas. Formerly it was necessary to go all the way from Guadalajara to Tepic and then down to Puerto Vallarta. The highway is quite winding in spots with deep cuts and big fills (watch for rocks on pavement). Thanks to Roger Morey of Austin TX for helping update this log.

0.0	0.0	Here at the junction with Hwy #80 (straight ahead), TURN LEFT and proceed north on Hwy #200. **GAS**, at right.
0.5	0.8	Thru village of Emiliano Zapata.
3.0	4.8	Nice view off to right of valley and ocean.
3.9	6.2	Community of Aguacatillo, a handful of houses at right. Then over two little bridges.
4.8	7.7	Road down to left goes to El Tamarindo, a private club.
5.0	8.0	Top! Now down – not too fast! **KM 7**.
8.5	13.6	Curve right past side road (left) to La Manzanilla, two kilometers away.
10.2	16.3	Curve right past side road to Hotel Bahía de Tenacatita (not functioning) down on nice beach among stately palms, and to Boca de Iguanas RV Park: 50 spaces among palms on lagoon with beach; some water and electrical hookups; showers; toilets; camping; fishing.
12.5	20.0	Pass entrance (left) to Fiesta Americana de los Angeles Locos ("The Crazy Angels"), a nice, secluded hotel: 221 rooms; restaurants; bars; SATV; pool; nice beach; AE, MC, VI; Ph: (315) 157-0021.
17.9	28.6	Over long bridge over Río Purificación.
18.5	29.6	Thru scattered settlement of Agua Caliente. Out and curve right. **KM 30**.
20.7	33.1	Pass paved side road (left) to Hotel El Tecuane, six miles thru beautiful mango trees; 32 rooms; restaurant; bar; pool; two landing strips; four miles beach frontage; several RV spaces w/o hookups; AE, MC, VI; Ph: (315) 337-0132. In Guadalajara Ph: (33) 3615-8872 or 3616-0085.
21.8	34.9	Puente ("bridge") El Seco.
25.0	40.0	Thru little village of Emiliano Zapata, mostly at right. Topes at both ends of town.
26.8	42.8	Sharp curve left, then over Río Cuitzmala. Another sharp left at end of bridge.

MI	KM	
33.4	53.4	Pass cobblestone side road (left) to top-notch Hotel Plaza de Careyes (see below) and to Club Mediterranean/Playa Blanca (the latter for members only) a little farther inland.

HOTEL PLAZA DE CAREYES, styled after a Mediterranean village, is an excellent facility covering 3,700 acres and include 8 miles of protected coastline. 104 A/C rooms, suites and kitchens; nice pool; restaurant; bar; disco; movie; "Noche Mexicana" with mariachis and cockfights on Saturday nights; horses; fishing; sailing; shops; AE, MC, VI.

MI	KM	
36.4	58.2	Pass side road (right) to University of Mexico's (UNAN) biology station.
39.3	62.8	Restaurante Mariscos En Servicio (sic) at right.
40.1	64.2	Another mariscos restaurant, also at right.
41.6	66.6	Pass side road (left) to Club Playa Chamela.
43.6	69.8	Pass village of San Mateo to the right.
44.6	71.3	Pass Bungalows Naryar Chamela: 18 bungalows, 2 bedroom, Ph: 3-7318 or 44-0044 in Guadalajara. **GAS**, at right.
45.0	72.0	Restaurant El Tejabán at left has chips, cold soft drinks and beer. Then pass side road (left) to Villa Polinesia RV Campground (eight spaces with all hookups; camping; showers; toilets; BBQ grills; palapas; laundromat; Ph: (33) 3622-3940 in Guadalajara).
47.3	75.6	Pass dirt side road (left) to beaches of Perula and La Fortuna. Also to Búngalos Playa Dorada, 18 bungalows and 18 rooms; ice; pool. Little town of Perula and La Punta Perla are also down this road.
51.9	83.0	Pass side road (left) to Las Alamandas.
52.6	84.1	Long bridge across Río San Nicolás, then curve right.
54.5	87.2	Then thru edge of José María Morelos, mostly at left.
62.6	100.1	Into booming farm village of Campo Acosta. Topes just before bridge. Another tope just after the bridge is followed by yet a third. Then out and up, curving slightly right.
64.7	103.5	Over Puente Toro 2.
71.9	115.0	Slow thru little town of La Cumbre (the "top" or "summit"). **GAS**, at left.
72.4	115.9	Pass side road (right) to Tomatlán, 12 kilometers. Then cross Puente Tomatlán. Incidentally, the first tomato is said to have been cultivated in this area around Tomatlán by the Aztecs, or so the legend goes.
77.3	123.7	Slow for topes and enter the community of José María Pino Suárez.
80.6	129.0	Campo Experimental Tomatlán at right.
85.9	137.4	Thru settlement of Tesquesquite. Small store on the right sells cold sodas.
88.8	142.1	Note ancient volcanic plug off to the right. Pass dirt side road (right) to San Rafael.
94.1	150.5	Cross Puente Las Jarillas. Up slightly, then curve right. From here into Puerto Vallarta, rocks on road are common, particularly during or just after rains.
100.0	160.0	Curve left, then over Río Las Juntas. Up hill and curve right.
105.7	169.1	Slow thru scattered town of El Tuito, mostly at left. Hotel Real Del Valle at right.
106.3	170.1	Pass school at right and curve left and out of El Tuito.
107.0	171.2	Slow for sharp right curve. Road begins considerable winding.
108.9	174.2	Over Puente La Hacienda.
110.1	176.2	Slow for sharp right curve.
113.9	182.3	Thru tiny brick making settlement.
115.7	185.1	Cross Puente La Puerta.
117.8	188.4	Curve right and over Río Los Horcones, followed by a sharp left curve.
118.6	189.8	Slow thru Las Juntas de Verano.
120.1	192.2	Pass side road (left) to famous Chico's Paraíso, an interesting restaurant set on a tropical hillside overlooking waterfall.
120.6	192.9	Cascade down at left. Watch for tour buses stopping on road.
122.0	195.2	Glimpse of Pacific thru narrow valley.
122.3	195.7	Sharp left curve across curved bridge.
124.0	198.4	The famous Arcos ("arches") islets can be seen ahead at left.
126.2	201.9	Mismaloya at left. It was on a small point that juts out into Banderas Bay near here that the set for the movie Night Of The Iguana was constructed. Then La Joya de Mismaloya Resort and Spa, also at left.
127.1	203.4	Good view of Los Arcos at left.
128.4	205.4	Presidente Inter-Continental Hotel at left.
129.1	206.5	Hotel Garza Blanca ("White Heron") at left. Across the street at right are hotel's hillside chalet-type suites, each with private pool.
131.8	210.9	Highrise Camino Real Hotel at left on Las Estacas Beach, with hotel entrance at right.

IF TO: Rincón de Guayabitos, Tepic, or Guadalajara, start Pto. Vallarta - Tepic Log. (See Mexico's Pacific Coast and Copper Canyon book, page 155).

End of Log 59

LOG 60 *START:* Tecomán, Col *END:* Guadalajara, Jal

UD-046

146.3 MI or 234.1 KM
DRIVE TIME 2 1/2 - 3 HOURS
SCENIC RATING — 2

MI	KM	
0.0	0.0	Starting at Tecomán Junction, head north on Hwy #110 a 4-lane divided highway.
1.2	1.9	Note large Coca Cola bottling plant on left.
3.4	5.4	Pass road (left) to Caleras and Madrid. Then thru coconut palms.
7.1	11.4	Pass town of Tecolapa over to left.
9.0	14.4	Pass side road (right) to Ixtlahuacan. **KM 26**.
13.1	21.0	Summit.
15.5	24.8	Pass side road (right) to Los Asmoles.
17.3	27.7	Pass another road (right) into Los Asmoles. **KM 13**.
18.2	29.1	**GAS** at left.
21.9	35.0	Pass side road (right) to Loma de Fátima.
23.5	37.6	Pass Colima golf course at left. Then **GAS** on right.
25.1	40.2	Come to junction of Hwy #54 and #110. Left takes you to downtown Colima. See Colima map (page 9) and Colima Eat & Stray (page 103) for accommodations.

IF TO: Jiquilpan, turn right and join Tecomán Jct.- Jiquilpan Log (page 54) at mile 25.1.

IF TO: Guadalajara, continue straight ahead on Hwy #54 bypass around Colima.

MI	KM	
25.2	40.3	Colima over on left, a peaceful city Don't hesitate to stop if it is growing late in the evening.
25.5	40.8	Pass another entrance into Colima at left.
26.5	42.4	Come to end of bypass. TURN RIGHT and ahead on Hwy #54. Left goes to downtown Colima.
29.6	47.4	Pass side road (right) to town of El Trapiche. Note crosses in center of road. Divided highway ends.
30.3	48.5	Pass exit (right) to Chiapa.
30.5	48.8	Pass exit (right) to free road to Guadalajara.
32.1	51.4	**GAS** on right. **KM 143**.
34.1	54.6	Pass exit (right) to airport and Cuauhtémoc. **KM 140**.
34.6	55.5	Over puente Cuauhtémoc.
40.1	64.2	Puente Los Lobos (The Wolves). **KM 131**.
41.5	66.4	Cross bridge over Barranca del Muerto. This is the state line. Leave state of Colima and enter state of Jalisco.
46.0	73.6	Come to tollbooth and pay toll (car $46, 2-axle $58, 3-axle $79).
47.8	76.5	Pass village of Volcán. Then Viaducto Beltrán. **KM 120**.
49.1	78.6	Pass Mountain top town of Pialla. Then over Puente Pialla, altitude 3,200 ft. **KM 117**.
52.2	83.5	Puente Los Hornos. Doesn't the rock formation on right look like an Indian guarding the bridge?
53.2	85.1	Pass paper mill town of Antenquique. Then cross El Nuevo bridge.
54.0	86.4	Puente Las Agates. **KM 113**.
54.3	86.9	Cross two magnificent bridges over deep canyons, Antenquique I and II.
55.9	89.4	Pass exit (right) to Atenquique and free road, but it's closed. **KM 107**.
66.1	105.8	Note electrical generator plant at left.
68.9	110.2	Fertilizer plant at right. Then pass exit (right) to Cd. Guzmán. **KM 87**.
71.3	114.1	Rest area and snack stand at left. **KM 85**.
80.3	128.5	Bypass town of Usmajac (or Uxmajac, the Indian spelling).
82.8	132.5	Curve left and pass exit (right) to Sayula and Usmajac. **KM 65**.
83.9	134.2	**GAS** at right and at left. This is a sand storm region.
92.8	148.5	Pass exit (right) to towns of Tapalpa and Atoyac over at left.
101.1	161.8	Pass exit (right) to village of Techaluta.
105.0	168.0	Thru the marshlands you may see egrets with no regrets or a brawny Brahma.
123.1	197.0	Bypass little town of Acatlán de Juárez. Note town down to left.
123.6	197.8	Topes! Pay Toll (car $44, 2-axle $54, 3-axle $75). Toll road ends here. Altitude: 1,370 m or 4,506 feet.
124.3	198.9	Pass exit left to Morelia and Jocotepec. Left for Barra de Navidad also. Straight for Guadalajara.
127.2	203.5	Birriera Los Chavos at left.
128.3	205.3	Thru village of Buena Vista.
129.7	207.5	Industrial park on right. Then Restaurante Mi Ranchito on left.
131.2	209.9	Thru town of Santa Cruz. **GAS** on both sides. Balneario Escondido and Vegetarian school at left.
135.0	216.0	Fancy new Dunas Motel on left.

MI   KM

135.7 217.1   Pass Garden Hotel at left.

136.9 219.0   Pass exit (right and up overpass) to fabulous Santa Ana Golf Course and subdivision.

137.7 220.3   Good **GAS** on left.

138.6 221.7   Pass side road (left) to San José del Tajo Trailer Park.

IF TO: San José del Tajo Trailer Park, do not try to turn across traffic. Continue straight ahead past the Siemans factory to the next overpass (El Palomar exit), exit right and up onto overpass and over highway. Continue to the opening, which is the entrance to Gigante supermarket, and make a U-turn and back to the highway and turn right. Retrace your steps past the Siemans plant, then pass Parrilla de Tajo restaurant on your right. Turn right at the entrance to San José del Tajo trailer park and follow the cobblestone road back to the office and turn right again.

139.3 222.9   Pass exit (right) to El Palomar. Gigante is over on left.

140.3 224.5   Pass exit (right) to Ciudad Bugambilias and shopping center.

141.3 226.1   On right before pedestrian crossing is Restaurant and Bar La Camarada and Mercedes Benz dealer. Careful now! Come to junction with Periférico. (There is usually a traffic cop here.)

IF TO: Chapala, Mexico City, Querétaro or San Luis Potosí, exit right and join the Guadalajara Bypass Counterclockwise Log at mile12. See Mexico's Huasteca Potosina Book (page 77).

IF TO: Zacatecas, go under overpass, exit right and join Guadalajara Bypass Clockwise Log at mile 13. See Mexico's Huasteca Potosina Book (page 67).

IF TO: Tepic, go under overpass, exit right and join Guadalajara Bypass Clockwise Log at mile 13. See Mexico's Pacific Coast Book (page 77).

141.7 226.7   Pass Coca Cola plant on left.

142.0 227.2   Comercial Mexicana on right. Then **GAS** and Restaurante Real Cazadores on left.

142.6 228.2   Gigante on left. Then Administration building for Zapopan.

142.8 228.5   You pass thru impressive eagle road markers (which used to be the city limits of Guadalajara). Then Holiday Suites del Real on left.

143.0 228.8   Bolerama La Calma on left.

143.4 229.4   Exit here for Hyatt Hotel.

143.6 229.7   Guadalajara Grill at right.

143.8 230.1   Chrysler dealer is on right and Ford on the left.

144.0 230.4   Pass Holiday Inn at left and Motel Plaza del Sol at right. Exit here for Holiday Inn Crown Plaza and pass statue of Mariano Otero at right. Plaza del Sol shopping center and Hotel Plaza del Sol are on the right.

145.0 232.0   There's a pretty fountain on left. Then Gigante on left.

145.2 232.3   Motel Campo is on right, Motel Chapalita beyond and Posada Guadalajara on the left.

145.5 232.8   Under Lázaro Cárdenas street. **GAS** on right.

146.0 233.6   Firestone is on the right. El Caballo Restaurant will be on left along with Price Club.

146.3 234.1   Come to Fiesta Americana on left and Danessa Ice Cream ahead of you on the right, Burger King on the left and Tok's Restaurant on right.

IF TO: Jalpa, Zacatecas continue straight and start Guadalajara - Zacatecas Log (See Mexico's Huasteca Potosina, page 206).

IF TO: San Luis Potosí, Aguascalientes, turn right at circle and start Guadalajara -San Luis Potosí Log (See Mexico's Huasteca Potosina, page 201).

IF TO: Querétaro, turn right at circle and start Guadalajara - Querétaro Log (See Mexico's Colonial Heart, page 2).

IF TO: Mexico City or Morelia, Turn right and start Guadalajara - Morelia (toll) Log (See Mexico's Colonial Heart, page 33) or Guadalajara - Jiquilpan (free road) Log (See Mexico's Colonial Heart, page 40).

IF TO: Tepic or Pto. Vallarta turn left at circle and start Guadalajara - Tepic Log (See Mexico's Pacific Coast and Copper Canyon, page 151).

End of Log 60

LOG 61 *START:* Acapulco, Gro *END:* Iguala, Gro

UD-087

126.2 MI or 201.9 KM
DRIVE TIME 4 — 4 1/2 HOURS
SCENIC RATING — 1

MI	KM	
0.0	0.0	At Diana Circle on Costera Miguel Alemán in Acapulco, with a parking lot at right and Comercial Mexicana at left, proceed ahead, northward, past **GAS**, station (watch 'em!) at left.
0.9	1.4	Keep right for Mexico (vía rápida) thru tunnel.
1.2	1.9	Enter tunnel.
3.0	5.0	Emerge from tunnel.
3.2	5.1	Come to tollbooth and pay toll (cars $23, buses $42, 3-axle $70). (Locals pay 1/2 price.) After tollbooth merge with traffic coming from right from Pto. Marquez.
3.8	6.1	**GAS** on right.
4.2	6.7	Another **GAS** on right. Then thru long tianguis area (roadside shops).
5.1	8.2	Under "Gracias por su Visita, Feliz Viaje" sign. Bid farewell to Acapulco.
5.3	8.5	Pass Colonia Jardines del Tiempo on left.
5.8	9.3	Pass exit (left) to Blvd. López Portillo and village of Las Cruces.
6.2	9.9	Pass exit (left) to Zihuatanejo, Tierra Colorada. Continue straight for toll road to Mexico City.

IF TO: Ixtapa, Zihuatanejo, turn left and start Acapulco - Ixtapa Log (page 142).

MI	KM	
6.7	10.4	Restrooms on right just before puente La Sábana
6.9	11.0	Pass exit right to Acapulco International Airport.
7.3	11.7	Come to tollbooth and pay toll (cars — $55, extra axle — $20, 2 axle — $75, 3 axle — $110). Nice 4-lane divided highway. This highway goes thru many rock cuts and hills but is flat with no sharp curves.
20.0	32.0	Small rest area and shrine on right. **KM 345**.
29.5	47.2	Thru tunnel. **KM 330**.
31.5	50.4	Cross bridge over Río Papagayo. **KM 327**.
34.9	55.8	Pass exit (right) to Tierra Colorada. **KM 321**.
48.3	77.3	Thru another tunnel. **KM 300**.
55.6	89.0	Come to second tollbooth and pay toll (cars — $60, 2 axle — $80, 3 axle — $125). Restrooms and snack bar at right. Altitude 4,200 feet. Sign says "Chilpancingo 18 Km." **KM 289**.
62.3	99.7	Pass exit (right) to Mochitlán and Petaquillas.
62.6	100.1	**GAS**, right and left. We're now in Chilpancingo.
63.3	101.3	Pass exit (right) to Chilpancingo
65.2	104.3	Pass another exit (right) to Chilpancingo
66.5	106.4	Pass Hotel Paradise Inn at right.
67.1	107.4	Pass Restaurant Las Brisas on left (use retorno). Altitude 4,400 feet.
67.4	107.8	**GAS** at left. **KM 276**.
68.6	109.8	Pass Hotel El Monasterio over on left.
69.1	110.6	Pass exit (left) to Chichihualco. Then **GAS**, right.
69.4	111.0	Pass exit (right) to free road to Iguala. **KM 267**.
77.2	123.5	Over puente El Zapote.
88.0	140.8	Pass exit (left) to return to Chilpancingo. Careful for high winds thru here. **KM 237**.
90.2	144.3	Over puente Barranca El Cañon. **KM 234**.
98.8	158.8	Pass exit right to Mirador Las Balsas.
99.4	159.0	Cross bridge over Río Mezcala. **KM 221**.
106.2	169.9	Pass rest area on right.
108.7	173.9	At left is another retorno.
124.0	198.4	Thru tunnel Los Querendas.
126.2	201.9	Come to exit (right) to Atenango del Río and Iguala. **GAS**, at right and left. Pay toll ahead.

IF TO: Taxco (also spelled Tasco), and if you want to avoid the toll, exit here and follow signs thru Iguala and up GRO Hwy #1 and start Iguala - Ixtapan de la Sal Log. Otherwise there's another exit ahead.

IF TO: Cuernavaca, Mexico City, start Iguala - Cuernavaca Log (page 157).

End of Log 61

LOG 62 *START:* Iguala, Gro *END:* Ixtapan de la Sal, Mex

66.5 MI or 106.4 KM
DRIVE TIME – 1 1/2 HOURS
SCENIC RATING – 3

MI	KM	
0.0	0.0	Starting here at Iguala junction Hwy #95 with **GAS** at left, proceed ahead under overpass.
1.0	1.6	Wind around historic little city of Iguala over to left. Pepsi plant at left.
2.3	3.7	Turn right at stop sign. Then pass military garrison at left.
4.0	6.4	School at left and slow for narrow bridge.
5.5	8.8	Over railroad (LOOK-&-LISTEN). Curve right and thru village of El Naranjo (The Orange Tree). Careful for topes and school zone.
8.0	12.8	Now start climbing. Sharp curves just ahead.
11.3	18.1	Wind down and past school at left. Then alongside pretty stream.
13.5	21.6	Spratling's famous silver factory at right – well worth a visit.
14.0	22.4	Pass side road (right) to Old Taxco, the forerunner of the present town of Taxco, off and up to right.
15.0	24.0	Pass side road (left) to village of Tecapulco. Note the silver shops all along here. Then over narrow bridge.
19.5	31.2	Thru village of Minas Viejas (Old Mines).
21.3	34.1	Pass side road (left) to Hacienda San Francisco Cuadra – fair inn built from ruins of an old mining village.
22.8	36.5	Enter town of Taxco on Av. J.F. Kennedy.
23.3	37.3	Bus station at right. **GAS** at left. For uptown Taxco, Hotels Rancho Taxco, Victoria, Santa Prisca, Meléndez, etc. turn left here and start uphill.
23.8	38.1	OK Motel Loma Linda at right. Then pass Secretariat of Tourism office at right.
24.3	38.9	Hotel De la Borda up lane at right. Street at left leads to zócalo (main plaza). **GAS** at right. Then Taxco's tourist office at left.
25.0	40.0	Under aqueduct arches and take leave of Taxco. Then wind up.
26.0	41.6	Come to entrance of Hotel Monte Taxco (previously Holiday Inn) at left. To get to hotel, stop and get visitor's pass, wind up right and then take left fork at top of hill.
26.5	42.4	Slow for sharp curves. Wind past village of Tehuilotepec down at left.
27.5	44.0	Highway Patrol station at right. Vendors along roadway sell quartz, rocks and other minerals.
31.0	49.6	Wind down thru community of La Azul. Then curve right over narrow stone bridge.
32.0	51.2	Settlement of Huajojutla at right. Thru desert-looking rock forest.
32.9	52.6	Right fork takes you to the Cuernavaca toll road. Straight is to Ixtapan de la Sal. Road narrows to two lanes.

IF TO: Cuernavaca, turn right and join Taxco-Hwy #95 Special (page 98) at mile 7.8.

MI	KM	
36.6	58.6	Thru Axixintla, mostly to right. **KM 65**.
38.2	61.1	Pass side road (right) to Cuernavaca. TAKE LEFT FORK for Ixtapan de la Sal and Toluca.
41.9	67.0	Pass turnoff right for famed Cacahuamilpa caves. These cave were discovered back in 1835 but still haven't been fully explored.
43.2	67.9	Pass junction (right) with Hwy #116 to Cuernavaca. Sharp curves ahead.
44.1	70.6	Thru village of Cacahuamilpa.
44.7	71.5	Leave Cacahuamilpa and wind up and up.
47.5	76.0	Summit and then down. Careful for sharp curves.
49.7	79.5	Thru tile-making village of El Mogote. Eight Topes.
51.3	82.1	Pass mirador, a nice lookout point on both sides of road where you can look down into deep Luluvar Canyon with Río Chontalcoatlán down in the bottom. **KM 104**.
52.5	84.0	Topes. Enter village of Piedras Negras. Note Abraham Lincoln school at right at far end. The Mexican people are great admirers of Lincoln who was a good friend of Benito Juárez, But they never met as Lincoln was assassinated before Juárez won his revolution.
53.2	85.1	After 5 topes take leave of Piedras Negras.
54.4	87.0	Cross state line – leave state of Guerrero and enter state of México.
56.3	90.1	Pass side road (right) to Grutas de la Estrella (Star Caves).
59.4	95.0	Careful for topes. **KM 90**.
59.8	95.7	Wind thru roadside village of Terrero.
61.7	98.7	Bend right and into Tonatico. Careful for several topes. Then turn right at TOLUCA sign and on up thru town. Then pass store Miel Vita-Real and restaurant El Amigo Toño at right.
63.3	101.3	Municipal Balneario on right – mineral baths for the nearby home folks.
65.5	104.8	Now into town of Ixtapan de la Sal. See Ixtapan de la Sal map (page 36) and Eat & Stray (page 125) for accommodations. **GAS,** left at junction with road (left) to Coatepec and Zacualpan.

MI   KM

65.8   105.3   Another **GAS** left.

66.1   15.8   Pass Hotel Ideal at right.

66.3   106.1   Now come to side street (left) leading to big Hotel Ixtapan.

IF TO: Hotel Ixtapan, turn left and up then turn in (right) at iron gate.

IF TO: Toluca, continue ahead and start Ixtapan de la Sal - Toluca Log.

IXTAPAN DE LA SAL is quite a place, one of Mexico's finest spas. The government owns the springs and the big bath house, so regardless of where you are staying, you can use the bath house.

End of Log 62

LOG 63 *START:* Ixtapan de la Sal, Mex *END:* Toluca, Mex

UD-017

55.8 MI or 89.3 KM
DRIVE TIME 1 1/2 – 2 1/2 HOURS
SCENIC RATING – 3

Wind thru farmland, then forested mountains. You also go thru many flower farms which raise carnations and daisies. There are many downhill grades where you must brake with motor.

0.0   0.0   Here at the turnoff left to big hotel Ixtapan, proceed ahead down beautiful flowered divided parkway. Then pass entrance street left to big public bathhouse. Pass hotel Kiss at right with hotel Sara Isabel next door. Then come to Bungalows Lolita a block to right. Note San Roman family mansion at right just before exit gates. (The San Román family owns hotel Ixtapan.)

0.5   0.8   Thru gates and leave Ixtapan de la Sal then curve left and wind. Come to exit to toll road.

IF TO: Toluca via toll road, hop to it! It saves a lot of time though it isn't as interesting. Start stub log below otherwise skip down to continuation of log.

IXTAPAN DE LA SAL – TOLUCA TOLL ROAD

1.3   2.1   Pass entrance to Balneario Ixtapan de la Sal. Then pass little statue of Diana.

8.4   13.4   **GAS** at right.

8.8   14.1   Begin divided.

9.3   13.3   Back to two lanes.

15.1   24.2   Pass exit to Villa Guerrero. There's a restaurant here.

27.8   44.5   Come to tollhouse and pay toll (car – $8; 2 axle – $16; 3 axle – $24; extra axle – $7).

33.3   53.3   Pass restaurant Las Codornices (The Quail).

34.4   55.0   Come to junction with free road. Join main log at mile 40.8.

End Ixtapan de la Sal – Toluca Toll Road

3.3   5.3   Village of San Diego down at right. Take right horseshoe curve and wind up.

5.0   8.0   Sharp right and over Arroyo Llano de la Unión.

5.3   8.5   Pass side road left to P. Díaz. Then thru community of Llano de la Unión. Down alongside Nenetzingo Canyon at right.

6.0   9.6   Curve right and slow for one-way bridge over Calderón Bridge, then right and wind up.

7.5   12.0   Now straight for a change.

12.0   19.2   Thru stretched out community of San Francisco.

13.5   21.6   Take left fork here for bypass around little town of Villa Guerrero.

14.8   23.7   Careful! Merge with road right coming from town.

16.5   26.4   Slow for right curving bridge. **KM 54**.

18.0   28.8   Down thru little town of Santa Ana. Buy your sweetie a bunch of flowers from here. Curve right-left at far end and wind down.

19.0   30.4   Slow now as you approach Tenancingo de Degollado, usually called "Tenancingo," known for its fruit wines, "rebozos" (made of cotton, rayon and silk) and tropical hardwood. It is also the home of Ken Baldin, a pre-Columbian artist and naturalist. His studio (or gallery) is up at left – worthwhile, but parking is a problem.

MI	KM	
19.3	30.9	Enter town proper. Furniture factory at right and left. Then turn right onto one-way Morelos. Pass plaza at right and then church. Continue thru town.
20.3	32.5	Power station at left and turn left onto divided parkway. Soccer field at right and ahead with pretty shady park at right.
21.0	33.6	Restaurant Vel-Mar at right. It used to be a balneario. Stop and eat at tables outside by the swimming pool. Past Morelos monument circle. Then curve right and up and out. VW agency at left.
26.5	42.4	Slow for a couple of sharp left curves.
27.5	44.0	Top. Now wind down. Pass side road (right) to MALINALCO archeological zone, equipped with a public campground (no hookups).
29.8	47.7	Thru edge of San Pedro Zictepec, mostly up and over to right.
33.0	52.8	Little town of Atlatlahuca over to left.
35.3	56.5	Curve left and then straight stretch. Road's easier going now.
36.0	57.6	**GAS**, left. Into outskirts of Tenango de Valle over to left. Then at left is archeological site of TEOTENANGO. Begin 4-lane divided to Toluca.
40.8	65.3	Curve left past village of San Antonio la Isla at right. Fruit-processing plant at left. Here is where toll road rejoins us.
44.3	70.9	Thru edge of Mexicalcingo.
45.0	72.0	This is where the Tres Marías-Toluca special joins us. It's a shortcut to Cuernavaca.
47.0	75.2	Rocks to left and a nice view of Nevado de Toluca. Mexico's fourth highest mountain of 14,900 feet and an extinct volcano – you can drive right up to the crater's rim! The Indian name for this ex-volcano is "Xianatecatl," meaning Naked Man. Incidentally, Mexico's tallest mountain is Orizaba at 18,851 feet; second is "Popo" at 17,761 feet and third is "Izta" (Sleeping Lady) at 17,343 feet.
47.8	76.5	Pass side road (right) to town of Metepec, best known for its famous pottery depicting colorful tree-of-life works. Their Monday morning market is good.
47.9	76.6	Zoológico Metepec, right. Over *vibradores* (speed bumps). Straight to Toluca. **KM 5**.
48.1	77.0	Pass glass tower at left. Plaza Las Americas shopping center on right. Burger King, Toks, Gigante and Sam's Club. **KM 2**.
49.5	79.2	VW dealer at right.
49.7	79.5	Enter Toluca, capital of the state of Mexico, officially known as "Toluca de Lerdo" honoring Sebastián Lerdo de Tejada, a Mexican statesman. See Toluca map (page 34) and Eat & Stray (page 124) for accommodations.
49.8	79.7	Las Canetas restaurant, bar and grill at right. Refraccionaria California to left.
50.0	80.0	Super Kompras to right.
50.3	80.5	Intersection. Stoplight. Valle del Bravo to left. Mexico D.F., right. Keep going straight to Toluca.
50.8	81.3	Come to big **GAS** right and Paseo Tollocan (from where "Toluca" is derived) bypass around town (also jct Hwy #15). Hardware store left.

IF TO: Morelia and Valle del Bravo, turn left and start Toluca – Morelia Log (See Mexico's Colonial Heart, page 192).

IF TO: Mexico City, turn right onto bypass and start Toluca – Mexico City Log (page 63).

IF TO: Palmillas and Querétaro, turn right onto bypass and start Toluca – Palmillas Log.

IF TO: Cd. Altamirano, Ixtapa, Zihuatanejo and Hwy #200, start Toluca – Cd. Altamirano Log (page 66).

End of Log 63

LOG 64 *START:* Toluca, Mex *END:* Palmillas Jct, Qro

UD-017

83.1 MI or 133.0 KM
DRIVE TIME 2 1/2 – 3 1/2 HOURS
SCENIC RATING – 2

Besides being a good shortcut highway to Morelia and Querétaro (even though it is a little winding in spots and often congested with slow moving trucks), this is also a most historical road because it was along this route that Padre Miguel Hidalgo marched his ragtag revolutionary army from Dolores Hidalgo-San Miguel de Allende-Querétaro to Toluca and then across toward Mexico City.

MI	KM	
0.0	0.0	Having turned right onto bypass (Paseo Tollucán) proceed ahead past the National Chamber of Commerce at right.
0.8	1.3	Pass Hotel Central and cross overpass. **GAS** and SuperCompras a left.
1.0	1.6	Pass Comercial Mexicana department store at left.
1.2	1.9	Pass McDonald's with clean restrooms on right.
1.5	2.4	Pass modernistic sculpture and exit (right) to Mexico City. Then curve left and pass exit (right) to downtown Toluca.
1.8	2.9	Ford dealer at left and Mercedes dealer at right. **GAS** and GM plant at right.
2.0	3.2	Pass residential colonia Las Torres at left.
2.3	3.7	**GAS** at right. Then pass intersection of Vía José López Portillo. Toluca Centro to left.
2.7	4.3	Pass multi-storied bluff and red housing project at left. Then over very bumpy railroad crossing.
2.9	4.6	Come to Jct Hwy #55. TURN RIGHT and pass Cemento Cruz Azul at left. Straight would take you to Morelia.
3.6	5.8	College of Engineers at left.
4.0	6.4	Holanda (ice cream distributor) and John Deere at left.
4.4	7.0	Take leave of Toluca. Fedomex plant at right and left.
4.6	7.4	Real Hacienda La Puerta at left. Pass side road (left) to village of Calixtlahuaca. **GAS** at left.

A short way beyond this village, there are archeological discoveries called CALIXTLAHUACA. They're pretty neat, but not worth a special trip.

8.6	13.8	Slow now. LOOK-&-LISTEN as you cross the bumpy railroad.
10.2	16.3	Pass tollbooth (tollbooths were not open when we came thru, so I can't tell you the cost).
14.8	23.7	Cross stone bridge over Río Lerma. **KM 24**.
19.7	31.5	Hacienda La Purísima to left.
22.6	36.2	Veer right to bypass village of Ixtlahuaca. If you're interested, market day is Monday. You will see red-winged blackbirds thru here.
29.1	46.6	Pass big factory at left. They make electrical things like switch boxes, meters and insulation material, etc.
30.8	49.3	**GAS** at left.
33.3	53.3	Little village of Mavoro over to right.
37.1	59.4	Pass exit to S.A. Enchise. Go under overpass. Lots of cops on this road. Watch your speed.
37.3	59.7	Slow for topes. Pay toll at tollhouse.
37.6	60.2	**GAS** right.
38.9	62.2	Pass Corona agency. Extinct Volcano at right.
39.1	62.6	At left is Hotel-Spa Fiesta Mexicana – quite a deal! It has a real spa with Swedish showers, jacuzzi, steam, massage, facials, weight reduction etc. They also have a nice hotel with 44 rooms and 6 suites with jacuzzi, restaurant, tennis courts, pool and gym. Ph: (712) 122-2236, 122-2238 Fax: 122-2337.
39.2	62.7	Pass shopping center with Super Kompras, right. Uniroyal left. Then highway patrol and **GAS** at right.
39.4	63.0	Pass restaurant Los Arcos.
40.3	64.5	Pottery sellers at left. Then electrical generating station at left.
40.4	64.6	Come to junction with Marativo highway. Straight goes to Atlacomulco.

IF TO: Palmillas, Querétaro, TURN RIGHT and ahead.

IF TO: Maravatio, Morelia (free road), turn left. FOLKS, WE DON'T RECOMMEND THIS ROUTE. IT'S PRETTY SCENERY BUT HAS MANY CURVES. Just ahead is the Morelia toll road.

40.5	64.8	Having turned right, curve left and up past La Cabaña restaurant. Then pass Gerardo's restaurant at left.
41.8	66.9	Pass fringes of Atlacomulco. Then turn right and come to exit to Morelia toll road.

IF TO: Morelia and on to Guadalajara via toll road – exit here. Exit right following "Marativo, Morelia" signs. It's a dandy road. If you want to save some time (and are willing to pay for it), then hop to it.

MI	KM	
43.8	70.1	Now up on winding road. Top. 8,500 feet.
47.9	76.6	BUMPY! BE READY FOR CURVY ROAD. Left. CAREFUL! Then SHARP RIGHT!
49.1	78.6	DOWN, then UP. CAREFUL! SHARP RIGHT!
54.3	86.9	Straight thru edge of little town of Acambay (population 47,915) and a Larga Distancia office. Topes. Emergency hotel. More topes. Wind up. Often bumpy road surface.
60.1	96.2	El Acosten to left. GO STRAIGHT.
62.6	100.2	Old stone hacienda 'way off to right. You'll be able to look down on it in a moment when the road winds up around over there.
63.8	102.1	Thru rocky community of El Bosque (The Forest). For the next few miles, you'll climb and climb and wind and wind. Looks a little like the forests outside two of my favorite U.S. places – Santa Fe, New Mexico or some spots in Washington state.
66.3	106.1	Thru a beautiful stand of trees!
66.6	106.6	Old stone aqueduct on right.
67.0	107.2	Pass side road (right) to Aculco. Altitude about 8,000 feet. Then little community of Nado.
78.3	125.3	Past Río Blanco "barranca" (canyon) over to left.
81.3	130.1	Cross state line at a little bridge; leave state of Mexico and enter state of Querétaro. CAREFUL! Slow for a sharp right curve. Down and down and then left.
83.1	133.0	Come to junction with Hwy #57 Expressway.

IF TO: Querétaro, San Luis Potosí, start Mexico City – Querétaro Log (See Mexico's Colonial Heart, page 174). There's a toll road from just south of Querétaro that bypasses the city and goes to the San Miguel junction. Then there's another that bypasses San Luis Potosí on the way to Saltillo.

IF TO: Ixmiquilpan, Pachuca, or Zimapán, go north on Hwy #57 for a couple of miles, turn right at PACHUCA exit, and start Palmillas - Ixmiquilpan Log (See Mexico's Huasteca Potosina, page 89).

End of Log 64

LOG 65 *START:* Iguala, Gro *END:* Cuernavaca, Mor

UD-087

60.3 MI or 96.5 KM
DRIVE TIME 1 1/4 HOURS
SCENIC RATING – 1

0.0	0.0	After **GAS**, head for MEXICO CUOTA slot and onto old Hwy #95D. (left fork here would take you into Iguala and up to Taxco). Come to tollbooth and pay toll (cars – $90, extra axle – $60, 2 axle – $135, 3 axle – $205).
13.1	21.0	Cross state line – leave state of Guerrero and enter state of Morelos.
27.5	44.0	Pass exit (right) to Lake Tequesquitengo and Tehuixtla.
33.1	53.0	Pass exit (right) to Taxco and Iguala.
39.4	63.0	Come to Alpuyeca tollhouse. Slow for topes and pay toll (cars – $35, extra axle – $18, 2 axle – $50, 3 axle – $80). If you wish to go over to Vista Hermosa (5 miles), Jojutla or to Lake Tequesquitengo (9 miles), turn off right after tollbooth. **GAS**, right and left.
46.3	74.1	Exit right to subdivision of Santa Fe. **KM 73**.
49.0	78.4	Curve right and over Río Zacatepec. Then another retorno to pull over for a stop.
51.0	81.6	Suburban community of Xochitepec over at left. For El Paraíso RV Park, take next exit. Turn right, Go about 2 miles (east) towards Chiconcoac, then turn right (south) towards Zacatepec. After 1 1/2 miles, turn right (SW) towards Atlacholoaya. Entrance to trailer park will be on you right after about 1/4 mile.
54.3	86.9	Las Brisas subdivision off to right. The Cuernavaca RV Park is 10 miles ahead.
55.8	89.3	Burgos subdivision at right.
56.5	90.4	Enter Cuernavaca. See Cuernavaca map (page 22) and Cuernavaca Eat & Stray (page 128) for accommodations.
57.0	91.2	CAREFUL NOW: TAKE RIGHT FORK and up over bridge. Ahead past VW and GM dealers. **GAS**, right. TAKE RIGHT FORK to bypass Cuernavaca. Left lane goes into town on Calle Morelos (Note: You can turn off and go into town here, but the turn off at end of log, 3 miles ahead, is better). Ahead under overpass and careful for traffic merging from your left.

MI	KM	
59.0	94.4	Pass exit (right) to Tabachines and under overpass.
60.3	96.5	Now come to east interchange and turnoff to Cuautla and Yautepec and to Camino Real Sumiya Hotel.

IF TO: Sumiya Hotel, exit off toll road toward Cuautla. Then turn right at the first stoplight.

IF TO: Cuernavaca Trailer Park, or north end Cuernavaca interchange (6 miles ahead), DO NOT turn off here, but continue ahead.

IF TO: Mexico City, continue ahead and start Cuernavaca - Mexico City Log.

End of Log 65

LOG 66 *START:* Cuernavaca, Mor *END:* Mexico City, DF

UD-087

43.8 MI or 70.1 KM
DRIVE TIME 1 – 2 HOURS
SCENIC RATING – 2

The best time to arrive in Mexico City is between 1-3 PM because traffic is less congested during these hours ("siesta" time). Negotiating the streets there after dark can be harrowing.

Warning: Pollution controls have been implemented in D.F. and they do apply to tourists. The fine for disregarding is U.S. $120.00. If your plate ends in the "right" number, it's wrong to drive that day. Subject to change, the "day without a car" will be extended if a smog emergency is declared. How to tell? Hopefully The News or local paper will advise. All you can do is ask at the tollbooth. If your plate ends with a letter you cannot circulate on Fridays.

Day	Monday	Tuesday	Wednesday	Thursday	Friday
Color	Yellow	Pink	Red	Green	Blue
Last #	5 & 6	7 & 8	3 & 4	1 & 2	9 & 0
Sometimes	7 & 8	9 & 0	1 & 2	3 & 4	5 & 6

Any time you think a cop is being too eager, We suggest you write the cop's badge # down. See "cops" section in the filler. Also you must have a fire extinguisher in your vehicle while in Mexico City. It's a good idea to carry one anywhere you go.

The way to use retornos on this highway is to pull off to right till traffic clears, then cross left over 2 lanes. Don't make the left turn from left lane.

0.0	0.0	On the toll road, at east Interchange into Cuernavaca with hospital at left, proceed ahead on divided. **KM 90**.
0.3	0.5	Corona agency at left.
1.1	1.8	Pass exit (right) to Unidad Morelos and Firestone at right. Take this exit for Cuernavaca RV Park. **KM 88**.
4.5	7.2	Under overpass, then up and over bridge over the railroad.
5.3	8.5	Exit (right) to Ahuatepec and Tepoztlán.

IF TO: Oaxtepec Vacation center, RV park and Hotel Hacienda Cocoyoc, exit here and follow log in Cuernavaca Eat & Stray.

6.2	9.9	Chrysler dealer, right. Begin three lanes.
7.0	11.2	OK **GAS**, at right and left. If you need gas, fill up here as the Mexico City stations are usually very congested.
9.8	15.7	Altitude 6,600 feet. Now down.
12.0	19.2	Here is the junction with #115-D expressway to Cuautla and Cocoyoc Huaxtepec at right. Exit to right. Then curve left. Take MEXICO slot.
12.7	20.3	Red Cross medical service at right.
14.0	22.4	Retorno, left and mirador at right – nice spot to park and take a breather if you like. **KM 68**.
14.5	23.2	Roadway narrows to 2-lane divided. Slow now for sharp left horseshoe curve called the pear and on up.

MI	KM	
14.8	23.7	Altitude 7,200 feet.
19.8	31.7	Retorno. Pedestrian crossing. Altitude 8,400 feet.
23.0	36.8	Up thru little town of Tres Cumbres (3 Peaks), also known as Tres Marías. Altitude 8,900 feet. There's an exit here to Toluca and Zempoala (Hwy #4). **KM 53**.

IF TO: Toluca, in order to avoid Mexico City, take this Tianguistengo shortcut. Go to next retorno (left) and come back. Take the first exit for Tres Marías. Pass a row of restaurants. Go 1/4 mile to first right. There's a concrete tourism marker and a map. Then turn right. Start the Tres Marías-Toluca Special.

23.3	37.3	Cross bridge over railroad and wind up into the pines.
26.3	42.1	Retorno. Altitude 10,000 feet.
26.5	42.4	Nice park and monument to Morelos up at left, one of Mexico's Top heroes of the revolution against the Spaniards and of whom Napoleon said, "Give me five generals like Morelos and I'll conquer the world!."
27.0	43.2	Come now to state line – leave Morelos and enter Distrito Federal (DF).
30.0	48.0	Parres bus stop. Then Estación Parres, the highest point on highway (9,900 feet). Nice skyline drive.
38.0	60.8	Majestic views off to right. Altitude now about 8,400 feet.
43.8	70.1	Thru village of San Pedro Mártir and ahead to tollhouse. Stop and pay toll (car – $47, 2 axle – $80, 3 axle $140, extra axle – $23). Restrooms at right. See Mexico City maps (pages 19 and 20) **KM 24**.

IF TO: Querétaro, start Mexico City Periférico South to North (See Mexico's Colonial Heart, page 97), which takes you to Hwys #15-57 or downtown and avoids busy, congested Insurgentes Avenue.

IF TO: Mexico City, continue ahead and start Insurgentes-North Special (See Mexico's Colonial Heart, page 98).

End of Log 66

LOG 67 *START:* Tehuantepec, Oax *END:* Oaxaca, Oax

UD-087

158.0 MI or 252.8 KM
DRIVE TIME 4 – 5 HOURS
SCENIC RATING – 3

The highway from Tehuantepec to Oaxaca is quite winding, so don't plan to make a fast trip. Plan to get a reasonably early start from Tehuantepec so you can stop off and see the Mitla Ruins and the famous Tule Tree. The only worthwhile accommodations or restaurant between here and Oaxaca are at Mitla.

0.0	0.0	Having taken right fork here in Tehuantepec at junction with Hwy #185, ahead past truck inspection station at right. **GAS** at left. There is also a hotel of left. Sign says "Oaxaca 250 Km, Mexico 700 Km." **KM 250**.
0.5	0.8	Pass Col. Juárez on left.
1.5	2.4	Penitentiary at left.
2.2	3.5	Cross twin bridges over Río Las Tortugas ("The Turtles").
5.0	8.0	Ruins of Guien Gola to right (7 km).
6.5	10.4	Down over Puente ("bridge") Las Tejas. **KM 240**. Start winding up foothills.
8.5	13.6	Pass community of Paso Alicia.
9.5	15.2	Pass side road left to village of San Miguel Tenango.
12.5	20.0	Note marble mine up at right.
17.3	27.7	Pass side road (right) down to big Benito Juárez Dam, 5 km. (Dam is 88 meters high and has created Mexico's twelfth largest artificial reservoir, with 942,000 cubic meters of water and is used for irrigation only.)
18.7	29.9	Thru little lake-side town of Jalapa del Marquez (population 23,000). Note big lake, sometimes called Lake Marquez and sometimes Lake Benito Juárez. Topes.
23.2	37.1	*Vibradores* (speed bumps) as you enter community of Llano Grande.
24.3	38.9	Pass Restaurant Mary at right. Then Col. San José off to right.
30.0	48.0	Pass exit (right) to Tequisistlán (over on left) and down. Cross Río Tequisistlán and wind on up past a marble and onyx mill at left.
31.3	50.1	Over one-way bridge and thru bus stop community and Restaurant Marilú on right.
32.4	51.8	Pass side road (left) to Tlacolula. **KM 200**.
35.0	56.0	Thru village of Las Flautas. **KM 195**.

MI	KM	
38.3	61.3	Slow for sharp left curve. Then thru Las Majadas. **KM 188**.
42.0	67.2	Thru village of La Reforma. Restaurant Reforma at right (not bad). Skip truck inspection at right.
47.5	76.0	Cross narrow bridge over Río Hondo and thru Río Hondo. Then Puerto San Bartolo.
56.0	89.6	Community of Las Minas ("The Mines") at left. Then road workers' village of El Coyul.
63.5	101.6	Portillo Nejapán with little shrine at left.
71.0	113.6	Thru village of Camarón ("shrimp") and cross narrow bridge. **GAS** at left.
76.0	121.6	Pass side road (right) to Najapán. Then cross bridge and thru settlement of El Gramal.
77.0	123.2	Settlement of Las Animas over at right and across Río Camarón. Then wind alongside Boquerón ("Big Hole") Canyon for a spell. Down and thru El Boquerón – where?
79.3	126.9	Over one-lane bridge over Río Boquerón (flash your lights for right-of-way). Watch for rocks on road ahead.
82.5	132.0	Thru settlement of San Jose de García. Casa de Huéspedes (Guest House) at right.
88.5	141.6	Over one-lane Las Catarinas Bridge.
101.3	162.1	Thru San Juan Guegoyache. Then big village of Totolapan. **GAS** at left.
109.5	175.2	Left horseshoe curve here at La Ceiba. Then Agua Santa and shrine at right.
116.5	186.4	Pass side road (left) to San Dionisio Ocotepec. Then some easy winding for a change.
121.2	193.9	Top hill. Altitude is 6,200 feet. Then down. **KM 62**.
125.0	200.0	Thru Mezcal brewing village of Matatlán. You can smell it a mile away. Topes (3 sets) (Mezcal is a low-grade form of Tequila.)
133.4	213.4	**GAS** at right and come to junction with road to Mitla Ruins.

IF TO: Mitla Ruins, turn right onto this side road (4 kilometers).

MITLA, from the civilizations of the Zapotecas (first) and Mixtecas (later) is interesting and worth a short visit. Just wind about 4 miles along this side road and thru little town of Mitla (open daily, 9-5; admission charged).

Of prime significance at Mitla is the great mystery regarding why it's the only large archeological find in Mexico where there are no carvings or paintings of people and animals or symbols of mythology or the universe. In the big Hall of Monoliths, everything is geometric (lace-like) and more like the fretwork of ancient Greece. And another mystery is how the huge 20-foot stone columns over the big doorways were lifted into place, as some must weigh at least 15 tons!

There's an interesting little museum of Mixtec and Zapotec items and artifacts in the middle of town run by the University of the Americas. An American, the late E.R. Frissell, did much of the early work here and the museum was once his private collection.

And also in the village adjacent to the museum is Posada La Sorpresa, an ancient hacienda converted to an interesting little inn, especially its library. Don't hesitate to stay the night, as the rooms are comfortable and its charming patio restaurant serves good American-style specialties.

137.9	220.6	Pass side road (right) to ruins of Zapotec-Mixtec YAGUL archeological site off to right on hillside, somewhat similar to Mitla but not quite as large nor as well restored.
138.7	221.9	Cross narrow bridge and past little town of Tlacolula, mostly at left. Maguey Azul Mezcal distillery at right.

It's been said that the only place nowadays to buy COCHINEAL DYE is right here in Tlacolula's Sunday market. Cochineal is the famous old red color dye that was once the basis of the economy in this area. The magenta color of the uniforms of the British Red-coats that our colonists whipped back in 1776 came from Oaxaca's cochineal dye; likewise, the "liberty red" in the first tricolor of the French Republic. Since the development of synthetic dyes, however, there's not much demand for the genuine cochineal variety except by the natives. (Cochineal is a little mite that attaches itself to the red bloom of the cactus which is where it absorbs its vivid coloring. The natives then gather jillions of them, boil them and dry them in the sun and then package them. Fortunes were made on these tiny ticks in the olden days!)

139.7	223.5	**GAS** at left and pass side road (right) to Díaz Ordaz.
140.5	224.8	Pass mezcal distillery at right. Then archeological ruins of LAMBITYECO at left.
146.1	233.7	Pass side road (right) to Benito Juárez.
149.4	239.0	Pass side road (left) to towns of Abasolo and San Juan Tepetac.
150.4	240.6	Topes. Pemex storage plant at left.
152.1	243.4	Come to village of El Tule. Veer left to bypass town. Straight for a close-up look at famous TULE TREE in front of church, whose base is said to be of greater circumference than any other tree in the world! (At least it's the biggest in Mexico, for sure!) It's an "ahuehuete" (cypress) said to be over 2000 years old with a circumference of 160 feet.

MI	KM	
152.6	244.2	Come to end of bypass and entrance to town of El Tule. Then pass Restaurant Florencia.
154.9	247.8	Thru suburban village of San Sebastián. Posada Los Arcos at left.
155.6	249.0	Then come to fancy mural monument at left to Benito Juárez. Then pass junction (right) Hwy #175 to Textepec and Guelatao, Benito Juárez' birthplace (50 miles). Then Restaurant Los Venados.
156.0	249.6	Motel Internacional at left, use retorno to get there.
156.8	250.9	Topes. Hotel Del Bosque at left.
157.0	251.2	Military garrison at right. **GAS** at left (more ahead) and enter Oaxaca (population 240,000), capital of Oaxaca state and a terrific town! Oaxaca was the home state of two of Mexico's most famous presidents, Benito Juárez and Porfirio Díaz.
157.2	251.5	Now thru Oaxaca's famous green rock quarries – many of their public buildings as well as fancy mansions have been constructed of this green stone.
157.5	252.0	Under "Welcome to Oaxaca de Juárez" sign.
157.6	252.2	Careful for topes. Pass Euzkadi dealer. Then side street Violeta (right) to Oaxaca Trailer Park (up about mile). Come to Junction with Periférico.

IF TO: Pochutla, Pto. Angel, turn left and start Oaxaca - Pochutla Log (page 69).

157.8	252.5	Pass bus station and Hotel Veracruz at left. Then pass road (right) to Col. Reforma.
158.0	252.8	**GAS** at left and come to important intersection of Av. Juárez (left) and Calz. Porfirio Díaz (right). If to Misión de los Angeles, turn right; if to downtown, turn left.

IF TO: Cuautla, Puebla, or Mexico City via Huajuapan, continue ahead and start Oaxaca - Huajuapan de León Log (page 81).

IF TO: Puebla, Orizaba, Veracruz, via toll road, start Oaxaca - Puebla toll Log (page 161).

IF TO: Tehuacan via free road, start Oaxaca - Tehuacan Free Log (page 71).

Note: Plan to stay here in Oaxaca at least a couple of days, as you'll thoroughly enjoy this unusual place. See Oaxaca Eat & Stray (page 134) for accommodations.

End of Log 67

LOG 68 START: Oaxaca, Oax END: Puebla, Pue (toll)

UD-087

216.5 MI or 346.4 KM
DRIVE TIME 3 1/2 HOURS
SCENIC RATING — 3

0.0	0.0	Starting in Oaxaca City (altitude 5,000 feet) at traffic light at junction Hwy 190 and Av Juárez with downtown to your left, proceed ahead on Hwy 190. **GAS** on left. This street is called Av. Niños Héroes de Chapultepec. Then social security hospital at right.
0.4	0.6	Euzkadi tire and Chrysler, Dodge and Jeep dealer at right. Then pass Hotel Fortín Plaza on right.
0.7	1.1	Pass Hotel Victoria on right up on hill.
1.1	1.8	Pass Auditorio Guilguetza on right.
1.3	2.1	Pass scenic overlook to left. This is a nice view of Oaxaca City, the valley and Río Atoyac.
1.6	2.6	Dangerous curve to left and then right.
2.3	3.7	Note huge purple building at left as you approach monument glorieta junction.
2.5	4.0	Come to monument glorieta junction. A left will take you to turnoff to Monte Albán archeological ruins (a very interesting site) or down Madero to hotels Los Olivos and Primavera. Continue straight for toll road.
2.7	4.3	Pass sports center and stadium, left. Then **GAS** at right.
3.6	5.8	Pass big Mercado Santa Rosa at right. Then Motel Bel Air at left.
4.1	6.6	Hotel La Cabaña on left.
4.3	6.9	Breñamiel Arboledas next to tennis club, left.
4.6	7.4	Pass Hotel Villas del Sol at left. Then trailer park Rosa Isabel on left. Use retorno to get there.
4.7	7.5	Hotel Loma Bonita on right.
5.8	9.3	Restaurant El Nixtequito on right. Then pass monument to Hidalgo.
6.1	9.8	Higueras Motel at left.
6.5	10.4	**GAS** on left and right. **KM 243**.
7.7	12.3	Welcome sign to toll road.

162

MI	KM	
8.0	12.8	Come to junction with toll road. Stay in the left lane and follow the signs to Nochixtlan. Do not take the right fork to Huajuapan, that is the free road.

IF TO: Tehuacán, Puebla via toll road, stay in left lane.

IF TO: Huajuapan de León, take right fork and join Oaxaca - Huajuapan de León Log (page 81) at mile 8.0

IF TO: Huautla or Tehuacán via free road, take right fork and join Oaxaca - Tehuacán Log (page 71) at mile 8.0.

8.8	14.1	Cross bridge over Oaxaca-Mexico City railroad.
9.3	14.9	Cross bridge over Río Seco.
19.3	30.9	Over puente Ochimilco.
22.6	36.2	Come to first tollhouse and pay toll (cars $46, 2-axle $95, 3-axle $110) and exit (right) to Huitzo. Then cross bridge over Río Negro. Then restrooms and first aid station. The road narrows to a wide 2-lane roadway.
23.4	37.4	Cross bridge over a branch of Río Negro. Note dam over on left.
24.1	38.6	Curve left and signs warning of falling rocks ahead. Sign says "Tehuacán 175 km."
29.7	47.5	Cross bridge that curves to left over deep canyon of Arroyo Carbonera with small reservoir over to left. Rock cuts are covered with wire mesh.
32.3	51.7	Cross bridge over Barranca Cruz de Piedra (Rock Cross Canyon).
33.8	54.1	Over Río Díaz. We are now going thru landscapes with tall trees. Altitude 6,000 feet.
37.9	60.6	Over Arrollo Surco. **KM 196**.
39.2	62.7	Over Arrollo Tinu. **KM 194**.
40.2	64.3	Cross bridge over Río Salinas at an altitude of 6,500 feet.
49.6	79.4	**GAS** at right. There is an exit here to town of Nochixtlán. **KM 178**.
51.2	81.9	Pass exit (right) to Nochixtlán. Under second overpass is exit to Huacuapan. Altitude 7,000 feet. **KM 175**.
52.3	83.7	Sign says "Puebla, 240 km."
54.8	87.7	Over puente Yotonchi. **KM 170**.
60.0	96.0	Note strange looking green rock thru here (Is it Mars?).
63.2	101.1	We are now at 7,800 feet and climbing.
64.0	102.4	Careful for about 1/2 mile of rough road thru landslide area. Then some dangerous curves.
66.3	106.1	Pass exit (right) to Nativitas and Monteverde. **KM 152**. Sign says "Puebla 261 km."
68.8	110.1	Altitude 7,400 feet and we start heading down.
72.8	116.5	Come to exit (right) to Coixtlahuaca and Suchixtlahuaca and second tollhouse. Pay toll (cars $38, 2-axle $74, 3-axle $95) Then restrooms on right.
73.9	118.3	Cross bridge over Arroyo Grande. **KM 140**.
83.0	132.8	Pass exit (right) to Tepelmeme and Tamazulapan. Then over Río Grande bridge.
84.3	134.9	Pass exit (right) to Tepelmeme Concepción. **KM 124**. Sign says "Tehuacán 73 km."
86.3	138.1	Over Río Chiquito. **KM 121**.
95.0	152.0	Over puente Otates curving to left. Altitude 6,900 feet.
100.2	160.3	Over puente Santa Lucía bridge curving to left. Beware of possible landslides.
102.6	164.2	Careful for a short 1/2 mile detour to left due to recent landslides. There had been a tunnel but it caved in.
106.0	169.6	Rough 1/2 mile of road.
108.5	173.6	Cross puente Carizarillos curving to left over a deep canyon. We now enter an organ cactus forest.
110.3	176.5	Cross long Calapa bridge curving to left over another deep canyon. This is also the state line. Leave state of Oaxaca and enter state of Puebla.
117.0	187.2	Down into wide horizon valley.
118.7	189.9	Come to exit (right) to Tetitlán and Miahuatlán. Come to third tollhouse and pay toll (cars $15, 2-axle $26, 3-axle $30) Parking and restrooms are on right.
124.8	199.7	Pass exit (right) to village of San Gabriel Xilac. Sign says "Tehuacán 23 km."
127.6	204.2	Note chicken farms on left and right. **KM 55**.
133.4	213.4	Gravel mill on left. Then pass exit (right) to Huajuapan and Tehuacán. Don't hesitate visit this city of thermal water spas. See Tehuacán Eat & Stray, (page 133) for accommodations. **KM 48**.

IF TO: Huajuapan de León, exit right and join Tehuacán - Huajuapan de León Log (page 90) at mile 4.0.

IF TO: Tehuacán, exit right and join Huajuapan de León - Tehuacán Log (page 92) at mile 70.0.

136.3	218.1	You can see the tops of the houses of Tehuacán in the valley over to right.
138.7	221.9	Pass exit (right) to Tehuacán and Francisco Madero. Come to fourth tollhouse and pay toll (Cars, $24, 2-axle $48, 3-axle $72). Altitude just under 6,000 feet. Restrooms on right. Army check point here. **KM 40**.
139.0	222.4	Over puente Tehuacán and under overpass. **KM 39**.

MI	KM	
139.4	223.0	**GAS** on right and a 24-hour restaurant Los Arcos. Now we start climbing again.
142.1	227.4	Cross bridge over Puebla-Tehuacán railroad.
143.0	228.8	Cross another bridge over Puebla-Esperanza railroad. Altitude 5,000 feet.
148.0	236.8	Begin series of curves.
155.2	248.2	Altitude 8,000 feet. **KM 14**.
160.5	256.8	Cross bridge over Barranca del Salto.
162.9	260.6	Pass gravel pit mine over on left.
163.3	261.3	Pass exit (right) under overpass to Cuacnopalan. **KM 2**.
164.0	262.4	Come to junction with Hwy 150D. Left lane goes to Mexico and Puebla. Right lane goes to Córdoba, Orizaba and Veracruz. **KM 0**.

IF TO: Mexico, Puebla, stay in left lane which curves around to left and merge with traffic coming from left and ahead.

IF TO: Córdoba, Orizaba or Veracruz, stay in right lane which curves around to right and merge with traffic coming from left. Join Puebla - Veracruz Log (See Mexico's Colonial Heart, page 20) at mile 52.5.

172.2	275.5	**GAS**, on both sides of highway. Then Popular Oasis truck stop restaurant, right. **KM 192**.
173.5	277.6	Pass exit (right) to San Miguel Jaltepec.
175.7	281.1	Thru maguey fields and under a flock of overpasses.
179.5	287.2	Pass exit (right) to Quecholac and Temachalco.
187.0	299.2	Village of Acatzingo at right.
187.9	300.6	Come now to Hwy #140 Interchange.

IF TO: Perote, Teziutlán, or Jalapa, exit here (also if to Tehuacan via old (free) Hwy #150).

IF TO: Puebla, Mexico City, continue ahead on #150-D toll road.

201.2	321.9	Now over bridge over usually dry tributary of Río Atoyac.
203.2	325.1	Head for MEXICO slot and pay toll (cars — $24; 2-axle — $46; 3-axle — $89). Then SLOW for tollhouse ahead at Amozac Interchange. Cross bridge over railroad.
205.3	328.5	**GAS**, right and left. **KM 134**.

"La Malinche" (really "Malintzi") was Cortes' Indian mistress, and has always been considered a traitor — hence the appellation "Wicked Woman."

207.9	332.6	Little town of Nopaluca 'way over to left. Note mountain over at right — that's famous MT. LA MALINCHE ("The Wicked Woman"), Mexico's fifth highest mountain at 13,700 feet. The other four are Orizaba, Popo, Sleeping Lady, and Nevado Toluca, in that order.)

Now is a good time to tell you about General Zaragoza, the Texas-born hero of famed Cinco de Mayo (5th of May) Battle of Puebla when Mexico defeated the French on these plains. The good general wasn't really born in Texas but in Goliad in what is NOW Texas. In those days it was part of Mexico, so Mexico always takes a good-natured ribbing about having to come to Texas for its very best general.

211.5	338.4	Turnoff left into Puebla, but stay in CENTER LANE marked MEXICO CUOTA, then up and over and ahead. Come to big monument at left to General Zaragoza.
212.3	339.7	Big NCR plant and stadium, left.
214.0	342.4	Over railroad (LOOK-&-LISTEN).

IF TO: Pachuca, exit right and start Puebla - Pachuca Log (See Mexico's Huasteca Potosina, page 193) at mile 2.

215.0	344.0	Junction with Hwy #119 right to Tlaxcala and left into Puebla.
216.5	346.4	Come to junction with Hwy #190 to Izucar de Matamoros and Oaxaca, continue ahead following 150D/MEXICO signs.

IF TO: Izucar de Matamoros, Cholula, or Las Americas RV Park, follow PUEBLA 150D signs which will feed you into town on Hermanos Serdán Boulevard (Hwy #190). Start Puebla - Izucar de Matamoros Log (page 88).

IF TO: Mexico City, follow MEXICO signs and start Puebla - Mexico City Log.

End of Log 68

LOG 69 *START:* Puebla, Pue *END:* Mexico City, DF

UD-087

78.0 MI or 124.8 KM
DRIVE TIME 1 3/4 – 2 1/2 HOURS
SCENIC RATING – 3

Beautiful multi–lane expressway that climbs and goes through a forest. Well engineered. Some steep grades.

Warning: Pollution controls have been implemented in D.F. and they do apply to tourists. The fine for disregarding is U.S. $120.00. If your plate ends in the "right" number, it's wrong to drive that day. Subject to change, the "day without a car" will be extended if a smog emergency is declared. How to tell? Hopefully The News or local paper will advise. All you can do is ask at the tollbooth. If your plate ends with a letter you cannot circulate on Fridays.

Day	Monday	Tuesday	Wednesday	Thursday	Friday
Color	Yellow	Pink	Red	Green	Blue
Last #	5 & 6	7 & 8	3 & 4	1 & 2	9 & 0
Sometimes	7 & 8	9 & 0	1 & 2	3 & 4	5 & 6

Any time you think a cop is being too eager, We suggest you write the cop's badge # down. See "cops" section in the filler. Also you must have a fire extinguisher in your vehicle while in Mexico City. It's a good idea to carry one anywhere you go.

MI	KM	
0.0	0.0	Here at junction Hwy #190, proceed ahead. **GAS**, and self-serve snack restaurant at left (restrooms in restaurant cleaner than those in gas station).
0.5	0.8	Now down and over bridge over Río Atoyac.
2.0	3.2	Pass huge Volkswagen factory at right.
5.0	8.0	Ocotlán at left with its hilltop church.
8.0	12.8	Thru village of Xoxtla "shoaks-tla," left. Big steel mill off to left.
16.2	25.9	Wide curve left. Over bridge over railroad.
17.7	28.3	Pull up at green light slot at tollhouse and pay Puebla toll (cars – $13, 2 axle – $26, 3 axle – $39, Extra axle – $7). Restrooms at left.
28.0	44.8	Over bridge over Río Emperador – go a little slow and note its deep, deep gorge.
29.0	46.4	"Mirador" at left. Village of Santa Rita de Tlahuapan, left.
35.5	56.8	Under old road and cross state line – leave state of Puebla and enter state of Mexico. Careful here! Pass turnoff left to Río Frío rest area – **GAS**, food, arts-and-crafts, lodging, camping.
41.2	65.9	Up in here is the highest point on the road – 10,700 feet above sea level. This is the CONTINENTAL DIVIDE, the backbone of the North American continent. Then start winding down stretch – not too fast! You're in a National Park. Remember to shift to a lower gear if you want to have any brakes right at the bottom! Easy does it!
45.5	72.8	Now more curves and down into majestic pine forest. 9,200 feet. You'll see a sign that says "Caution with ice on road." Welcome to sunny Mexico. Beware of fog as you descend this mountain!
46.5	74.4	"Mirador" at left, where you can stop and park and enjoy the lovely view. Altitude 8,000 feet.
58.0	92.8	Restrooms are at left – park at left just before tollhouse. Pull up at green light slot at tollhouse and pay toll (car – $15, 2 axle – $30, 3 axle $45, extra axle – $8). **KM 32.**
62.5	100.0	On a clear day you can see famed snow-capped Mts. Popocatepetl "Popo" and Ixtaccihuatl "Ixty," or "sleeping Lady" off to left Then a straight stretch. Curve right around mini-mountain.
64.5	103.2	Now down gradually. Cross state line here – leave Mexico and enter state of Federal District (DF). Then UNDER OVERPASS. Pass **GAS**, at left.
65.5	104.8	Curve around left and careful for traffic from right. Follow airport signs
66.5	106.4	Burger Boy, right. Pass **GAS**, at left.
67.9	108.6	Then TOK'S restaurant, Gigante and McDonald's at right.
68.5	109.6	Federal government radio monitoring station over to left. Huge ISSSTE hospital at left.
69.5	111.2	Come to junction with Canal de San Juan which is also the Periférico.

IF TO: Xochimilco or north part of town via the Periférico, turn left and start Mexico City Periférico

South to North Log (See Mexico's Colonial Heart, page 97). Otherwise continue straight on Zaragoza.

MI	KM	
71.0	113.6	Go under *Metro* . Now come to Río Churubusco. Pantitlán to right. Left lane to Viaducto. Stoplight – a few more ahead. Keep straight on Zaragoza.
71.5	114.4	Another stoplight. Bear left. Ahead and wide curve right. STOPLIGHT at end of sports complex.
75.0	120.0	Pass Aurrera shopping center at right and Vip's Restaurant also at right.
75.3	120.5	For airport or Basílica of Guadalupe, turn right at next light. Go under overpass and TURN LEFT for down town on Fray Servando. Pass Aeropuerto Metro stop and Zapateros Morelos. Go one block and curve right and merge left onto Fray Servando.
75.7	121.1	Pass Esso on left. Follow Centro Histórico signs.
76.0	121.6	Pass Hotel Kennedy at right.
76.6	122.6	Cross Av. Congreso de la Unión and under Metro. Then Mercado La Merced, left and **GAS** at left
77.0	123.2	Go under overpass (Calz. Tlalpan). Then Hotel Costa Azul at left. Follow La Villa signs, stay in center lane. Take next right onto Isabel la Católica (a one-way street to zócalo). Chapultepec saloon on left.
77.2	123.5	Pass Baños Señorial at right. Cross Regina street. Then public parking at left and pass Hotel Isabel at left. Then cross Uruguay.
77.5	124.0	Pass Sanborn's at left. Corona sign dead ahead. Turn right onto Madero with Church La Profesía in front of you. Vip's on right. Cross La Palma street with parking lot 1/2 block down.
78.0	124.8	Come to Hotel Majestic, right with zócalo and Palacio Nacional dead ahead.

IF TO: Toluca, start Mexico City – Toluca Log.

IF TO: Pachuca, go around block, then go to Eje Central Lázaro Cárdenas, turn right and follow Eje Central till you come to Insurgentes where you turn right and join Mexico Pachuca Log (See Mexico's Colonial Heart, page 191) at mile 3.0 just north of La Raza Monument.

IF TO: Zona Rosa and angel monument. Follow stub log below:

TO ANGEL MONUMENT

0.0	0.0	Starting at zócalo with church behind you, Palacio Nacional at left and Hotel Majestic behind at right, cross Calle 16 de Septiembre, proceed ahead on 5 de Febrero, going south.
0.2	0.3	Gigante store on left. Then cross Uruguay with Hotel Montecristo to right.
0.5	0.8	Turn right at Chapultepec-Insurgentes sign onto Fray Servando with 6-story building on left and tree-lined divided street to left. Pass Calle Isabel La Católica at first light. Ahead is Eifel Tower (actually TV tower – channel 2).
0.8	1.3	Cross Eje Central, Av. Lázaro Cárdenas, with Dodge dealer at right.
1.0	1.6	Nissan agency on left. The name of street you're on changes to Río de la Loza. Keep following Chapultepec-Insurgentes signs. Cross Balderas with TV tower in front. Balderas Metro station is one block to right.
1.2	1.9	Go one block, TURN RIGHT at antenna onto Dr. Lucio. Go one block and turn left onto Av. Chapultepec. Cross Bucareli. Stay in middle lane.
1.5	2.4	Go through tunnel at Insurgentes glorieta. Just past the tunnel, exit right onto Florencia (Eje 2 pte). Pass Hotel Plaza Florencia. Two blocks farther on at Hamburgo, turn left for Gallerías. The Independence Angel is dead ahead. Suites San Marino ahead.

IF TO: Querétaro, San Luis Potosí, at angel monument start Mexico City – Querétaro Log (See Mexico's Huasteca Potosina, page 178).

End of Log 69

Index

A

Acapulco, Gro 15, 24, 25, 40, 140, 142, 152
Acatlán, Pue 78, 83
Atlacomulco, Mex 33, 156
Atlixco, Pue 87, 89

B

Barra de Navidad, Jal 3, 148

C

Cd. Altamirano, Mich 61, 62, 66, 67
Chilpancingo, Gro 25, 152
Cholula, Pue 88, 89
Coajinicuilapa, Gro 26, 141
Colima, Col 8, 54, 56, 150
Cuautla, Mor 23, 77, 84
Cuernavaca, Mor
   18, 23, 76, 84, 96, 157, 158, 159
Cuyutlán, Col 4, 147

E

EAT & STRAYS
   Acapulco 110
   Barra de Navidad 99
   Colima 103
   Cuautla 132
   Cuernavaca 128
   Huatulco 122
   Ixtapa 104
   Ixtapan de la Sal 126
   Manzanillo 101
   Oaxaca 134
   Puerto Angel 121
   Puerto Escondido 119
   Salina Cruz 124
   Taxco 127
   Tehuacán 133
   Toluca 125
   Zihuatanejo 107
Esperanza, Pue 89, 93

G

Guadalajara, Jal 7, 50, 52, 150

H

Huajuapan, Oax 78, 79, 81, 83, 90, 92
Huatulco, Oax 29, 139
Huautla, Oax 72, 75

I

Iguala, Gro 23, 24, 38, 40, 152, 153, 157

Ixtapa, Gro 12, 15, 61, 67, 142, 144
Ixtapan de la Sal, Mex 35, 38, 96, 153, 154
Izucar de Matamoros, Pue 83
Izucar de Matamoros, Pue 76, 78, 84, 87, 88

J

Jiquilpan, Mich 54, 55
Juchitán, Oax 32, 138

L

La Mira Jct, Mich 10, 12, 57, 59, 144, 145
La Ventosa, Oax 31, 138
Lázaro Cárdenas, Mich 12, 144

M

Manzanillo, Col 4, 147
MAPS
   Acapulco 17
   Colima 9
   Cuautla 85
   Cuernavaca 22
   Downtown Oaxaca 47
   Guadalajara 6
   Ixtapa 13
   Ixtapan de la Sal 36
   Manzanillo 5
   Mexico City 20
   Mexico City Downtown 19
   Oaxaca 46
   Puebla 43
   Puerto Escondido 27
   Puerto Vallarta 1
   Salina Cruz 30
   Taxco 39
   Tehuacan 73
   Toluca 34
   Uruapan 58
   Zihuatanejo 14
Melaque Jct, Jal 2, 3, 50, 52, 147, 148
Mexico City, DF 18, 41, 63, 64, 158, 159, 164
Mitla, Oax 48, 160

N

Nueva Italia, Mich 59, 60

O

Oaxaca, Oax
   44, 48, 68, 69, 71, 74, 79, 81, 159, 160, 161, 162

P

Palmillas Jct, Qro 32, 156
Pinotepa Nacional, Oax 26, 141
Playa Azul, Mich 11, 60, 145
Pochutla, Oax 68, 69, 139
Pto Escondido, Oax 138
Pto. Escondido, Oax 140
Puebla, Pue 41, 44, 87, 88, 161, 162, 164
Puerto Angel, Oax 28, 71, 139
Puerto Escondido, Oax 25, 28
Puerto Vallarta, Jal 2, 148

S

Salina Cruz, Oax 29, 139
San Bartolo Coyotepec, Oax 69
Santiago Tianguistengo 94, 96

T

Taxco, Gro 38, 98, 153
Tecomán Jct, Col 3, 7, 10, 54, 55, 145, 147, 150
Tehuacán, Pue 45, 71, 74, 89, 90, 92, 93, 162, 163
Tehuantepec, Oax 28, 31, 48, 138, 159, 160
Toluca, Mex 32, 35, 62, 63, 64, 66, 94, 95, 154, 156
Tres Marías, Mor 94, 95

U

Uruapan, Mich 57, 59

Z

Zihuatanejo, Gro 15, 143

Notes